# Attention, Genes, and ADHD

# Attention, Genes, and ADHD

Edited by
Florence Levy and David A. Hay

Published in 2001 by Brunner-Routledge
27 Church Road, Hove, East Sussex, BN3 2FA

Simultaneously published in the USA and Canada
by Taylor & Francis Inc
325 Chestnut Street, Suite 800, Philadelphia, PA 19106

*Brunner-Routledge is an imprint of the Taylor & Francis Group*

© 2001 by Brunner-Routledge

Associate Editor to Florence Levy and David A. Hay:
Jillian Pearsall-Jones

Cover design by Sandra Heath
Typeset in Times by RefineCatch Limited, Bungay, Suffolk
Printed and bound in Great Britain by
Biddles Ltd, Guildford and King's Lynn

*British Library Cataloguing in Publication Data*
A catalogue record for this book is available from the British Library

*Library of Congress Cataloging-in-Publication Data*
Attention, genes and ADHD / editors, Florence Levy, David A. Hay.
    p.   cm.
  Includes bibliographical references and index.
  ISBN 1–84169–193–3
    1. Attention-deficit hyperactivity disorder. 2. Attention deficit
  hyperactivity disorder—Genetic aspects. 3. Attention.   I. Levy,
  Florence, M.M.B.S.   II. Hay, David A.
    [DNLM:   1. Attention Deficit Disorder with Hyperactivity—
  genetics. 2. Genetics, Medical. 3. Twins. 4. Child. WS 350.8.A8
  A8837 2001]
  RC394.A85 A885 2001
  616.85'89042—dc21                                    00–065135

ISBN 1–84169–193–3

Cover image: Microsatellite Genotypes. *Computer generated image of a
polyacrylamide gel run on an Applied Biosystems 377 DNA Sequencer.
The gel contains DNA microsatellite markers amplified using the
polymerase chain reaction. Each vertical lane contains samples from a
single individual for between 6 and 15 different DNA markers. Each
marker is labelled with blue, green or yellow fluorescent dye. The markers,
which differ in size are separated on the gel according to size, with each
coloured band representing a different marker. Size standards, labelled with
a red fluorescent dye, are run in each lane in order to calculate the size of
the individual bands representing the markers. The microsatellite markers
on this gel were used in a genetic linkage analysis study performed at the
Garvan Institute of Medical Research, Sydney, Australia.*

To our mothers,
Manya Waldman Levy and Patricia Mary McGregor Hay

**George F. Still, MA, MD Cantab., FRCS Lond.**
From a speech delivered before the Royal College of Physicians of London
on 4th, 6th, and 11th March, 1902.

> Whatever the cause of the defect may be, it seems clear that in these cases
> there is a morbid limitation of the capacity for the development of moral
> control, and the fact that this limitation is not necessarily proportionate to the
> limitation of the capacity for the development of moral control, and the fact
> that the mental processes involved in moral control may be affected altogether
> apart from those concerned with more general intellectual acquirements.
>
> (G.F. Still, 1902. Some abnormal physical conditions in children.
> *Lancet*, *I*, 1077)

# Contents

# List of contributors

**John P. Alsobrook II PhD**, Child Study Center, Yale University School of Medicine, New Haven, Connecticut, USA

**Cathy Barr PhD**, Assistant Professor, Department of Psychiatry, University of Toronto, Canada.

**Robert Cohen PhD, MD**, Lead Clinical Investigator, Laboratory of Cerebral Metabolism and Geriatric Psychiatry Branch, National Institute of Mental Health, USA.

**Monique Ernst MD**, PhD, Associate Director, Brain Imaging Center, National Institute of Drug Abuse, National Institutes of Health, USA.

**Nancy Fredine, MA**, Child Study Center, Yale University School of Medicine, New Haven, Connecticut, USA.

**David A. Hay PhD**, Professor, School of Psychology, Curtin University of Technology, Perth, Western Australia, Australia.

**Charles R. Hurst BSW**, Child Study Center, Yale University School of Medicine, New Haven, Connecticut, USA.

**James Kennedy MD, FRCP(C)**, I'Anson Associate Professor, University of Toronto, Head, Neurogenetics Section, Center for Addiction and Mental Health, Canada.

**Florence Levy MBBS, MD, FRANZCP**, Associate Professor, School of Psychiatry, University of New South Wales, Prince of Wales and Sydney Children's Hospitals, Australia.

**Barbara A. Lewis PhD**, Department of Pediatrics, Case Western Reserve University, Rainbow Babies and Childrens Hospital, Cleveland, Ohio, USA.

**Kimberly Lynch MSN**, Child Study Center, Yale University School of Medicine, New Haven, Connecticut, USA.

**Michael McStephen BSc(Hons)**, Mental Health Research Institute, Melbourne, Australia.

**David Pauls PhD**, Professor of Psychiatric and Neurobehavioral Genetics, Child Study Center, Yale University School of Medicine, New Haven, Connecticut, USA.

**Soo Hyun Rhee PhD**, Department of Psychology, Emory University, Atlanta, Georgia, USA.

**Professor Sir Michael Rutter MD, FRS**, Social, Genetic and Developmental Psychiatry Research Centre, Insitute of Psychiatry, De Crespigny Park, Denmark Hill, London, UK.

**Jim Stevenson PhD**, Professor, Centre for Research into Psychological Development, Department of Psychology, University of Southampton, UK.

**James Swanson PhD**, Professor of Pediatrics and Cognitive Sciences, Director of the University of California Irvine Child Development Center, USA.

**Irwin D. Waldman PhD**, Associate Professor of Psychology, Department of Psychology, Emory University, Atlanta, Georgia, USA.

**Alan Zametkin MD**, Senior Staff Psychiatrist, Office of the Clinical Director, National Institute of Mental Health, Bethesda, Maryland, USA.

# Preface

Recent decades have seen a resurgence of interest and research in behaviour genetics. This has coincided with striking advances in molecular genetic technologies, with potential for advances for both fields to compliment each other's findings. Behaviour genetic techniques have advanced from examining twin correlation and concordances to the use of powerful modelling techniques, which allow simultaneous examination of genetic, shared, and unique environmental influences, as well as developmental and comorbidity issues.

Attention Deficit Hyperactivity Disorder (ADHD) is a particularly exciting and relevant syndrome for behaviour genetic investigation. Early studies have indicated unusually high heritability. Also, phenotypic studies have shown a considerable degree of comorbidity with Oppositional Defiant Disorder, Conduct Disorder, Learning Disability, and, in adults, Personality Disorder. The sources and influences on comorbidity of ADHD are not well understood, and behaviour genetic methods offer potential for a better understanding of these issues.

The present text contains an introductory chapter on the history and current concepts of ADHD by Florence Levy (Chapter 1). This is followed by three chapters by David Hay, Michael McStephen, and Florence Levy: an introduction to methodology in behaviour genetics (Chapter 2); discussion of the potential of "Diagnostic Genetics" to examine issues of diagnostic validity, including the validity of the *DSM-IV* classification system of ADHD subtypes, as well as a genetic item analysis of *DSM-IV*. The latter analysis is of interest in showing differences at subtype and symptom level (Chapter 3); and, in Chapter 4, a discussion of the applications of behaviour genetics to the understanding of developmental issues in ADHD providing examples from the Australian Twin Study of ADHD.

Barbara Lewis outlines the familial and genetic basis of speech and language disorders in Chapter 5 and provides pilot data from a study of children and their families, ascertained through a proband with preschool phonology disorder, suggesting a comorbid speech and language/ADHD subtype.

Jim Stevenson provides an important discussion of the genetics of reading, spelling and ADHD in Chapter 6, including evidence of high comorbidity, early linkage findings, and evidence for shared genetic influences on ADHD, reading and spelling. The overlap among symptoms of ADHD, Oppositional Defiant Disorder, and Conduct Disorder are investigated in Chapter 7 by Irwin Waldman, Soo Hyun Rhee, Florence Levy, and David Hay, using multivariate genetic analyses and Cholesky decomposition.

In Chapter 8, the same authors examine the fascinating question of why there are striking sex differences (4:1 incidence in boys vs girls) in the prevalence of ADHD. They compare polygenic multiple threshold and constitutional variability models.

Two chapters are devoted to an examination of molecular genetic advances in ADHD. Alan Zametkin, Monique Ernst, and Robert Cohen outline the history and relevance of single gene studies of ADHD in Chapter 9, including molecular studies, gene to brain function in resistance to thyroid hormone, and Fragile-X Syndrome as a molecular model. In Chapter 10, Cathy Barr, James Swanson, and James Kennedy provide a primer on Molecular Genetics, including problems defining the phenotype of ADHD for genetic studies and their own studies of the D4 receptor gene. They also outline a pharmacologic model based on stimulant therapy and the dopamine hypothesis.

The genetics of ADHD and Gilles de la Tourette Syndrome (GTS) has been of great interest to investigators and the natural history, neuropsychological phenotypes, and recent research on co-occurrence of ADHD and TS are described by David Pauls and colleagues in Chapter 11. David Hay and Florence Levy discuss the implications of the genetics of ADHD for education and intervention in Chapter 12, including implications of subtype differences and comorbidity, as well as ethical implications of the "genetic revolution". Throughout the book, the issue of comorbidity is a recurring theme, and a challenge for genetic investigation.

Chapter 13, by Professor Sir Michael Rutter, provides a Commentary which synthesises the material offered in the text, and makes suggestions for future directions of a combined behaviour and molecular genetic approach to the questions posed in relation to Attention, Genes, and ADHD. The implications of a genetic/environmental model for the future of Child Psychiatry following the sequencing of the human genome are discussed.

FLORENCE LEVY MBBS, MD, FRANZCP
*School of Psychiatry, University of New South Wales,*
*Prince of Wales and Sydney Children's Hospitals, Australia*
DAVID A. HAY PhD
*Curtin University of Technology,*
*Perth, Australia*

# Acknowledgements

We would like to express our appreciation for the considerable contribution made by our Associate Editor Jillian Pearsall-Jones, and Michael McStephen, in producing this volume.

We gratefully thank the National Health and Medical Research Council of Australia (NHMRC) for 9 years of support for the Australian Twin Attention Deficit Hyperactivity Disorder Project (ATAP, 1994–2003), which was the inspiration for this book.

Thanks to Professor John Hopper, Palma Ragno, and all others associated with the NHMRC-funded Australian Twin Registry (ATR), without whose cooperation this project could not have been undertaken. We also thank the Government Employees' Medical Insurance Fund for their initial support.

Special appreciation goes to the many families on the ATR who participated and continue to participate in our reported studies. Over the past 10 years they have responded more than admirably to our requests for information, and have given so openly of themselves in order to enrich our understanding of twins and their families, ADD/ADHD, and comorbid conditions.

# 1    Introduction

*Florence Levy*

Clinical interest in problems of overactivity and attention goes back to lectures to the Royal Academy of Physicians by George Still (1902), who described a group of children manifesting a deficit in "volitional inhibition" or a deficit of moral control! According to Barkley (1997), Still's observations were astute in describing many of the associated features of ADHD, now corroborated in research more than 50–90 years later. These features include an over representation of males, an aggregation of alcoholism, criminal conduct and depression among biological relatives, a familial predisposition to the disorder, and the possibility of the disorder arising from acquired injury to the nervous system.

Since that time, there have been many theories about the nature of similar syndromes. A syndrome of overactivity and distractibility was described following the pandemic of encephalitis lethargica that swept Europe in 1917–1918, giving rise to theories of Minimal Brain Dysfunction (MBD) (Kessler, 1980). In the 1950s and 1960s hyperactivity and poor impulse control were thought to be due to poor thalamic filtering of stimuli entering the brain (Laufer, Denhoff, & Solomons, 1957).

Another milestone in the history of ADHD was the observation of Charles Bradley (1937) that benzedrine, a central nervous system stimulant, had a calming affect on the behaviour of overactive children. This finding led to the use of dexamphetamine and methylphenidate as a treatment for hyperactivity, and the use of these medications has been particularly developed in North America (Wilens & Biederman, 1992; Greenhill, 1992). A multisite study (Arnold et al., 1997; MTA Cooperative Group, 1999) has compared the use of stimulant medication alone, with stimulant medication combined with multimodal treatments. A recent text by Solanto, Arnsten and Castellanos (2001) provides an excellent review of the basic and clinical neuroscience of stimulant drugs and ADHD.

There has been a continuing divergence between North American clinicians, who view Attention Deficit Hyperactivity Disorder (ADHD) as a developmental disorder with substantial biological origins, and UK clinicians, who place greater emphasis on conduct problems originating from poor parental management. The shift to an emphasis on inattention in North

American studies began with the work of Virginia Douglas (1972), who hypothesised that a deficit in the capacity to sustain attention underlay observed symptoms of hyperactivity and impulse control. The work of Douglas (1972, 1983) influenced the re-categorisation of the disorder in the third edition of the Diagnostic and Statistical Manual (*DSM-III*; American Psychiatric Association [APA], 1980) as Attention Deficit Disorder (ADD) with and without Hyperactivity. The *DSM-III* conceptualised ADD with Hyperactivity as a tri-dimensional disorder characterised by developmentally inappropriate inattention, impulsivity and hyperactivity with symptoms and cut-offs described to operationalise the diagnosis. The revised edition (*DSM-III-R*, APA, 1987) on the other hand, listed 14 symptoms, some related to attention and some to impulsivity and hyperactivity in descending order of discrimination (according to field trials), requiring 8 symptoms for a diagnosis. The fourth edition of the Diagnostic and Statistical Manual (*DSM-IV*, APA, 1994) includes separate diagnostic criteria for symptoms of inattention and hyperactivity/impulsivity. Thus, ADHD is now diagnosable as three subtypes: Predominantly Inattentive, Predominantly Hyperactive/Impulsive, and a Combined type.

Swanson (1997) has pointed out that while the *DSM-IV* and *International Classification of Disease—10th revision* (*ICD-10*; World Health Organisation [WHO], 1992) use similar classification schemes for ADHD and Hyperkinetic Disorder (HD), the *ICD* also describes a combined Hyperkinetic Conduct Disorder category. This has important implications for the diagnosis of comorbid disruptive behaviour disorders. A substantial proportion of children with a diagnosis of ADHD and referred to clinics have comorbid Oppositional Defiant Disorder and/or Conduct Disorder on *DSM-IV* diagnosis, yet in Europe might rather obtain a diagnosis of Hyperkinetic Conduct Disorder. This makes a diagnosis of HD less likely in European countries, when children have comorbid symptoms, than in the US, despite virtually identical symptoms. Thus, the issue of the relationship with ADHD of comorbid symptomatology remains an important theoretical and classification issue, which may be clarified by behaviour genetic studies.

In his 1997 monograph, Barkley made a number of critiques of the *DSM-IV* approach. He pointed out that it was not clear that ADHD-I, the predominantly inattentive type of ADHD, was actually a subtype of ADHD sharing a common attention deficit with other types. The Inattentive subtype manifests greater stability over time and is more predictive of school performance problems and possibly reading difficulties. He questioned whether young ADHD—predominantly Hyperactive/Impulsive (ADHD-HI)—children, who do not require Inattention symptoms for diagnosis, eventually move into the ADHD-Combined type (ADHD-C) over time, and why hyperactive-impulsive symptoms decline sharply over time. He also asked how applicable were the diagnostic thresholds set for the two main *DSM-IV* subtypes to age groups outside those used in the *DSM-IV* field trial (ages 4–16 years). An adult outcome study by Barkley, Fisher, Fletcher, and Smallish (1997) showed that when self-report of *DSM* criteria was used, persistence into adulthood was 3%, but when an empirical (age referenced) definition was used, persistence was increased to 28%.

Barkley (1997) suggested that ADHD may need to be defined as a developmentally relative disorder at the extreme end of a normal psychological trait. This trait probably undergoes developmental elaboration and maturation with age, as do language ability, memory, and intelligence. He suggested that current criteria are descriptive and atheoretical, and do not make predictions about associated features or life course.

A paper by Hill and Schoener (1996) has sparked controversy about whether or not there is an age-dependent decline of attention deficit hyperactivity disorder in adolescence and adulthood. The authors analysed data from nine prospective ADHD studies in which original diagnosis was made in childhood, and follow-up evaluations were made into late adolescence. They fitted an exponential function which predicted a decline in symptoms with age such that, assuming a mean prevalence of 4% at age 9, this would drop to 0.84% at age 20; to 0.21% at age 30; to 0.05% at age 40; and to 0.01% at age 50.

Barkley (1997) has queried the Hill and Schoener conclusions, on the grounds of unreliability of measurement of the disorder across time, and insensitivity of *DSM* criteria with increasing age. The controversy raises issues about whether or not fundamental changes in the expression of ADHD occur with development, or whether compensatory mechanisms minimise expression of the disorder. Therefore, important developmental issues in relation to ADHD still require resolution.

Sergeant (1995) has discussed the difference between quantitative and categorical approaches to the diagnosis of ADHD. He pointed out that while categorical approaches may be useful, their validity should be tested by prospective checks on stability and family studies. He also pointed out that in instances where classification studies introduce major shifts (as has happened with the *DSM*), it may be useful to use a broad array of quantitative symptom scores, as are employed by the Child Behaviour Checklist (CBCL; Achenbach, 1991). The CBCL provides quantitative scores on scales reflecting different domains of psychopathology, allowing an examination of comorbidity issues.

Taylor, Sandberg, Thorley, and Giles (1991) have pointed out that the predictive significance of attention deficit vs hyperactive symptoms varies in different studies (Fergusson & Horwood, 1993; Gittelman, Mannuzza, Shenker, & Bonagura, 1985; McGee, Williams, & Silva, 1987). British and North American studies have emphasised Conduct Disorder/Attention Deficit Disorder as outcomes of hyperactivity. Taylor et al. (1991) pointed out that prospective longitudinal studies of epidemiologically defined groups, and of a clinical series, are needed to answer questions of predictive significance, including clinical case controls and subthreshold levels of hyperactivity. Such studies would examine the predictive implications of heterogeneity and comorbidity with associated behaviour disorders. Comorbid aggression, conduct disorder, learning disability or anxiety may represent subtypes of ADHD.

Taylor (1998) has also discussed confusion arising from the terminology "attention deficit disorder", particularly since the advent of *DSM-IV* subtypes, inattentiveness and overactivity/impulsivity. He pointed out that it is possible to have ADHD without being inattentive. On the other hand, *ICD-10* requires inattentiveness for a diagnosis of hyperkinetic disorder. The hypothesis of a unitary attention deficit may be misleading because of the complexities of determining the transition from brain dysfunction, through cognitive dysfunction, into behavioural presentation.

The development of operational criteria is complex. Taylor (1998) pointed out that the distinction between oppositional behaviour and inattentiveness is a frequent challenge to the clinician, because a very oppositional child may not engage in tasks long enough to allow satisfactory judgements about task orientation. In other words, motivation may interact with attention. Many definitions used in rating scales and diagnostic schemes refer to inferences and value judgements, rather than to observable behaviour. For example, distractibility, short attention span, and sensation seeking might all be terms used to describe similar behaviour.

Hudziak and Todd (1993) have discussed possible phenotypic subtyping of ADHD, including subtyping by comorbidity, family studies, relationship to mood disorders, learning disability, gender, parental ADHD, laboratory methods, or biological markers. They concluded that available data supported subtyping by comorbidity, but familial relationships did not support co-segregation in families. While these critiques in relation to developmental, classification, and comorbidity issues are challenging and heuristic, they indicate a fundamental problem in assigning diagnostic criteria on the basis of factor-analytic studies of parent and teacher ratings. Many of the questions posed may not be answerable by phenotypic investigations. According to Taylor (1998) the development of molecular genetics means that different genetic influences will be measured rather than inferred, while developments in experimental psychology should allow for clearer descriptions of what is impaired by different genes.

Rutter, Silberg, O'Connor, and Simonoff (1999) have reviewed advances in quantitative and molecular genetics, in relation to shifts in research strategies, multifactorial disorders (affected relative linkage designs, association strategies, and quantitative trait loci studies), and new molecular techniques.

The present authors believe that behavioural and molecular genetic approaches enable examination of genetic and environmental influences on latent behavioural traits, as well as genetic and environmental influences on comorbidity and outcome, more adequately than can phenotypic approaches alone.

# REFERENCES

Achenbach, T.M. (1991). *Manual for the Child Behaviour Checklist 4–18 and 1991 Profile*. Burlington, VT: University of Vermont, Department of Psychiatry.

American Psychiatric Association. (1980). *Diagnostic and statistical manual of mental disorders* (3rd ed.) [*DSM-III*]. Washington, DC: Author.

American Psychiatric Association. (1987). *Diagnostic and statistical manual of mental disorders* (3rd ed., rev.) [*DSM-III-R*]. Washington, DC: Author.

American Psychiatric Association. (1994). *Diagnostic and statistical manual of mental disorders* (4th ed.) [*DSM-IV*]. Washington, DC: Author.

Arnold, L.E., Abikoff, H.B., Cantwell, D.P., Conners, C.K., Elliott, G., Hechtman, L., Hinshaw, S.P., Hoza, B., Jensen, P.S., Kraemer, H.C., March, J.S., Newcorn, J.H., Pelham, W.E., Richters, J.E., Schiller, E., Severe, J.B., Swanson, J.M., Vereen, D., & Wells, K.C. (1997). National Institute of Mental Health collaborative multi-modal treatment study of children with ADHD (the MTA): Design challenges and choices. *Archives of General Psychiatry, 54*, 865–870.

Barkley, R.A. (1997). *ADHD and the nature of self-control*. New York/London: Guildford Press.

Barkley, R.A., Fischer, M., Fletcher, K., & Smallish, L. (1997). *Adult outcome of hyperactive children: I. Psychiatric status and psychological adjustment*. Unpublished manuscript.

Bradley, C. (1937). The behaviour of children receiving benzedrine. *American Journal of Psychiatry, 94*, 557–585.

Douglas, V.I. (1972). Stop, look and listen: The problem of sustained attention and impulse control in hyperactive and normal children. *Canadian Journal of Behavioural Science, 4*, 259–282.

Douglas, V.I. (1983). Attention and cognitive problems. In M. Rutter (Ed.), *Developmental neuropsychiatry* (pp. 280–329). New York: Guilford Press.

Fergusson, D.M., & Horwood, L.J. (1993). The structure, stability and correlations of the trait components of conduct disorder, attention deficit and anxiety/withdrawal reports. *Journal of Child Psychology and Psychiatry, 34*, 749–766.

Gittleman, R., Mannuzza, S., Shenker, R., & Bonagura, N. (1985). Hyperactive boys almost grown up. *Archives of General Psychiatry, 42*, 937–947.

Greenhill, L.L. (1992). Pharmacotherapy: Stimulants. *Child and Adolescent Psychiatric Clinics of North America, 1*, 411–447.

Hill, J., & Schoener, E. (1996). Age dependent decline in ADHD, *American Journal of Psychiatry, 15*, 1143–1146.

Hudziak, J.J., & Todd, R.D. (1993). Familial subtyping attention deficit hyperactivity disorder. *Current Opinion in Psychiatry, 6*, 489–493.

Kessler, J.W. (1980). History of minimal brain dysfunction. In H. Rie & E. Rie (Eds.), *Handbook of minimal brain dysfunctions: A critical view* (pp. 18–52). New York: Wiley.

Laufer, M., Denhoff, E.S., & Solomons, G. (1957). Hyperkinetic impulse disorder in children's behaviour problems. *Psychosomatic Medicine, 19*, 38–49

McGee, R., Williams, S., & Silva, P.A. (1987). A comparison of girls and boys with teacher-identified problems of attention. *Journal of the American Academy of Child and Adolescent Psychiatry, 26*, 711–717.

MTA Cooperative Group. (1999). A 14 month randomised clinical trial of treatment strategies for Attention-Deficit/Hyperactivity Disorder. *Archives of General Psychiatry, 56*, 1073–1086.

Rutter, M., Silberg, J.L., O'Connor, T., & Simonoff, E. (1999). Genetics and child psychiatry: I. Advances in quantitative and molecular genetics. *Journal of Child Psychology and Psychiatry*, *40*, 3–18.

Sergeant, J. (1995). Hyperkinetic disorder revised. In J.A. Sergeant (Ed.), *Eunethydis*. Amsterdam: University of Amsterdam.

Solanto, M.V., Arnsten, A.F.T., & Castellanos, F.X. (2001). *Stimulant drugs and ADHD: Basic and clinical neuroscience*. Oxford/New York: Oxford University Press.

Still, G.F. (1902). Some abnormal physical conditions in children. *Lancet*, *I*, 1008–1012, 1077–1082, 1163–1168.

Swanson, J.M. (1997). Hyperkinetic disorders and attention deficit hyperactivity disorders. *Current Opinion in Psychiatry*, *10*, 300–305.

Taylor, E. (1998). Clinical foundations of hyperactivity research. *Behavioral Brain Research*, *94*, 11–24.

Taylor, E., Sandberg, S., Thorley, G., & Giles, S. (1991). *The epidemiology of childhood hyperactivity*. Oxford/New York: Oxford University Press.

Wilens, T.E., & Biederman, J. (1992). The stimulants. *Psychiatric Clinics of North America*, *15*, 191–222.

World Health Organisation. (1993). *International classification of diseases: Classification of mental and behavioural disorders—diagnostic criteria for research* (10th ed.) [*ICD-10*]. Geneva: Author.

# 2 Introduction to the genetic analysis of attentional disorders

*David A. Hay, Michael McStephen, and Florence Levy*

## THE AIMS OF BEHAVIOUR GENETIC ANALYSIS

There are at least two disparate approaches to genetic analysis of behaviour—one focused on discrete behaviour characteristics, the other on characteristics as a continuum in the population.

Molecular genetics focuses on the biochemistry of discrete characteristics, features, or disorders that one either has or has not. Advances in molecular genetics and publicity about major initiatives, such as the Human Genome Project, would suggest that most work pertaining to this approach takes place in the laboratory, seeking to find specific genes that influence behaviour. Several chapters of this text deal with the application of such methodology and technology to attentional problems.

In contrast, analyses in other chapters of this text assume that an apparently discontinuous variable, such as the diagnosis of ADHD, should best be seen as the end of a continuum of behaviour throughout the population. Twin and other approaches to continuous traits do not deal with the clearly defined genetic sequences of molecular genetics, but with a much more abstract view of genetics in the theory of polygenic inheritance ("poly" = "many"). A basic assumption of such an approach is that behaviour is a complex characteristic, influenced by many genes of small but cumulative effect, as well as by environmental influences.

This is a key point, as different research strategies may be required, depending on how ADHD is viewed. This issue is even more important when the focus turns to comorbidity and the relationship between ADHD and other disorders. To date, molecular approaches have met with only modest success in clarifying continuous or quantitative characteristics that include most human behaviours, such as intelligence, personality, social attitudes, and temperament, all of which have been implicated in ADHD. That is, genes reported for "intelligence" or "personality" are usually found to have very small effects, and studies identifying such genes have rarely been replicated. This is different from molecular genetics, in that we have no idea of the number of genes involved, far less what such genes do biochemically. We hypothesise that for each gene, its alleles (different forms) add to, or subtract from, the overall expression of the behaviour characteristic. It is also crucial to bear in mind that finding a genetic contribution to such behaviours is quite different from the claim that a gene has been found for a particular disorder. How large is the effect of such a gene? This can be illustrated by the work by Plomin (1997, 2000) on intelligence. It is clear that there is no *one* gene involved, but rather several contributing genes have been identified, each of which may have effect on only a few IQ points.

Another issue raised in this chapter is that of synergy, and how these different approaches could best be integrated (Martin, Boomsma, & Machin, 1997; Spector, Sneider, & MacGregor, 1999). That is, means by which twin and related research could help direct molecular studies, given that there are many ongoing studies using both approaches for ADHD.

Polygenic inheritance implies environmental as well as genetic effects (without specifying the magnitude of these environmental effects), blurring distinctions between genotypes. The term heritability is often used to sum-marise the proportion of the total differences between people attributed to genetic, rather than to environmental, factors. Thus adult height and weight are both polygenic, despite the fact that weight has a far lower heritability than does height, and has more scope for environmental influences from diet and lifestyle. While such genetic effects may seem very abstract, until recently such effects have formed the basis of most selective breeding of plants and animals. The cost of racehorses has long reflected their genetic "form", despite the lack of any clearly identified genes.

Traditionally, the issue of determining the relative contributions of her-edity and environment to a particular behaviour has been dismissed as too complex and totally entwined. Crude estimates of heritability were developed, comparing the resemblance in identical and non-identical twins (see Hay, 1985). But in the last 30 years there have been significant advances in the analyses of data from twin, sibling, and other family rela-tionships, such as adoptions and the nuclear family. This chapter outlines these new methods of analysis, and emphasises that behaviour genetics is concerned with testing models of behavioural interest concerning the determinants of particular behaviours, and their relationship to other behaviours.

Specific examples of this, such as the determinants of the relationship between ADHD and reading problems, are considered in this text by Steven-son (Chapter 6) and by Hay and Levy (Chapter 12). The key issue is not whether ADHD or reading disability are to some extent genetic, but rather to what extent the overlap between these disorders can be attributed to common genes. By asking this question we are moving far beyond the conventional debate about whether children with reading problems are more likely to be classified as ADHD, or whether ADHD children are more likely to develop reading problems (Dykman & Ackerman, 1991). Rather, we are asking whether the overlap between the two conditions is primarily due to genes that contribute to both, and whether both conditions share a common cause, rather than one causing the other. This has fundamental implications for both research and intervention.

It would be fair to say that this approach to behaviour genetics is most advanced in the areas of personality (Loehlin, 1992), and intelligence (Hay, 1999). Loehlin has made a major contribution by identifying the key issues for personality, and his text is recommended as an insightful (and reader-friendly) introduction into the potential of this methodology. This multivariate approach to behaviour genetics is less advanced in adult psycho-pathology than is the approach to single disorders, and least so in child psychopathology, with such disorders as ADHD. The methodology can be highly mathematical and daunting, but is becoming increasingly easier to comprehend.

The present chapter is designed to help interpret what has been, and could yet be, done in the quantitative genetics of attentional disorders. We do not aim to review studies to date, which has been recently done by Tannock (1998), Thapar, Holmes, Poulton, and Harrington (1999), and in the context of a wider review of genetic methodology and results in childhood psycho-pathology by Rutter, Silberg, O'Connor, and Simonoff (1999a, b). One point of emphasis in evaluating the studies discussed in these reviews is the defin-ition of ADHD. This is the topic of Chapter 3 in this text (Levy, McStephen, & Hay), on diagnostic genetics. Because of the extensive time required for completion of genetic studies, most published studies to date are not based on the more recent fourth edition of the *Diagnostic and Statistical Manual* (*DSM-IV*, American Psychiatric Association [APA], 1994). Many are not even based on the third edition—revised (*DSM-III-R*, APA, 1987), but on behaviour checklists that can have widely different degrees of overlap with current conceptions of ADHD.

## WHY ARE PEOPLE DIFFERENT?

Behaviour genetics is concerned with differences, rather than similarities, between people. Thus it may say little about reasons for gender differences (however, see Chapter 8, by Rhee, Waldman, Hay, & Levy), and nothing at all about ethnic group differences. Rather, behaviour genetics is concerned with what contributes to differences between members of *one* population, on *one* particular measure of behaviour, at *one* point in time. Such a focus cannot be emphasised too strongly, as it is not the aim of this text, nor of empirical approaches to behaviour genetics in general, to imply how one such subgroup may be genetically different from another. Without the impossibility of identical twins of different sexes or different ethnic groups, conventional behaviour genetic methods can contribute little to such contentious issues.

## THE TOOLS OF BEHAVIOUR GENETICS

Contemporary behaviour genetics has gone far beyond simply calculating "the heritability", using traditional formulae such as those provided by Holzinger or by Nichols, with all the problems and pitfalls these entail (Hay, 1985). The usual approach nowadays is by model-fitting, which provides a test of the adequacy of the genetic model as a parsimonious explanation of the data. While full details can be found in texts such as Neale and Cardon (1992), the most common procedure is based around the ACE model, hypothesising three influences on behaviour:

Additive genetic effects—the increase in the observed phenotype or trait due to an increase in the number of alleles that influence that trait.

Common family environment—sometimes called "shared" environment, since it concerns the environmental factors which family members share, and which make them more similar for the behaviour under study.

Environmental influences unique to the individual—also called "non-shared" environment. One of the main contributions of behaviour genetics has been to distinguish between the latter two types of environmental effect, focusing attention in developmental psychology on why children growing up in the same family may be so different from each other.

The three approaches to estimating A, C, and E are shown schematically in Figure 2.1, which describes basic genetic methodologies. In (a), the traditional nuclear family, parents pass genes to their children, and the children share half their genes. (To simplify the diagram, the path from parent to child is the midparent value, the average of the two parents.) But parents also pass on the common environment C, and the children share C as well as their genes, making it difficult to distinguish the effects of shared genes from the effects of shared environment. The only way to achieve this is to "disrupt" nuclear family patterns. Traditionally this has been done in one of two ways—the adoption design and the twin method.

In (b), the adoption design, children receive their genes from one set of parents, but share the environment of another family. Of course, this is an oversimplification, especially for recent adoptions, where many of the children have experienced traumatic events prior to their placement (Rutter, Roy, & Kreppner, in press). Many are inter-country adoptees, with little known about their biological parents.

The main method of behaviour genetic analysis is (c), the twin design, which is becoming increasingly popular with the rising number of twin births and the declining number of adoptions. Between 1980 and 1995, the incidence of twins rose from 1 birth in 100 to 1 in 72. The basics of the twin design are discussed in detail elsewhere (Hay, 1985; Plomin, De Fries, McClean, & Rutter, 1997). Essentially, monozygotic (MZ) twins result from the splitting in two of a single fertilised egg shortly after conception, and thus

(a) Nuclear Family

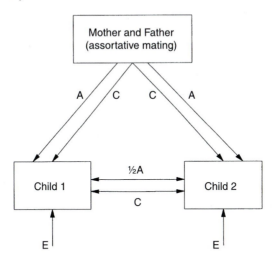

(b) Adoption (Two unrelated children in the same family)

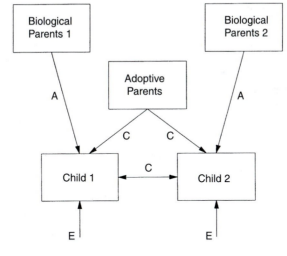

(c) Twins

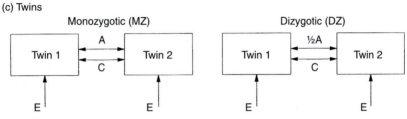

*Figure 2.1* Diagram of major designs in behaviour genetic analysis.

are genetically identical, whereas dizygotic (DZ) twins result from the independent fertilisation of two eggs by two sperm. Apart from the fact that the two eggs happened to be released in the same cycle, DZ twins are no more alike than any other brothers or sisters.

There are a number of assumptions underlying the twin method. For example, twins are often born pre-term, and one has to be sure that their similarities in behaviour characteristics are a consequence of shared genes, rather than of biological insults associated with pre-term birth (Bryan, in Bouchard & Propping, 1993). A widely debated issue is the "equal environments" assumption, and whether C, the common environment, is really the same in MZ and DZ twins. As reviewed by Kendler (1993), there is surprisingly little evidence that the similarities in MZ twins are a consequence of people perceiving them as similar. MZ twins may well be treated more similarly than DZ twins, but this is far more a consequence of their genetic similarity in behaviour (and of ensuing responses by parents and others) than a cause of such similarity. Apart from MZ twins being treated more similarly than are DZ twins, the converse is true—that differences between DZ twins may be exaggerated. Work on maternal rating bias in assessing hyperactive symptoms is discussed later in this chapter.

Statistical methodology to achieve analyses in heritability studies has also developed over the past 30 years. The first and landmark publication of Jinks and Fulker (1970) used methods that required sophisticated algebraic computations. The obvious difficulty in implementing such methods, by scientists more interested in the psychology than in the mathematics, has led to the widespread use of the LISREL statistical software to compare confirmatory factor analysis models. Analysis of these models using LISREL allows the evaluation of the relative merits of competing structural models of the determinants of a behaviour (Eaves, Eysenck, & Martin, 1989). Still more flexible software programs have recently become available, such as Mx (Neale, Baher, Xie, & Maes 1999), which handles data from more complex or more varied family relationships. The actual methodology of such statistical methods is beyond the scope of this chapter. None the less, the rationale behind them follows for anyone who has encountered structural equation modelling in general, with its logic that one is seeking the most parsimonious set of parameters that explain the relationship between the scores of individuals (such as sets of twins) on one or more measures.

## Sample size in behaviour genetics and implications for study design

Contemporary behaviour genetics is far more complex than simply testing a few sets of twins and comparing the resemblance in identical and nonidentical twins. The sophistication of the mathematical analysis in genetic research is such that very large numbers are needed to accurately estimate the genetic and environmental effects, and to ensure that all possible factors be tested. In her recent review of European Twin Registers, Boomsma (1998) calculates that together they include over 350,000 twin pairs. Current large twin studies focusing on childhood behaviour include:

Australian Twin ADHD Project (Levy, Hay, McStephen, Wood, & Waldman, 1997) (ATAP)
Greater Manchester Twin Register (Thapar, Harrington, Ross, & McGuffin, 2000)
Virginia Twin Study of Adolescent Behavioural Development (Simonoff et al., 1998) (VTSABD)
Minnesota (Sherman, Iacono, & McGue, 1997)
Colorado (Schmitz, Fulker, & Mrazek, 1995)
Norwegian Twin Registry (Gjone, Stevenson, & Sundet, 1996)
Dutch Twin Registry (van der Valk, Verhulst, Stroet, & Boomsma, 1998)
Missouri Twin Study (Hudziak et al., 1998)
UK Twins Early Development Study (Dale et al., 1998) (TEDS).

The need for large sample size introduces two further issues—how to collect the data, and from whom.

## Method of data collection

Visiting families to obtain information in face-to-face structured interview can become prohibitively expensive in all but a few studies, such as the Virginian Twin Study. Instead, one may resort to interview by telephone (Hudziak et al., 1998), or mailing questionnaires (Levy et al., 1997). Kaprio, Verkasalo, and Koskenvuo (in Spector et al., 1999) discuss some of the issues that may confound studies, such as twins colluding on their responses to items on questionnaires! A payoff is necessary between the value of formal interviews, the limitations that may be imposed because of the additional cost, and the potential reluctance of families to be involved in such possibly invasive procedures. Our experience (Levy, Hay, McLaughlin, Wood, & Waldman, 1996) is that questionnaires can provide a conservative estimate of the extent of behavioural problems, in that parents report more symptoms at interview than in a questionnaire. On average, parents who reported five *DSM-III-R* ADHD symptoms in the questionnaire reported the eight needed to reach criterion at interview. It is reassuring that our rates of the *DSM-IV* subtypes in 8- to 16-year-old Australian female twins, obtained by questionnaire, were very close to the rates obtained by Hudziak and colleagues in telephone interviews with US adolescent twins.

## Subjects

Traditionally, most twin families on twin registers and participating in research have been volunteers. Some of the largest databases, such as the

Australian Twin Registry with over 25,000 sets enrolled, are still based on volunteers. This raises potential biases. For instance, families with reading problems are less likely to participate if they have to complete written questionnaires, or families in which both twins have problems being more likely to volunteer because they are acutely aware of their circumstances. Gleeson, Hay, Johnston, and Theobald (1990) suggested that some basic measures routinely be collected in all twin studies, to check comparability. An alternative is the move to population-based registries, often based on birth records as in the Virginia and the UK-based Twins Early Development Study (TEDS). This may reduce biases in the identification of families, but biases in participation may remain. Of the 7756 twin pairs identified and approached in the TEDS project, only 3442 families returned the background and test booklets containing vocabulary questions (Dale et al., 1998).

As Strachan (in Spector et al., 1999) emphasises, there are advantages and disadvantages to each potential source of twins. Although each method of subject selection has the potential to bias estimates of both prevalence and genetic effects, too few studies to date have compared data from different recruitment methods.

## AN EXAMPLE OF GENETIC ANALYSIS OF ADHD

What follows is an example of the genetic analysis of ADHD, regarding it first as a continuum throughout the population and then as a discrete disorder. The genetic relationship between ADHD and speech/language problems is used to introduce multivariate genetic modelling.

### What is ADHD?

Throughout the example we shall deal with the unitary ADHD defined in *DSM-III-R* diagnosis, which required 8 out of 14 symptoms to reach criterion, with no distinction made between Inattention and Hyperactivity–Impulsivity. Use of the *DSM-III-R* definition is not meant to argue against *DSM-IV*, which classifies ADHD into three types as discussed by Levy et al. in Chapter 3 of this text, on diagnostic genetics. Rather, it is used because it is far simpler to introduce genetic analysis with one disorder than it is to do so with three inter-related disorders reflecting two underlying dimensions (Inattention and Hyperactivity/Impulsivity). The data come from our Australian Twin ADHD Project (ATAP), described by Levy et al. (1996), and some discussion of the genetic analysis of *DSM-IV* Inattention and Hyperactivity-Impulsivity in ATAP can be found in Chapter 3 of this volume.

## The Australian Twin ADHD Project (ATAP)

Most family-genetic studies have been too small and have involved varied and often inconsistent definitions of ADHD. It was partly the need for a better designed study, large enough for the current sophisticated methods of behaviour genetic analysis, which led to us in 1990 to establish ATAP. Identifying sufficient twins with ADHD to reliably assess both genetic and developmental features is possible only with access to large-scale twin registries. In 1991, we approached all eligible, 4- to 12-year-old twin pairs on the Australian National Health and Medical Research Council (NH&MRC) funded Australian Twin Registry (ATR). Consenting parents were asked to complete a questionnaire that included the ADHD questions from *DSM-III-R*, so screened for ADHD. The same information was obtained about siblings in the same age-range, to provide further relationships for genetic analysis. A detailed description of the process by which families were identified for the present study is provided by Levy et al. (1996). In total 1938 families, comprising 5067 children, responded to the questionnaire in 1991—a response rate of 73.5%. This number derives from the 3049 contactable families recruited to the ATR through a number of sources (e.g., media-releases, maternity hospitals, Australian Multiple Birth Association), of which 2350 families expressed interest in our study. Of the 2350 families who responded, 412 were excluded from the study as one or more children (usually twins) in the family had a major disability, such as cerebral palsy or intellectual disability. These are disabilities for which twins are at high risk (Bryan, in Bouchard & Propping, 1993), an issue to be considered in any study, especially those in which there is little direct contact with the families. When working with families of young twins there is the definite possibility that behavioural similarities may be due less to genetics, than to such pre- and perinatal correlates of the twin situation.

## How common are symptoms of ADHD in these families?

Table 2.1 shows the distribution of symptoms for boys, girls, twins, and singleton siblings. Levy et al. (1996) discussed these results further, as well as the association of these symptoms with the well-known differences between twins and singletons in speech and language development (Mogford-Bevan, 1999, and later in this text). What matters for genetic analysis is not whether there is a twin–singleton difference in means, but whether the same factors are determining the causes of individual differences in both groups. We have shown elsewhere (Rhee, Waldman, Hay, & Levy, 1999) that the same estimates of genetic effects are obtained from the twin data as from analysis of the data on twins and singleton siblings combined. In other words, the mean may be changed, but the pattern of familial effects can remain the same.

Table 2.1 shows that the number of symptoms follows the negative exponential distribution that one would expect, where many children have no

*Table 2.1* Distribution of *DSM-III-R* symptoms in twins and their singleton siblings in the Australian Twin ADHD Project. In bold are the symptoms for *DSM-III-R* cut off

| Number of symptoms | Twin | | | | Sibling | | | |
|---|---|---|---|---|---|---|---|---|
| | Male | | Female | | Male | | Female | |
| | Count | % | Count | % | Count | % | Count | % |
| 0 | 635 | 29.5 | 933 | 42.7 | 437 | 46.7 | 489 | 55.9 |
| 1 | 302 | 14.1 | 372 | 17.0 | 139 | 14.9 | 134 | 15.3 |
| 2 | 225 | 10.5 | 232 | 10.6 | 82 | 8.8 | 91 | 10.4 |
| 3 | 198 | 9.2 | 170 | 7.8 | 61 | 6.5 | 49 | 5.6 |
| 4 | 156 | 7.3 | 106 | 4.9 | 55 | 5.9 | 30 | 3.4 |
| 5 | 107 | 5.0 | 97 | 4.4 | 30 | 3.2 | 20 | 2.3 |
| 6 | 120 | 5.6 | 73 | 3.3 | 31 | 3.3 | 17 | 1.9 |
| 7 | 96 | 4.5 | 58 | 2.7 | 23 | 2.5 | 10 | 1.1 |
| **8** | **60** | **2.8** | **43** | **2.0** | **19** | **2.0** | **13** | **1.5** |
| **9** | **72** | **3.4** | **38** | **2.0** | **18** | **1.9** | **6** | **0.7** |
| **10** | **58** | **2.7** | **16** | **0.7** | **8** | **0.9** | **10** | **1.1** |
| **11** | **48** | **2.2** | **24** | **1.1** | **11** | **1.2** | **1** | **0.1** |
| **12** | **43** | **2.0** | **13** | **0.6** | **9** | **1.0** | **1** | **0.1** |
| **13** | **17** | **0.8** | **6** | **0.3** | **3** | **0.3** | **3** | **0.3** |
| **14** | **12** | **0.6** | **4** | **0.2** | **9** | **1.0** | | |
| Total | 2149 | 100 | 2185 | 100.1 | 935 | 100 | 874 | 100 |
| % meeting criterion | | 15.5 | | 6.6 | | 8.3 | | 3.8 |

symptoms and very few have a majority of symptoms. There has been much discussion in behaviour genetics about the appropriateness of statistically transforming data such as these to something closer to a normal distribution before analysis. Such transformations made no difference to the genetic analysis here. For clarity, they are used because of the difficulties in the clinical context of interpreting transformed values.

### Are there key correlated behaviours?

In developing this example of genetic analysis, a major issue is that ADHD does not exist in isolation and that any model must include other behaviours. Throughout the developing literature on ADHD, a key question has been the relationship to speech/language disability (Levy et al., 1996). Table 2.2 identifies the key questions for speech/language development that will be used later in this chapter in multivariate analyses.

### Testing for zygosity

DNA testing to determine the zygosity of twins is not a routine clinical procedure. For example, DNA collection by blood sampling may be

*Table 2.2* The six speech items in the Australian Twin ADHD Project and means for twins and their singleton siblings

| Q1 | Does this child need to have instructions or questions repeated because he/she doesn't follow them? |
|---|---|
| Q2 | Does this child have trouble putting words and sentences together? |
| Q3 | (a) For their age, can this child tell you a reasonable story about a recent event? (b) Do you need to ask questions to understand what has happened to their story? |
| Q4 | Has your child ever had Speech Therapy? |
| Q5 | In your opinion, does this child require extra work/remedial instruction in Speech and Oral Language? |

|  | *Mean* | *SD* | *Cases* |
|---|---|---|---|
| MZ |  |  |  |
| Male | 1.05 | 1.46 | 888 |
| Female | 0.56 | 1.04 | 1011 |
| Total | 0.79 | 1.28 | 1899 |
| DZ |  |  |  |
| Male | 0.93 | 1.30 | 1258 |
| Female | 0.60 | 1.11 | 1155 |
| Total | 0.77 | 1.22 | 2413 |
| Siblings |  |  |  |
| Male | 0.66 | 1.05 | 927 |
| Female | 0.36 | 0.70 | 864 |
| Total | 0.51 | 0.91 | 1791 |
| Total | 0.70 | 1.16 | 6103 |

considered too invasive for some children. Thus, despite the growing number of clinics that offer such assessment, many families will have no precise information on zygosity. As an alternative, it is common to rely on questionnaire assessment of zygosity. Although studies of adult twins have found that reliable information is obtained with only a few questions, we have found that this is not the case with children (as explained below). We rely on the 12 questions listed in Table 2.3, six on similarity and features and six on confusion by others (Cohen, Dibble, Grawe, & Pollin, 1975). We then use Discriminant Function Analysis (DFA) to combine these to maximise the adequacy of diagnosis. We can also identify two common causes of confusion, namely placentation and blood group polymorphisms such as ABO and Rhesus. The old myth that all MZ twins have one placenta is still common (Bryan, as cited in Bouchard & Propping, 1993), and parents may not recognise that being the same on common blood group systems does not mean the twins are necessarily MZ.

The lower part of the table shows the distribution of zygosity in the same-sex pairs and it is clear that there is one common cause of confusion. Almost all the twins about whose zygosity parents were unsure, were rated MZ by the

*Table 2.3* Zygosity questions in the Australia Twin ADHD Project

| Question | Responses | | |
|---|---|---|---|
| I believe the twins to be: | Genetically identical (one egg) | Genetically Nonidentical (two eggs) | Not sure |
| To what extent are the twins similar at this time for the following features? | | | |
|   Height | Not at all similar | Somewhat similar | Exactly similar |
|   Weight | Not at all similar | Somewhat similar | Exactly similar |
|   Facial appearance | Not at all similar | Somewhat similar | Exactly similar |
|   Hair colour | Not at all similar | Somewhat similar | Exactly similar |
|   Eye colour | Not at all similar | Somewhat similar | Exactly similar |
|   Complexion | Not at all similar | Somewhat similar | Exactly similar |
| Do they look as alike as two peas in a pod? | | Yes | No |
| Does their mother ever confuse them? | | Yes | No |
| Does their father ever confuse them? | | Yes | No |
| Are they sometimes confused by other people in the family? | | Yes | No |
| Is it hard for strangers to tell them apart? | | Yes | No |
| Do they have very similar personalities? | | Yes | No |
| Did they have one placenta? | Yes | No | Don't know |
| Do they have the same blood group? | Yes | No | Don't know |

| | *Parent report* | | | | |
|---|---|---|---|---|---|
| DFA estimate | MZ | DZ | Unsure | Total | % |
| Identical | 551 | 72 | 103 | 726 | 59.1 |
| Non-identical | 27 | 395 | 23 | 445 | 36.2 |
| Unsure | 26 | 24 | 8 | 58 | 4.7 |
| Total | 604 | 491 | 134 | 1229 | |
| % | 49.1 | 40.0 | 10.9 | | 100 |

Discriminant Function. That is, parents observed some small differences between their MZ twins, differences that were too small to lead them to label the twins DZ, but enough for them to be unsure if they were MZ.

## How similar are the twins in their ADHD symptomatology?

We present the degree of similarity of the twins in two complementary ways, graphically and through the correlations that form the basis of genetic analysis.

Figure 2.2 shows scatterplots of the ADHD scores of both members of each twin pair, with the MZ twins in (a) clearly clustering far more around the

(a) DSM-III-R ADHD
Identical Twin Pairs

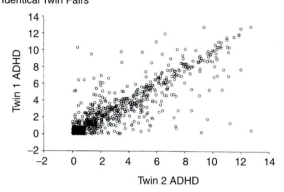

(b) DSM-III-R ADHD
Non-identical Twin Pairs

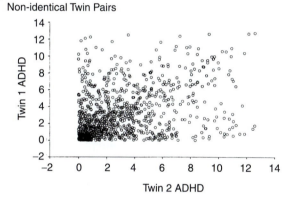

(c) DSM-IV Inattention Scale (SWAN)
Identical Twin Pairs

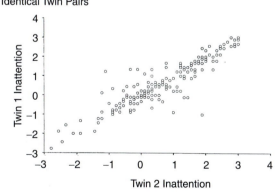

*Figure 2.2* Scatterplot of the scores of each member of a twin pair. (a) and (b) are the number of DSM-III-R symptoms present (0–14) and (c) is the score on the strengths and weaknesses of ADHD and normal (SWAN) behaviour questionnaire (–3 for above average severity to 3 for below average severity).

diagonal than the DZ twins in (b). To describe the similarity between twins in a different way, 61% of the MZ twins had exactly the same score, compared to 32% of the DZ twins. Conversely, only 10% of the MZ twins differed by three or more items, compared to 34% of the DZ twins.

It is worth considering why so many twins have no symptoms and obviously one consideration is how the questions have been developed. A more recent approach by Swanson (2001) extends the scale in another direction, considering the extent to which the person is *more attentive* or *less distractible* than average. Figure 2(c) shows the MZ scatterplot for this new scale. The difference is obvious, but why is this important? As increasing numbers of molecular designs (Chapter 9 and 10, present volume) seek more concordant or discordant twin or sibling pairs, this approach will allow for more detail in defining the meaning of these terms. In the usual approach, concordant for no symptoms may none the less reflect quite different persons, some average and some better than average.

Resemblance is most often expressed as correlations, and Table 2.4 gives the MZ and DZ correlations, not just for ADHD symptom number, but also for the speech data discussed later. There are 14 ADHD categories, but only six speech types (see Table 2.2) and thus polychoric correlations, which assume the variables follow an underlying bivariate normal distribution (Neale & Cardon, 1992), are calculated using PRELIS.

## What are the genetics of ADHD symptom number?

The next step is to test the most parsimonious explanation for the MZ correlation of .91 and the DZ correlation of .52. In Box 2.1 there is a detailed description of how such correlations are interpreted at a formal level. This introduces the topic of path analysis, which estimates the various genetic and environmental pathways through which the scores of two individuals may be related. This theme is extended in Chapter 7 of this volume, with a more complex example of the relation of ADHD to other disruptive disorders.

This strategy can be used to compare different explanations of the observed correlations. Table 2.5 summarises the most likely models. A large chi square value (and correspondingly low *p* value) indicates a poor fit of the

*Table 2.4* Correlation matrix for speech and ADHD scores in MZ and DZ twins

| Correlation | T1ADHD | T2ADHD | T1Speech | T2Speech |
|---|---|---|---|---|
| T1ADHD | 1 | 0.91 | 0.48 | 0.40 |
| T2ADHD | 0.51 | 1 | 0.41 | 0.43 |
| T1Speech | 0.42 | 0.24 | 1 | 0.90 |
| T2Speech | 0.20 | 0.42 | 0.59 | 1 |

*Note*
DZ below diagonal; MZ above diagonal

*Box 2.1* Path diagrams to accompany the analysis in Table 2.5 and the diagrams in Figure 2.3).

Path diagrams are a way of visually representing relationships between variables. They are useful in conceptualising theories but they can also be extended to show mathematical relationships among variables. They consist of variables connected by arrows, which depict the causal relationships among those variables. There are two types of arrows depicting different things. A straight, single-headed arrow that indicates a causal relationship and a curved double-headed arrow that indicates correlation without implied causation. Variables are named in one of two ways; a rectangle surrounding a variable name indicates an observed variable, where as a circle surrounding a variable name indicates that the variable is a latent (unobserved) variable.

**Reading path diagrams**
The conventions of tracing paths from one variable to another using path diagrams are:

No loops (cannot include the same variable twice in a path)
Paths can't go forward (in the direction of an arrow) and then backward (opposite direction of an arrow)
Paths can only contain one double headed arrow

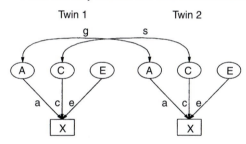

This diagram shows the relationships between a variable (X) observed for each twin of a twin pair and three unobserved variables; A, C, and E. As seen by the arrows, the observed variable, X, is caused by three other variables A, C, and E. A and C are correlated between the twins, but there is no inferred causation due to this correlation. This is a common genetic model in which the A refers to additive genetic causes of an observed trait, C refers to a common environmental influence and E refers to a non-genetic cause unique to each twin. The correlations between the twins exist because of their shared genes and, where twins are brought up in the same family, shared environmental influences. Other influences that are not shared by the twins, make up the effect on the trait (X) represented by E.

   The coefficient g is set to 1.0 for MZ twins and 0.5 for DZ twins representing their genetic similarity. The s coefficient is set to 1.0 for both MZ and DZ because the C term is representing the environmental influences which are shared by the twins (this makes the equal environment assumption, that MZ twins are not treated any more alike than are DZ twins, so the size of c is the same in both twin types).

   From this model, we can calculate the relationships between the twins by tracing the paths. There are two paths for each type of twin:

For MZ: $a \times g \times a = a^2$ and $c \times s \times c = c^2$
For DZ: $a \times g \times a = 0.5a^2$ and $c \times s \times c = c^2$

Thus, the correlations between the MZ and DZ twins are:

$$r_{DZ} = 0.5a^2 + c^2$$
$$r_{MZ} = a^2 + c^2$$

With two equations and two unknown parameters, there are no degrees of freedom left to test the model. That is, there is no other observation which can contradict the estimated parameter estimates. A model that has positive degrees of freedom is one in which it is assumed that $c^2$ is equal to 0. In this case the model reduces to:

$$a^2 = 2 \times r_{DZ}$$
$$a^2 = r_{MZ}$$

Either one of these equations is sufficient to estimate $a^2$, which leaves the other to test the accuracy of the estimate.

*Table 2.5* Results of univariate genetic models of ADHD and speech, fitting the three most common models (ACE, AE, CE)

| Variable | Model | $\chi^2(1)$ | p | $a^2$ | $c^2$ | $e^2$ |
|----------|-------|-------------|-------|-------|-------|-------|
| ADHD | ACE | 0.000 | 1.000 | 0.774 | 0.137 | 0.090 |
| | AE | 1.699 | 0.192 | 0.914 | 0.000 | 0.085 |
| | CE | 54.761 | 0.000 | 0.000 | 0.882 | 0.118 |
| Speech | ACE | 0.000 | 1.000 | 0.621 | 0.276 | 0.104 |
| | AE | 6.313 | 0.012 | 0.906 | 0.000 | 0.094 |
| | CE | 28.807 | 0.000 | 0.000 | 0.856 | 0.145 |

data to the model; models with a *p* value below .05 are rejected as inadequate. The question is whether the similarity between twins can be explained purely environmentally in the CE model (with environmental effects that make twins similar to each other—C, or different from each other—E). Alternatively, whether a genetic model should incorporate similarity due to environmental (C) as well as additive genetic (A) effects. One of the advantages of this approach is that it can be validated by showing that models fit some behaviours but not others. Table 2.5 shows that the basic AE model is adequate for the symptoms of ADHD, but not for the number of speech problems in terms of the chi-squared goodness of fit. For both behavioural traits, the purely non-genetic CE model is inadequate, with significant chi-squared values for the differences between observed and expected. For the speech measure, the simple genetic (A) and environmental (E) model is not enough, and the ACE model is needed to explain the behaviours. That is, growing up as a twin contributes to similarities in speech development, consistent with the extensive literature on what has been variously called "secret language" (Zazzo, 1960), or autonomous language (Mogford-Bevan, 1999).

The failure to find a common environmental effect on ADHD has important implications for explanations of the aetiology of ADHD. For example, it contradicts the hypothesis that ADHD is related to diet, unless one were to make the unlikely speculation that DZ twins growing-up together were more likely than MZ twins to eat different foods!

A graphic way of representing the outcome of genetic modelling is shown in Figure 2.3. Using the same representation as in Box 2.1, these are the best models derived from the analyses in Table 2.5, with AE for ADHD (a) and ACE for Speech Problems (b). This and similar approaches are used in other chapters of this text, as well as in many other behaviour genetic publications.

(a) DSM-III-R ADHD
   Chisq(1) = 1.69, p = 0.192

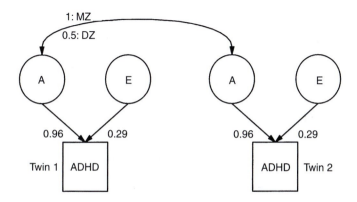

(b) Speech Problems
   Chisq(0) = 0, p = 1.0 (Saturated Model)

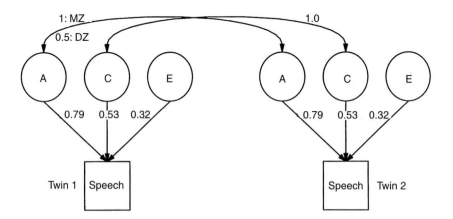

*Figure 2.3* Best fitting genetic models for ADHD (AE model) and for speech (ACE).

Here we have chosen to show the model that shows both twins and their interrelationships, genetic and environmental. Another common format is to show only half of the model, in which instance the relationships are the same for both twins.

One point for the unwary is the manner in which coefficients between latent and observed variables are quoted. This is not the place to discuss the rules of path analysis which underlie Box 2.1 and Figure 2.3. In Box 2.1 the coefficients are squared. When working with correlations, adding these will equal 1.0, and thus the "a" estimate directly gives the heritability ("a") is a parameter estimate (strength of an affect) whereas "A" is the label for the latent variable causing that affect). In presenting diagrams such as Figure 2.3, the values are often not squared. Without discussing the reasoning behind these different methods, the easiest way to avoid confusion is to add all values directed to one observed variable, and establish whether they add up to 1.0 directly, or only if squared.

An interesting aspect of these models is that there is no direct path between the behaviour of one twin and the behaviour of the other. That is, having a twin with ADHD does not directly affect one's own behaviour. Is this realistic or should we give more thought to the dynamics of the twin situation?

## What is it like being a twin?

Since much current genetic analysis is based on the relationship between twins rather than on other relationships, it is important to identify variables that may make the twin relationship different from those of singletons. The most commonly cited criticism of the twin design is that MZ twins are more similar than DZ twins because they have been treated similarly, rather than because they share the same genes. Kendler (1993) emphasised the point that to date little evidence has been found for differences in the MZ versus DZ environment, and very few cases could not be explained by genetic similarity. That is, MZ twins are treated alike in response to their genetically mediated similarities in behaviour, rather than the converse of behavioural similarities resulting from environmental factors, such as similar treatment.

In contrast, Simonoff et al. (1998) analysed a very different type of environmental bias affecting DZ twin scores. On their measure of hyper-activity (discussed further in this text in Chapter 3 by Levy et al.), the DZ correlation was very low compared with the MZ value. When more complex models were used, and data were gathered from sources other than parents, they showed that this was due to parental bias. Parents overestimated the differences between their DZ twins, for instance polarising them as "One is the quiet one and the other is the active one." Obviously, this is not the case in the present data, with the DZ correlation for ADHD symptom number being almost half the MZ correlation for ADHD. Thus, it is important to be alert to ways in which the dynamics of the twin family situation may influence reported resemblance and consequently genetic estimates. Hay and O'Brien

(1987) reported a very different bias in parental reports of temperament in younger twins, with factors such as birth order being a determinant of differences reported in MZ twins. The most likely explanation was that parents wanted their twins to be individuals, and would therefore emphasise any potential discriminators.

Although Simonoff et al. (1998) addressed parental variables affecting the report of ADHD in twins, little has been done concerning what it is like for a child to have a co-twin with ADHD. As part of the ATAP study, parents were asked to comment upon several situations regarding the relationship between the twins themselves, and between the twins and other children. Table 2.6 shows that ADHD brings with it some problems in interpersonal inter-actions, especially if both have ADHD. In this respect, they were more likely to follow each other around and to be compared by other children. Unfortunately when split by zygosity, numbers became too small to incorpor-ate this factor into genetic modelling and to determine whether this was a consequence of the ADHD rather than a causative influence.

## IS ADHD A CONTINUUM OR A DISCRETE CATEGORY?

The analyses to date have been based around the perspective of ADHD in terms of *DSM-III-R* symptom number rather than emphasising the eight-symptom cut-off. The debate over whether childhood psychopathology is best regarded as dimensional or categorical continues (Jensen, Salzberg, Richters, & Watanabe, 1993). The limitations of the alternative categorical approach become evident in genetic analysis. This is especially so for *DSM-IV* with the concept of two disorders, Inattentive and Hyperactive/Impulsive types (plus a Combined type), each of the first two types requir-ing six out of nine specific symptoms to reach criteria. This can potentially give rise to the bizarre situation of a pair of twins (or siblings) where the affected one has six symptoms of one category, while the "unaffected" sib-ling has ten symptoms, five Inattentive and five Hyperactive/Impulsive. Thus the decision as to whether both twins are "affected" is much more difficult if one has to rely on cut-off scores for diagnoses, than if one can take a dimensional approach to the resemblance for an underlying continuous variable.

Box 2.2 introduces methodology that has been developed in behaviour genetics to approach the question of whether a variable should be seen as continuous or dichotomous (De Fries & Fulker, 1985). If a behaviour is inherited as something one "has" or "has not", there are different implica-tions for the predicted score of co-twins of "affected" individuals than would be the case were the behaviour is continuous throughout the population. Furthermore, the ability to predict co-twin score will vary with zygosity, depending upon the heritability of the behaviour. The results in Box 2.2 show that the heritability of *DSM-III-R* ADHD is essentially the same

*Table 2.6* Effects of ADHD on maternal reports of the relationship between twins and the reactions of other children

Do other children compare the twins?

|  | *N* | *A little* | *As much as expected* | *A lot* |
|---|---|---|---|---|
| MZ Male | 290 | 27.9% | 54.8% | 17.2% |
| DZ Male | 279 | 41.2% | 44.1% | 14.7% |

Who is dominant?

|  | *N* | *Neither* | *Twin 1* | *Twin 2* | *Both* |
|---|---|---|---|---|---|
| MZ Male | 303 | 45.9% | 31.0% | 22.1% | 1.0% |
| DZ Male | 306 | 32. 7% | 38.9% | 27.5% | 1.0% |

Do other twins follow each other?

|  | *Neither ADHD* | *One ADHD* | *Both ADHD* | *p* |
|---|---|---|---|---|
| Male | 1.96 | 2.04 | 2.23 | <0.0001 |

Do other children compare the twins?

|  | *Neither ADHD* | *One ADHD* | *Both ADHD* | *p* |
|---|---|---|---|---|
| Male | 1.76 | 1.72 | 2.04 | <0.0001 |

Absolute dominance (score of the most dominant twin)

|  | *Neither ADHD* | *One ADHD* | *Both ADHD* | *p* |
|---|---|---|---|---|
| Male | 0.89 | 1.33 | 1.12 | <0.0001 |

Total competitiveness (4 measures)

|  | *Neither ADHD* | *One ADHD* | *Both ADHD* | *p* |
|---|---|---|---|---|
| Male | 0.82 | 1.09 | 1.27 | <0.0001 |

irrespective of whether it is seen as a continuous trait or as a disorder. However, there are other behaviours where this is not the case. In a recent study of 2-year-old twins in the TEDS project (Dale et al., 1998), the heritability of language acquisition was 25% in the entire population. However, it was 73% in the lowest 5% of the population distribution of vocabulary

---

*Box 2.2* The DeFries and Fulker multiple regression approach to behaviour genetic analysis and the question of whether a disorder or trait is inherited

- This approach involves three basic questions:
    (1) Can one predict the score of one twin from the other (a measure of familiarity)?
    (2) Is the acuracy of prediction influenced by knowing whether the twins are identical or not (a measure of genetic effects)?
    (3) Is the heritability of the disorder the same as that of the trait (the dichotomy-continuum controversy)?

- Results

| | |
|---|---|
| Heritability of the disorder is | 0.91 (±0.12) |
| Heritability of the trait is | 0.75 (±0.21) |
| Difference between the heritabilities is | 0.16 (±0.24) |
| Effect of shared environment is | 0.13 (±0.16) |

---

scores, an important index of language development. That is, there is a genetic component to language delay, which is specific to this group and not found in the determinants of language in the entire population. Consistent with the analyses presented in Table 2.5, there was a large common environment term in the general twin group that was much less among those with significant delay.

The example of intelligence may clarify the distinction between the continuum and the disorder perspectives. Intellectual disability is not just the lower end of the normal range of intelligence test performance (except for those with the so-called "cultural-familial intellectual disability" [Hay, 1985], who have fewer of the genetic and environmental advantages most of us experience). There are other groups who have suffered insults to chromosomes e.g. Down Syndrome; insults to single genes, for instance phenylketonuria (PKU); or insults through environmental effects, such as maternal rubella. Individuals in these groups have in common something that does not relate to the distribution of intelligence in the general population, and gives rise to a "hump" in the lower end of the distribution curve. In ADHD we have much less evidence of its relationship to such disorders (with the exception of the disorders discussed by Zametkin, Ernst, and Cohen in Chapter 9 of this volume). The evidence to date suggests that ADHD is best interpreted as the end of a continuum throughout the entire population. That is, we all inherit some attentional capacity, but for some these difficulties are sufficiently severe to provide "clear evidence of clinically significant impairment in social, academic or occupational funtioning" (*DSM-IV*; APA, 1994, p. 84). Individuals who meet sufficient criteria for a diagnosis are the ones who acquire the label of ADHD.

## Multivariate genetic analysis and the relationship between measures

A powerful aspect of current quantitative genetics is the ability to examine the relationship between behaviours at levels broader than the phenotype. While the observed relationship between two behaviours may be modest, the implications for understanding both aetiology and intervention would be of major significance if this relationship were found to be entirely genetic. Our aim here is to introduce the methodology of multivariate genetic analysis and relationships between measures, whereas examples are developed in other chapters.

We return to Table 2.4, the correlation matrix for ADHD and speech problems. What we observe here is that one individual's ADHD score predicts that individual's speech problem score reasonably well, with a correlation between .42 and .48. Furthermore, for MZ twins, one twin's ADHD score predicts the speech problem score of the identical co-twin almost as well (correlation .40 from twin 1 to twin 2 and .41 from twin 2 to twin 1). But, in DZ twins the values are far less (correlation .20 and .24), essentially half that of MZ twins. Figure 2.4 shows the modelled relationship between these two behaviours. The good chi-square fit indicates the adequacy of this model, and one can use

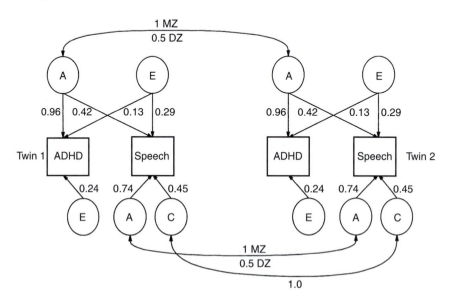

*Figure 2.4* Best fitting genetic model for the relationship between ADHD and speech.

the rules discussed earlier to determine the effects on a specific behaviour. Thus, the differences between twins in speech problems comprise:

17%   $(0.42^2)$   Genetic effects common to ADHD and speech
 8%   $(0.29^2)$   Environmental effects specific to the individual but common to both ADHD and speech
55%   $(0.74^2)$   Genetic effects unique to speech
20%   $(0.45^2)$   Common family environmental effects unique to speech problems
100%            Total

The previous analysis is of value both theoretically and in clinical practice for identifying variables in the family that should be addressed in any intervention programme. For example, it is important to establish which environmental variables contribute to only one child in a twin pair having problems with ADHD and speech, or which result in both twins having speech problems but not ADHD.

Table 2.7 shows that these issues are more complex when one turns to more rigid diagnostic categories, even though these may be more useful at the clinical level. Because of the complexities of defining speech problems, we have used the simplest dichotomous variable, namely whether or not that twin has had speech intervention. (Fortunately the figures in Table 2.7 are consistent with using cut-offs based on the number of speech symptoms in Table 2.2.) The genetic analysis of categorical data raises many issues that cannot be explored here, the most obvious of which is the actual estimation of concordance. This needs to take into account the extent to which the disorder (or combination of disorders) is commonly found. If a disorder is very rare, then only a few concordant twin pairs may be vitally important. There is dispute over the various measures of concordance (McGue, 1992) and the genetic analysis of such concordance data (Neale & Cardon, 1992). In fact, much can be gained by just inspecting the percentages. For example, we can see in Table 2.7(b) that only 13% of DZ twins share the same pattern of ADHD and/or speech problems, compared with 25.2% of MZ twins.

Another way of viewing the situation is that there are substantial groups of individuals who experience one but not both of these problems. As discussed in Chapter 12 of this volume, more attention should to be paid to extreme groups, both clinically, and in understanding comorbidity in ADHD.

## Extensions of the twin design

Although twin design remains the major approach to genetic analysis, more comprehensive approaches to analyses are developing. Analyses that incorporate other relatives besides twins are logical ways of testing the adequacy of the twin design. Siblings are the most obvious group (Rhee et

*Table 2.7* Categorical analyses of the concordances between ADHD and Speech problems, defined either as two or more of the symptoms in Table 2.2 or as having had speech intervention

(a) Using 2/6 speech symptoms present

| Concordance between twins | Speech − ADHD − | Speech − ADHD + | Speech + ADHD − | Speech + ADHD + |
|---|---|---|---|---|
| Speech − ADHD − | 261 / 313 | 14 | 22 | 6 |
| Speech − ADHD + | 33 | 9 / 42 | 0 | 3 |
| Speech + ADHD − | 25 | 3 | 8 / 25 | 4 |
| Speech + ADHD + | 13 | 4 | 3 | 9 / 15 |

(b) Using the presence of specific speech therapy

| Concordance between twins | Speech − ADHD − | Speech − ADHD + | Speech + ADHD − | Speech + ADHD + |
|---|---|---|---|---|
| Speech − ADHD − | 222 / 283 | 16 | 22 | 6 |
| Speech − ADHD + | 37 | 10 / 41 | 0 | 3 |
| Speech + ADHD − | 43 | 4 | 29 / 56 | 6 |
| Speech + ADHD + | 5 | 3 | 6 | 9 / 16 |

*Note*
DZ below diagonal; MZ above diagonal.

al., 1999), and another option is the extended twin design, which incorporates relatives from other generations. The merits, and the problems, of such designs become most noticeable when there are questions concerning how behaviour is manifested and interpreted in different generations. This issue will be explored more in this volume in Chapter 4, which deals with developmental issues.

## DISCUSSION

It is clear from this chapter that a number of issues underlie common statements such as "Twin studies show a substantial genetic component to behaviour X." The issues include: (1) where and how the twins are recruited;

(2) how and by whom the behaviour is assessed; (3) the means by which zygosity is determined; (4) the method used to determine heritability; and (5) confounding factors that have or have not been considered for the specific behaviour being assessed. When we progress to the analysis of multiple measures the situation becomes even more complex, especially when categorical as well as continuous measures are considered.

None the less, such complexities and potentials are fundamental to behaviour-genetic analysis, a theme that will be developed throughout this text. Issues considered include the relationship between Inattention and Hyperactivity-Impulsivity (Chapter 3); ADHD, Oppositional Defiant Disorder and Conduct Disorder, (Chapter 7); ADHD and learning disability (Chapter 6); and symptoms at different ages (Chapter 4).

The behaviour-genetic models can be extended considerably further, as was done in the following studies:

- Simonoff et al.'s (1998) analyses of parental bias in the rating of behavioural symptoms of hyperactivity.
- Eaves et al.'s (1993) analyses of exactly how many genetic latent classes underlie the range of ADHD symptoms.
- Kendler's (1995) identification of environmental factors that interact with genotypic differences.
- The approach developed by Zahn-Waxler, Schmitz, Fulker, Robinson, and Emde (1996), in which twin data are used to develop a wider concept of an individual's control over the environment in which he or she developed.

These newer approaches still have some way to go in statistical methodology. Nonetheless, they do identify the extent to which behaviour-genetic approaches have developed a far more informed analysis of ADHD, and will continue to do so.

What is the impact of quantitative advances on molecular approaches to ADHD? A further *rapprochement* with molecular genetics is developing with the strategy of quantitative trait loci (QTLs). This argues that even if behaviour is polygenic, some of the genes involved may be of sufficiently large effect, such that their specific contribution can be identified. For example, promising results have come from the personality dimension, novelty seeking. Two separate studies (Benjamin, Patterson, Greenberg, Murphy, & Hamer, 1996; Ebstein et al., 1996), which used different measures of this behaviour, have identified variation in behaviour between individuals differing at the dopamine DRD4 receptor gene.

A fundamental question then arises as to whether behaviour genetic or molecular genetic approaches should be primary. For example, given the limited and equivocal data on specific dopamine genes, should future quantitative research focus only on the personality dimensions putatively associated with ADHD, or alternatively, on developing family data for both quantitative and molecular analyses? Another question revolves around exactly who should be assessed, and more importantly, who should be regarded as "affected". This seemingly simple question is the crux of genetic investigation of ADHD. One of the key aims for the future should be to explore its implications. The answers go beyond our current information, but appreciating the complexities of ADHD and comorbid conditions is a task for more detailed future analyses. Given that the definition of ADHD has changed and will continue to evolve over time, this chapter should be seen as an indication only of what could be done, rather than of what has been done to date. There is great potential in genetic methodology, both quantitative and molecular, and the challenge is how best to integrate these approaches.

## REFERENCES

American Psychiatric Association. (1987). *Diagnostic and statistical manual of mental disorders* (3rd ed., rev.). Washington, DC: Author.

American Psychiatric Association. (1994). *Diagnostic and statistical manual of mental disorders* (4th ed.). Washington, DC: Author.

Benjamin, J., Li, L., Patterson, C., Greenberg, B.D., Murphy, D.L., & Hamer, D.H. (1996). Population and familial association between the D4 dopamine receptor gene and measures of novelty seeking. *Nature Genetics, 12*, 81–84.

Boomsma, D.I. (1998). Twin registers in European overview. *Twin Research, 1*, 34–51.

Bouchard, T., & Propping, P. (Eds.). (1993). *Twins as a tool of behavioral genetics.* Chichester, UK: Wiley.

Cohen, D.J., Dibble, E., Grawe, J.M., & Pollin, W. (1975). Reliably separating identical from fraternal twins. *Archives of General Psychiatry, 32*, 1371–1375.

Dale, P., Simonoff, E., Bishop, D.V.M., Eley, T., Oliver, B., Price, T., Purcell, S., Stevenson, J., & Plomin, R. (1998). Genetic influence on language delay in two-year-old children. *Nature Neuroscience, 1*, 324–328.

De Fries, J.C., & Fulker, D.W. (1985). Multiple regression analysis of twin data. *Behavior Genetics, 15*, 467–473.

Dykman, R.A., & Ackerman, P.T. (1991). Attention deficit disorder and specific learning disability: Separate but often overlapping disorders. *Journal of Learning Disabilities, 24* 96–103.

Eaves, L.J., Eysenck, H.J., & Martin, N.G. (1989). *Genes, culture and personality: An empirical approach.* London: Academic Press.

Eaves, L.J., Silberg, J.L., Hewitt, J.K., Meyer, J.M., Rutter, M., Simonoff, E., Neale, M.C., & Pickles, A. (1993). Genes, personality and psychopathology: A latent class analysis of liability to symptoms of Attention Deficit Hyperactivity Disorder in twins. In R. Plomin & G. McClean (Eds.), *Nature, nurture and psychology* (pp. 285–303). Washington, DC: American Psychological Association.

Ebstein, E.B., Novick, O., Umansky, R., Priel, B., Osher, Y., Blaine, D., Bennett, E.R., Nemanov, L., Katz, M., & Belmaker, R.H. (1996). Dopamine D4 receptor (D4 DR) exon III polymorphism associated with the human personality trait of novelty seeking. *Nature Genetics, 12*, 78–80.

Gjone, H., Stevenson, J., & Sundet, J.M. (1996). Genetic influence on parent-reported attention-related problems in a Norwegian general population twin sample. *Journal of the American Academy of Child and Adolescent Psychiatry, 35*, 588–596.

Gleeson, C., Hay, D.A., Johnston, C.J., & Theobald, T.M. (1990). Twins in school: An Australia-wide program. *Acta Geneticae Medicae et Gemellologiae, 39*, 231–224.

Hay, D.A. (1999). The developmental genetics of intelligence. In M. Anderson (Ed.), *The development of intelligence* (pp. 75–104). Hove, UK: Psychology Press.

Hay, D.A. (1985). *The essentials of behaviour genetics.* Oxford, UK: Blackwell Scientific.

Hay, D.A., & O'Brien, P.J. (1987). Early influences on the school social adjustment of twins. *Acta Geneticae Medicae et Gemellologiae, 36*, 239–248.

Hudziak, J.J., Heath, A.C., Madden, P.A.F. Reich W.C., Bucholz, K.K, Slutske W., Bierut, L.J., Neuman, R.J., & Todd, R.D. (1998). Latent class and factor analysis of DSM-IV ADHD: A twin study of female adolescents. *Journal of the American Academy of Child and Adolescent Psychiatry, 37*, 848–857.

Jensen, P.S., Salzberg, A.D., Richters, J.E., & Watanabe, H.K. (1993). Scales, diagnoses and child psychopathology: I. CBCL and DISC relationships. *Journal of the American Academy of Child and Adolescent Psychiatry, 32*, 397–406.

Jinks, J.L., & Fulker, D.W. (1970). Comparison of the biometrical genetical, MAVA, and classical approaches to the analysis of the human behavior. *Psychological Bulletin, 73*(5), 311–349.

Kendler, K.S. (1993). Twin studies of psychiatric illness: Current status and future directions. *Archives of General Psychiatry, 50*, 905–915.

Kendler, K.S. (1995). Genetic epidemiology in psychiatry: Taking both genes and environment seriously. *Archives of General Psychiatry, 52*, 895–899.

Levy, F., Hay, D., McLaughlin, M., Wood, C., & Waldman, I.D. (1996). Twin–sibling differences in perinatal reports of ADHD, speech, reading and behaviour problems. *Journal of Child Psychology and Psychiatry, 37*, 569–578.

Levy, F., Hay, D., McStephen, M., Wood, C., & Waldman, I.D. (1997). Attention Deficit Hyperactivity Disorder (ADHD): A category or a continuum? Genetic analysis of a large scale twin study. *Journal of the American Academy of Child and Adolescent Psychiatry, 36*, 737–744.

Loehlin, J.C. (1992). *Genes and environment in personality development.* Newbury Park, CA: Sage.

Martin, N., Boomsma, D., & Machin, G. (1997). A twin-pronged attack on complex traits. *Nature Genetics, 17*, 387–392.

McGue, M.K. (1992). When assessing twin concordance, use the probandwise not the pairwise rate. *Schizophrenia Bulletin, 18*, 171–176.

Mogford-Bevan, K. (1999). Twins and their language development. In A.C. Sandbank (Ed.), *Twin and triplet psychology: A professional guide to working with multiples* (pp. 36–60). London: Routledge.

Neale, M.C., Baker, S.M., Xie, G., & Maes, H.H. (1999) Mx: Statistical modeling, 5th edn. Box 126 MCV, Richmond, Virginia VA 23298.

Neale, M.C., & Cardon, L.R. (1992). *Methodology for genetic studies of twins and families.* Dordrecht, The Netherlands: Kluwer.

Plomin, R. (1997). Identifying genes for cognitive abilities and disabilities. In R.J. Sternberg & E. Grigorenko (Eds.), *Intelligence, heredity, and environment* (pp. 89–104). New York/Cambridge: Cambridge University Press.

Plomin, R. (2000) Behavioural genetics in the 21st century. *International Journal of Behavioral Development, 24*, 30–34

Plomin, R., De Fries, J.C., McClean, G.E., & Rutter, M. (1997). *Behavioural genetics* (3rd ed.). New York: Freeman.

Rhee, S.H., Waldman, I.D., Hay, D.A., & Levy, F. (1999). Sex differences in genetic and environmental influences on DSM-III-R Attention-Deficit Hyperactivity Disorder (ADHD). *Journal of Abnormal Psychology, 108*, 24–41.

Rutter, M., Roy, P., & Kreppner, J. (in press). Institutional care as a risk factor for inattention/overactivity. In S. Sandberg (Ed.), *Hyperactivity and attention disorders in childhood* (2nd ed.). Cambridge, UK: Cambridge University Press.

Rutter, M., Silberg, J.L., O'Connor, J., & Simonoff, E. (1999a). Genetics and child psychiatry: I. Advances in quantitative and molecular genetics. *Journal of Child Psychology and Psychiatry, 40*, 3–18.

Rutter, M., Silberg, J.L., O'Connor, J., & Simonoff, E. (1999b). Genetics and child psychiatry: II. Empirical research findings. *Journal of Child Psychology and Psychiatry, 40*, 19–55.

Schmitz, S., Fulker, D.W., & Mrazek, D.A. (1995). Problem behavior in early and middle childhood: An initial behavior genetic analysis. *Journal of Child Psychology and Psychiatry, 36*, 1443–1458.

Sherman, D.K., Iacono, W.G., & McGue, M.K. (1997). Attention-Deficit Hyperactivity Disorder dimensions: A twin study of inattention and impulsivity-hyperactivity. *Journal of the American Academy of Child and Adolescent Psychiatry, 36*, 745–753.

Simonoff, E., Pickles, A., Hervas, A. Siberg, J.L., Rutter, M., & Eaves, L. (1998). Genetic influences on childhood hyperactivity: Contrast effects imply parental rating bias, not sibling interaction. *Psychological Medicine, 28*, 825- 837.

Spector, T.D., Snieder, H., & McGregor, A.J. (Eds.). (1999). *Advances in twin and sib-pair analysis*. London: Greenwich Medical Media.

Swanson, J., McStephen, M., Hay, D., & Levy, F. (2001) The potential of the SWAN rating scale in genetic analysis of ADHD. Poster at the International Society for Research in Child and Adolescent Psychiatry. 10th Scientific Meeting, Vancouver June 2001.

Tannock, R. (1998). Attention Deficit Hyperactivity Disorder: Advances in cognitive, neurobiological and genetic research. *Journal of Child Psychology and Psychiatry, 39*, 65–99.

Thapar, A., Holmes, J., Poulton, K., & Harrington, R. (1999). Genetic basis of attention deficit and hyperactivity. *British Journal of Psychiatry, 174*, 105–111.

Thapar, A., Harrington, R., Ross, K., & McGuffin, P. (2000). Does the definition of ADHD affect heritability? *Journal of the American Academy of Child and Adolescent Psychiatry, 39*, 1–12.

Van der Valk, J.C., Verhulst, F.C., Stroet, T.M., & Boomsmsa, D.I. (1998). Quantitative genetic analysis of internalising and externalising problems in a large sample of 3-year-old twins. *Twin Research, 1*, 25–33.

Zahn-Waxler, C., Schmitz, S., Fulker, D., Robinson, J., & Emde, R. (1996). Behavior problems in five-year old monozygotic and dizygotic twins: Genetic and environmental influences, patterns of regulation and internalization of control. *Developmental Psychopathology, 8*, 103–122.

Zazzo, R. (1960). *Les jumeaux: Le couple et la personne*. Paris: Presses Universitaire de France.

# 3    The diagnostic genetics of ADHD symptoms and subtypes

*Florence Levy, Michael McStephen, and David A. Hay*

## INTRODUCTION

In recent years, behaviour genetic methods have advanced to the extent that, given sufficiently large twin samples, underlying genetic and environmental effects on phenotypic traits can be examined. These approaches can also be used to examine whether diagnostic subtypes, or individual items in a diagnostic scale, differ in heritability. The focus of this chapter is the analysis of the criteria used for diagnosing Attention Deficit Hyperactivity Disorder (ADHD) as defined by the fourth edition of the *Diagnostic and Statistical Manual of Mental Disorders* (*DSM-IV*, American Psychiatric Association [APA], 1994.)

Diagnostic criteria for ADHD have undergone a number of changes since the advent of the *Diagnostic and Statistical Manual of Mental Disorders*; third edition (*DSM-III*; APA, 1980), which described operational criteria for diagnostic categories. *DSM-III* listed symptoms of inattention, impulsivity, and hyperactivity, and required that three inattention and three impulsivity symptoms, and two hyperactivity symptoms, be present to attain a diagnosis.

The revised third edition of the *Diagnostic and Statistical Manual* (*DSM-III-R*; APA, 1987), described a single list of fourteen items, incorporating symptoms of inattention, impulsivity, and hyperactivity, with an eight-item cut-off for diagnosis. Although not explicit, this change implied that symptoms of ADHD were on a continuum from low to high numbers of symptoms in normal vs clinical populations, and might thus be manifestations of a single behavioural trait. Although symptoms were chosen in order of discriminability from field trial data, any eight symptoms were sufficient to obtain a diagnosis.

*DSM-IV* (APA, 1994) has, based on factor analyses of field trials, returned to a categorical classification, describing Predominantly Hyperactive-Impulsive, Predominantly Inattentive, and Combined subtypes of ADHD. Both the Predominantly Hyperactive-Impulsive and Predominantly Inattentive subtypes require that six out of nine symptoms, specific to those domains, be present for diagnosis. Symptoms causing impairment must be present before 7 years of age, and significant impairment from symptoms must be present in two or more settings—at school, and/or work, and/or home. These diagnostic criteria are almost identical with the *International Classification of Diseases*, 10th revision (*ICD-10*, World Health Organisation, 1993) research criteria, reflecting a *rapprochement* between North American and European approaches.

*DSM-IV* defines a syndrome as a cluster of symptoms, which co-occur and may be aetiologically linked, and therefore may respond to similar treatments. It is currently unclear whether the *DSM-IV* defined subtypes of ADHD are aetiologically linked syndromes, or rather a cluster of co-occurring symptoms, with aetiological heterogeneity amongst them. It is also unclear whether the subtypes show differential treatment responses. In terms of the heritable aspects of ADHD, we raise a number of questions. For instance, do the same genes determine the Inattention and Hyperactivity/ Impulsivity symptoms, and is there a difference in aetiology between the six Hyperactivity items and the three Impulsivity items that constitute the Hyperactive-Impulsive subtype?

## DIAGNOSTIC GENETICS

As suggested in Chapter 1 of this text, diagnostic issues can best be approached by a combination of factor analysis of the phenotypes, and behaviour genetic methods. In studies of schizophrenia and depression, the introduction of operational criteria for use in psychiatric research (Feighner et al., 1972; McGuffin et al., 1993) has made achievable the goal of reliability, as reflected in agreement between pairs of clinicians. According to McGuffin et al. the central problem concerning diagnosis of psychiatric disorders with a genetic component is not one of reliability, but of validity. That is, do our modern definitions of clinical entities (phenotypes) accurately reflect the action of some underlying combinations of alleles (genotypes)? This raises at least two issues. That is, does one genotype underlie a clinical entity, and is the optimal clinical definition the one that maximises heritability (Kaprio et al., 1993)?

McGuffin et al. (1993) examined heritability for both schizophrenia and depression, and showed that apparently reliable criteria, which define varieties of schizophrenia, have best estimates of heritability as different as 0% and 80%. Similarly, for definitions of unipolar depression, estimates of heritability may range from 20% to 80%. For ADHD, Faraone et al. (1992) have shown that different, albeit closely related, phenotypic definitions show different modes of inheritance when diagnostic algorithms are modified.

According to Sonuga-Barke (1998), there are a number of features of categorical systems, which might help explain such problems. For instance a mismatch between clinicians' mental representations and the decision rules of the system. Alternatively, differences between clinicians in the way in which sets of symptoms of a disorder are interpreted, leading to diagnoses not based on the formal criteria. Judgement may be affected by the clinician's theoretical perspective, or relationship with the client (Mumma, 1993), or by the ethnicity and gender of the client (Malgady, 1996). Clarke, Watson and Reynolds (1995) have argued that high levels of comorbidity between, and heterogeneity within, disorders undermines the validity of the categorical approach.

## CATEGORICAL VERSUS DIMENSIONAL SYSTEMS

Sonuga-Barke (1998), in discussing the scientific status of categorical models of childhood disorder, argued that assumptions underpinning the "medical model"—namely categorical, endogenous, and dysfunctional syndromes—constrain empirical study and development of theory. For example, the claim that adopting *DSM-IV* criteria provides a commonly used and generally accepted way of defining disorders, and so encourages good science, is undermined if these criteria are not reliable or valid. Cantwell (1996) has claimed diagnostic validity for ADHD based on internal validity of symptoms, which can be differentiated from closely related problems. However, Sonuga-Barke (1998) pointed out that those attributes do not establish whether ADHD is qualitatively different from normality.

Achenbach, Conners, Quay, Verhulst, and Howell (1989), Edelbrock and Costello (1988), and others have proposed a dimensional approach to classification. This work comes from a psychometric background, and proposes that the severity of an individual's disorder can be placed along a continuous dimension. This dimension may not always be observed, and observed categories may represent the crossing of a threshold on the dimension. While dimensions derived within the psychometric approach are often roughly equivalent to categories, Sonuga-Barke (1998) pointed out that the total adoption of the dimensional view raises concern about the transparency and communicability of research findings. This would make communication between clinic and laboratory more difficult. The most influential attempt to design a dimensionally based diagnostic system is the Achenbach Child Behaviour Checklist (CBCL; Achenbach,1991). Although this has been extensively used in academic settings (Sergeant, 1995), it has not been routinely adopted in clinical settings. This is possibly because administration is relatively time-consuming, and because its fundamental assumption—that disorders of psychopathology differ from the normal by degree—conflict with assumptions of bimodality implied by the categorical approach. Nonetheless, the CBCL has been very influential in providing an alternate dimensionally based diagnostic system, and dimensional ratings of disruptive behaviour disorder have been shown to have better predictive validity than is the case with categorical measures (Fergusson & Horwood, 1995).

The use of latent class analysis in genetically informative designs is proposed by Sonuga-Barke (1998) as an approach to the investigation of nonlinear relations between symptoms and underlying aetiological factors. For example, Eaves et al. (1993) have explained the latent structure of ADHD by successively fitting models that best characterise the distribution of symptoms. By successively fitting models that assumed one to four classes, they established that the distribution of symptoms was best characterised by three classes, each increasing their likelihood of displaying a subset of ADHD symptoms. By comparing the pairwise membership of latent classes in MZ and DZ twins, they postulated that ADHD could be accounted for by a single gene of reduced penetrance.

## HERITABILITY

De Fries and Fulker (1985, 1988) described a statistical approach that can be applied to twin data and other simple behavioural genetic designs. This is described by Hay (1985) and in Chapter 2 of this text. This technique utilises multiple regression to predict a co-twin's score, based on the genetic relationship between members of twin pairs and the expected statistical regression toward the mean. It compares behavioural assessments of MZ and DZ co-twins of affected probands. To the extent that a trait is heritable, MZ and DZ co-twins regress differentially toward the population mean (i.e., MZ within-pair resemblance is greater than DZ within-pair resemblance). The proportion of variance due to shared environmental influences, too, can be estimated. The multiple regression approach can also be used to address one of the core issues in psychopathology, namely the relationship between the normal and the abnormal. It does this by assessing the extent to which genetic and environmental factors that affect the disorder are the same as those that affect normal variability. In other words, the procedure tests whether the disorder is merely the extreme of a normal distribution of variability. This approach was utilised by Gjone, Stevenson, and Sundet (1996) and by Levy, Hay, McStephen, Wood, and Waldman (1997), to investigate heritability of ADHD defined as either a trait or a category.

## AUSTRALIAN TWIN ADHD PROJECT (ATAP)

Levy et al. (1997) investigated the heritability of ADHD in a large-scale twin sample (2350 families), utilising a *DSM-III-R*-based maternal rating scale. At the phenotypic level, Cronbach alpha (intercorrelations of symptoms) calculations for ADHD symptoms derived separately for MZ and DZ first-born and second-born twins were all close to 0.9, indicating a consistently homogeneous scale. Heritability, when ADHD was defined as a trait, was examined using the De Fries and Fulker (1985, 1988) regression technique. The results indicated a heritability of 0.75 as part of a continuum, and 0.91 for disorder, with no significant difference between the heritabilities. The analysis suggested that *DSM-III-R* ADHD be best viewed as the extreme of a behaviour, which varied genetically throughout the extent of the population, rather than as a disorder with discrete determinants. The effect of shared environment was statistically nonsignificant.

## CONCORDANCE DATA

The traditional way of examining heritability for a diagnostic category is to compare the degree of similarity in MZ vs DZ twins. However, the choice of the statistical measure of twin concordance has been questioned, depending on whether or not there is an assumption of an underlying or unobservable trait that is unidimensional with a normal distribution (Kraemer, 1997). According to Kraemer, the tetrachoric correlation coefficient (TCC) should be used if diagnosis is based on a univariate continuous latent trait that operates on a threshold or "on–off" switch. On the other hand, more conventional intraclass correlation coefficients should be used if this assumption is not met, and if measures are categorical. In the ATAP, we examined probandwise concordances, i.e., concordance between twins meeting diagnostic criteria, in our *DSM-IV*-based twin data, obtained from the second wave of data in 1994 for 1167 same-sex twin pairs (see McGue, 1992 for a discussion of methods of calculating concordances).

We found that concordances in Table 3.1 were consistently at least twice as great in MZ twins as in DZ twins, for Inattentive (I) Hyperactive-Impulsive (H/I) and Combined (C) subtypes of ADHD. The observed values were consistently higher than values expected by chance, far more so for the MZ twins than the DZ twins, thus there were few MZ twins with the Inattentive subtype whose co-twin had the Hyperactivity-Impulsivity subtype. This also applied to the Combined subtype, indicating that *DSM-IV* Inattentive, Hyperactive-Impulsive and Combined subtypes of ADHD may breed true, and may be genetically distinct. Cross-concordances were consistently low for all subtypes. Barkley (1997) has suggested that the predominantly Hyperactive-Impulsive type of ADHD may be a developmental precursor of the Combined type, which was found more frequently in school-aged children. However, in our data the average age was the same for the three subtypes, suggesting that the Hyperactive-Impulsive subtype is not a precursor of the Combined type.

Interestingly, Hudziak et al. (1998) have described a latent class and factor analysis of *DSM-IV* ADHD, in female adolescent twins. Their results suggest that *DSM-IV* subtypes can be thought of as existing on separate dimensions of Inattention, Hyperactivity-Impulsivity, and Combined types. Membership in the severe Inattention subtype predicted academic problems, family problems and referral to health care providers, whereas membership in the severe Hyperactivity-Impulsivity and Combined subtypes predicted impaired social relations.

*Table 3.1* Casewise concordances and cross-correlations

| Twin 2 | No diagnosis | Inattentive | Hyperactive impulse | Combined | Total |
|---|---|---|---|---|---|
| **Identical twins** | | | | | |
| No diagnosis | 567 | 26 | 7 | 8 | 608 |
| | (511.4) | (57.8) | (17.2) | (21.6) | 86.2% |
| Inattentive | 14 | 39 | 2 | 3 | 58 |
| | (48.8) | (5.5) | (1.6) | (2.1) | 8.2% |
| Hyperative-impulse | 5 | 0 | 10 | 0 | 15 |
| | (12.6) | (1.4) | (0.4) | (0.5) | 2.1% |
| Combined | 7 | 2 | 1 | 14 | 24 |
| | (20.2) | (2.3) | (0.7) | (0.9) | 3.4% |
| Total | 593 | 67 | 20 | 25 | 705 |
| | 84.1% | 9.5% | 2.8% | 3.5% | 100.0% |
| | | | | | |
| **Fraternal twins** | | | | | |
| No diagnosis | 353 | 19 | 10 | 0 | 391 |
| | (334.3) | (27.1) | (14.4) | (15.2) | 84.6% |
| Inattentive | 22 | 10 | 1 | 2 | 35 |
| | (29.9) | (2.4) | (1.3) | (1.4) | 7.6% |
| Hyperative-impulse | 4 | 0 | 1 | 2 | 7 |
| | (6.0) | (0.5) | (0.30) | (0.3) | 1.5% |
| Combined | 16 | 3 | 5 | 5 | 29 |
| | (24.8) | (2.0) | (1.1) | (1.1) | 6.3% |
| Total | 295 | 32 | 17 | 18 | 462 |
| | 85.5% | 6.9% | 3.7% | 3.9% | 100.0% |

*Note:*
Chi-square (9) = 700.84, $p <0.000\ 01$ for MZ twins; and Chi-square (9) = 79.06, $p <0.000\ 01$ for DZ twins) Observed data given with expected data in parenthesis

| | Inattention | Hyperactive-impulsive | Combined |
|---|---|---|---|
| **Identical twins** | | | |
| Base rates | 0.09 | 0.03 | 0.04 |
| Casewise concordances | 0.62 | 0.57 | 0.57 |
| | | | |
| **Fraternal twins** | | | |
| Base rates | 0.07 | 0.03 | 0.05 |
| Casewise concordances | 0.30 | 0.08 | 0.21 |

Although the Hudziak et al. (1998) study has some limitations, because it investigated adolescent girls only, it tends to replicate the ATAP findings of separate genetic influences on *DSM-IV* subtypes. These may have different relationships to academic and social variables.

## Contrast versus interaction effects

Unlike our own data, (see Chapters 2 and 4 by Hay and colleagues in this text), a pattern of high intraclass correlations for MZ twins and low intra-class correlations for DZ twins has been reported in a number of studies. These studies used maternal ratings of hyperactivity (Goodman & Stevenson, 1989; McGue, 1992; Thapar, Hervas, & McGuffin, 1995). For example, correlations of .71 in male MZ twins and –.22 in male DZ twins were reported by Thapar et al. (1995). They suggested that the best explanation for this pattern of correlations was a model that incorporates sibling competitive or contrast effects, which lower correlations between DZ twins. Contrast effects tend to exaggerate true differences between DZ twins. Although disproportionately low DZ correlations may also result from genetic dominance effects or non-additive genetic interactions, this would not lead to correlations less than zero.

Structural modelling has been used to clarify the role of genetic and environmental factors in the aetiology of ADHD, and the influence of contrast effects on hyperactivity ratings (Neale & Cardon, 1992). The Thapar et al. (1995) study earlier suggested that, for the maternally rated hyperactivity scores from the Rutter A scale (Rutter, Tizard, & Whitmore, 1970), contrast effects accounted for approximately 6% of the total variance. It is important to note that both the Goodman and Stevenson (1989) and Thapar et al. (1995) studies derived their "hyperactivity" measure by summing three items only on the Rutter A questionnaire (Rutter et al., 1970). These were "very restless, has difficulty staying seated for long", "squirmy fidgety child", and "cannot settle to anything for more than a few moments". Recent studies, such as ATAP, and the Virginia Twin Study of Adolescent Behavioural Development (VTSABD) used complete *DSM-IV* or similar data, allowing differentiation between Hyperactive-Impulsive and Inattentive subtypes of ADHD.

In a sample of 900 twin pairs from the VTSABD, Nadder, Silberg, Eaves, Maes, and Meyer (1998) found that a model that incorporated contrast effects provided the best fit for ADHD symptomatology. It was also marginally better than a model incorporating additional dominance effects. The effects were small, and the power of the study was not sufficient to detect the significance of both dominance and contrast effects. Nadder et al. (1998) pointed out that data using only one rater cannot distinguish between contrast effects that are a function of the rater, versus those derived from competitive sibling interactions. Unlike ADHD, contrast effects did not play a significant role in parental ratings of Oppositional Defiant Disorder or Conduct Disorder symptomatology.

Silberg et al. (1996) have pointed out that the tendency for an informant to rate twins as more or less similar can be due to the influence of one twin's behaviour on his/her co-twin. This can affect twins' correlations and variances, and thus resemble the effects of either shared environment or genetic nonadditivity. Thus a model which includes a shared environment parameter, to account for a DZ correlation greater than half the MZ correlation, has similar implications to one which postulates a "positive" influence of one twin's phenotype on the co-twin. Very high DZ correlations can be accounted for by shared environmental influences, positive interaction, or rater bias. It could also be that there is a relationship between shared environment and rater bias, in that positive sibling interactions are a component of common environment. On the other hand, a model that specifies nonadditive genetic effects—based on a DZ twin correlation significantly lower than half the MZ twin correlation, and lower DZ variances—can be compared against a model that includes "negative" or contrasting influence of one twin's parental rating on the co-twin. However, for an extremely low DZ correlation, the only tenable explanation is negative comparison effects, since a DZ correlation that approximates zero is not consistent with any genetic model.

In the ATAP data, DZ correlations were generally about half the MZ correlations for both categorical and continuous measures. For the continuous data, the DZ correlation was greater than half the MZ, indicating a common family environment effect for Hyperactivity-Impulsivity (see Figure 3.1 later, and associated discussion). There may be differential contrast effects at categorical or high symptom levels. None the less, as pointed out by Nadder et al. (1998), maternal, paternal, and teacher ratings may be required to separate the effects of rater bias from the common environmental component of variation in the childrens' behaviour.

Simonoff et al. (1998) used hyperactivity ratings from mothers and teachers for 1644 twin pairs in the VTSABD to explore the origin of contrast effects, making use of independent teacher reports in a proportion of twins. Models for maternal data suggested that contrast effects were operative, whereas teacher ratings were influenced by twin confusion or by rater bias. On the other hand, a recent genetic study by Thapar, Harrington, Ross, and McGuffin (2000) found rater contrast effects (AE-s model) for the Rutter A scale (which contains only three hyperactivity items). They did not find this for the Du Paul ADHD rating scale, which is *DSM-III-R* based. This suggests that maternal rating effects vary for different instruments used with the same set of twins. This conclusion is supported by Hudziak, Rudiger, Neale, Heath, and Todd (2000). They found no evidence of rater contrast effects in a study of 498 same-sex 8- to 12-year-old twins, rated by their mothers using the Child Behaviour Check List (CBCL). The authors attribute this result to the fact that the CBCL presents symptoms alphabetically, rather than by syndrome groupings, thereby minimising bias.

## GENETIC ANALYSIS

Quantitative genetics allows the testing of explicit simultaneous models of genetic and environmental parameters, utilising latent trait analysis to examine questions of underlying patterns of association, such as in Thapar et al. (1995). Eaves, Silberg, Meyer, and Maes (1997) reported extensive data from the VTSABD. They derived a *DSM-III-R* diagnosis of ADHD from the Child and Adolescent Psychiatric Assessment (CAPA) interviews with both parents, as well as obtaining Conners and Rutter "B (2)" scale teacher data (Rutter et al., 1970). Analyses of five scales assessing symptoms of ADHD showed highly significant twin contrast comparison effects for maternal and paternal ratings. These results were relatively homogeneous over the sexes, and were similar for interviews and questionnaire assessment. The contribution of additive genetic factors, after removing the effects of contrast from the data, was between 60% and 80%. Teacher ratings gave slightly lower estimates of genetic and environmental components, but showed no evidence of significant contrast effects. The investigators commented that future multivariate genetic analyses of multimethod/multirater data should shed further light on determining which genetic and social effects are measurement-dependent, and which are stable across sources of data. Added to this, the inclusion of more "objective" laboratory-based measures of attention should help to separate primary genetic and environmental influences from those generated or exaggerated by the process of measurement.

Tannock (1998) has pointed out that, although high heritability estimates for ADHD imply a very strong genetic contribution, and a low level of measurement error, the extent of genetic influence appears to vary by informant source and diagnostic criteria (Goodman & Stevenson, 1989; Sherman, Iacono, & McGue, 1997; Sherman, McGue, & Iacono, 1997). Schmitz, Saudino, Plomin, Fulker, and DeFries (1996) investigated genetic influence on teacher and "tester" ratings of temperament in 7-year-old children. Their study utilised a sibling adoption design to investigate teacher and tester ratings, and showed significant genetic influence on both teacher and tester ratings of activity. Bivariate genetic analysis showed that the modest covariance between teacher and tester ratings of activity was entirely mediated genetically.

According to Hay et al. (Chapter 2, this volume), the contentious issues of whether C, the common environment, is really the same in MZ and DZ twins has been widely debated. MZ twins may well be treated more similarly, but this is more a *consequence* of their genetic similarity in behaviour (and consequent responses by parents and others) than a *cause* of similarity.

To date there has been little genetic evidence for the *DSM-IV* distinction of Inattention and Hyperactivity-Impulsivity, possibly reflecting the long time required for completion of a genetic study based on these new criteria. Sherman, Iacono, and McGue (1997) have found some evidence for a genetic correlation between Inattention and Hyperactivity-Impulsivity, although this differed considerably between teacher and mother reports, with maternal reports suggestive of rater bias effects.

Neuman et al. (1999) applied latent class analysis to ADHD symptom profiles obtained from parent or best informant in three samples. These were:

a population-based set of female adolescent twins; child and adolescent male; and child and adolescent female offspring, ascertained from high-risk alcoholic families. The pattern of latent classes suggested that ADHD consisted of Inattentive and Combined subtypes, within each of which was a dimensional domain. This is consistent with the ATAP concordance data reported previously, in which *DSM-IV* subtypes appeared to breed true, rather than the Combined subtype merely representing a combination of symptoms from the Inattentive and Hyperactive-Impulsive types. In the Neuman et al. (1999) study, a large proportion of the MZ siblings (80%), versus a smaller proportion of DZ siblings (52%), were assigned to the same latent class. Interestingly, the high-risk families contained a class in which members heavily endorsed the ADHD "fidget" item, but not other ADHD items. The relatively low prevalence of the Hyperactive-Impulsive class in the study was thought to reflect the older age of the samples, and possibly a gender bias.

Data from the ATAP has been used to fit models of genetic and environmental factors to *DSM-IV* ADHD data. This model described the factors shared by the two dimensions Inattention and Hyperactivity/Impulsivity, as well as those factors specific to each of the disorders.

A path diagram representing the best fitting model is shown in Figure 3.1. This model shows that additive genetic (A), common environmental (C) and non-shared environmental (E) factors all contribute to the overlap between

DSM-IV ADHD
Chi Square (5) = 5.283, p = 0.382

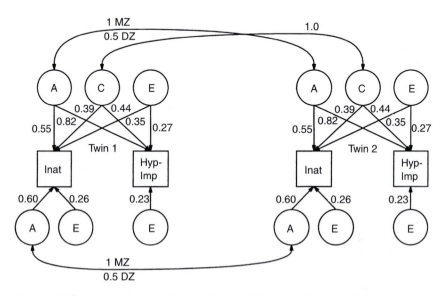

*Figure 3.1* The overlap between Inattention and Hyperactivity/Impulsivity.

Inattention and Hyperactivity/Impulsivity. There are also specific genetic (g) and non-shared environmental (e) factors affecting Inattention, and specific non-shared environmental (e) factors which affect Hyperactivity/Impulsivity.

Demonstrating this different mixture of effects on the two dimensions prompted closer examination of genetic and environmental effects on individual items in both scales. Inattention and Hyperactivity-Impulsivity scales are designed to describe the manifestation of the underlying disorders and the most basic descriptors of these disorders are the items of the scale. These items are known to be highly inter-correlated, because the scales were derived from factor analytic techniques and other techniques designed to show uniformity of scale. What is not known is the extent to which the inter-correlation of items has a genetic basis. Genetic item analysis seeks to elucidate the mechanisms underlying the phenotypic inter-correlation of items.

## ITEM ANALYSIS

Loehlin (1992) has discussed the major designs that have been applied to the study of behaviour genetics of personality traits. A review of behaviour genetic studies of extraversion-related traits of impulsivity, dominance and sociability showed that, although heritabilities of these traits were modest but respectable at 20 to 40%, there were differences among the subtraits. These differences were not apparent when extroversion was modelled as a trait. This raised the question of the optimal level for analysis of personality traits or subtraits.

Conventional studies of personality traits compute correlations between twin pairs or other relatives for scale scores obtained as the weighted (or unweighted) sum of responses to a number of items. Heath and Martin (1990) have pointed out that implicit in this approach is the assumption that the observed ("phenotypic") personality trait and the underlying genetic and environmental factors are not qualitatively different. It is assumed that phenotypic common factor loadings and corresponding genetic common factor loadings differ only by a scale factor. That is, the same genetic factor is influencing subphenotypes. However, in reality, in an extreme case the genetic factors underlying subphenotypes may differ so markedly that they are acting independently. Under these conditions the concept of heritability would no longer be applicable at the trait level, and would be better interpreted at the item level.

Genetic item analysis has been proposed as an alternative to traditional methods for analysing the influence of heredity on behavioural traits. Differences in item heritability can arise, however, through differences in item reliability, through item loadings on one or more underlying genetic common factors, or through item-specific genetic influences.

Waller and Reise (1992) have pointed out that a unidimensional scale may be composed of multidimensional items at the genetic level. Furthermore, the scale variance is frequently dominated by a common factor that can be partitioned into separate Common genetic and Common environmental influences. The item variance may nonetheless have substantial loadings on genetic and/or environmental factors that are specific to each item. It is only by examining all of the factors that influence item response behaviour, that investigators will be able to understand completely the full determinants of response pattern variation. For example, identical twins produce more like responses than do fraternal twins because identical twins share 100% of genetic factors relating to the underlying trait, and 100% of item-specific genetic factors. Fraternal twins share only (on average) 50% of their genes and therefore are (on average) half as similar on underlying trait and *item-specific* genetic factors as identical twins. These differences in item-specific genetic effects only become apparent when analysis is done at the item level. For some items, the influence of an item's specific factor score will add significantly to that of the common factor score, whereas other items are influenced predominantly by the common factor.

According to Heath and Martin (1990) multivariate genetic analysis permits the estimation of separate genetic and environmental, common and specific, factor loadings from data on twin pairs. When applied to items, rather than to scale scores, this avoids some of the pitfalls of univariate item analysis. For example, their results, when applied to the items of the Psychoticism scale (P scale) of the Eysenck Personality Questionnaire, showed marked lack of correspondence between the dimensions of genetic variation influencing the P scale. That is, some loadings were positive and some negative, which suggested that specific effects were important at the item level.

## UNIVARIATE ITEM ANALYSIS

We considered an analysis of individual ADHD items from our 1994 *DSM-IV*-based maternal ratings of 1167 same sex twin pairs. Mx (Neale, Boker, Xie, & Maes, 1999) was used to fit genetic models with three sources of variance: A, additive genetic effects ($h^2$); C, shared family environmental effects ($c^2$); and E, environmental effects ($e^2$) unique to the individual. (See Chapter 2, this volume, for more discussion of estimation of these parameters.) The results are summarised in Table 3.2. Of the Hyperactivity-Impulsivity items, only one showed reasonable fit to an AE model. This was item 14, "Fidgets with hands or feet or squirms in seat". Although item 10, "On the go—driven by a motor." had a nonsignificant chi-square value for the AE model, it had a large standardised residual (3.85), which indicated a substantial mismatch between the observed and predicted correlation.

Of the Inattention items, the chi-square for the AE model indicated acceptable fit for five out of nine items. Of these five items (1, 2, 5, 7, and 9),

Table 3.2 Genetic item analysis

| Item | MZr | DZr | $A^2$ | $C^2$ | $E^2$ | $AE\ X^2$ | $AE\ p$ | $A^2$ | $E^2$ |
|---|---|---|---|---|---|---|---|---|---|
| **Inattention items** | | | | | | | | | |
| 1 Easily distracted | 0.867 | 0.536 | 0.66 | 0.21 | 0.13 | 3.526 | 0.060 | 0.88 | 0.12 |
| 2 Trouble following instructions | 0.857 | 0.531 | 0.65 | 0.21 | 0.14 | 3.326 | 0.068 | 0.86 | 0.13 |
| 3 Difficulty keeping attention | 0.890 | 0.588 | 0.60 | 0.29 | 0.11 | 7.180 | 0.007 | 0.91 | 0.09 |
| 4 Does not seem to listen when spoken to directly | 0.912 | 0.729 | 0.37 | 0.54 | 0.09 | 24.523 | 0.000 | 0.96 | 0.04 |
| 5 Loses things | 0.855 | 0.526 | 0.66 | 0.20 | 0.14 | 2.644 | 0.104 | 0.87 | 0.13 |
| 6 Difficulty organising tasks | 0.876 | 0.555 | 0.64 | 0.23 | 0.12 | 3.938 | 0.047 | 0.89 | 0.11 |
| 7 Fails to give attention to detail | 0.812 | 0.476 | 0.67 | 0.14 | 0.19 | 1.468 | 0.226 | 0.82 | 0.18 |
| 8 Forgetful in daily activities | 0.882 | 0.608 | 0.55 | 0.33 | 0.12 | 7.451 | 0.006 | 0.90 | 0.10 |
| 9 Reluctant with prolonged concentration | 0.885 | 0.487 | 0.80 | 0.09 | 0.11 | 0.525 | 0.469 | 0.89 | 0.11 |
| **Hyperactivity/impulsivity items** | | | | | | | | | |
| 10 On the go–driven by a motor | 0.918 | 0.539 | 0.76 | 0.16 | 0.08 | 1.966 | 0.161 | 0.92 | 0.08 |
| 11 Leaves seat in classroom | 0.911 | 0.643 | 0.53 | 0.38 | 0.09 | 8.001 | 0.005 | 0.93 | 0.07 |
| 12 Difficulty playing quietly | 0.966 | 0.682 | 0.57 | 0.40 | 0.03 | 12.483 | 0.000 | 0.97 | 0.03 |
| 13 Runs about or climbs | 0.971 | 0.776 | 0.39 | 0.58 | 0.03 | 28.389 | 0.000 | 0.98 | 0.02 |
| 14 Fidgets with hands or feet or squirms in seat | 0.903 | 0.481 | 0.84 | 0.06 | 0.10 | 0.207 | 0.649 | 0.90 | 0.09 |
| 15 Talks excessively | 0.875 | 0.542 | 0.67 | 0.21 | 0.12 | 3.441 | 0.064 | 0.89 | 0.12 |
| 16 Difficulty awaiting turn | 0.905 | 0.617 | 0.57 | 0.33 | 0.10 | 8.945 | 0.003 | 0.92 | 0.08 |
| 17 Blurts out answers | 0.894 | 0.589 | 0.61 | 0.28 | 0.11 | 6.101 | 0.014 | 0.91 | 0.09 |
| 18 Interrupts or intrudes | 0.905 | 0.655 | 0.50 | 0.40 | 0.09 | 14.977 | 0.000 | 0.94 | 0.07 |

only two items (7 and 9) had standardised residual less than 3. The fit of the other three of the five items was marginal, and the standard residuals were greater than 3.0. Item 5 was close to acceptable, in that the chi-square was $p > .05$ and standard residual 3.094.

In this circumstance, the ACE model is to be preferred, for two reasons. Firstly, an *a priori* reason is that these data were collected using the same rater for both twins in the pair, thus there will be some rater effect that is environmental and common to both twins. (i.e., a C component). Second, since most AE models do not fit, using the ACE model for all items allows comparability of parameter estimates across items. If a C term is not present in the model, then the observed relationship between twin covariance is solely explained by the A path. This A path will be higher than the parameter from an A path of an ACE model, which has some variance explained through the C path. Grayson (1989) makes the point that the "twins reared together" design tends to overestimate the genetic influence, so in the absence of strong evidence for a consistent AE model, the ACE model is preferred.

As can be seen from Table 3.2, the unique environment parameter ($e^2$), which represents random variation in twin similarity and unreliability of measurement, is small and does not vary much among items (mean = 0.11, standard deviation = 0.037). Since the parameters of the model were standardised, the common environment terms in the table are small for large heritability values and *vice versa*.

The items relating to Inattention had an average heritability of 0.62. Six of the nine items showed heritabilities between 0.6 and 0.7. Item 8 "Forgetful in daily activities" had a heritability of 0.55; item 4 "Does not seem to listen when spoken to directly" had a heritablity of 0.37; and "Reluctant with prolonged concentration", 0.8. The unique environmental variance was about 10% for all items, so most nongenetic variance was due to family environmental influences.

The items relating to Hyperactivity-Impulsivity showed a similar average heritability (0.61), but more variation. Six of the nine items had heritabilities between 0.5 and 0.7 (0.2–0.4 common environment) with three having values outside this range. These three were item 10, "On the go—driven by a motor" (heritability = 0.76), item 14, "Fidgets with hands or feet or squirms in seat" (heritability = 0.84), and item 13, "Runs about or climbs" (heritability = 0.39). The distributions of heritability values for the items are shown in Figure 3.2. It was unexpected that item 10, "On the go—driven by a motor" and item 13, "runs about or climbs" were quite different in heritability. However, both items combine questions about two separate behaviours, and it could be that part of a compound item such as "climbs" has a confounding affect on mothers' ratings.

It is easier to propose a reason for low heritability, rather than considering high heritability as being due to poor item design, because there is no obvious reason why an ambiguous item should affect MZ correlations more than DZ correlations. Item 4, "Does not seem to listen when spoken to directly" and

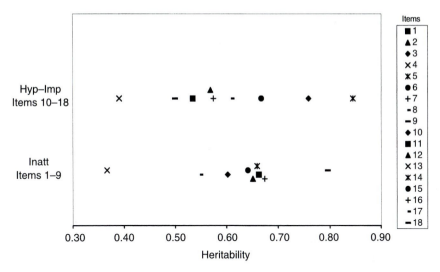

*Figure 3.2* Heritability of Inattention and Hyperactivity-Impulsive items.

item 13, "Runs about or climbs" are both low heritability items (i.e., high common environment). Thus, either this behaviour is not genetic in origin, or the ratings are more sensitive to bias, such that both twins are rated highly regardless of zygosity (i.e., a "positive" affect).

The other outstanding items are 9, "Reluctant with prolonged concentration", 14 "Fidgets with hands or feet or squirms in seat", and 10 "On the go—driven by a motor". These have the highest heritability (0.80, 0.84, and 0.76 respectively) and therefore lowest common environment (0.09, 0.06, and 0.16). Thus, either these behaviours are genetic in origin, or parents of MZ twins rate twins more similarly for them than do parents of DZ twins. Interestingly, these items are most similar to the Rutter A scale items (Rutter et al., 1970); (Very restless, difficulty staying seated for long; Squirmy fidgety child; Cannot settle to anything to more than a few minutes). In our data, these items do not appear to show DZ contrast effects.

All the extreme value items (4 and 13 and 9, 14, and 10) have average "error" terms, so these are not simply items that do not fit into any model. The effect of common family environment was generally larger than for Inattention items.

## MULTIVARIATE ITEM ANALYSIS

The multivariate genetic models discriminate components of the genetic and environmental variance on the items measuring *DSM-IV* ADHD subtypes. This model describes the relationship between items in terms of their association with the underlying trait (Inattention or Hyperactivity-Impulsivity), and putative genetic and environmental variance specific to the items. The phenotypic trait is described in terms of the affects of putative genetic and environmental effects. These factors affect the variation among the items through the item loadings on the phenotype. Thus, the variance of each item (and covariance among the items) is partitioned into variance due to the trait, and genetic and environmental factors specific to the items.

The Inattention and Hyperactive-Impulsive subtype items were modelled to determine the extent to which items shared genetic and shared environmental influences within each subtype. Mx (Neale et al., 1999) allows examination of the hypothesis that there is a set of genetic and environmental factors common to all nine items of each subtype. Figures 3.3 and 3.4 illustrate these models. The middle level of the model shows the phenotypic loading of each item on the putative trait. The top level of the diagram shows the A, C and E contributions common to the overall Inattention and Hyperactive-Impulsive traits. The bottom level of the model shows the genetic and environmental effects specific to each item. The multivariate model for the Inattention items is shown in Figure 3.3.

Note that there is considerable discussion over the best goodness-of-fit measures. The chi-square statistic is sensitive to degrees of freedom. The residual mean square analysis (RMSEA) is less influenced by population assumptions, and values of the RMSEA less than 0.05 indicate a good fit of the model to the data (Joreskog & Sorbom, 1993).

As can be seen from Figure 3.3, most of the additive genetic variance (A) of the items describing the *DSM-IV* Inattention scale is explained by the genetic variation of the trait. The amount of genetic variance specific to the items ranges from 10% (item 2) to 25% (item 1). A similar pattern is observed with the common environmental (C) influences with most of the variance being due to the trait and some variance specific to individual items. The specific C variance ranged from 0% (items 7 and 9) to 16% (item 8). There was very little item-specific variance due to other environmental variance (E). Variance due to these non-shared environmental influences had little affect on the overall phenotype (7.0%). The negative direction of the path coefficient indicated that this variation was associated with dissimilarity (negative correlation) between the twins.

The path coefficient for the relationship between the phenotype and the items gives an indication of the amount of item variance due to the phenotype, and therefore how much variance is specific to the item (specific variance = 100% − phenotypic variance). This gives an indication of which items are core items of *DSM-IV* ADHD Inattention. There are five items with loading of approximately 80% on the phenotype. For these items, only 20% of the variance is not due to the underlying phenotype. One point to note is that although item 9 "Reluctant with prolonged concentration" has a loading of 79%, all of the 21% of variance specific to the item is genetic.

The three items with the lowest loading (1, 5, and 8) have less variance

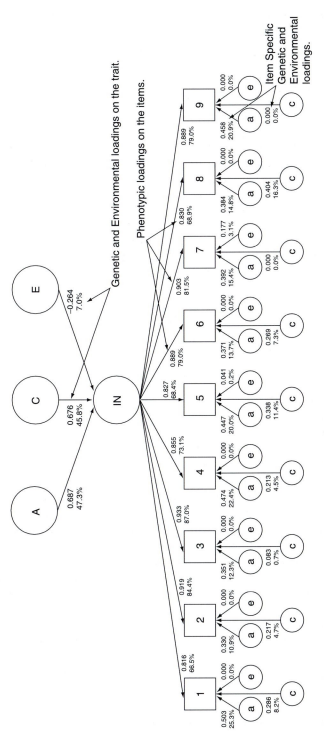

*Figure 3.3* Standardised common path diagram for Inattention items.

associated with the phenotype, and have a combination of relatively high specific genetic and common environmental variance.

The multivariate model for the Hyperactive-Impulsive items is shown in Figure 3.4. The item variance for the Hyperactivity-Impulsivity scale was also predominantly due to the latent phenotype. The specific item variances showed a stronger effect of common environment than did Inattention, with item-specific C variance ranging from 4.8% (item 14, "Fidgets with hands and feet or squirms in seat") to 25.8% (item 15, "Talks excessively"). There was a greater range of item-specific genetic variance than that shown by the Inattention scale items (2.6% for item 18 to 29.2% for item 14). The pheno-typic loadings were correspondingly smaller, reflecting the greater item-specific variance. Items 10, 11, 12, 13, and 18 had phenotypic loadings of 75.3%, 75.5%, 75.9%, 74.6%, and 76.7% respectively, whereas items 14, 15, and 17 ("Blurts out answers to questions") had lower loadings; 59.8%, 66.7%, and 65.9% respectively. These three had high specific genetic variances 29.2%, 25.8%, and 20.4% as did item 16 ("Difficulty awaiting turn") at 20.3%, which had a phenotypic loading of 71.8%, which was intermediate to the two groups of items. These items, 14, 15, 17, and possibly 16, may represent an associated but distinct aspect of Hyperactivity-Impulsivity (possibly the Impulsive component), with some genetic influences specific to these items. It may be relevant that Neuman et al. (1999) reported a latent class in high-risk alcoholic families, in which members heavily endorsed the ADHD item "fidgets", but not other ADHD items.

## DISCUSSION

The previous data illustrate very clearly that, while a putative syndrome may appear homogeneous at the phenotypic level, a genetic latent trait analysis reveals much more heterogeneity for ADHD. This of course has implications for finding a gene for ADHD. From the findings, it would seem that Inatten-tion is a more homogeneous construct than is Hyperactivity-Impulsivity at a latent genetic level. Both the concordance data from the ATAP, and the gen-etic analyses at scale and item level, support the *DSM-IV* division into Pre-dominantly Inattentive, Predominantly Hyperactive-Impulsive, and Com-bined subtypes, which are shown to breed true. The findings in the Gjone et al. (1996) and Levy et al. (1997) studies, that *DSM-III-R* heritability does not significantly differ regardless of whether ADHD is defined as a trait or a category, might appear to be at variance with these *DSM-IV* data. However, as can be seen from Figure 3.1, there is shared genetic variance between Inattention and Hyperactivity-Impulsivity, thus the latent traits are geneti-cally related, but still have unique genetic variance. Although heritability may not differ significantly, different or additional genes might operate at the extremes of behaviour, which may then breed true when classified according to *DSM-IV* criteria. Given the results of Hudziak et al. (1998) and Neuman

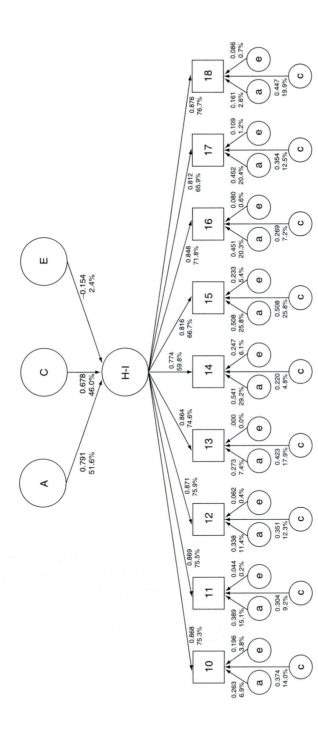

*Figure 3.4* Standardised common path diagram for Hyperactive-Impulsive items.

et al. (1999), the jury is still out on whether there is a continuum for the Combined subtype, separate from the Inattentive and Hyperactive-Impulsive subtypes.

In general, similarities among items within subtypes outweigh differences, and support the *DSM-IV* categorisation into Inattentive and Hyperactive-Impulsive subtypes. However, the comparatively lower phenotypic loadings for items 14, 15, 16, and 17 could suggest a possible subtype related to Impulsivity. Interestingly, items 15, 16, 17, and 18 represent the *ICD-10* (WHO, 1992) Impulsivity subtype symptoms, whereas items 16, 17, and 18 represent the *DSM-IV* Impulsivity symptoms. The possibility of a separate subtype could be further investigated at the molecular genetic level, and may too have implications for treatment. For example, items 15 and 18 have larger specific common environment effects, which may need specific interventions.

Additive genetic influences are of major importance for both Inattention and Hyperactivity-Impulsivity, but the more significant common environment effects for most Hyperactivity-Impulsivity items raise a number of intriguing questions about the nature of these effects on both classification and treatment. These effects remain in the multivariate analysis, and are particularly noticeable for items 10, 13, 15, 17, and 18. Certainly, at a clinical level, the more impulsive items reflecting interruption or intrusion are likely to impact on siblings. However, the question of whether these effects are "real", or reflect rater or instrument effects, remains unanswered. It may be that the greater heterogeneity of the Hyperactive-Impulsive items leaves them more liable to rater effects, be these interactive, or contrast effects. None the less, the findings could suggest that greater attention should be paid to the behaviour management of Hyperactive-Impulsive symptoms, which may be partially maintained by adverse interactions in a family setting than may be the case for the Inattentive symptoms. The implications of subtype differences for treatment and education are discussed in Chapter 12 of this volume, "Implications of Genetic Studies of Attentional Problems for Education and Intervention".

The search for a gene for ADHD should continue to differentiate Inattentive and Hyperactive-Impulsive and Combined subtypes (and possibly an Impulsive subtype), despite the considerable shared additive genetic influences shown in Figure 3.1. The findings discussed here demonstrate the power of genetic designs to differentiate latent influences on phenotypic presentations, which can reflect both genetic and environmental influences, at both scale and item levels, and may help to define genetic phenotypes for molecular studies. A collaborative relationship between quantitative genetic and molecular genetic approaches is an encouraging outcome of advances in both areas.

# REFERENCES

Achenbach, T.M. (1991). *Manual for the Child Behaviour Checklist 4–18 and 1991 profile*. Burlington, VT: University of Vermont, Department of Psychiatry.

Achenbach, T.M., Conners, C.K., Quay, H.C., Verhulst, F.C., & Howell, C.T. (1989). Replication of empirically derived syndromes as a basis for taxonomy of child/adolescent psychology. *Journal of Abnormal Child Psychology, 17,* 299–320.

American Psychiatric Association. (1980). *Diagnostic and statistical manual of mental disorders* (3rd ed.). Washington, DC: Author.

American Psychiatric Association. (1987). *Diagnostic and statistical manual of mental disorders* (3rd ed., rev.). Washington DC: Author.

American Psychiatric Association. (1994). *Diagnostic and statistical manual of mental disorders* (4th ed.). Washington DC: Author.

Barkley, R.A. (1997). *ADHD and the nature of self-control*. New York: Guilford Press.

Cantwell, D.P. (1996). Classification of child and adolescent psychopathology. *Journal of Child Psychology and Psychiatry, 37,* 3–12.

Clark, L.A., Watson, D.S., & Reynolds, S. (1995). Diagnosis and classification in psychopathology: Challenges to the current system and future directions. *Annual Review of Psychology, 46,* 121–153.

De Fries, J., & Fulker, D.W. (1985). Multiple regression analysis of twin data. *Behaviour Genetics, 15,* 467–472.

De Fries, J.C., & Fulker, D.W. (1988). Multiple regression analysis of twin data: Aetiology of deviant scores versus individual differences. *Acta Geneticae Medicae Gemellologiae (Roma), 7,* 205–216.

Eaves, L., Silberg, J.L., Hewitt, J.K., Meyer, J.M., Rutter, M., Simonoff, E., Neale, M.C., & Pickles, A. (1993). Genes, personality, and psychopathology: A latent class analysis of liability to symptoms of Attention-Deficit Hyperactivity Disorder in twins. In R. Plomin & G.E. McLern (Eds.), *Nature, nuture, and psychology* (pp. 285–303). Washington, DC: American Psychiatric Association Books.

Eaves, L.J., Silberg, J.L., Meyer, J.M., & Maes, H.H. (1997). Genetics and developmental psychopathology: 2. The main effects of genes and environment and behavioural problems in the Virginia twin study of adolescent behavioural development. *Journal of Child Psychology and Psychiatry, 38,* 965–980.

Edelbrock, C.S., & Costello, A.J. (1988). Convergence between statistically derived problem syndromes and child psychiatric diagnosis. *Journal of Abnormal Child Psychology, 16,* 219–231.

Faraone, S.V., Biederman, J., Chen, W.J., Krifcher, B., Keenan, K., Moore, C., Sprich, S., & Tsuang, M.T. (1992). Segregation analysis of Attention Deficit Hyperactivity Disorder. *Psychiatric Genetics, 2,* 257–275.

Feighner, J.P., Robins, E., Guze, R.A., Woodruff, G., Winokur, G., & Mundz, R. (1972). Diagnostic criteria for use in psychiatric research. *Archives of General Psychiatry, 26,* 57–63.

Fergusson, D.M., & Horwood, L.J. (1995). Predictive validity of categorically and dimensionally scored measures of disruptive childhood behaviors. *Journal of the American Academy of Child and Adolescent Psychiatry, 34,* 477–485.

Gjone, H., Stevenson, J., & Sundet, J.M. (1996). Genetic influences on parent reported attention—related problems in a Norwegian, general population twin sample. *Journal of the American Academy of Child and Adolescent Psychiatry, 35,* 588–596.

Goodman, R., & Stevenson, J. (1989). A twin study of hyperactivity: II. The aetiological role of genes, family relationships and peri-natal adversity. *Journal of Child Psychology and Psychiatry, 30*, 691–709.

Grayson, D.A. (1989) Twins reared together: Minimizing shared environmental effects. *Behavior Genetics, 19*, 593–604.

Hay, D.A. (1985). *Essentials of behaviour genetics.* Oxford, UK: Blackwell Publications.

Heath, A.C., & Martin, N.G. (1990). Psychoticism as a dimension of personality: A multivariate genetic test of Eysenck and Eysenck's psychoticism construct. *Journal of Personality and Social Psychology, 58*, 1–11.

Hudziak, J.J., Heath, A.C., Madden, P.A.F., Reich, W., Bucholz, K.K., Slutske, W., Bierut, L.J., Neuman, R.J., & Todd, R.D. (1998). Latent class and factor analysis of DSM-IV ADHD: A twin study of female adolescents. *Journal of the American Academy of Child and Adolescent Psychiatry, 37*, 848–857.

Hudziak, J.J., Rudiger, L.P., Neale, M.C., Heath, A.C., & Todd, R.D. (2000). A twin study of inattentive, aggressive and anxious/depressed behaviours. *Journal of the American Academy of Child and Adolescent Psychiatry, 39*, 469–476.

Joreskog, K.G. (1993). *LISREL 8: Structural equation modelling with the SIMPLIS command language.* Chicago: Scientific Software International.

Kaprio, J., Buchsbaum, M.S., Gottesman, A.C., Heath, A. C., Korner, J., Kringlen, E., McGuffin, P., Propping, P., Rietzschel, H.H., & Stassen, H.H. (1993). Group report: What can group studies contribute to the study of aduly psychopathology? In T.J. Bouchard Jr. & P. Propping (Eds.), *Twins as a tool of behaviour genetics.* New York: John Wiley & Sons.

Kraemer, H. (1997). What is the "right" statistical measure of twin concordance (or diagnostic reliability and validity)? *Archives of General Psychiatry, 54*, 1121–1124.

Levy, F., Hay, D., McLaughlin, M., Wood, C., & Waldman, I.D. (1996). Twin–sibling differences in parental reports of ADHD, speech, reading and behaviour problems. *Journal of Child Psychology and Psychiatry, 37*, 569–578.

Levy, F., Hay, D.A., McStephen, M., Wood, C., & Waldman, I.D. (1997). Attention Deficit Hyperactivity Disorder: A category or a continuum? Genetic analysis of a large-scale twin study. *Journal of the American Academy of Child and Adolescent Psychiatry, 36*, 737–744.

Loehlin, J.C. (1992). *Genes and environment in personality development.* London/New Delhi: Sage Publishers.

Malgady, R.G. (1996). The question of cultural bias in assessment and diagnosis of ethnic minority clients—let's reject the null hypothesis. *Professional Psychology: Research and Practise, 27*, 73–77.

McGue, M.K. (1992). When assessing twin concordance, use the probandwise not the pairwise rate. *Schizophrenia Bulletin, 18*, 171–176.

McGuffin, P., Katz, R., Rutherford, J., Watkins, S., Farmer, A.E., & Gottesman, I.I. (1993). Twin studies as vital indicators of phenotypes in molecular genetic research. In T.J. Bouchard Jr. & P. Propping (Eds.), *Twins as a tool of behaviour genetics.* New York: John Wiley & Sons.

Mumma, G.H. (1993). Categorization and rule induction in clinical diagnosis and assessment. *Psychology of Learning Motivation, 29*, 283–326.

Nadder, T.S., Silberg, J.L., Eaves, L.J., Maes, H.H., & Meyer, J.M. (1998). Genetic effects on ADHD symptomatology in 7- to 13-year old twins: Results from a telephone survey. *Behavior Genetics, 28*, 83–99.

Neale, M.C., Boker, S.M., Xie, G., & Maes, H.H. (1999). *Mx: Statistical Modeling.* (Available from Department of Psychiatry, Box 126 MCV, Richmond VA 23298)

Neale, M.C., & Cardon, L. (1992). *Methodology for genetic studies of twins and families.* London: Kluwer Academic Press.

Neuman, R.J., Todd, R.D., Heath, A.C., Reich, W.C., Hudziak, J.J., Bucholz, J.J., Madden, P.A.F., Begleiter, H., Porjesz, B., Kuperman, S., Hesselbrock, V., & Reich, T. (1999). Evaluation of ADHD typology in three contrasting samples: A latent class approach. *Journal of the American Academy of Child and Adolescent Psychiatry, 38,* 25–33.

Rutter, M., Tizard, J., & Whitmore, K. (1970). *Education, health and behaviour.* London: Longman.

Schmitz, S., Saudino, K.J., Plomin, R., Fulker, D.W., & DeFries, J.C. (1996). Genetic and environmental influences on temperament in middle childhood: Analyses of teacher and tester ratings. *Child Development, 67,* 409–422.

Sergeant, J.A. (1995). *Eunethydis, European approaches to hyperkinetic disorder.* Amsterdam: University of Amsterdam.

Sherman, D.K., Iacono, W.G., & McGue, M.K. (1997). Attention Deficit Hyperactivity Disorder dimensions: A twin study of inattention and impulsivity–hyperactivity. *Journal of the American Academy of Child and Adolescent Psychiatry, 36,* 745–753.

Sherman, D.K., McGue, M.K., & Iacono, W.G. (1997). Twin concordance for Attention Deficit Hyperactivity Disorder: A comparison of teachers' and mother's report. *American Journal of Psychiatry, 154,* 532–535.

Silberg, J.L., Rutter, M., Meyer, J.M., Maes, H.H., Hewitt, J.K., Simonoff, E., Pickles, A., Loeber, R., & Eaves, L. (1996). Genetic and environmental influences on the covariation between hyperactivity and conduct disturbance in juvenile twins. *Journal of Child Psychology and Psychiatry, 37,* 803–816.

Simonoff, E., Pickles, A., Hervas, J.L., Silberg, J.L., Rutter, M., & Eaves, L. (1998). Genetic influences on childhood hyperactivity: Contrast effects imply parental rating bias, not sibling interaction. *Psychological Medicine, 28,* 825–837.

Sonuga-Barke, E.J.S. (1998). Categorical models of childhood disorder: A conceptual and empirical analysis. *Journal of Child Psychology and Psychiatry, 39,* 115–133.

Tannock, R. (1998). Attention Deficit Hyperactivity Disorder: Advances in cognitive, neurobiological and genetic research. *Journal of Child Psychology and Psychiatry, 39,* 65–99.

Thapar, A., Harrington, R., Ross, K., & McGuffin, P. (2000). Does the definition of ADHD affect heritability? *Journal of the American Academy of Child and Adolescent Psychiatry, 39,* 1–12.

Thapar, A., Hervas, A., & McGuffin, P. (1995). Childhood hyperactivity scores are highly heritable and show sibling competition effects: Twin study evidence. *Behaviour Genetics, 25,* 537–544.

Waller, N., & Reise, S.P. (1992). Genetic and environmental influences on item response scalability. *Behavior Genetics, 22,* 135–152.

World Health Organisation. (1993). *International classification of diseases: Classification of mental and behavioural disorders—diagnostic criteria for research.* (10th ed.) [ICD-10]. Geneva: Author.

# 4 The developmental genetics of ADHD

*David A. Hay, Michael McStephen, and Florence Levy*

## INTRODUCTION

ADHD is a developmental disorder. In the *Diagnostic and Statistical Manual of Mental Disorders*, fourth edition (*DSM-IV*; American Psychiatric Association [APA], 1994) by definition symptoms must appear before the age of 7 years. However, there is much controversy over what happens to children with ADHD as they grow up (Hechtman, 1996), and over the diagnosis of ADHD in adults as there are changes in the symptom pattern during development. This has lead to the suggestion by Barkley (1995) that the diagnostic criteria for ADHD should change with age and possibly with gender. Children, and especially girls with Inattentive symptoms, may manage in the structured environment of the primary (elementary) school. It is often only in secondary (senior) school that organisational problems become obvious, so diagnoses by age 12 or 13 rather than age 7 may be appropriate.

During the past 20 years there have been massive longitudinal genetic studies of the development of cognition, both in twins and in adopted children (reviewed by Hay, 1999). Certainly, we have moved from the Wechsler Intelligence Scale for Children—revised (WISC-R; Wechsler, 1974) to the Wechsler Intelligence Scale for Children—third edition (WISC-III; Wechsler, 1991) in this time, but the construct remains the same. These studies, and parallel studies of personality, reviewed by Loehlin (1992), have relied upon stable definitions of the phenotype during this period. Because of the lack of stability of the definition of the phenotype for ADHD in many ways, it is unfair to ask for a similar developmental genetic analysis of ADHD at present.

The definition of ADHD has progressed through *Diagnostic and Statistical Manual of Mental Disorders*, second edition (*DSM-II*; APA, 1968), *Diagnostic and Statistical Manual of Mental Disorders*, third edition (*DSM-III*; APA, 1980), *Diagnostic and Statistical Manual of Mental Disorders*, third edition revised (*DSM-III-R*; APA, 1987) and *DSM-IV* (APA, 1994). In many ways we are studying a maturing approach to the definition of ADHD and this makes it difficult for any longitudinal study to have a consistent definition of the disorder. The change has been from the view of *DSM-III-R*, introduced in 1987 with a single category of ADHD, to the 1994 *DSM-IV* with its three categories. These are Primarily-Inattentive (ADHD I), Primarily Hyperactive-Impulsive (ADHD H/I), and for those individuals that meet the criteria for both ADHD I and ADHD H/I, the Combined type (ADHD C). This makes it clear that definitive developmental genetic analysis must await continuity in diagnosis.

This raises the related issue of whether ADHD should be viewed as part of a continuum throughout the population, or as a discrete disorder. In event of the latter, a rigid application of the diagnostic criteria implies that the loss or addition of only one symptom could mean the difference between a classification of "unaffected" and "affected". The problem was raised in Chapters 2 and 3 of this volume, and affects longitudinal analysis particularly. The problem is that a pair of twins might differ from each other very slightly in number of ADHD symptoms (by as little as one symptom). At the critical cut-off point, the difference of one symptom would result in the pair being labelled "discordant" for ADHD. Adhering strictly to a defined number of symptoms has important implications in follow-up studies too. In these a child may "recover" on follow-up by "losing" just one symptom. This despite the evidence, not accounted for in *DSM-IV*, that changes in symptom number (Barkley, 1995) occur as the child gets older. It is for these sorts of reasons that Jensen (1995) reminded us that symptom number should not be followed slavishly. Furthermore, clinical diagnosis also takes into account age of onset, duration, severity, and impairment, all of which have the potential to introduce even greater genetic and environmental variation into the analysis.

This is one reason why longitudinal studies of childhood psychopathology have frequently taken the approach of using questionnaires, such as the Achenbach Child Behavior Checklist (CBCL; Achenbach, 1991). Achenbach's approach is based not on clinical consensus, as in the DSM criteria, but rather on dimensions identified through factor analysis of item responses from many children, or from their parents or teachers. With the general availability of parallel report forms, this approach lends itself to multiple informants (Fergusson & Horwood, 1993). The question of the extent of appropriateness of questionnaires for the identification of childhood psychopathology is a key issue, and one well beyond the scope of this text (see Jensen, Salzberg, Richters, & Watanabe, 1993 for a discussion on this issue). Although high scores on the appropriate dimensions of the CBCL are predictive of a diagnosis of ADHD (Chen, Faraone, Biederman, & Tsuang, 1994), this is not the same as implying that studying the aetiology of CBCL scores is necessarily the same as studying the aetiology of ADHD. For example, the parent rating form includes few *DSM-IV* Inattention items. Yet its Attention Scale includes items on learning problems and clumsiness, which often occur in children with ADHD (see Chapter 6 by Stevenson in this volume, and Piek, Pitcher, & Hay, 1999). Thus, these items may well be identified in a factor analysis as part of a factor labelled "Attention" but are in reality part of commonly comorbid conditions.

The advantages of a questionnaire approach to longitudinal genetic analysis are obvious, in that one has a continuous measure of behaviour across all ages, and some of these studies are reviewed in this chapter. When we discuss data from our own Australian Twin ADHD Project (ATAP), introduced in Chapters 2 and 3 of this text, we use analyses that regard ADHD both as a continuum in terms of symptom number, and as a diagnosis. Issues for and against these two approaches are well covered by Fergusson and Horwood (1995) with an accompanying discussion by Jensen (1995) as well as by Nigg and Goldsmith (1998).

In this chapter we consider four approaches to developmental issues:

(1) Changes with age in the number of Inattention and Hyperactivity-Impulsivity symptoms, and corresponding membership of the associated diagnostic categories. This may seem conventional in terms of genetic analysis, since it simply requires assessing the same children a few years apart, but it raises two key questions:

- Do the same genes operate throughout development to influence ADHD?
- Are there different phenotypes, some where the children "grow out" of their ADHD, and others where difficulties remain?

(2) The adult outcome for the child with ADHD, and mediating factors such as Conduct Disorder and learning problems, which contribute both to stability of symptoms and to their change and/or amelioration. Studies of the long-term outcomes clearly indicate that considerable problems remain into adulthood for a significant proportion of those diagnosed with ADHD during childhood (Hechtman, 1996). Many of the chapters in this book deal with genetic and other contributions to comorbidity, and, clearly, comorbidity should be considered as a genetic mediator, even though the genetic models to deal with this complexity do not yet exist (see Rutter, Chapter 13 this volume).

(3) Psychopathology in adult relatives of young people with ADHD. Family, twin and adoption studies have all suggested that genetic factors are involved in ADHD (Faraone, Biederman, & Chen, 1995; Levy, Hay, McStephen, Wood, & Waldman, 1997 and Chapter 3 in this volume), with exceptionally high heritabilities compared to most behavioural traits (75–90% depending on the form of analysis). This begs the question: "If ADHD is so heritable, surely some signs should be readily identifiable in adult relatives?"

(4) Implications from molecular genetic studies. The plethora of suggested associations between single genes and behavioural phenotypes provides a unique perspective to longitudinal research when the same allele is found to be associated with different behaviours in infancy, childhood, and adulthood.

One way of viewing these different scenarios is shown in Figure 4.1 which

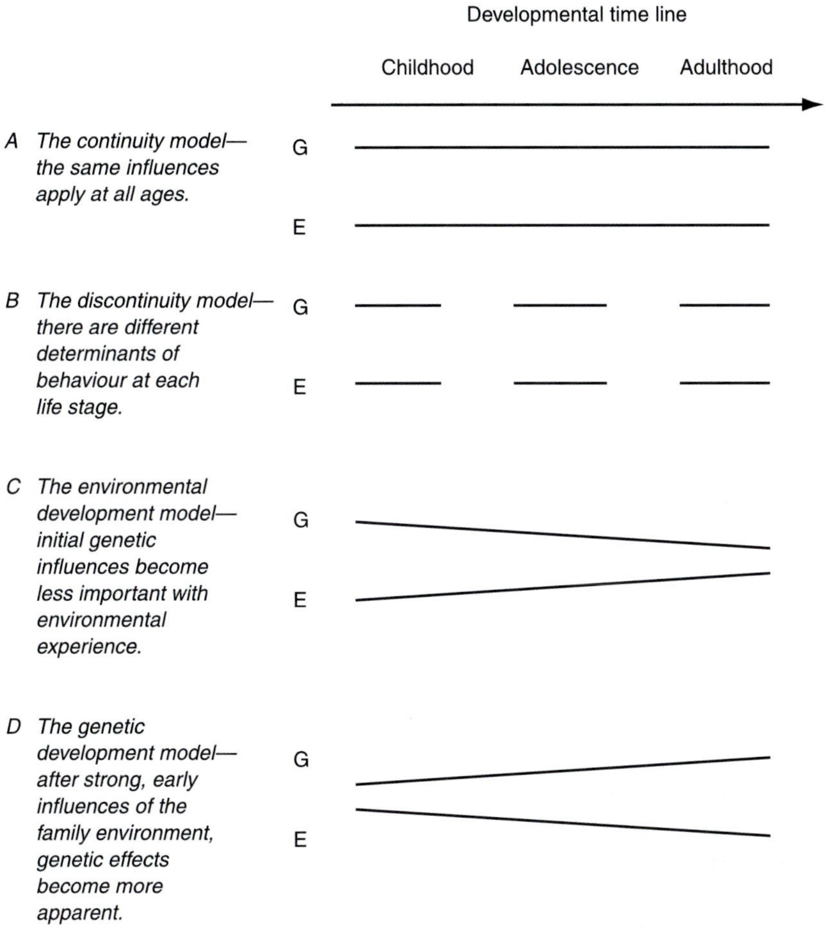

Developmental time line

Childhood     Adolescence     Adulthood

A   *The continuity model—*   G
    *the same influences*
    *apply at all ages.*

                              E

B   *The discontinuity model—*   G
    *there are different*
    *determinants of*
    *behaviour at each*   E
    *life stage.*

C   *The environmental*
    *development model—*   G
    *initial genetic*
    *influences become*
    *less important with*   E
    *environmental*
    *experience.*

D   *The genetic*
    *development model—*   G
    *after strong, early*
    *influences of the*
    *family environment,*   E
    *genetic effects*
    *become more*
    *apparent.*

*Figure 4.1* Hypothetical models for the change of genetic and environmental influences during development.

presents, in schematic form, four potential models for developmental change (Hay, 1985). Model A has complete continuity, with the same genetic and environmental influences operating all the way from childhood to adolescence. Note that this model does not imply that the same behavioural symptoms are necessarily present throughout development. For example, there could be a high correlation between one measure in parents and a very different measure in their children (Kendler, 1993; Neale, Walters, Eaves, Maes, & Kendler, 1994). There might also be a high correlation between a measure of behaviour in one MZ twin at time one, and quite a different behaviour in the co-twin at time two. Thus genetic continuity does not require that there be phenotypic continuity, nor does phenotypic continuity imply genetic continuity. A good example of the former arises with the molecular data discussed later, where the same gene may be associated with infant temperament, with ADHD in childhood/adolescence, and with personality/temperament measures in adulthood.

Model B is the converse, arguing for complete discontinuity. Obviously there can be many combinations of A and B. While ADHD data are limited, on other behavioural traits data are increasing. Hay (1999) reviews the evidence that there may be additional genetic factors that influence cognitive development that come into effect at age 7 or 8, effectively new genes being "switched on". Loehlin's excellent (1992) summary of genetic approaches to personality introduces the same issue.

Models C and D show the more traditional views on behavioural development (Nigg & Goldsmith, 1998), assuming continuity of both genetic and environmental factors, but appreciating that the relative impact of each, and hence the "heritability", would change. Model C assumes initial genetic influences, with environmental effects gradually increasing and overtaking in importance; Model D is the opposite. In Model D the family environment is assumed to matter most in the very young child, and as the child develops independence, genetic influences become more obvious.

## STABILITY AND CHANGES IN SYMPTOMATOLOGY

Assessment of developmental changes in ADHD symptomatology has been greatly complicated by changes in the diagnostic systems discussed previously, so that studies prior to 1994 and many published subsequently are more often based on the unitary model of *DSM-III-R*. Barkley (1997) summarises the evidence that Hyperactivity-Impulsivity symptoms appear earlier (at age 3–4 years), with Inattention becoming apparent later at the time of starting school (age 5–7 years), and the associated attention problems later still. Correspondingly, the Hyperactivity-Impulsivity symptoms decline more during childhood than do Inattention symptoms (Gjone, Stevenson, & Sundet, 1996; Hart, Lahey, Loeber, Applegate, & Frick, 1995; Hechtman, 1996; Levy, Hay, & Rooney, 1996b). This decline in Hyperactivity-Impulsivity is not the consequence of medication or other treatment, and thus is likely to be developmental (Hart et al., 1995). The only changes in Inattention, reported by Hart et al. (1995), occurred in the year after the children first were seen in the clinic. This was irrespective of age.

However, these studies only describe changes at the phenotypic level, and say nothing about what underlies the developmental progression. Evidence on genetic continuity of ADHD symptomatology is sparse. Schmitz, Fulker, and Mrazek (1995) collected both cross-sectional and longitudinal data on Colorado twins with the Child Behavior Checklist (CBCL) forms for 2- to 3- and 4- to 18-year-olds. (Their Fig. 2 and the accompanying discussion are an excellent introduction to path analysis in longitudinal data.) One problem is that the factors do not correspond between the two age groups, there being no

Attentional factor in the younger group, and hence no possibility of longitudinal analysis of attentional problems. It is interesting that there was a considerable role for common family environment (C) on the externalising factor (the overt behavioural problems which include attention and activity) in the younger children. In the older group there was a lesser, but still significant, role. That is, the effects of being reared together diminish. In fact, there was no C term at all for the Attention subscale of the externalising factor in the older group.

A very different study design was used in the Virginia Twin Study of Adolescent Behavioral Development (VTSABD; Silberg et al., 1996), to examine age changes from age 8 to age 16 years in the genetics of hyperactivity, conduct disturbance, and their covariance. This cohort of 1412 families, on whom there are extensive questionnaire and interview data, is a uniquely important present and future resource for longitudinal analysis of developmental psychopathology. As there is such extensive assessment, it is important to be clear as to what is being used in a particular analysis. For Silberg et al. (1996), Hyperactivity was defined by the same three Rutter scale items as discussed in Chapter 3 of this text, and characterised by a very low DZ correlation. Conduct Disturbance was not Conduct Disorder alone, but included Oppositional Defiant Disorder (ODD) symptoms, such as temper tantrums and disobedience.

The univariate results were complex, varying between behaviour, ages, and genders. However, the bivariate models for the relationship between the Hyperactivity and Conduct Disturbance traits showed that essentially all of the relationship between the two behaviours was genetic in the younger group (aged 8–11 years). In the older group, a different picture emerged, with far more genetic specificity to each behaviour. The authors discussed the concept of a genetically influenced developmental pathway that begins with multiple symptoms in childhood, with further genes becoming active in adolescence. This typifies the dynamic philosophy now becoming apparent in developmental behaviour genetics, and it is worth relating this to changes in clinical presentation. The decline in Hyperactivity symptoms in adolescence has already been discussed. *DSM-IV* makes a distinction between Conduct Disorder with early onset, and that which begins towards adolescence. It would be interesting to know if there are changes in the pattern of ODD and CD symptoms from the younger to the older group and whether these are genetically distinct phenotypes. As Irwin Waldman, Rhee, Levy and Hay discuss in Chapter 7 of this volume, ADHD has different patterns of genetic relationship to ODD and to CD, which may explain this pattern of change in "Conduct Disturbance".

A second issue that emerged in the 12- to 16-year-olds was that of gender differences in genetic effects. Whilst Chapter 8 in this volume, by Rhee, Waldman, Hay, and Levy, deals with gender differences in ADHD, most of the twins and siblings in this analysis were aged 4–12 years, and differences between boys and girls in symptomatology and genetic effects were more quantitative than qualitative. It is much more likely that gender differences would emerge at adolescence, with the differences in maturation between boys and girls.

The majority of longitudinal genetic analyses are now based on twins, since most of the children in adoption studies are now reaching adulthood, reflecting changes in birth and adoption practices, with fewer healthy Western children now available for adoption. The most notable exception is the Dutch study of international adoptees (van der Valk, Verhulst, Neale, & Boomsma, 1998), which comprised two sets of data collected 3 years apart, starting when the adoptees were aged 10–15 years. With children coming to the Netherlands from so many countries, primarily from Korea and Columbia, this is clearly not a representative sample of children. For example, the CBCL score increases in these adopted young people at adolescence, whereas it decreases in nonadoptees, and the authors discuss some of the specific issues facing adoptees at this age that may contribute to this. Nevertheless, this sample is a unique resource. Not only is the adoptive sample so large, but there are also three distinct groupings, with the placement in the same family of biological siblings (111 pairs), of unrelated children—called nonbiological siblings (221 pairs), as well as the traditional adoption situation of a single child (1484 individuals). Even without data on the biological parents (a type of missing data that often complicates adoption research), these three resources provide a powerful means of analysing both genetic and common family environment.

There are two caveats about the van der Valk et al. (1998) longitudinal analysis of CBCL data. First, they used a conventional Cholesky decomposition model (Loehlin, 1996), which hypothesises two sources of variation, namely that which remains constant over the 3 years, and that which only comes into play at the second point in time. Figure 4.1, discussed earlier, raises an alternative model of genetic factors found only in younger children, and lost by the time of the subsequent assessment. The second issue was selective attrition, with the families that participated in both assessments reporting slightly fewer problems at the first assessment. Loss of families with more difficulties is a common problem in longitudinal research, and emphasises the point from Chapter 2 in this volume, that heritability is population and time-specific. Nevertheless, this is a unique sample, and the authors discussed at length some of the issues in genetic analysis of such a specific cohort of children. Our chief interest here is the Attention scales of the CBCL, where there was considerable genetic variance (53%) at the first assessment, but much less 3 years later (28%) with only 19% that was common to both times. Common family environmental influences were small (7% on both assessments), so made little contribution to continuity over time. Given the limitations of the Attention scale discussed earlier, it is worth considering the broad-band externalising problems, where there was 55% genetic variance at the first assessment, and 48% at the second, with 26% being in common. In contrast, the internalising problems showed little genetic continuity, but much continuity was attributable to common and nonshared family environment. In other words, what mattered considerably for continuity of internalising features was how the adolescent was perceived by others in the environment or perceived him or herself. Van der Valk and colleagues rightly emphasise the importance of replication from other genetically informative sources, and cite twin studies that support their conclusion. But how much of this is method-specific?

O'Connor, Neiderhiser, Reiss, Hetherington, and Plomin (1998) used a very similar design with twins in the same age-range, but from a different perspective, focusing on antisocial and depressive symptoms. Their Figures 2 and 3 reveal quite different pictures for the antisocial and depression measures, the externalising and internalising foci respectively. On both measures there were age-specific genetic effects almost as large as those common to both times (except for the second Depression assessment). The finding of genetic effects specific to the first assessment would not have been identified in the van der Valk approach, which did not include these in the model. More significantly, although there were common family environment effects for antisocial behaviour across both times (one twin could not be exhibiting antisocial behaviour without influencing the other twin), there were absolutely no common family environmental effects for depression.

The last two studies emphasise that there are significant methodological issues concerning both research design (twins or adopted children), and what is measured. Insufficient time has lapsed since the publication of *DSM-IV* in 1994 to allow for completion of a longitudinal study on the subtypes of Inattention and Hyperactivity-Impulsivity. As discussed in Chapter 3 of this volume, even the relationship between Inattention and Hyperactivity-Impulsivity remains a matter of debate. Sherman, Iacono, and McGue (1997) factor analysed teacher ratings and parent interviews (although without all *DSM-IV* items) and found the genetic correlation between teacher and mother reports on these two ADHD dimensions differed considerably.

The Australian Twin ADHD Project collected data from twins and their siblings in 1990–1991 when the children were aged 4–12 years (Levy, Hay, McLaughlin, Wood, & Waldman, 1996a), and again some 4 years later as *DSM-IV* was being introduced. As all *DSM-IV* items had not been included at time 1, the Hart et al. (1995) classification was used to distinguish Inattention and Hyperactivity-Impulsivity (Morgan, Hynd, Riccio, & Hall, 1996).

Table 4.1 is based on 711 MZ and 460 same-sex DZ twin pairs, and shows how striking is the genetic continuity. For example, the correlation between the first and second Inattention scores of MZ twin 1 (the first-born), measured 4 years apart, was .637. This is little different from the .58 reported by Fergusson and Horwood (1993) for a different maternal rating of Attention, over a similar period in singletons. The correlation of the first Inattention score of MZ twin 1, with the second Inattention score of the co-twin twin 2, measured 4 years later, was not much less (.552). For DZ twins, the

*Table 4.1* Continuity of Inattention over time in MZ and same-sex DZ twins

|  | Twin 1 | | | | Twin 2 | | | |
| --- | --- | --- | --- | --- | --- | --- | --- | --- |
|  | Time 1 | | Time 2 | | Time 1 | | Time 2 | |
|  | Inatt | Hyplmp | Inatt | Hyplmp | Inatt | Hyplmp | Inatt | Hyplmp |
| **Twin 1** | | | | | | | | |
| Time 1 | | | | | | | | |
| Inatt | 1 | 0.726 | 0.637 | 0.540 | 0.881 | 0.706 | 0.552 | 0.548 |
| Hyplmp | 0.691 | 1 | 0.531 | 0.645 | 0.710 | 0.927 | 0.495 | 0.628 |
| Time 2 | | | | | | | | |
| Inatt | 0.658 | 0.524 | 1 | 0.759 | 0.583 | 0.503 | 0.829 | 0.652 |
| Hyplmp | 0.539 | 0.663 | 0.747 | 1 | 0.519 | 0.586 | 0.653 | 0.868 |
| **Twin 2** | | | | | | | | |
| Time 1 | | | | | | | | |
| Inatt | 0.470 | 0.362 | 0.207 | 0.174 | 1 | 0.729 | 0.643 | 0.571 |
| Hyplmp | 0.401 | 0.587 | 0.192 | 0.225 | 0.645 | 1 | 0.511 | 0.665 |
| Time 2 | | | | | | | | |
| Inatt | 0.209 | 0.194 | 0.438 | 0.353 | 0.610 | 0.389 | 1 | 0.730 |
| Hyplmp | 0.294 | 0.323 | 0.405 | 0.522 | 0.445 | 0.605 | 0.684 | 1 |

|  | Twin 1 | | Twin 2 | |
| --- | --- | --- | --- | --- |
|  | Time 1 | Time 2 | Time 1 | Time 2 |
| **Twin 1** | | | | |
| Time 1 | 1 | 0.637 | 0.881 | 0.552 |
| Time 2 | 0.658 | 1 | 0.583 | 0.829 |
| **Twin 2** | | | | |
| Time 1 | 0.470 | 0.207 | 1 | 0.643 |
| Time 2 | 0.209 | 0.438 | 0.610 | 1 |
| **Twin 1** | | | | |
| Time 1 | 1 | 0.645 | 0.927 | 0.628 |
| Time 2 | 0.663 | 1 | 0.586 | 0.868 |
| **Twin 2** | | | | |
| Time 1 | 0.587 | 0.225 | 1 | 0.665 |
| Time 2 | 0.323 | 0.522 | 0.605 | 1 |

*Note:*
  MZ above diagonal, DZ below.

correlation of the twin 1 scores over the same time was similar (.658) as would be expected (it is the same individual at the two times), but the correlation with the co-twin's score at time 2 was much less (.209).

Genetic analysis is much more than just comparing correlations. Figure 4.2 gives the best-fitting genetic models (Neale & Cardon, 1992) for both Inattention and Hyeractivity-Impulsivity. The modest chi-squares show that

(a) Inattention

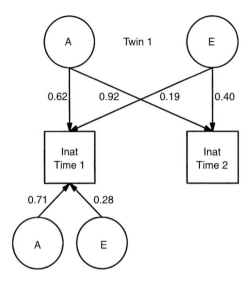

(b) Hyperactivity

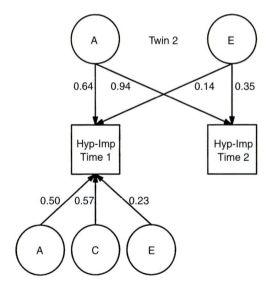

*Figure 4.2* Longitudinal models for the change of (a) Inattention and (b) Hyperactivity-Impulsivity in the Australian Twin ADHD Project. Chi-squares for the fit of the models were 11.165 (df = 8, *p* = 0.193) for Inattention and 12.683 (df = 7, *p* = 0.08) for Hyperactivity-Impulsivity.

they adequately describe what is happening. These models had specific genetic variation in the younger groups; alternative models—with specific genetic effects being more evident at later ages—did not fit nearly as well. How can this be interpreted in terms of the behaviour? The Hyperactivity-Impulsivity scores do decrease a little with age and this may explain to some extent the changes on this dimension. If symptoms decline over time, it may be because of multiple and nongenetic factors such as family, school, or medication-intervention. Supporting this is analysis that shows that the role of common family environment increases over time in Hyperactivity-Impulsivity. It is difficult to think of a twin whose behaviour would not gradually be changed by the presence of a Hyperactive-Impulsive co-twin.

There was no role for common family environment for Inattention and no increasing role for this parameter with age, which again is consistent with the fact that one can live with an Inattentive co-twin without one's own behaviour being affected. It is more difficult to explain why there was initial genetic variance for Inattention at time 1. Many families do not seek help for young people with Inattentive symptoms. On the other hand, the Inattentive (and the Combined) types are more strongly associated with reading and other school-based problems and so there may again be nongenetic influences or indeed different genetic influences. Symptoms of Inattention may only be recognised when the child is old enough for to detect common comorbid conditions such as Reading Disorder. As pointed out by Stevenson in Chapter 6 of this volume, this may lead to some confounding genes for ADHD and reading.

Although the studies described so far are research-based, in that they derive from families volunteering for research, one very important initiative has been that of Biederman and his colleagues. They have developed a family study around children presenting clinically for ADHD and other childhood conditions. While familiality may be environmental rather than genetic, the strength of this approach is obviously its clinical relevance. One of their analyses (Biederman et al., 1996) identified a family history of ADHD as one of the most important predictors of whether ADHD persisted or diminished over a 4-year period. There are certainly nongenetic explanations, such as parents with a history of ADHD being less structured and less compliant with interventions for their child. This notwithstanding, their study does raise key questions about the potential practical implications of behaviour genetic analyses.

## THE LONG-TERM OUTCOME OF ADHD

There has been considerable recent interest in the diagnosis and psychopathology of adult ADHD (Murphy & Barkley, 1995) and also in predictors of continued psychopathology in children and adolescents with ADHD, as well as personality outcome in adolescence and adulthood. Adolescents with

ADHD have patterns of psychiatric comorbidity including Oppositional Defiant Disorder, Conduct Disorder, Depression, and Anxiety Disorders (Barkley, 1990; Biederman, Newcorn, & Sprich 1991). Several recent investigations with ADHD adults have also found a substantial presence of comorbid conditions including Depression, Anxiety, Substance Abuse, and Antisocial Personality Disorders (Biederman et al., 1993; Tzelepis, Schubiner, & Warbasse, 1994).

The best summary of the developmental perspective on ADHD is that there is no single outcome. Hechtman (1996) summarises the results by identifying three groups in adulthood: (1) those who function as well as those without a childhood history of ADHD; (2) those with significant psychopathology; and (3) the largest group, those who have some difficulties with concentration, impulse control, and social functioning. The actual percentages vary extensively between different studies. Hechtman discusses many of the methodological issues, a key one being variation in how adults have been identified (through their own children, through follow-up studies based on their own childhood behaviour, through self-referral, through clinical surveys, etc.).

Could it be the case that Hechtman's groups are genetically distinct? Biederman et al. (1996) identified a family history of ADHD as a major predictor of who did or did not improve in their symptomatology, implying some genetic variation in the longitudinal trajectory. Using the Australian Twin ADHD Project, we identified twins who changed in *DSM-III-R* diagnosis in the four years between the assessments. We chose to use *DSM-III-R*, as there are not the numbers for a breakdown around the *DSM-IV* subtypes. The basic message in Table 4.2 is clear. In the MZ twins, there are some 11 times more pairs that have the same pattern of change over the 4 years, either remaining unaffected, reaching *DSM-III-R* criterion, dropping from it, or retaining the 8/14 symptoms. (Furthermore, it is interesting that the three groups in which at least one twin has ADHD, are essentially the same size.) Expressed in another way, only 8% of MZ twins differ in developmental trajectory compared with 20% of DZ twins, a difference which is highly significant (chi squared = 65.61, df = 1, $p < .001$). Although the arbitrariness of the cut-off scores has already been discussed, the difference between MZ and DZ twins means that this is a real genetically programmed change or source of developmental heterogeneity, and not just an artefact of the unreliability of the scoring system.

Identifying changes in ADHD symptomatology is actually the easiest part of longitudinal studies. As Biederman, Faraone, and Kiely (in Hechtman, 1996) explain, considering patterns of comorbidity is vital in understanding the outcome of ADHD. Although many of the comorbid conditions themselves have a significant genetic component, issues of statistical power mean it will not necessarily be easy to incorporate these into longitudinal genetic analyses. We summarise some of the key moderating behaviours. In one of the major phenotypic (as distinct from genetic) longitudinal studies,

*Table 4.2* MZ and DZ twin pair diagnosis at two time points, counts and expected values

|  | Twin 2 | | | | |
|---|---|---|---|---|---|
|  | *Not at Time 1 Not at Time 2* | *Not at Time 1 ADHD Time 2* | *ADHD Time 1 Not at Time 2* | *ADHD Time 1 ADHD Time 2* | *Row total* |
| *Twin 1* | | | | | |
| **MZ** | | | | | |
| Not at Time 1/ | **589** | 6 | 7 | 5 | 607 |
| Not at Time 2 | *519.9* | *24.8* | *29.9* | *32.4* | 85.40% |
| Not at Time 1/ | 13 | **22** | 0 | 2 | 37 |
| ADHD Time 2 | *31.7* | *1.5* | *1.8* | *2.0* | 5.20% |
| ADHD Time 1/ | 3 | 0 | **22** | 10 | 35 |
| Not at Time 2 | *30.0* | *1.4* | *1.7* | *1.9* | 4.90% |
| ADHD Time 1/ | 4 | 1 | 6 | **21** | 32 |
| ADHD Time 2 | *27.4* | *1.3* | *1.6* | *1.7* | 4.50% |
| Column total | 609 | 29 | 35 | 38 | 711 |
|  | 85.70% | 4.10% | 4.90% | 5.30% | 100.00% |
| **DZ** | | | | | |
| Not at Time 1/ | **346** | 18 | 12 | 9 | 385 |
| Not at Time 2 | *323.9* | *23.4* | *17.6* | *20.1* | 83.70% |
| Not at Time 1/ | 14 | **7** | 1 | 3 | 25 |
| ADHD Time 2 | *21.0* | *1.5* | *1.1* | *1.3* | 5.40% |
| ADHD Time 1/ | 10 | 0 | **7** | 5 | 22 |
| Not at Time 2 | *18.5* | *1.3* | *1.0* | *1.1* | 4.80% |
| ADHD Time 1/ | 17 | 3 | 1 | **7** | 28 |
| ADHD Time 2 | *23.6* | *1.7* | *1.3* | *1.5* | 6.10% |
| Column total | 387 | 28 | 21 | 24 | 460 |
|  | 84.10% | 6.10% | 4.60% | 5.20% | 100.00% |

*Notes:*
  MZ Chi-square (9) = 904.924, *p* = .0001. DZ chi-square (9) = 112.795, *p* = .0001.

Mannuzza, Klein, Bessler, Malloy, and LaPadula (1998) found that childhood ADHD predicted specific adult psychiatric disorders, namely antisocial and drug abuse disorders. Lambert (1988) found that hyperactive children had significantly poorer educational outcomes and more Conduct Disorders than their age peers. Lie (1992) found that criminality was related to school and conduct problems in childhood rather than to ADHD *per se* with a major role for comorbid Conduct Disorder in final prognosis. To date there have been no behaviour genetic analyses that take into account the ongoing controversy as to whether ADHD is a distinct risk factor for substance abuse, or whether all its effects are due to comorbid Conduct Disorder (Mannuzza et al., 1998).

The extensive studies of psychiatric comorbidity in ADHD by Biederman et al. (1993) found major depression, bipolar disorder, anxiety disorders, and personality disorders may be present concurrently with adult ADHD. They also found high rates of antisocial and substance use disorders, as well as lower full-scale IQ and vocabulary and reading scores. There has been little systematic research on personality outcome of ADHD children. Rey, Morris-Yates, and Stewart (1995) reported that those with disruptive behaviour disorders during adolescence showed high rates of personality disorder as young adults particularly the Cluster B disorders (antisocial, borderline, hysterical, and narcissistic).

This raises the issue of whether the adult manifestations of ADHD should best be viewed as versions of the childhood symptoms, or as aspects of personality. Downey, Stelson, Pomerleau, and Giordani (1997) identified a specific profile for adults with ADHD on Cloninger's Temperament and Personality Questionnnaire (TPQ), and on the Minnesota Multiphasic Personality Inventory—2 (MMPI-2). On the TPQ, they had high scores on novelty seeking and harm avoidance, whereas on the MMPI-2, there were four scales (depression, psychopathy, psychasthenia, and schizophrenia), where scores were above normal. Downey and colleagues raised a very interesting question. That is, are these the personality features of adults with ADHD, or are these the personality variables that contribute to young people with ADHD going on to have problems in adulthood? Rutter (Chapter 13, this volume) raises the same issue in a different way when he discusses models of genetic risk factors. Are such temperament/personality variables just risk factors that increase the risk of ADHD only in the presence of other genetic and environmental risk factors? As Downey et al. observed, a behaviour genetic analysis is one of the few ways of differentiating these two possibilities, and the concomitant significant clinical implications. Although such a study has yet to be done, the family-study information presented next does begin to address this issue.

## PSYCHOPATHOLOGY IN ADULT RELATIVES OF YOUNG PEOPLE WITH ADHD

The major studies in this area are those of Biederman and his group. As previously mentioned, these are not behaviour genetic studies in the strict sense, since they are based exclusively upon families attending clinics. The most relevant summary of their many years of research is in Milberger, Faraone, Biederman, Testa, and Tsuang (1996) where they sought to define "the phenotype of the more genetic form of ADHD". In other words, what best characterises mothers, fathers, sisters, and brothers of young people with ADHD. There were two key points. First, no one pattern was common to all relatives. For example, panic disorder was a main feature of the mothers, but not of the fathers, in whom a different anxiety disorder, separation anxiety, was more common. Second, many of the variables that defined these relatives were internalising symptoms, such as anxiety and depression, as well as the anticipated problems in reading ability (see Chapter 6 of this text, by Stevenson). Given the modest size of the clinical sample there is no doubt that this

*Table 4.3* Table of means of parents TPQ scores for parents ADHD subtype

| | No category (NC) n = 229 (71.8%) | Inattentive (PI) n = 28 (8.8%) | Hyperactive- Impulsive (PHI) n = 44 (13.8%) | Combined (PC) n = 18 (5.6%) | Total n = 319 | Significant differences (p < .025) |
|---|---|---|---|---|---|---|
| Novelty seeking (NS) | 7.21 | 7.64 | 9.36 | 8.39 | 7.61 | NC < PHI |
| Harm avoidance (HA) | 6.20 | 9.04 | 5.50 | 8.72 | 6.50 | NC = PHI < PI = PC |
| Reward dependence (RD) | 10.74 | 9.89 | 12.34 | 10.56 | 10.87 | PI < PHI |

study needs replication before it can be termed definitive in terms of which relatives to classify as "affected" in family and linkage studies of ADHD.

One difficulty has been that the vast majority of their diagnoses were based on *DSM-III-R*, and the question arises as to whether distinct profiles can be found for family members on the *DSM-IV* categories. Table 4.3 introduces data from a new study in which adult twins and their children are the focus of our research, rather than twin children. This cohort of adult twins has been the focus of a great deal of previous research on measures of temperament and personality (Heath, Cloninger, & Martin, 1994). Table 4.3 shows that adults with *DSM-IV* ADHD subtypes differ in temperament profiles (analysis of *DSM-IV* disorders is still in progress). It should be emphasised that the rates of "adult" ADHD in this sample have no relationship to those in the general population. These twins had been chosen for study because of their high scores on previous TPQ studies following the Downey et al. (1997) study discussed earlier. Thus, the prevalence of the *DSM-IV* subtypes is specific to this population. What matters is the relationship between these personality variables and the *DSM-IV* categories. It is clear from Table 4.3 that differences among the ADHD subtypes occur across all three of the Cloninger scales. Thus studies of ADHD symptomatology in adults should be complemented with analyses of temperament/personality variables and genetic analyses of whether these represent complementary expressions of the same genotype.

## TRENDS IN MOLECULAR STUDIES

In this volume, Chapter 10 by Barr, Swanson, and Kennedy, and Chapter 9 by Zametkin, Ernst, and Cohen summarise recent developments in the molecular genetics of ADHD. Both the Dopamine D4 receptor gene (DRD4) and the Dopamine Transporter gene poymorphisms have been extensively replicated.

Two other series of molecular genetic studies give a clue as to how the genetic factors in ADHD may be expressed at different ages. Ebstein et al. (1998) studied temperament in 2-week-old babies. They found significant associations of the DRD4 polymorphism with several behavioural clusters, including orientation and motor organisation. In adults, the Temperament and Character Inventory (TCI; summarised in Cloninger, Pryzbeck, Sorakie, & Wetzel, 1994) includes a measure of novelty-seeking. Ebstein et al. (1996) and Benjamin, Li, Patterson, Greenberg, Murphy, and Hamer (1996) noted that adults with a high number of exons, or repetitions of DNA subunits on the D4 receptor gene, were significantly more likely to report aspects of novelty-seeking (for instance, aspects such as impulsive, quick-tempered, fickle, and extravagant) than were those with fewer repetitions.

There is no doubt that these studies need replication, nor that the associations may turn out to be far more complex. On one of the other TCI scales, reward dependence, Benjamin, Ebstein, and Lesch (1998) found some evidence for an interaction between DRD4 and the Serotonin 2C receptor gene. This occurred in an Israeli sample, and was not replicated in a US sample. Nevertheless, these studies do indicate the potential of molecular genetic approaches to extend the developmental genetic perspective on the phenotype of ADHD.

## DISCUSSION

The basic issue of whether the same genes are expressed in different ways at different ages turns out to be more complex. Given that other behaviours are comorbid with ADHD, the ultimate behaviour genetic model needs to incorporate good measures of ADHD, as well as of key comorbid conditions.

The analyses of the Australian Twin ADHD Project raise basic questions over developmental genetic analyses of ADHD symptomatology. ADHD children frequently have clinical problems, and often families will seek help during the time between longitudinal assessments. Not only is this a significant (but ethically important) confound in the genetic analysis, but it also raises at least two issues for genetic analysis. First, how can intervention be included in the genetic analysis, with the possibility of genotype–environment interaction, and the fact that some families may respond better than do others to intervention?

The second issue is more significant. Who seeks intervention, and what are the personality characteristics in the family (the parents as well as the children) that may contribute to this? We all know of families, in which one parent says, "But I was just like that as a child, so we don't need to worry." Developmental genetic analyses in general are susceptible to such issues, and we would argue that ADHD is especially susceptible because of its symptomatology, and the controversies over providing services to such families. Behaviour genetic designs have not yet come to terms with the complexity of modelling childhood behaviours (Rutter, 1995). In adult disorders, it is the client who provides data on the symptoms and the intervention. For children, and especially in ADHD, the situation is very different. Woodward, Taylor, and Dowdney (1998) raised the role of parental attitudes and behaviour in shaping all aspects of ADHD, including prognosis and treatment outcomes. They approached the issue as being psychosocial, but of course there is likely to be a significant genetic contribution to parenting behaviours. We thus have a classic case of genotype–environment correlation (Loehlin, 1992), where genotypes are likely to co-exist with aspects of the home environment that encourages particular behaviours. Rutter develops this theme in Chapter 13 of this volume.

The large E effect common to both times warrants discussion, since it implies a very general difference between the members of a twin pair. E incorporates many effects, including unreliability of measurement, although this cannot be the case with something consistent across time and trait. One possible factor may be maternal stereotyping of differences between twins, which has been found to be very common, with one being the "quiet" and the other the "restless" one (Hay & O'Brien, 1987). A way of approaching this would appear to be to obtain ratings from another informant, such as a teacher (Sherman et al., 1997). However, Hay and O'Brien (1987) showed that stereotyping of twin differences was found in teacher ratings of behaviour. Presumably, intrafamilial differences in expectations of behaviour had become entrenched enough to be seen in behaviour at school as well as at home.

It may therefore be preferable to use a different research design, less dependent upon the features of the child. Figure 4.3 illustrates the co-twin design. Here adult twins are identified, and the behaviour of their children assessed. Thus the impact of parents on their children is being assessed both environmentally and genetically. If only the parent is affected, it is impossible to determine whether any behavioural problems in the child are environmental or genetic. If the parent is a twin, it is another matter entirely. We can then ask the genetically more informative question of whether having an uncle or aunt with ADHD (MZ twin of one of the child's parents) is fundamental to ADHD symptomatology in the child. This helps filter out environmental versus genetic influences—and in this instance it is not growing up with an affected parent that matters, as much as does having an affected biological uncle or aunt that matters in distinguishing whether familial influences are genetic or environmental.

An intriguing aspect of results discussed in this chapter is that they are contrary to those found in the personality disorders, especially in antisocial personality disorder. Kendler (1995) argued that there would be more shared (common) environment in childhood, and that genetic effects would thereafter grow in significance (Model D in Figure 4.1). Kendler's comments were

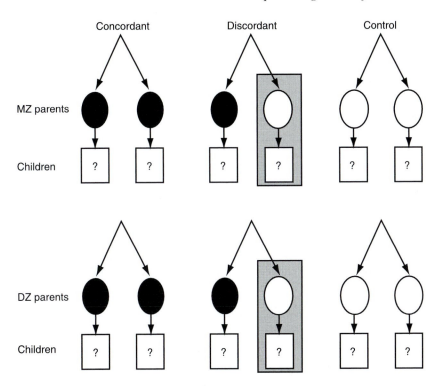

*Figure 4.3* The co-twin control design with affected individuals shown as shading.

based around problems other than ADHD, which is unique in that all the phenotypic evidence suggests that symptoms diminish with age (Levy, Hay, & Rooney, 1996b). The data discussed here also offers little support for the suggestion by Barkley (1997), and van den Oord and Rowe (1997), that common environment may contribute to the continuity of behaviour over time. Rather, most of the continuity, as well as most of the change over time, is genetic.

However, the story is far from complete. A full developmental genetic study of ADHD must consider not only the *DSM-IV* subtypes, but also their differential comorbidities (Willcutt, Pennington, Chhabildas, Friedman, & Alexander, 1999) together with conditions that affect prognosis. To adequately model the complex genetic contributions to these relationships over time, while considering the psychosocial impact of family members with ADHD, needs a major evaluation of the optimal research design.

Results need extension and replication, but at least this chapter has begun to indicate the potential for developmental genetic analysis of ADHD and its age-related changes in expression.

# REFERENCES

Achenbach, T.M. (1991). *Manual for the Child Behavior Checklist 4–18 and 1991 profile.* Burlington, VT: University of Vermont, Department of Psychiatry.

American Psychiatric Association. (1968). *Diagnostic and statistical manual of mental disorders* (2nd ed.). Washington, DC: Author.

American Psychiatric Association. (1980). *Diagnostic and statistical manual of mental disorders* (3rd ed.). Washington, DC: Author.

American Psychiatric Association. (1987). *Diagnostic and statistical manual of mental disorders* (3rd ed., rev.). Washington, DC: Author.

American Psychiatric Association. (1998). *Diagnostic and statistical manual of mental disorders* (4th ed.). Washington, DC: Author.

Barkley, R.A. (1990). *Attention Deficit Hyperactivity Disorder: A handbook for diagnosis and treatment.* New York: Guilford Press.

Barkley, R.A. (1995). A closer look at the DSM-IV criteria for ADHD: Some unresolved issues. *The ADHD Report, 3,* 1–15.

Barkley, R.A. (1997). *ADHD and the nature of self-control.* New York: Guilford Press.

Benjamin, J., Ebstein, R.P., & Lesch, K.-P. (1998). Genes for personality traits: Implications for psychopathology. *International Journal of Neuropsychopharmacology, 1,* 153–168.

Benjamin, J., Li, L., Patterson, C., Greenberg, B.D., Murphy, D.L., & Hamer, D.H. (1996). Population and familial association between the D4 dopamine receptor gene and measures of novelty seeking. *Nature Genetics, 12,* 81–84.

Biederman, J., Faraone, S., Milberger, S., Curtis, S., Chen, L., Marrs, A., Oullette, C., Moore, P., & Spencer, T.J. (1996). Predictors of persistence and remission of ADHD into adolescence: Results from a four-year prospective follow-up study. *Journal of the American Academy of Child and Adolescent Psychiatry, 35,* 343–351.

Biederman, J., Faroane, S.V., Spencer, T.J., Wilens, T.E., Norman, D., Lapey, K.A., Mick, E., Lehman, B.K., & Doyle, A. (1993). Patterns of psychiatric comorbidity, cognition and psychosocial functioning in adults with Attention-Deficit Hyperactivity Disorder. *American Journal of Psychiatry, 150,* 1792–1798.

Biederman, J., Newcorn, J., & Sprich, S. (1991). Comorbidity of Attention Deficit Hyperactivity with conduct depressive, anxiety and other disorders. *American Journal of Psychiatry, 148,* 564–577.

Chen, W.J., Faraone, S.V, Biederman, J., & Tsuang, M.T. (1994). Diagnostic accuracy of the Child Behavior Checklist Scales for Attention-Deficit Hyperactivity Disorder: A receiver-operating characteristic analysis. *Journal of Consulting and Clinical Psychology, 62,* 1017–1025.

Cloninger, C.R., Pryzbeck, T.R., Sorakie, D.M., & Wetzel, R.D. (1994). *The Temperament and Character Inventory (TCI): A guide to its development and use.* St Louis, MO: Centre for Psychobiology of Personality, Washington University.

Downey, K.K., Stelson, F.W., Pomerleau, O.F., & Giordani, B. (1997). Adult Attention Deficit Hyperactivity Disorder: Psychological test profiles in a clinical population. *Journal of Nervous and Mental Disease, 185,* 32–38.

Ebstein, E.B., Novick, O., Umansky, R., Priel, B., Osher, Y., Blaine, D., Bennett, E.R., Nemanov, L., Katz, M., & Belmaker, R.H. (1996). Dopamine D4 receptor (D4 DR) exon III polymorphism associated with the human personality trait of novelty seeking. *Nature Genetics, 12,* 78–80.

Ebstein, R.P., Levine, J., Geller, V. Auerbach, J., Gritsenko, I., & Belmaker, R.H.

(1998). Dopamine D4 receptor and serotonin transporter promoter in the determination of neonatal temperament. *Molecular Psychiatry, 3,* 238–246.

Faraone, S.V, Biederman, J., & Chen, W.J. (1995). Genetic heterogeneity in Attention-Deficit Hyperactivity Disorder (ADHD): Gender, psychiatric comorbidity and maternal ADHD. *Journal of Abnormal Psychology, 104,* 334–345.

Fergusson, D.M., & Horwood, L.J. (1993). The structure, stability and correlations of the trait components of Conduct Disorder, attention deficit and anxiety/withdrawal reports. *Journal of Child Psychology and Psychiatry, 34,* 749–766.

Fergusson, D.M., & Horwood, L.J. (1995). Predicitive validity of categorically and dimentionally scored measures of disruptive childhood behaviors. *Journal of the American Academy of Child and Adolescent Psychiatry, 34,* 477–487.

Gjone, H., Stevenson, J., & Sundet, J.M. (1996). Genetic influence on parent-reported attention-related problems in a Norwegian general population twin sample. *Journal of the American Academy of Child and Adolescent Psychiatry, 35,* 588–596.

Hart, E.L., Lahey, B.B., Loeber, R., Applegate, B., & Frick, P.J. (1995). Developmental change in Attention-Deficit Hyperactivity Disorder in boys: A four-year longitudinal study. *Journal of Abnormal and Child Psychology, 23,* 729–749.

Hay, D.A. (1985) *The essentials of behaviour genetics.* Oxford, UK: Blackwell Scientific.

Hay, D.A. (1999). The developmental genetics of intelligence. In M. Anderson (Ed.), *The development of intelligence* (pp. 75–104). Hove, UK: Psychology Press.

Hay, D.A., & O'Brien, P.J. (1987). Early influences on the school social adjustment of twins. *Acta Geneticae Medicae et Gemellologiae, 36,* 239–248.

Heath, A., Cloninger, C.R., & Martin, N.C. (1994). Testing a model for the genetic structure of personality: A comparison of the personality systems of Cloninger and Eysenck. *Journal of Personality and Social Psychology, 66,* 762–775.

Hechtman, L. (1996). Attention-Deficit/Hyperactivity Disorder. In L. Hechtman (Ed.), *Do they grow out of it? Long-term outcomes of childhood disorders* (pp. 17–38). Washington, DC: American Psychiatric Press.

Jensen, P.S. (1995). Scales versus categories? Never play against a stacked deck. *Journal of the American Academy of Child and Adolescent Psychiatry, 34,* 485–487.

Jensen, P.S., Salzberg, A.D., Richters, J.E., & Watanabe, H.K. (1993), Scales, diagnoses and child psychopathology: I. CBCL and DISC relationships. *Journal of the American Academy of Child and Adolescent Psychiatry, 32,* 397–406.

Kendler, K.S. (1993) Twin studies of psychiatric illness: Current status and future directions. *Archives of General Psychiatry, 50,* 905–915.

Kendler, K.S. (1995). Genetic epidemiology in psychiatry: Taking both genes and environment seriously. *Archives of General Psychiatry, 52,* 895–899.

Lambert, N.M. (1988). Adolescent outcomes for hyperactive children. *American Psychologist, 4,* 786–799.

Levy, F., Hay, D., McLaughlin, M., Wood, C., & Waldman, I.D. (1996a). Twin–sibling differences in perinatal reports of ADHD, speech, reading and behaviour problems. *Journal of Child Psychology and Psychiatry, 37,* 569–578.

Levy, F., Hay, D., McStephen, M., Wood, C., & Waldman, I.D. (1997). Attention Deficit Hyperactivity Disorder (ADHD): A category or a continuum? Genetic analysis of a large scale twin study. *Journal of the American Academy of Child and Adolescent Psychiatry, 36,* 737–744.

Levy, F., Hay, D.A., & Rooney, R. (1996b). Predictors of persistence of ADHD symptoms in a large-scale twin study: Preliminary report. *The ADHD Report, 4*(6), 12.

Lie, N. (1992). Follow-ups of children with Attention Deficit Hyperactivity Disorder. *Acta Psychiatrica Scandinavia, 368* (Suppl.), 1–40.

Loehlin, J.C. (1992) *Genes and environment in personality development.* Newbury Park, CA: Sage.

Loehlin, J.C. (1996) The Cholesky approach: A cautionary note. *Behavior Genetics, 26,* 65–69.

Mannuzza, S., Klein, R.G., Bessler, A., Malloy, P., & LaPadula, M. (1998). Adult psychiatric status of hyperactive boys grown up. *American Journal of Psychiatry, 155,* 493–498.

Milberger, S., Faraone, S.V., Biederman, J., Testa, M., & Tsuang, M.T. (1996). New phenotypic definition of Attention Deficit Hyperactivity Disorder in relatives for genetic analysis. *American Journal of Medical Genetics (Neuropsychiatric Genetics), 67,* 369–377.

Morgan, A.E., Hynd, G.W., Riccio, C.A., & Hall, J.H. (1996). Validity of DSM-IV ADHD predominantly inattentive and combined types: Relationship to previous DSM diagnoses/subtype differences. *Journal of the American Academy of Child and Adolescent Psychiatry, 33,* 325–333.

Murphy, K., & Barkley, R.A. (1995). Preliminary normative data on DSM-IV criteria for adults, *The ADHD Report, 3*(3), 6–7.

Neale, M.C., & Cardon, L.R. (1992) *Methodology for genetic studies of twins and families.* Dordrecht, The Netherlands: Kluwer.

Neale, M.C., Walters, E.E., Eaves, L.J., Maes, H.H., & Kendler, K.S. (1994). Multivariate genetic analysis of twin-family data on fears: Mx models. *Behavior Genetics, 24,* 119–139.

Nigg, J.T., & Goldsmith, H.H. (1998). Developmental psychopathology, personality, and temperament: Reflections on recent behavioral genetics research. *Human Biology, 70,* 387–413.

O'Connor, T.G., Neiderhiser, J.M., Reiss, D., Hetherington, E.M., & Plomin, R. (1998). Genetic contributions to continuity, change and co-occurrence of antisocial and depressive symptoms in adolescence. *Journal of Child Psychology and Psychiatry, 39,* 232–336.

Piek, J.P., Pitcher, T.M., & Hay, D.A. (1999). Motor coordination and kinaesthesis in boys with Attention Deficit Hyperactivity Disorder. *Developmental Medicine and Child Neurology, 41,* 159–165.

Rey, J.M., Morris-Yates, A., & Stewart, G.W. (1995). Continuities between psychiatric disorders in adolescents and personality disorders in young adults. *American Journal of Psychiatry, 152,* 895–900.

Rutter, M. (1995). Relationships between mental disorders in childhood and adulthood. *Acta Psychiatrica Scandinavia, 91,* 73–85.

Schmitz, S., Fulker, D.W., & Mrazek, D.A. (1995). Problem behavior in early and middle childhood: An initial behavior genetic analysis. *Journal of Child Psychology and Psychiatry, 36,* 1443–1458.

Sherman, D.K., Iacono, W.G., & McGue, M.K. (1997). Attention-Deficit Hyperactivity Disorder dimensions: A twin study of Inattention and Impulsivity-Hyperactivity. *Journal of the American Academy of Child and Adolescent Psychiatry, 36,* 745–753.

Silberg, J.L., Rutter, M., Meyer, J.M., Maes, H.H., Hewitt, J.K., Simonoff, E.,

Pickles, A., Loeber, R., & Eaves, L. (1996). Genetic and environmental influences on the covariation between hyperactivity and conduct disturbance in juvenile twins. *Journal of Child Psychology and Psychiatry, 37*, 803–816.

Tzelepis, A., Schubiner, H., & Warbasse, L. (1994). Differential diagnosis and psychiatric co-morbidity patterns in adult Attention Deficit Disorder. In K. Nadeau (Ed.), *A comprehensive guide to attention deficit disorders in adults* (pp. 35–57). New York: Brunner/Mazel.

van den Oord, E.J.C.G., & Rowe, D.C. (1997). Continuity and change in children's social maladjustment: A developmental behavior genetic study. *Developmental Psychology, 33*, 319–332.

van der Valk, J.C., Verhulst, F.C., Neale, M.C., & Boomsma, D.I. (1998). Longitudinal genetic analysis of problem behaviors in biologically related and unrelated adoptees. *Behavior Genetics, 28*, 365–380.

Wechsler, D. (1974). *The Wechsler Intelligence Scale for Children—Revised*. New York: Psychological Corporation.

Wechsler, D. (1991). *Wechsler Intelligence Scale for Children—third edition*. San Antonio, TX: The Psychological Corporation.

Willcutt, E.G., Pennington, B.F., Chhabildas, N.A., Friedman, M.C., & Alexander, J. (1999). Psychiatric comorbidity associated with DSM-IV ADHD in a non-referred sample of twins. *Journal of the American Academy of Child and Adolescent Psychiatry, 38*, 1355–1362.

Woodward, L., Taylor, E., & Dowdney, L. (1998). The parenting and family functioning of children with hyperactivity. *Journal of Child Psychology and Psychiatry, 39*, 161–169.

# 5 Familial and genetic bases of speech and language disorders[1]

*Barbara A. Lewis*

Speech and language disorders represent two of the most common developmental problems of childhood. Despite this, in the vast majority of instances a causal factor for the communication problem is not identifiable. Historically, disorders with no identifiable aetiology were termed functional disorders, and were attributed to environmental influences and faulty learning. In the 1990s, a growing body of research has suggested that familial and/ or genetic, as well as environmental, factors may contribute to some of these disorders. Currently, advances in molecular genetics enable researchers to investigate genetic factors that may contribute to some of these speech and language disorders, and genetic studies promise to illuminate the underpinnings of these uniquely human attributes.

These advances aside, as with exploration into many complex human traits, scientific examination in this field is limited by different understandings of the concepts being studied and by limitations of the measures used to assess them. The search for genetic bases to speech and language disorders particularly, has been complicated by inconsistencies of definition and methodology, and by a dearth of standardised assessment measures that span a broad age range. Added to this, there are few clear-cut phenotypic boundaries of comorbid conditions such as ADHD, dyslexia, and other learning disabilities. Nor can shared aetiological factors always be identified.

This chapter reviews current knowledge relating to the familial and genetic bases of speech and language disorders, and suggests possible relationships with ADHD. We examine phenotypes and phenotype definitions, as well as incidence and prevalence of speech and language disorders. We also look at gender as a risk factor, family aggregation, and twin and adoption studies. Segregation and linkage analysis are covered briefly. Some attention is given to comorbid conditions, such as reading disorders. Finally, we consider the implications for ADHD. We present some pilot data on the relationship between ADHD and speech and language disorders in our own cohort—

1 This project was supported by research grant number RO1 DC00528–06A1 from the National Institute on Deafness and Other Communication Disorders, National Institutes of Health.

children enrolled in a longitudinal family study of phonology disorders, with a comorbid diagnosis of ADHD.

## THE SEARCH FOR PHENOTYPE DEFINITIONS

Developmental speech and language difficulties in children include a heterogeneous group of disorders that affect speech sound production, as well as receptive and expressive language skills. Traditional classification systems divide disorders into those of articulation/phonology; disorders affecting the speech sound system; language disorders including difficulties with syntax, semantics, or pragmatics; disorders of fluency including stuttering and prosody disturbances; and voice disorders. These conditions are not mutually exclusive, and more often than not a child presents with a combination of two or more difficulties with speech and language.

Critical to genetic studies of speech and language disorders are the phenotype definitions—definitions that are not universally agreed on. Some investigators have used a broad phenotype definition that includes all speech and language disorders, as well as related language learning difficulties such as reading and spelling (Tallal, Ross, & Curtiss, 1989). Others have narrowed the phenotype definition to a specific speech or language disorder, such as stuttering or phonology (Lewis, Ekelman, & Aram, 1989).

Added to this lack of constancy of phenotype definition is inconsistent application of phenotype definitions within investigations. Some studies, although applying a narrow definition of the phenotype for the proband, have utilised a broad phenotypic definition for nuclear family members who, as is the case with the probands, often present with a wide spectrum of disorders.

Identification of affected family members presents another challenge to genetic studies in the field. For instance, as speech and language disorders are often remediated by 7 or 8 years of age, in many instances older siblings and parents no longer demonstrate speech sound deficits or grammatical errors in their conversational speech.

In light of this "vanishing phenotype", researchers have often relied on historical reports, rather than on direct observation of the speech or language disorder. When compared to standardised testing of speech and language disorders, historical reports may underestimate affected adults (Plante, Shenkman, & Clark, 1996). Even when direct testing is possible, there is a lack of norm-referenced tests specifically designed to identify residual speech and language disorders in adults (Plante et al., 1996). Furthermore, few speech and language measures span the age range from preschool through adulthood. This makes it difficult to compare family members of various ages on similar measures. Despite, and no doubt because of, these methodological difficulties, interest in genetic contributions to a complex trait such as speech and language is growing.

## STUDIES OF PHENOTYPES

Studies of the familial transmission of speech and language disorders have examined probands selected for stuttering (Kidd, Kidd, & Records, 1978); phonology disorders (Lewis et al., 1989); and/or specific language impairment (SLI; Tomblin, 1989). They describe difficulty in the acquisition of language skills in the absence of abnormalities of hearing, nonverbal IQ, social environment, or motor skills (Tomblin, 1996). These disorders, especially phonology and SLI, are often found to co-occur, and boundaries within and between conditions are not always clear.

Various criteria have been utilised in attempts to define SLI. These have ranged from cut-off scores of between 1 standard deviation (SD) below the mean and 2 SD below the mean, on a norm-referenced test (Bloom & Lahey, 1978). Tomblin, Records, and Zhang (1996) recommended a cut-off of 1.24 SD below the mean, on two or more composite scores, on a standardised test such as the Test of Language Development—P:2. However, even when applying these criteria, SLI remains a heterogenous group with individuals presenting with a variety of profiles of semantic, syntactic, phonologic, and pragmatic skills.

In contrast to utilising cut-off scores on standardised tests, some authors have suggested that linguistic impairment specific to grammar may provide the basis for phenotype definitions of SLI. Rice and Wexler (1996) proposed that specific grammatical characteristics, such as the extended optional infinitive, be used as clinical markers to identify children with SLI. They demonstrated that these markers appeared at a lower rate in the grammar of children with SLI, than in typically developing children.

However, use of specific grammatical characteristics as clinical markers may not be useful for the identification of affected older children and adults. Gopnik and Crago (1991) reported on a large multigenerational British pedigree with a specific linguistic impairment in marking tense. The pedigree was consistent with a dominant mode of transmission. However, since family members had difficulty with speech sound production, in addition to the linguistic impairment, interpretation of these data as transmission within the family of a specific grammatical impairment is obscured. Affected individuals may have been incapable of producing the grammatical marker in question.

Children with SLI also demonstrate various degrees of receptive and expressive language problems. Some investigators have explored subtyping children with language disorders into those with receptive language problems, or with receptive-expressive language difficulties. There is evidence to suggest that receptive language disorders may differ from expressive language disorders in familial aggregation. Lahey and Edwards (1995) examined the families of 53 probands with either mixed receptive-expressive language delay, or expressive-only delay. They found that children in the group with an expressive only delay were more likely to have an affected family member.

However, Whitehurst, Arnold, Smith, and Fischel (1991), failed to find a greater number of affected members in the families of 63 children with expressive language delay only, when compared to families of control children.

A co-mingling analysis (i.e., matching of assumed distributions) of receptive and expressive language scores of children with histories of preschool phonology disorders, and their siblings ($n = 172$) was done. This provided further evidence that receptive and expressive language disorders may have distinct aetiologies (Lewis et al., 1997). The finding that a single distribution was adequate would be consistent with the interpretation that the scores of children with phonology disorders represent the lower end of a single distribution. It could also be accounted for by the normal variation of verbal skills within the population. In contrast, a finding that the distribution of scores would better be described by a mixture of two or more distributions, would suggest that skills of some children with speech and language disorders reflect a distinct aetiology, rather than variation along the normal continuum. The results differed for receptive and expressive language measures. The mixture analyses failed to provide evidence that a mixture of distributions fit better than a single distribution for the receptive language score. On the other hand, for the expressive language measures, a model that assumed mixture of two distributions fit the data significantly better than did a model that assumed a single distribution. These results suggested that the expressive deficits noted in these families were not merely representative of the lower end of the normal continuum of verbal skills, but instead possibly reflected distinct aetiologies. In addition, these results suggested that the underlying aetiology for expressive deficits was different to that of receptive deficits.

Some reasons for the inconsistency of expressive or receptive language problems found in previous studies of familial aggregation are the differing criteria that have been used in proband selection. In our study (see later), probands were selected for a phonology disorder and therefore, not surprisingly, have expressive language deficits. Shriberg and Austin (1998) found that children with speech involvement had a two–three times greater risk for expressive language problems than for receptive language problems. Estimates of the comorbidity of receptive language disorders with speech disorders ranged from 6% to 21%, based on whether receptive language was assessed by vocabulary, grammar, or both. Estimates of comorbidity of expressive language disorders with speech disorders ranged from 38% to 62% depending on the methods used to assess expressive skills.

The heterogeneous nature of speech and language disorders suggests that several different underlying genetic aetiologies may be involved. The development of well-specified phenotypes, based on clinically valid subtypes of speech and language disorders, is essential for progress in this area.

## INCIDENCE/PREVALENCE

Accurate estimates of the prevalence of speech and language disorders in the general population are essential in conducting behavioural genetic research, and prevalence rates vary, based on the type of disorder and the comorbid conditions associated with it (Leske, 1981). Again, diagnostic criteria for determining affected status of individuals must be well specified and reliable (Aram, Morris, & Hall, 1993). Prevalence rates for specific language impairment range from 2.5% (Randall, Reynell, & Curwen, 1974) to 12.6% (Beitchman, Nair, Clegg, & Patel, 1986), based on the diagnostic criteria applied, and on the age of the subjects. In a recent epidemiologic study that screened 7218 kindergarten children for specific language impairment, Tomblin et al. (1997) reported a prevalence rate of 7.4%. The prevalence rate for SLI was slightly higher for males (8%) than for females (6%).

## GENDER AS A RISK FACTOR

A robust finding of studies of familial speech and language disorders has been a higher prevalence of disorders in males than in females. This has ranged from a ratio of 2:1 to 3:1 (Lewis, 1992; Neils & Aram, 1986; Tallal et al., 1989; Tomblin, 1989). Explanations for this increased prevalence in males include referral bias (Shaywitz, Shaywitz, Fletcher, & Escobar, 1990); immunoreactive theories (Robinson, 1991); differences in rates and patterns of neurological maturation (Plante, 1996); variation in cognitive phenotypes (Bishop, North, & Donlan, 1995); and differences in genetic transmission of the disorders. An X-linked mode of transmission of speech and language disorders has not been supported by pedigree studies (Lewis, 1992; Beitchman, Hood, & Inglis, 1992).

However, there has been support for a gender specific, threshold hypothesis. This proposes that girls have a higher threshold for expression of the disorder, and therefore require a higher genetic loading (more risk genes) before the disorder is expressed (Beitchman et al., 1992; Lewis, 1992; Tomblin, 1989). Consistent with this hypothesis, a higher percentage of affected relatives are reported for female than for male probands (since females carry a higher genetic loading). This has been found in studies of dyslexia (Decker & DeFries, 1981); stuttering (Kidd, et al. 1978); language disorders (Tomblin, 1989); and phonology disorders (Lewis, 1992). Our family study of phonology disorders supports a threshold model, with female probands reporting a greater percentage of affected nuclear family members—26% for male probands and 37.6% for female probands. Differing gender ratios may be found for various subtypes of phonology disorders (Shriberg & Austin, 1998). Hall, Jordan, and Robin (1993), reported a 3:1 male to female ratio for developmental apraxia of speech.

Similarly, boys with phonology disorders were found to have a higher rate of comorbid language disorders than did girls with phonology disorders (Shriberg & Austin, 1998). In our family study, probands with phonology disorders alone demonstrated a more equal gender ratio (59% male and 41% female), than did probands with phonology disorders together with language disorders (71% male and 29% female).

## FAMILIAL AGGREGATION

The familial aggregation of speech and language disorders has been well established. Researchers have estimated that 23%–40% of first-degree family members of individuals with speech and language disorders are affected (Felsenfeld, McGue, & Broen, 1995; Gopnik & Crago, 1991; Lahey & Edwards, 1995; Lewis, 1992; Neils & Aram, 1986; Rice, Haney, & Wexler, 1998; Spitz, Tallal, Flax, & Benasich, 1997; Tallal, et al., 1989; Tomblin, 1989). Tomblin (1989) reported that brothers and sisters of probands with language impairment were 30 and 16, respectively, times more likely to be affected than were siblings of control children. Risk estimates reported for parents were seven times greater for mothers, and five times greater for fathers, than was the case for parents of control children. Only one study (Whitehurst et al., 1991), which examined probands with expressive vocabulary deficits, found no differences in rates of impairment between relatives of probands and relatives of control children. Differences in rates of affected family members again may be attributed to differences in definitional criteria for probands and family members.

## STUDIES THAT SUGGEST A GENETIC COMPONENT/ GENETIC STUDIES

### Twin studies

The twin study paradigm has been employed to identify genetic and environmental contributions to speech and language disorders. Twin studies of speech/language disorders (Bishop et al., 1995; Lewis & Thompson, 1992; Tomblin & Buckwalter, 1998) have consistently reported higher concordance rates for monozygotic (MZ) than for dizygotic (DZ) twin pairs, confirming a genetic contribution to these disorders. Concordance rates for MZ twins range from .70 (Bishop et al., 1995), to .86 (Lewis & Thompson, 1992), and .96 (Tomblin & Buckwalter, 1998). Concordance rates reported for DZ twin pairs are as follows: .46 (Bishop et al., 1995); .48 (Lewis & Thompson, 1992); and .69 (Tomblin & Buckwalter, 1998). In the Tomblin study, heritability was calculated to be .45, employing the DeFries and Fulker method (1985). Bishop et al. (1995), calculated heritabilities for individual language skills to be .56 for repeating sentences, to 1.35 for a word finding measure (see later discussion of a heritability finding greater than 1).

Gathercole and Baddeley (1990) have argued that specific language impairment (SLI) involves a specific deficit in the phonological loop component of working memory. The importance of phonemic awareness for language (and likely reading) development is emphasised by the work of Bishop et al. (1995). Bishop's group used the Children's Nonword Repetition (CNRep) task, where children are asked to repeat nonwords of increasing syllable length. The test was initially administered to two groups: a group of 17 MZ and 13 DZ, SLI twin pairs, aged from 7 to 9 years, where at least one twin met criteria for SLI; and a control group. Children with resolved SLI, as well as those with persistent SLI, were significantly impaired on the CNRep. Comparisons of MZ and DZ twins indicated significant heritability of a CNRep deficit. A subsequent study (Bishop, Bishop, Bright, Delaney, & Tallal 1999), compared two groups on the CNRep test and Tallal's Auditory Repetition Test. These were 37 same-sex twins previously selected because one or both met criteria for language impairment, and 104 same-sex twin pairs in the same age range (7–13 years) from the general population. The CNRep was shown to better predict low language test scores, and gave high estimates of group heritability (.71). Interestingly, extreme scores gave highly significant group heritability scores, greater than 1, possibly reflecting measurement error.

In a study of twins with typical verbal skills, Nichols and Broman (1974) estimated heritability to be .38 for verbal comprehension, .30 for verbal fluency, and .46 for language achievement. These studies, while supporting a genetic contribution to language skills, also indicated a moderate environmental influence. Environmental factors working with genetics may determine language impairment in an individual. However, environmental determinants of speech and language disorders are not well specified, and in some cases may be more obscure than are genetic factors.

Similarly, twin studies of reading disorders (Bakwin, 1973; Decker & Vandenberg, 1985; DeFries & Fulker, 1985; DeFries, Fulker, & LaBuda, 1987) have reported a higher concordance rate in MZ than in DZ twins. These rates ranging from .84 to 1.00 for MZ twin pairs, and from .29 to .40 for DZ pairs. Studies of reading disorders have demonstrated that phonological processing skills are the heritable component of dyslexia, and that orthographic abilities are more closely related to environmental factors (Olson, Wise, Connors, & Rack, 1989). Heritabilities of different component reading skills are reported as follows: .45 for word decoding skills and .27 for reading comprehension, with heritabilities for overall reading skills ranging from .27 to .55 (Brooks et al., 1990). Heritability of spelling skills has been estimated to fall between .21 and .62 (Brooks, Fulker, & DeFries, 1990; Petrill & Thompson, 1994). Reading and spelling problems are often comorbid with speech and language impairment, and with ADHD, as is described by Jim

Stevenson in Chapter 6. These skills may share common linguistic bases that are in part genetic.

## Adoption Studies

Consistent with these findings, an adoption study by Felsenfeld and Plomin (1997) demonstrated that a positive family history for speech and language disorders in the biological parent, best predicted whether the child was affected. Such a relationship was not found when the family history of the adoptive parents was considered.

## Segregation analyses

Segregation analyses were conducted on 45 pedigrees of children ascertained on the basis of a preschool phonology and language disorder. Children were required to demonstrate normal hearing, intelligence, speech mechanism, and neurological functioning. Segregation analyses confirmed familial aggregation of speech and language disorders, and supported both a major locus model, and a polygenic model, of transmission of the disorders (Lewis, Cox, & Byard, 1993). The failure to obtain a definitive mode of transmission may have been due to genetic heterogeneity (i.e., more than a single underlying genetic basis).

## Linkage analyses

Only one study to date has reported a molecular genetic analysis of a family with specific language impairment. Recently, Fisher, Vargha-Khadem, Watkins, Monaco, and Pembrey (1998) examined a large three generational pedigree, in which half of the members presented with a severe speech and language disorder. Besides deficits in grammar, affected family members demonstrated a dyspraxia of speech. A genome wide search identified a region on chromosome 7, which co-segregated with the speech and language disorder. Dominant inheritance, with full penetrance, was supported. This study provides the initial step for the application of molecular genetic techniques to the study of speech and language disorders.

## COMORBID DISORDERS

In recent years, researchers and clinicians have recognised that speech, language, and reading disorders often co-occur, or are comorbid within individuals. The study of comorbid disorders may provide insights into the aetiology of the primary disorder, and might lead to the development of better treatment and educational plans (Shriberg & Austin, 1998). Although associations between oral and written language abilities are well documented

(Kamhi & Catts, 1986), questions remain with regard to the possibility of common linguistic, cognitive, neurological, and genetic bases for these disorders.

One of the more fundamental issues in this area, is whether oral and written language disorders represent a single verbal trait deficit with variable expression, or whether each disorder has a distinct aetiology. The general verbal trait deficit hypothesis holds that there is a common underlying genetic and cognitive basis that may result in either an isolated speech, language, or reading disorder, or in a combination of these disorders. An alternative explanation is that each disorder has a unique underlying genetic and cognitive basis. Study of the comorbidity of these disorders may shed light on these hypotheses. If a single verbal deficit is responsible for various disorders, and their combinations, then family members should be equally affected across proband types, and speech and language profiles should be similar across probands.

## Studies of children with comorbid speech and language disorders

Follow-up studies show that 40% to 100% of children with preschool speech and language disorders have persistent language problems. In addition, 50% to 75% have academic difficulties (Aram & Hall, 1989; Bishop & Adams, 1990; King, Jones, & Lasky, 1982; Menyuk et al. 1991). In general, children with isolated phonology disorders tend to have better outcomes than do children with histories of phonology disorders accompanied by additional language problems. Children with isolated phonology disorders, for example, are less likely than are children with combined phonology and language disorders to have reading and writing difficulties (Aram & Hall, 1989). The latter finding suggests that the language impairment, rather than the phonology disorder, is responsible for academic deficits. One study by Magnusson and Naucler (1990) reported a good reading outcome for children whose errors were segmental in nature, and a poorer outcome for children whose errors were nonsegmental (i.e., crossed phoneme boundaries). These findings suggested that rule-based errors were more closely associated with later reading performance than were articulatory difficulties.

In summary, phonology disorders appear to be comprised of two distinct subtypes: isolated phonology disorders, and phonology disorders accompanied by more pervasive language disorders (Lewis & Freebairn, 1997).

## Studies of children with reading disorders

Numerous investigators have suggested that reading disability in children may be viewed as a developmental language disorder characterised primarily by deficits in phonological processing skills (Catts, 1993; Kamhi & Catts, 1986; Torgesen & Wagner, 1992). Phonological processing skills that are associated with reading include phonological encoding, phoneme awareness, and speed of naming or phonological recoding (Bradley & Bryant, 1983; Denkla & Rudel, 1976; Wagner, Torgesen, Laughon, Simmons, & Rashotte, 1993).

## Comorbidity with ADHD

Speech and language disorders are frequently reported as comorbid conditions of Attention Deficit Hyperactivity Disorder (ADHD; Berry, Shaywitz, & Shaywitz, 1985; Biederman, Newcorn, & Sprich, 1991; Cantwell & Baker, 1991; Flicek, 1992; Levy, Hay, McLaughlin, Wood, & Waldman, 1996; Pennington, Grossier, & Welsh, 1993). However, the underlying mechanisms for the association between speech and language disorders and ADHD is not known. Does the child have a speech/language problem that results in inattention, or does inattention result in reduced language skills? Alternatively, do these disorders share a common underlying genetic mechanism?

Studies examining the comorbidity of ADHD and speech and language disorders have employed different recruitment strategies. Some studies have surveyed clinical populations of children enrolled in speech and language therapy, to determine the prevalence of ADHD in children with speech and language disorders. Cantwell, Russell, Mattison, and Will (1979) reported that 16% of children enrolled for speech and language therapy also had a diagnosis of ADD. Another study (Beitchman et al., 1986), examined 5-year-old kindergarten children—with and without speech and language disorders—for behavioural and emotional disturbances. These researchers found that children with speech and language disorders were more likely to show behavioural disturbances, including Attention Deficit Disorder (ADD), than were control children. The percentage of children with comorbid conditions of speech/language disorders and ADD (30.4%) was much higher than was the percentage reported by Cantwell et al. (1979).

Other studies have examined populations, with known diagnoses of ADHD, for concomitant diagnoses of speech and language disorders. One study by Levy et al. (1996) surveyed a nonselected sample of 1938 families for both ADHD and speech and language disorders, as well as for Oppositional Defiant Disorder (ODD), Conduct Disorder (CD), and Separation Anxiety (SA). They found a strong association between ADHD symptoms and speech and reading problems, but not between ODD, CD, or SA.

Other studies have failed to find a relationship between ADHD and speech and language disorders. Benasich, Curtiss, and Tallal (1993) examined 99 8-year-old children, who were diagnosed as specifically language impaired, for behavioural-emotional disorders including ADHD. No significant comorbid relationship was found between ADHD and language impairment. These authors concluded that neurodevelopmental delay, and lower IQ, may account for behaviour/emotional problems in learning impaired children.

These studies have failed to account for subtypes of ADHD and speech and language disorders. As noted earlier, speech and language disorders represent a heterogeneous group of disorders with multiple aetiologies. ADHD is also a heterogeneous disorder of unknown aetiology. It is plausible that there may be a subgroup of speech and language disorders that is comorbid with ADHD.

Alternatively, a third disorder—such as dyslexia—may be comorbid with both speech and language disorders, and ADHD. This reading or phonological disorder, rather than the speech and language disorder, may be related to ADHD. This issue is further explored by Jim Stevenson in Chapter 6. Since many of the studies reporting comorbidity of speech and language disorders and ADHD did not test speech and language skills directly, the type of speech and language disorder that the child with ADHD exhibited cannot be identified.

## PILOT DATA

In order to investigate the relationship between ADHD and speech and language disorders in our own cohort, children enrolled in a longitudinal family study of phonology disorders, who had a comorbid diagnosis of ADHD, were examined. Children were initially recruited between preschool and first grade (ages 4.0 to 6.11 years), on the basis of having received speech/language therapy for a moderate to severe phonology disorder.

Additional inclusion criteria were: (1) a score of 1 SD or more below the mean on the Goldman-Fristoe Test of Articulation—Sounds in Words Subtest (GFTA; Goldman & Fristoe, 1986), evidence for at least three phonological error types, and a rating of moderate to severe as identified by the Khan-Lewis Phonological Analysis (Khan & Lewis, 1986); (2) a normal hearing acuity, as defined by passing a pure tone audiometric screening test at 25 dBHL ISO for 500, 1000, 2000, and 4000 Hz bilaterally, with fewer than six reported episodes of otitis media prior to age 3 as reported by the parent; (3) normal peripheral speech mechanism, as documented by the Oral Speech and Motor Control Protocol (Robbins & Klee, 1987); and (4) absence of a history of neurological disorders or developmental delays, other than speech and language as reported by the parent. Parents completed a family history interview, and a pedigree was constructed. Children were tested on a battery of speech and language tests upon enrolment in the study, and again 4 years later. At time 2 testing, children received reading and spelling tests, in addition to the speech and language measures.

Parents of eight of the children (8/47 or 17%), reported that their child had received the diagnosis of ADHD. As shown in Table 5.1, seven of those children were boys, and one was a girl. Only one child (ID = 1), had a negative history for the other comorbid conditions of language disorder, stuttering, reading disorder, spelling disorder, and learning disability. The remaining seven children reported language difficulties. Six reported reading and spelling problems, and five were labelled as learning disabled. Only one child

*Table 5.1* Comorbid disorders by report of probands with ADHD

| ID | Gender | Language | Stuttering | Reading | Learning disabilities | % nuclear |
|----|--------|----------|-----------|---------|-----------------------|-----------|
| 1 | M | – | – | – | – | 0 |
| 2 | M | + | – | + | + | 0 |
| 3 | M | + | – | ? | ? | 67 |
| 4 | M | + | + | + | – | 25 |
| 5 | M | + | – | + | + | 40 |
| 6 | M | + | – | + | + | 25 |
| 7 | F | + | – | + | + | 0 |
| 8 | M | + | – | + | + | 0 |

*Table 5.2* Test scores[1] of probands with phonology disorders comorbid with ADHD

| ID | Language (4–6 years) | Language (7–10 years) | Reading | Spelling | Articulation[2] |
|----|----------------------|------------------------|---------|----------|-----------------|
| 1 | 115 | 106 | 107 | 88 | 32 |
| 2 | 72 | 70 | 86 | 76 | 17 |
| 3 | 67 | – | –1 | – | <1 |
| 4 | 78 | 84 | 86 | 75 | 3 |
| 5 | 70 | 91 | 73 | 76 | <1 |
| 6 | 95 | 61 | 67 | 62 | 11 |
| 7 | 116 | 129 | 122 | 129 | 99 |
| 8 | 84 | 72 | 77 | 64 | 39 |

*Notes:*
[1] Scores are standard scores unless otherwise noted.
[2] Articulation score is a percentile score from the Goldman-Fristoe Test of Articulation.

stuttered. The percentage of nuclear family members reporting speech and language disorders ranged from 0% to 67%, with four children reporting a negative family history for speech/language disorders.

Direct testing of subjects is presented in Table 5.2. Five children at enrolment into the study scored less than 1 SD below the mean on a standard language measure. At elementary school (ages 8.0–10.0 years), four children scored less than 1 SD below the mean or greater on the language measure. Performance on reading and spelling measures revealed significant difficulties in these areas for six of the children. These results suggested that these children had pervasive speech, language, and learning disorders, which continued to impact reading and spelling skills, despite improvements in spoken language abilities.

Family history for ADHD was also examined for all children (N = 47) participating in the longitudinal follow-up phonology study. Twenty-five per cent of the families reported one or more nuclear family members with a diagnosis of ADHD. Examples of family pedigrees are presented in Figures 5.1 and 5.2. The most frequently reported family member affected was the

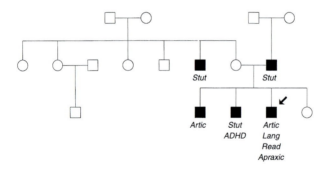

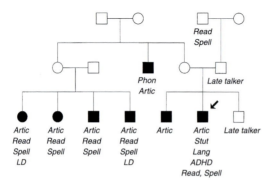

*Figure 5.1* Example pedigrees of children with comorbid conditions of ADHD, speech and language disorders. Aprax = apraxia; Artic = articulation disorder; Lang = language disorder; LD = learning disability; Phon = phonetic disorder; Read = reading disorder; Speech = speech disorder; Spell = spelling disorder; Stut = stuttering

brother of the proband (*n* = 9). Mothers and fathers were equally affected. No sisters were reported as affected. These results should be viewed as preliminary, as larger studies directly testing individual family members for ADHD are needed. However, preliminary results demonstrated that probands selected on the basis of a speech/language disorder, and their families, have a higher incidence of ADHD than expected based on the incidence in the general population. The presence of ADHD in these children cannot be attributed to lower IQ or to neurodevelopmental disorders, as these were exclusionary criteria for the study.

## GENETIC EXPLANATIONS

Without molecular genetic studies, it is not possible to determine the genetic substrate of phonology/language, reading disorders and ADHD. At least two hypotheses, with regard to underlying genetic mechanisms, may be

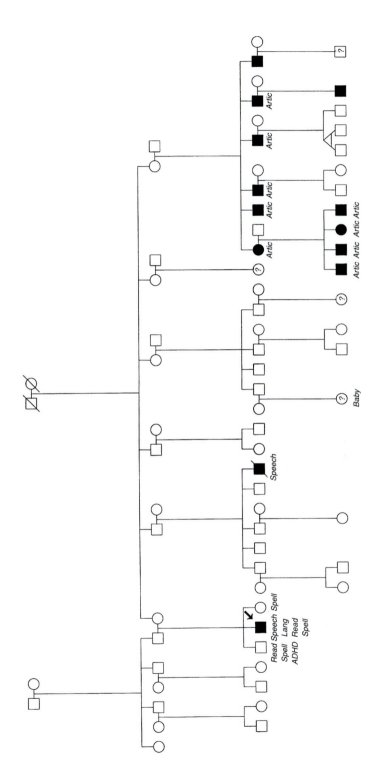

*Figure 5.1 (continued)*

proposed. The first hypothesis assumes that cognitive skills underlying speech, language, and reading—such as attention—are polygenic, or that many genes contribute to these skills. Individual families ascertained through the probands with speech/language disorders, such as in our study, may vary in the number of risk genes transmitted within any given family. According to this hypothesis, families presenting the highest number of affected members may have a greater loading of risk genes than do families without individuals with ADHD. If the action of a single set of genes influences attention, speech/language and reading disorders, comorbidity of disorders might result (Stevenson, Pennington, Gilger, DeFries, & Gillis, 1993).

An alternative hypothesis is that speech, language, reading, and attention disorders differ in their underlying genetic bases. Different abilities, such as phonological awareness, speech sound production, and receptive and expressive language skills, may have unique genetic bases with many different genes influencing speech, language and reading abilities. Understanding of genetic mechanisms will require further delineation of subtypes of disorders and the phenotypic boundaries of each.

## SUMMARY

Speech and language disorders represent a heterogeneous group of disorders that are often comorbid with other learning disabilities, such as dyslexia as well as ADHD. Studies of speech and language disorders have demonstrated a familial aggregation for the disorders, and suggested a genetic as well as an environmental component. Studies of the comorbidity of speech/language disorders and ADHD have been limited by the use of clinical populations, the lack of directly testing speech and language abilities, and the failure to control for other developmental problems. A pilot study of children and their families, ascertained through a proband with a preschool phonology disorder, suggested that a speech/language disorder comorbid with ADHD may represent a subtype of speech and language disorders. Future studies employing a population-based sample, with well-defined phenotypes and direct testing of all family members, are needed.

## REFERENCES

Aram, D.M., & Hall, N.E. (1989). Longitudinal follow-up of children with preschool communication disorders: Treatment implications. *School of Psychology Review, 19*, 487–501.

Aram, D.M., Morris, R., & Hall, N.E. (1993). Clinical and research congruence in identifying children with specific language impairment. *Journal of Speech and Hearing Research, 36*, 580–591.

Bakwin, H. (1973). Reading disability in twins. *Developmental Medicine and Child Neurology, 15*, 184–187.

Beitchman, J.H., Hood, J., & Inglis, A. (1992). Familial transmission of speech and language impairment: A preliminary investigation. *Canadian Journal of Psychiatry*, *37*, 151–156.

Beitchman, J.H., Nair, R., Clegg, M., & Patel, P.G. (1986). Prevalence of speech and language disorder in 5-year-old kindergarten children in Ottawa-Carleton region. *Journal of Speech and Hearing Disorders*, *51*, 98–111.

Benasich, A.A., Curtiss, S., & Tallal, P. (1993). Language, learning, and behavioral disturbances in childhood: A longitudinal perspective. *Journal of American Academy of Child and Adolescent Psychiatry*, *32*, 585–594.

Berry, C.A., Shaywitz, S.E., & Shaywitz, B.A. (1985). Girls with Attention Deficit Disorder: A silent minority? A report on behavioural and cognitive characteristics. *Paediatrics*, *76*, 801–809.

Biederman, J., Newcorn, J., & Sprich, S. (1991). Comorbidity of Attention Deficit Hyperactivity Disorder with conduct, depressive, anxiety, and other disorders. *American Journal of Psychiatry*, *148*, 564–577.

Bishop, D.V.M., & Adams, C. (1990). A prospective study of the relationship between specific-language impairment, phonological disorders, and reading retardation. *Journal of Child Psychology and Psychiatry*, *31*, 1027–1050.

Bishop, D.V.M., Bishop, S.J., Bright, P., Delaney, T., & Tallal, P. (1999). Different origin of auditory and phonological processing problems in children with language impairment: Evidence from a twin study. *Journal of Speech, Language, and Hearing Research*, *42*, 155–168.

Bishop, D.V.M., North, T., & Donlan, C. (1995). Non word repetition as a Behavioural marker for inherited language impairment: Evidence from a twin study. *Journal of Child Psychology and Psychiatry*, *37*, 391–403.

Bloom, L., & Lahey, M. (1978). *Language development and language disorders*. New York: Wiley.

Bradley, L.L., & Bryant, P.E. (1983). Categorizing sounds and learning to read: A casual connection. *Nature*, *301*, 419–421.

Brooks, A., Fulker, D.W., & DeFries, J.C. (1990). Reading performance and general cognitive ability: A multivariate genetic analysis of twin data. *Personality and Individual Differences*, *11*, 141–146.

Cantwell, D.P., & Baker, L. (1991). Association of attention deficit-hyperactivity disorder and learning disorders. *Journal of Learning Disabilities*, *24*, 88–95.

Cantwell, D.P., Russell, A.T., Mattison, R., & Will, L. (1979). A comparison of DSM-II and DSM-III in the diagnosis of childhood psychiatric disorders. I: Agreement with expected diagnosis. *Archives of General Psychiatry*, *36*, 1208–1213.

Catts, H.W. (1993). The relationship between speech-language impairments and reading disabilities. *Journal of Speech and Hearing Research*, *36*, 948–958.

Decker, S.N. & DeFries, J.C. (1981). Cognitive ability profiles in families of reading-disabled children. *Developmental Medicine and Child Neurology*, *23*(2), 217–227.

Decker, S.N., & Vandeberg, S.G. (1985). Colorado twin study of reading disability. In D.B. Gray & J. Kavanaugh (Eds.), *Biobehavioral measures of dyslexia* (pp. 123–135). Baltimore: York.

DeFries, J.C., & Fulker, D.W. (1985). Multiple regression analysis of twin data. *Behavior Genetics*, *15*, 467–473.

DeFries, J.C., Fulker, D.W., & LaBuda, M.C. (1987). Evidence for a genetic aetiology in reading disability of twins. *Nature*, *329*, 537–539.

Denkla, M.A., & Rudel, R.G. (1976). Naming of object drawing by dyslexic and other learning disabled children. *Brain and Language, 3*, 1–16.

Felsenfeld, S., McGue, M., & Broen, P.A. (1995). Familial aggregation of phonological disorders: Results from a 28-year follow-up. *Journal of Speech and Hearing Research, 38*, 1091–1107.

Felsenfeld, S., & Plomin, R. (1997). Epidemiological and offspring analyses of developmental speech disorders using data from the Colorado Adoption Project. *Journal of Speech and Hearing Research, 40*, 778–791.

Fisher, S.E., Vargha-Khadem, F., Watkins, K.E., Monaco, A., & Pembrey, M.E. (1998). Localization of a gene implicated in a severe speech and language disorder. *Nature Genetics, 18*, 168–170.

Flicek, M. (1992). Social status of boys with both academic problems and attention-deficit hyperactivity disorder. *Journal of Abnormal Child Psychology, 20*, 353–366.

Gathercole, S.E., & Baddeley, A.D. (1990). Phonological memory deficits in language disordered children: Is there a causal connection? *Journal of Memory and Language, 29*, 336–360.

Goldman, R., & Fristoe, M. (1986). *The Goldman-Fristoe Test of Articulation*. Circle Pines, MN: American Guidance Service.

Gopnik, M., & Crago, M. (1991). Familial aggregation of a developmental language disorder. *Cognition, 39*, 1–50.

Hall, P.K., Jordan, L.S., & Robin, D.A. (1993). *Development apraxia of speech: Theory and clinical practice*. Austin, TX: Pro-Ed.

Kamhi, A.G., & Catts, H.W. (1986). Toward an understanding of developmental language and reading disorders. *Journal of Speech and Hearing Disorders, 51*, 337–347.

Khan, L., & Lewis, N. (1986). *Khan-Lewis phonological analysis*. Circle Pines, MN: American Guidance Service.

Kidd, K.K., Kidd, J.R., & Records, M.A. (1978). The possible causes of the sex ratio in stuttering and its implications. *Journal of Fluency Disorders, 3*, 13–23.

King, R.R., Jones, C., & Lasky, E. (1982). In retrospect: A fifteen-year follow-up report of speech-language disordered children. *Language, Speech, and Hearing Services in Schools, 13*, 24–32.

Lahey, M., & Edwards, J. (1995). Specific language impairment: Preliminary investigation of factors associated with family history and with patterns of language performance. *Journal of Speech and Hearing Research, 38*, 643–657.

Leske, M. (1981). Prevalence estimate of communicative disorders in the US: Speech disorders. *American Speech and Hearing Association, 23*, 217–255.

Levy, F., Hay, D., McLaughlin, M., Wood, C., & Waldman, I.D. (1996). Twin–sibling differences in parental reports of ADHD, speech, reading, and behaviour problems. *Journal of Child Psychology and Psychiatry, 37*, 569–578.

Lewis, B.A. (1992). Pedigree analysis of children with phonology disorders. *Journal of Learning Disabilities, 25*, 586–597.

Lewis, B.A., Cox, N.J., & Byard, P.J. (1993). Segregation analyses of speech and language disorders. *Behavior Genetics, 23*, 291–297.

Lewis, B.A., Ekelman, B.L., & Aram, D.M. (1989). A familial study of severe phonological disorders. *Journal of Speech and Hearing Research, 32*, 713–724.

Lewis, B.A., & Freebairn, L. (1997). Subgrouping children with familial phonology disorders. *Journal of Communication Disorders, 30*, 385–402.

Lewis, B.A., Shriberg, L.D., Pollak, L.B., Freebairn, L., O'Donnell, B., & Dawson,

D.V. (1997, July). A mixture analysis of phonology disorders. Paper presented at the 27th annual meeting of the Behavior Genetics Association, Toronto, Canada.

Lewis, B.A., & Thompson, L.A. (1992). A study of developmental speech and language disorders in twins. *Journal of Speech and Hearing Research, 35*, 1086–1094.

Magnusson, E., & Naucler, K. (1990). Reading and spelling in language disordered children—linguistic and metalinguistic prerequisites, report on a longitudinal study. *Clinical Linguistics and Phonetics, 4*, 49–61.

Menyuk, P., Chesnick, M., Liebergott, J.W., Korngold, B., D'Agostino, R., & Belanger, A. (1991). Predicting reading problems in at-risk children. *Journal of Speech and Hearing Research, 34*, 893–903.

Neils, J., & Aram, D.M. (1986). Family history of children with developmental language disorders. *Perceptual and Motor Skills, 63*, 655–658.

Nichols, P.L., & Broman, S.H., (1974). Familial resemblance in infant mental development. *Developmental Psychology, 10*, 422–446.

Olson, R.K., Wise, B., Connors, F., & Rack, J. (1989). Specific deficits in component reading and language skills: Genetic and environmental influences. *Journal of Learning Disabilities, 22*, 339–348.

Pennington, B.F., Groisser, D., & Welsh, M.C. (1993). Contrasting cognitive deficits in Attention Deficit Hyperactivity Disorder versus reading disability. *Developmental Psychology, 29*, 511–523.

Petrill, S.A., & Thompson, L.A. (1994). The effect of gender upon heritability and common environmental estimates in measures of scholastic achievement. *Personality and Individual Differences, 16*, 631–640.

Plante, E. (1996). Phenotypic variability in brain–behavior studies of specific language impairment. In M. Rice (Ed.), *Toward a genetics of language*, Mahwah, NJ: Lawrence Erlbaum Associates Inc.

Plante, E., Shenkman, K., & Clark, M.M. (1996). Classification of adults for family studies of developmental language disorders. *Journal of Speech and Hearing Research, 39*, 661–667.

Randall, D., Reynell, J., & Curwen, M. (1974). A study of language development in a sample of three-year-old children. *British Journal of Disorders of Communication, 9*, 3–16.

Rice, M.L., Haney. K.R., & Wexler, K. (1998). Family histories of children with SLI who show extended optional infinitives. *Journal of Speech and Hearing Research, 41*, 419–432.

Rice, M. L., & Wexler, K. (1996). Toward tense as a clinical marker of specific language impairment in English-speaking children. *Journal of Speech and Hearing Research, 39*, 1239–1257.

Robbins, J., & Klee, T. (1987). Clinical assessment of oropharyngeal motor development in young children. *Journal of Speech and Hearing Research, 52*, 271–277.

Robinson, R.J. (1991). Causes and associations of severe and persistent specific speech and language disorders in children. *Developmental Medicine and Child Neurology, 33*, 943.

Shaywitz, S.E., Shaywitz, B.A., Fletcher, J.M., & Escobar, M.D. (1990). Prevalence of reading disability in boys and girls. *Journal of the American Medical Association, 264*, 998–1002.

Shriberg, L.D., & Austin, D. (1998). Comorbidity of speech-language disorders: Implications for a phenotype marker for speech delay. In R. Paul (Ed.), *Exploring the speech/language connection*. Baltimore: Paul S. Brooke.

Spitz, R., Tallal, P., Flax, J., & Benasich, A.A. (1997). Look who's talking: A prospective study of familial transmission of language impairments. *Journal of Speech and Hearing Research, 40*, 990–1001.

Stevenson, J., Pennington, B.F., Gilger, J. W., DeFries, J.C., & Gillis, J. (1993). ADHD and spelling disability: Testing for shared genetic aetiology. *Journal of Child Psychology, Psychiatry, and Allied Disciplines, 34*, 1137–1152.

Tallal, P., Ross, R., & Curtiss, S. (1989). Familial aggregation in specific language impairment. *Journal of Speech and Hearing Disorders, 54*, 167–173.

Tomblin, J.B. (1989). Familial concentration of developmental language impairment. *Journal of Speech and Hearing Disorders, 54*, 287–295.

Tomblin, J.B. (1996). Genetic and environmental contributions to the risk for specific language impairment. In M.L. Rice (Ed.), *Toward a genetics of language*. Mahwah, NJ: Lawrence Erlbaum Associates, Inc.

Tomblin, J.B., & Buckwalter, P. (1998). The heritability of poor language achievement among twins. *Journal of Speech and Hearing Research, 41*, 188–199.

Tomblin, J.B., Records, N.L., Buckwalter, P., Zhang, X., Smith, E., & O'Brien, M. (1997). Prevalence of specific language impairment in kindergarten children. *Journal of Speech and Hearing Research, 40*, 1245–1260.

Tomblin, J.B., Records, N.L., & Zhang, X. (1996). A system for the diagnosis of specific language impairment in kindergarten children. *Journal of Speech and Hearing Research, 39*, 1284–1294.

Torgesen, J.K., & Wagner, R.K. (1992). Language abilities, reading acquisition, and developmental dyslexia: Limitations and alternative views. *Journal of Learning Disabilities, 25*, 577–581.

Wagner, R.K., Torgesen, J.K., Laughon, P., Simmons, K., & Rashotte, C. A. (1993). Development of young readers' phonological processing abilities. *Journal of Educational Psychology, 85*, 83–103.

Weiner, P. (1974). A language-delayed child at adolescence. *Journal of Speech and Hearing Disorders, 39*, 202–212.

Whitehurst, G.J., Arnold, D.S., Smith, M., and Fischel, J.E. (1991). Family history in developmental expressive language delay. *Journal of Speech and Hearing Research, 34*, 1150–1157.

Woodcock, R.W. (1987). *Woodcock Reading Mastery Tests-Revised*. Circle Pines, MN: American Guidance Service.

# 6 Comorbidity of reading/ spelling disability and ADHD

*Jim Stevenson*

## DEFINING READING AND SPELLING DISABILITIES

Problems associated with literacy, such as reading and spelling disability (RSD), can be considered as extremes on a continuum of relative achievement. This makes the task of defining RSD that of applying a cutting point on this continuum, to identify children whose level of underachievement is of educational concern. An alternative formulation of RSD is that there are some children whose underachievement is a product of a set of disabilities that are distinct from those producing individual differences within the normal range. This formulation of a group of children with a distinct disorder of RSD underlies the concept of developmental dyslexia. The key distinction between these two positions is the judgement as to whether or not underachievement in some children is the product of a separate and distinctive set of difficulties.

Literacy is a complex and higher-order cognitive skill that consequently can be influenced by a wide range of underlying abilities. There is as yet no consensus as to which of these underlying abilities may be more strongly implicated for children with a qualitatively distinct RSD. Rather, a pattern is emerging from research into literacy development that suggests that, for all children, a primary influence on the acquisition of literacy skills is the ability to process phonological information. This formulation was best described by Stanovitch in his core deficit variable difference model (Stanovitch & Siegel, 1994).

A separate, but related, issue in the definition of RSD is the degree of deviation—between attainment in reading and spelling, and the child's general level of ability—required for the child to be considered to have a disability. The contrast here is between children whose reading is less good than one would expect given their overall ability, as indexed by IQ, and children who underachieve at reading, but are also generally less able intellectually. This distinction was most clearly made by Rutter and Yule (1975), who labelled the two difficulties specific reading retardation (SRR) and reading backwardness (RB). At that time, the distinction between SRR and RB was shown most clearly in terms of the associated characteristics. That is, if children were defined as SRR on the basis of a regression procedure, where their reading attainment was regressed onto IQ, and RB children were identified simply as having a reading age below their chronological age, then these two groups differed on a number of other variables. SRR was more strongly related to a history of language difficulties, whereas RB was often associated with a range of developmental delays; SRR was associated with antisocial behaviour, whereas RB was associated with a range of behavioural difficulties; and SRR was particularly prevalent in boys, whereas RB showed a more equal gender distribution.

Subsequent investigations (e.g., Stanovich, 1994) have suggested that when the cognitive processes concerned with reading are studied in SRR and RB children, it is difficult to identify specific deficits associated with SRR that are not shown by RB children.

These issues concerning the definition of RSD are crucial to any investigation into the epidemiology of RSD. Given the lack of a clear definition of how developmental dyslexia is to be identified, at present we have to rely on the cutting point on a continuum approach. The problem that this raises is where to place the cutting point. There are a number of possible approaches for solving this problem. The first is to look at concurrent validity, in terms of whether the child's level of attainment in reading and spelling represents a handicap to the child's general educational development. Another is prospective, that is, whether the children who are identified by a specific cutting point are those who are at continuing risk for either later RSD, or possibly later educational failure. Another alternative is to try to test more directly whether a specific cutting point identifies children whose reading problems arise from a distinct set of aetiological factors.

In this respect, genetic methodologies become particularly appropriate, as they can provide an estimate of the relative contributions to a disability of genetic and environmental influences. The methods—DF regression analysis, developed by DeFries and Fulker (1985, 1987)—are particularly appropriate for this application (this is covered in some detail by Levy and colleagues in Chapter 3). This DF analysis is based on the assumption that disability can be identified as the extreme score on an underlying continuum. Proband twins are identified as having scores that put them at an extreme and the estimate of the genetic contribution to proband status is determined by the score of the probands' co-twins. If the condition is strongly genetically influenced, then the scores of co-twins of monozygotic (MZ) pairs will regress back to the population mean to a lesser extent than will the scores of co-twins of dizygotic (DZ) probands. The estimate that is derived provides a numerical value for the extent to which proband status is determined by genetic influences—this is referred to as group heritability, or $h^2_g$.

DF analysis can then be used to test whether—as more extreme definitions of probands are used—children are identified whose disability stems more strongly or less strongly from genetic factors. Thus, a direct test can be made of the appropriateness of a specific cutting point in identifying children whose problems may have a distinct aetiology.

The previous approach was used by Stevenson (1991) to investigate heritability of RSD. The results indicated that whatever level of under-achievement was being adopted, the value of $h^2_g$ remained relatively constant. Therefore, in terms of relative reading achievement, there was no sharp demarcation between children with extreme underachievement and those within the normal range in terms of the strength of genetic factors.

None the less, these results using genetic methodology leave unresolved the problem of where to place the cutting point. Children vary in their level of reading attainment, and in a similar way vary for spelling ability, and it would appear that the definition of RSD is essentially arbitrary.

## EPIDEMIOLOGICAL EVIDENCE FOR THE HIGH COMORBIDITY OF ADHD AND RSD

A number of studies have attempted to identify the extent to which ADHD and RSD co-occur. It has to be recognised that the definition used for behaviours related to ADHD, such as inattention, impulsivity, and overactiv-ity, have not always been applied to conform to a strict ADHD definition. Various studies use a broader concept of hyperactivity, based upon scores on standardised questionnaires. There have also been studies that have used ter-minology of hyperkinetic disorder from the 1993 World Health Organisation (WHO) *International Classification of Disease*—10th revision (*ICD-10*).

The extent of the comorbidity between hyperactivity and RSD is uncertain, but the co-occurrence of these two is a well replicated finding, regardless of the specific criteria for RSD and hyperactivity that are used (Semrud-Clikeman et al., 1992). It is important to show that this comorbidity is relatively specific, by excluding the possibility that it simply arises because these children have a wide range of comorbid problems. An illustration that this is not the case comes from a study by Dykman and Ackerman (1991). They investigated the co-diagnoses of children with attention deficit disorder. Within this group some 40% showed RSD or were slow learners. However, this group did not show other psychiatric problems at a greater rate than did ADHD children without comorbid RSD. This finding therefore indicates that the association between RSD and ADHD is relatively specific.

The question as to whether there are certain forms of ADHD that are more likely to show comorbidity with RSD is as yet unclear. August and Garfinkel (1990) studied a large sample of 7- to 11-year-old American children. They divided their sample in a number of ways, including making a distinction between pervasive and situational ADHD; severe and mild ADHD; attention deficit disorder with hyperactivity versus attention deficit disorder without hyperactivity. They failed to find any differences in reading scores between any of these subcategories of ADHD. By contrast, Taylor, Sandberg, Thorley, and Giles (1991) found that children with attention deficit disorders alone had significantly lower reading scores than did children with a combined attention deficit disorder and Conduct Disorder. Bauermeister, Alegria, Bird, Rubiostipec, and Canino (1992) and Cantwell and Baker (1992) did not find any differences in the rate of RSD between different diagnostic subgroups of ADHD children.

There have been a number of studies of the relationships between ADHD and RSD, centring on whether the two groups show similar cognitive deficits. Such studies can shed some light on the question of the direction of effects. That is, when is it comorbid ADHD that leads to RSD, and when RSD that subsequently leads to the development of ADHD? The logic of such an approach is that if the comorbid group have a pattern of cognitive deficits more like one of the two conditions, then it is likely that that condition is developmentally the antecedent.

Some studies have shown that members of the comorbid group with ADHD and RSD are similar to children with RSD alone, in having a deficit in phonological processing and other verbal abilities (Pennington, Groissier, & Welsh, 1993; Shaywitz et al., 1995). Pennington et al. (1993) investigated whether the comorbid group would show the same deficits in executive function that are found in ADHD alone children. The pattern of results suggested that the ADHD and RD children had the phonological deficits associated with RD, but not the executive function deficits associated with ADHD. Based on this pattern of findings Pennington and colleagues concluded that the comorbid condition might arise as a phenocopy of reading disabilities. That is, that early developing reading difficulties led—in some children at least—to ADHD symptoms as a secondary consequence. However, there are nonreplications of this pattern of deficits (e.g., Reader, Harris, Schuerholz, & Denckla, 1995). There has been contrary evidence that comorbid ADHD and RSD groups show the pattern of deficits found in ADHD children alone (Purvis & Tannock, 1997).

One of the most careful examinations of the impact of comorbidities on the cognitive profile of ADHD children was undertaken by Nigg, Hinshaw, Carte, and Treuting (1998). They aimed to determine whether the pattern of deficits, in effortful tasks that require planning or controlled motor output, was still evident in ADHD children when the effects of conduct problems and reading disability were controlled. They suggested that such deficits do persist, and that the deficits shown by children comorbid for ADHD and RSD were not merely a secondary consequence of RSD, as suggested by the results presented by Pennington et al. (1993).

A bench-mark test of the phenocopy hypothesis is the use of longitudinal data. Here the results do not support a strong impact of reading disability on later ADHD behaviours. Chadwick, Taylor, Taylor, Heptinstall, and Danckaerts (1999) compared the developmental course of children at 7–8 years with hyperactivity alone; SRR alone; comorbid hyperactivity and SRR; and a comparison group with neither condition. They found no evidence that the presence of SRR affected the persistence or onset of hyperactivity, nor did hyperactivity affect the onset or course of SRR. Using data from the Christchurch Health and Development Study, Fergusson and Horwood (1992) did not support the Pennington phenocopy hypothesis of RSD leading to comorbid attention deficits.

There were, however, indications that attention deficits may have an adverse effect over time on reading. Smart, Sanson, and Prior (1996) have described similar findings. More marked effects of early reading difficulties on later antisocial behaviour in children with ADHD were found in the Dunedin Longitudinal Study (Pisecco, Baker, Silva, & Brooke, 1996). These longitudinal data provide very little support for the notion that RSD can lead to ADHD. Rather, RSD seems to elevate the chance of antisocial behaviour developing in these ADHD children, but does not increase the risk of new onset cases of ADHD. If anything, these longitudinal studies suggest that attention deficits may exacerbate RSD.

Given this conclusion, any considerations of the overlap between hyperactivity and RSD has also to take into account the association between each of these and Conduct Disorder or antisocial behaviour. Stevenson (1996) reviewed the possible origins of comorbidities between these three conditions. The framework developed by Caron and Rutter (1991) was used. Here, comorbidities could be postulated to arise because of common influences shared between two conditions, or from a situation where one condition directly influenced or resulted in the other. The comorbidity could be spurious where the two conditions represented the same basic nosological category, or the two conditions could have distinct but correlated causes. Finally, the comorbid condition could represent an aetiologically distinct group of children.

Stevenson (1996) concluded that both hyperactivity and RSD arose from basic underlying, but separate, cognitive deficits. In contrast, Conduct Disorder did not have a distinctive cognitive profile. The nature of the underlying cognitive deficit for RSD was essentially that of a phonological processing difficulty. For hyperactivity, it was less clear whether the underlying deficit was one of attentional control, executive function, or behavioural inhibition. The issue of the extent to which comorbidities arise as a result of shared genetic influences on these cognitive abilities will be discussed in more detail later in this chapter. However, a number of more distal causes of Conduct Disorder, Hyperactivity, and RSD were intercorrelated. These include factors most strongly related to Conduct Disorder, such as family dysfunction—including marital discord; disruptive parenting—such as inconsistent discipline, related to hyperactivity; and factors related to reading disability—such as maternal depression. The origin of the correlation between these more distal causes possibly lay in social disadvantage. A similar conclusion was reached by Biederman et al. (1995) was that aggregated environmental risk factors influence the likelihood of comorbidity with ADHD. It is thus seen that a number of environmental mechanisms lead to the association between

ADHD and RSD. These environmental factors will act alongside possible genetic mechanisms and these that will be considered next.

## QUANTITATIVE GENETIC STUDIES OF RSD

There have been reports on the familial nature of RSD since the earliest clinical accounts (Hinshelwood, 1907). The first firm evidence that this familiality was the result of genetic factors came from twin studies published in the 1980s. The Colorado Twin Reading study (DeFries & Fulker, 1987; DeFries, Fulker, & LaBuda, 1987), and the London Twin Reading Study (Stevenson, Graham, Fredman, & McLoughlin, 1987) provided evidence that approximately 50% of the factors producing RSD stemmed from genetic differences between children in the study. These findings have been replicated in other twin studies (e.g., Reynolds et al., 1996)

These studies went on to demonstrate that in reading—when comparing phonological processing (i.e., sublexical units), and orthography (i.e., whole word reading)—the former was more strongly influenced by genetic factors than was the latter (Castles, Datta, Gayan, & Olson, 1999; Olson, Wise, Conners, Rack, & Fulker 1989; Stevenson, 1991).

The quantitative genetic studies of RSD are now at a stage where factors that moderate the impact of genes on RSD are being investigated. Some of the initial inconsistencies in the heritabilities of spelling and reading disability were explained by Stevenson et al. (1987), as arising from an age-related decline in heritability for reading, and a sustained higher heritability for spelling disability. DeFries, Alarcon, and Olson (1997) tested this hypothesis, using the Colorado twin data. They found that the heritabilities of spelling and reading were significant for age, with reading having a higher heritability below age 11.5 years and by contrast spelling showed an increase in $h^2_g$ after this age.

Most behaviour genetic studies of the relationship between ADHD and RD have not incorporated the distinction between Inattention and Hyperactivity/Impulsivity. A recent study by Willcutt, Pennington, and DeFries (2000) utilised a sample of 313 same-sex twin pairs aged 8–16 years to assess the aetiology of comorbidity between reading disability (RD) and ADHD. RD was assessed by a discriminant function score, based on the Peabody Individual Achievement Test, a standardised measure of academic achievement. The American Psychiatric Association *Diagnostic and Statistical Manual of Mental Disorders*, Third Edition (*DSM-III*; APA 1980) version of the Diagnostic Interview for Children and Adolescents was used to assess symptoms of ADHD. Separate factor scores were computed for Inattention and Hyperactivity/Impulsivity. They found that individuals with RD were significantly more likely than individuals without RD to exhibit elevations on both symptom dimensions, but the difference was larger for Inattention than for Hyperactivity/Impulsivity. Behaviour genetic analyses indicated significant bivariate heritability of ADHD and Inattention ($h^2_g$ RD/Inatt.) = 0.39), whereas the bivariate heritability of RD and Hyperactivity/Impulsivity was minimal and nonsignificant. Approximately 95% of the phenotypic covariance between RD and symptoms of inattention was attributable to common genetic influences, whereas only 21% of the phenotypic overlap between RD and Hyperactivity/Impulsivity was due to the same genetic factors.

A reassuringly similar pattern of results has been found in an unpublished analysis of data from the Australian Twin ADHD Project. (See Chapters 2 and 3 of this volume for details of the project.) The results are summarised in Figure 6.1, which examines the relationship between a history of reading intervention and the *Diagnostic and Statistical Manual of Mental Disorders, Fourth Edition* (*DSM-IV*; APA; 1994) Inattention and Hyperactivity symptom numbers.

The symbols in this figure follow the conventions introduced in Chapter 2 of this volume. In the middle row, in squares, are the observed scores of both members of a twin pair. Above these are the best-fitting additive genetic and environmental effects common to all three measures. Below are the corresponding items, specific to each measure. Thus, *all* of the genetic variance in Inattention is shared with the genes affecting reading. Hyperactivity/Impulsivity is partly genetically independent. For reading, there is some evidence of shared environment, implying that growing up in the same home

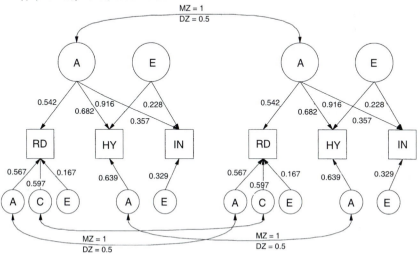

**Multivariate Genetic Model of Reading Intervention and ADHD**
Chi Sq (23) = 32.103, p < 0.098; RMSEA = 0.012

*Figure 6.1* Best fitting model (by M. McStephen) for the relationship of reading intervention to *DSM-IV* Inattention and Hyperactivity/Impulsivity symptoms in the Australian Twin ADHD Project.

with the same attitudes to reading has some affect. There are also some specific genetic effects, reflecting that part of reading ability is not necessarily related to ADHD.

This analysis was based on 1140 same-sex twin pairs, specifically to avoid issues that may arise with opposite-sex pairs, and gender differences in patterns of reading and ADHD.

An interesting study by Willcutt and Pennington (2000) provided some insight into the puzzling discrepancy between male:female ratios of individuals with reading disorder (RD) in clinic ADHD populations (approximately 4:1), versus those in nonreferred samples (1.2–1.5–1). They found the association of ADHD with RD to be stronger for the Inattentive symptoms. Analyses of gender differences revealed that RD was significantly associated with Inattention in males and females, but was associated with Hyperactivity/Impulsivity in males only. They suggested that the hyperactive and impulsive behaviours exhibited by males with RD may be more disruptive than were the inattentive behaviours exhibited by females, and may therefore precipitate more frequent referrals for clinical attention.

It has been suggested that the heritability of RSD may be greater for children with higher IQs. When the twin sample from the Colorado study was divided into those with a full-scale IQ greater than 100, and those with less than 100, the higher IQ children were found to have an $h^2_g$ of 0.72, and those of below 100 an $h^2_g$ of 0.43 ($p < .03$). It would appear that environmental factors had a greater role to play in the reading difficulties experienced by lower IQ children. Casto, Pennington, Light, and DeFries (1996) found evidence that for children with lower mathematical ability, $h^2_g$ for RSD is somewhat higher than for other children. The reverse was the pattern for IQ.

To facilitate studies on the molecular genetics of RSD, more quantitative genetic studies need to be undertaken to develop further understanding of the genetic architecture of reading and related abilities. Reading ability is correlated with a number of other cognitive skills. These range from the most general (e.g., IQ), through language abilities (e.g., syntactic ability), to specific aspects of processing text (e.g., phonological decoding). A study of two samples of twins age 6 years and 7 years has shown a complex pattern of genetic influences on reading and related cognitive abilities (Hohnen & Stevenson, 1999). They found that genes for general intelligence, and for general language, influenced individual differences in the early stages of reading ability. In this study, however, there was no evidence for a specific genetic association between phonological ability and literacy. Instead, these were associated via shared genetic influences on general language, and via a specific shared environmental influence. The latter is consistent with the evidence that experience of rhymes and specific training in phonological awareness can enhance reading development (e.g., Bryant, MacLean, Bradley, & Crossland 1990).

To summarise the position on the quantitative genetic study of RSD, it has been extensively replicated that genetic factors make a significant contribution to RSD, and that certain features of this phenotype show the genetic effects more strongly (e.g., spelling). Interest now centres on identifying the cognitive processes that mediate this genetic effect (e.g., phonological ability). Attention is also being paid to which factors interact with genetic influences to moderate heritability (e.g., age and IQ). The robust and substantial heritability of RSD has lead to it being the subject of intensive molecular genetic investigation, and this work will be outlined next.

## MOLECULAR GENETIC STUDIES OF RSD

Alongside these quantitative genetic studies, molecular genetic techniques have been applied to RSD. These are amongst the most extensive set of replicated molecular genetic investigations of complex cognitive abilities. There were initial linkage studies suggesting that a gene, on chromosome 15, might play a role in RSD (Smith, Kimberling, Pennington, & Lubs 1983). Subsequent analysis of this same set of families suggested that an additional gene, on chromosome 6, might play a role (Smith, Kimberling, Pennington 1991). In small samples, subsequent linkage to chromosome 1 was also suggested (Rabin et al., 1993).

The best evidence of linkage to date centres on chromosome 6. Using a sample of siblings, and an independent sample of twins, Cardon et al. (1994, 1995) found linkage to markers on a region of chromosome 6 (6p21.3). Subsequently, Grigorenko et al. (1997) also found evidence of linkage—for specific forms of RSD in six extended multiaffected families—to a similar region of chromosome 6. The Cardon et al. study was based upon a composite measure of RSD. A further analysis of the twins from that sample, this time using three more specific phenotypes (i.e., word recognition, phonological decoding and orthographic coding), found deficits in each facet of reading to be linked to the 6p21.3 region (Gayan et al., 1995).

One essential requirement for linkage studies of these complex characteristics is to obtain replication in independent samples. Gayan et al. (1999) obtained a new sample, of 126 sib-pairs, and found evidence for linkage—for orthographic, phonological, and word recognition—to markers D6S276 and D6S105. This overlaps with the region identified by Cardon et al. (1994, 1995). A similarly wide range of RSD-related deficits was found to be linked to exactly the same markers in a UK-based study by Fisher et al. (1999). The striking feature of this replication is that it has been found using different forms of linkage analysis, different measures of RSD, different samples and by different research teams. It should be noted that there has been a report, by Field and Kaplan (1998) of nonreplication of linkage to chromosome 6. They used a measure of pseudoword reading similar to the pronounceable non-words adopted by Gayan et al. (1999). They suggested that the nonreplication might have been due either to sample differences or possibly to differences in linkage analysis approaches. Until the Field and Kaplan (1998) data is analysed using the QTL approach adopted by Cardon et al. (1994, 1995), Gayan et al. (1999), and Fisher et al. (1999), the significance of this nonreplication is difficult to evaluate.

A different pattern of linkage results for RSD has been reported by Grigorenko et al. (1997). They too found linkage to chromosome 6, but only for a phonological awareness phenotype, not for single-word reading. The initial reports from this study suggested that the region, on chromosome 6, for which linkage was obtained was somewhat different from that identified by Cardon et al. (1994, 1995). It has subsequently been suggested that the positions of some the markers used in fact are in the same 6p21.3 region (Gayan et al., 1999).

Grigorenko et al. (1997) found single-word reading to be linked to a marker on chromosome 15 (D15S143). Using spelling disability in seven multiply affected families, Schulte-Korne et al. (1997) found linkage to the same marker on chromosome 15 (marker D15S143). Grigorenko et al. (1998) also have reported findings on an enlarged sample of eight families, and found linkage to chromosome 1 (marker D1S199) for a phonological decoding phenotype. Previous reported linkage of RSD to chromosome 1 had been made by Rabin et al. (1993).

As reviewed earlier, the quantitative genetic evidence suggests some shared, and some independent, genetic influences on different features of RSD. The molecular genetic studies seem to indicate that the shared genetic influence may be situated on chromosome 6. Additional specific genes may also be on chromosome 6, or possibly located on chromosome 15 and 1.

## EVIDENCE FOR SHARED GENETIC INFLUENCES ON ADHD AND RSD

The first attempt to identify shared genetic influences for RSD and ADHD came from Gilger, Pennington, and DeFries (1992). They compared the cross-concordances for MZ and DZ pairs—that is, if one twin was ADHD, did the co-twin show RSD? They found that the effects were in the direction of shared genetic effects, as the cross-concordances were higher for MZ than for DZ twin pairs. However, the power of the study was insufficient to detect these differences as significant.

Gillis, Silger, Pennington, and DeFries (1992) confirmed the findings of Goodman and Stevenson (1989) and Stevenson (1992), of substantial heritability for ADHD. They found a very high $h^2_g$ for ADHD in their sample of reading disabled twins (.98). However, that does not provide direct evidence that ADHD and RSD might share common genetic influences.

The first estimate of the size of the genetic correlation between RSD and hyperactivity was made by Stevenson, Pennington, Gilger, DeFries, and Gillis (1993). They used a bivariate extension of the DF analysis. The analysis assumes that those with a condition, either hyperactivity or RSD, are simply the extreme scorers on a continuum. The means of MZ and DZ twins are compared on one continuum measure (e.g., degree of hyperactivity) for those who are co-twins of twins with the other condition e.g., reading disability. If the DZ co-twins' mean is significantly closer to the population mean than that of MZ co-twins, then there is direct evidence for the role of genetic factors in producing the joint occurrence of the two conditions. The continuum assumption has been supported by genetic studies on RSD (Stevenson, 1988), and on ADHD (Gjone, Stevenson, and Sundet 1996; Levy, Hay, McStephen, Wood, & Waldman, 1997).

Using this approach, Stevenson et al. (1993) were able to show that on the Colorado and the London Twin Reading Studies, values for the bivariate group heritability were .32 and .21 respectively. Pooling these results produced a significant result ($p < .02$), indicating that the observed comorbidity between RSD and hyperactivity was due at least in part to common genetic influences.

The analysis by Stevenson et al. (1993) used spelling disability as the index of RSD. Using the Colorado sample, and a reading-based definition of RSD, Light, Pennington, Gilger, and DeFries (1995) were able to show that approximately 70% of the covariation between reading and hyperactivity arose from shared genetic factors. This figure is close to the 75% estimated by Stevenson et al. (1993) for the covariation between spelling disability and hyperactivity. These findings have been replicated in a large study of twins form the Australian Twin Registry (Levy, Hay, Waldman, & McLaughlin, 1995) using a hyperactivity measure able to identify ADHD rather than simply hyperactivity.

Despite the suggestion of correlated genetic influences, for RSD and hyperactivity, or ADHD replicated within twin studies, a rather different result emerged from a family study (Faraone et al., 1993). They investigated the extent to which RSD and ADHD tended to co-occur within ADHD affected families. They found no evidence for co-segregation of these two conditions, and concluded that ADHD and RSD were aetiologically distinct. At present this incompatibility between the results of twin and family studies has yet to be resolved.

To date there is no molecular genetic evidence that might help to decide this issue. It has been suggested, since the 6p21.3 locus is close the HLA region on chromosome 6, that genes affecting immune system dysfunction might play a role. In addition, there is evidence of a possible deficiency in C4B complement protein in children with ADHD (Warren et al., 1996). This has led Warren and colleagues (1995) to suggest that this gene, situated in the HLA region, is a good candidate for a shared genetic influence on ADHD and RSD. Efforts to test this hypothesis have not been fruitful. For example, Gilger et al. (1998) failed to identify any shared genetic influence on reading disability and immune disorders (see also Biederman et al., 1995).

There have been attempts to reformulate and subdivide the ADHD phenotype, to maximise genetic loadings (Milberger, Faraone, Biederman, Testa, & Tsuang 1996). This approach may prove fruitful in specifying the most appropriate cases for linkage and association analyses. To date this approach has not been extended to the issue of comorbidity between ADHD and RSD.

## CONCLUSIONS

The evidence for comorbidity between RSD and ADHD is well established. The key question remains as to how to account for this comorbidity. A number of possible experiential factors might account for part of this association. There is, however, also evidence to support the role of shared genetic factors. At present the quantitative genetic studies by themselves cannot differentiate between mechanisms where common genes cause both conditions, and where, developmentally, one phenotype leads to the other. However, both cross-sectional and longitudinal studies have failed to support the notion that comorbidity arises via this phenocopy mechanism. There are now two main issues to address. First, just which of the genes that are emerging as influencing RSD (e.g., at 6p21.3), and ADHD (e.g., DRD4), are responsible for the genetic correlation? Second, how do these genetic factors act with environmental risk factors, either additively, or in combination with gene–environment correlations and interactions, to produce children with complex combinations of disabilities such as RSD and ADHD?

## REFERENCES

American Psychiatric Association. (1980). *Diagnostic and statistical manual of mental disorders* 3rd edn. Washington, DC: Author.

American Psychiatric Association. (1994). *Diagnostic and statistical manual of mental disorders* 4th edn. Washington, DC: Author.

August, G.J., & Garfinkel, B.D. (1990). Comorbidity of ADHD and reading-disability among clinic-referred children. *Journal of Abnormal Child Psychology, 18*, 29–45.

Bauermeister, J.J., Alegria, M., Bird, H.R., Rubiostipec, M., & Canino, G. (1992). Are attentional hyperactivity deficits unidimensional or multidimensional syndromes—empirical-findings from a community survey. *Journal of the American Academy of Child and Adolescent Psychiatry, 31*, 423–431.

Biederman, J., Milberger, S., Faraone, S.V., Kiely, K., Mick, E., Albon, S., Warburton, R., & Reed, E.D. (1995). Family environment risk factors for ADHD—a test of Rutter's indicators of adversity. *Archives of General Psychiatry, 52*, 464–470.

Bryant, P.E., MacLean, M., Bradley, L.L., & Crossland, J. (1990). Rhyme and alliteration, phoneme detection, and learning to read. *Developmental Psychology, 26*, 429–438.

Cantwell, D.P., & Baker, L. (1992). Attention-deficit disorder with and without hyperactivity—a review and comparison of matched groups. *Journal of the American Academy of Child and Adolescent Psychiatry, 31*, 432–438.

Cardon, L.R., Smith, S.D., Fulker, D.W., Kimberling, W.J., Pennington, B.F., & DeFries, J.C. (1994). Quantitative trait locus for reading-disability on chromosome-6. *Science, 266*, 276–279.

Cardon, L.R., Smith, S.D., Fulker, D.W., Kimberling, W.J., Pennington, B.F., & DeFries, J.C. (1995). Reading-disability, attention-deficit hyperactivity disorder, and the immune-system—response. *Science, 268*, 787–788.

Caron, C., & Rutter, M. (1991). Comorbidity in child psychopathology—concepts, issues and research strategies. *Journal of Child Psychology and Psychiatry and Allied Disciplines, 32*, 1063–1080.

Castles, A., Datta, H., Gayan, J., & Olson, R. K. (1999). Varieties of developmental reading disorder: Genetic and environmental influences. *Journal of Experimental Child Psychology, 72*, 73–94.

Casto, S.D., Pennington, B.F, Light, J.G., & DeFries, J.C. (1996). Differential genetic etiology of reading disability as a function of mathematics performance. *Reading and Writing, 8*, 295–306.

Chadwick, O., Taylor, E., Taylor, A., Heptinstall, E., & Danckaerts, M. (1999). Hyperactivity and reading disability: A longitudinal study of the nature of the association. *Journal of Child Psychology and Psychiatry. 40*, 1039–1050.

DeFries, J.C., Alarcon, M., & Olson, R.C. (1997). Genetic aetiologies of reading and spelling deficits: Developmental differences. In C. Hulme & M. Snowling (Eds.), *Dyslexia: Biology, cognition and intervention* (pp. 20–37). London: Whurr.

DeFries, J.C., & Fulker, D.W. (1985). Multiple regression analysis of twin data. *Behavior Genetics, 15*, 467–473.

DeFries, J.C., & Fulker, D.W. (1987). Multiple regression analysis of twin data: Etiology of deviant scores versus individual differences. *Acta Geneticae Medicae et Gemellologiae, 37*, 1–13.

DeFries, J.C., Fulker, D.W., & LaBuda, M.C. (1987). Evidence for a genetic aetiology in reading disability of twins. *Nature, 329*, 537–539.

Dykman, R.A., & Ackerman, P.T. (1991). Attention-deficit disorder and specific reading-disability—separate but often overlapping disorders. *Journal of Learning Disabilities, 24*, 96–103.

Faraone, S.V., Biederman, J., Lehman, B.K., Keenan, K., Norman, D., Seidman, L.J., Kolodny, R., Kraus, I., Perrin, J., & Chen, W.J. (1993). Evidence for the independent familial transmission of attention-deficit hyperactivity disorder and learning-disabilities—results from a family genetic-study. *American Journal of Psychiatry, 150*, 891–895.

Fergusson, D.M., & Horwood, L.J. (1992). Attention deficit and reading achievement. *Journal of Child Psychology and Psychiatry, 33*, 375–385.

Field, L.L., & Kaplan, B.J. (1998). Absence of linkage of phonological coding dyslexia to chromosome 6p23-p21.3 in a large family data set. *American Journal of Human Genetics, 63*, 1448–1456.

Fisher, S.E., Marlow, A.J., Lamb, J., Maestrini, E., Williams, D.F., Richardson, A.J., Weeks, D.E., Stein, J.F., & Monaco, A.P. (1999). A quantitative-trait locus on chromosome 6p influences different aspects of developmental dyslexia. *American Journal of Human Genetics, 64*, 146–156.

Gayan, J., Olson, R.K., Cardon, L.R., Smith, S.D., Fulker, D.W., Kimberling, W.J., Pennington, B.F., & DeFries, J.C. (1995). Quantitative trait locus for different measures of reading-disability. *Behavior Genetics, 25*, 266.

Gayan, J., Smith, S.D., Cherny, S.S., Cardon, L.R., Fulker, D.W., Brower, A.M., Olson, R.K., Pennington, B.F., & DeFries, J.C. (1999). Quantitative-trait locus for specific language and reading deficits on chromosome 6p. *American Journal of Human Genetics, 64*, 157–164.

Gilger, J.W., Pennington, B.F., & DeFries, J.C. (1992). A twin study of the etiology of comorbidity—attention-deficit hyperactivity disorder and dyslexia. *Journal of the American Academy of Child and Adolescent Psychiatry, 31*, 343–348.

Gilger, J.W., Pennington, B.F., Harbeck, R.J., DeFries, J.C., Kotzin, B., Green, P., & Smith, S.D. (1998). A twin and family study of the association between immune system dysfunction and dyslexia using blood serum assay and survey data. *Brain and Cognition, 36*, 310–333.

Gjone, H., Stevenson, J., & Sundet, J.M. (1996). Genetic influence on parent-reported attention-related problems in a Norwegian general population twin sample. *Journal of the American Academy of Child and Adolescent Psychiatry, 35*, 588–596.

Gillis, J.J., Gilger, J.W., Pennington, B.F., & DeFries, J.C. (1992). Attention deficit disorder in reading-disabled twins: Evidence for a genetic etiology. *Journal of Abnormal Child Psychology, 20*, 303–315.

Goodman, R., & Stevenson, J. (1989). A twin study of hyperactivity: 2. The aetiological role of genes, family relationships and perinatal adversity. *Journal of Child Psychology and Psychiatry, 30*, 691–709.

Grigorenko, E.L., Wood, F.B., Meyer, M.S., Hart, L.A., Speed, W.C., Shuster, A., & Pauls, D.L. (1997). Susceptibility loci for distinct components of developmental dyslexia on chromosomes 6 and 15. *American Journal of Human Genetics, 60*, 27–39.

Grigorenko, E.L., Wood, F.B., Meyer, M.S., Pauls, J.E.D., Hart, L.A., & Pauls, D.L. (1998). Linkage studies suggest a possible locus for dyslexia near the rh region on chromosome 1. *Behavior Genetics, 28*, 470

Hinshelwood, J. (1907). Four cases of congenital word-blindness occurring in the same family. *British Medical Journal, 1*, 608–609.

Hohnen, B., & Stevenson, J. (1999). The structure of genetic influences on general cognitive, language, phonological, and reading abilities. *Developmental Psychology, 35*, 590–603.

Levy, F., Hay, D.A., McStephen, M., Wood, C., & Waldman, I.D. (1997). Attention-deficit hyperactivity disorder: A category or a continuum? Genetic analysis of a large-scale twin study. *Journal of the American Academy of Child and Adolescent Psychiatry, 36*, 737–744.

Levy, F., Hay, D.A., Waldman, I.D., & McLaughlin, M. (1995). To what extent does attention-deficit hyperactivity disorder have the same genetic-basis as speech and reading problems? *Behavior Genetics, 25*, 274

Light, J.G., Pennington, B.F., Gilger, J.W., & DeFries, J.C. (1995). Reading-disability and hyperactivity disorder—evidence for a common genetic etiology. *Developmental Neuropsychology, 11*, 323–335.

Milberger, S., Faraone, S.V., Biederman, J., Testa, M., & Tsuang, M.T. (1996). New phenotype definition of Attention Deficit Hyperactivity Disorder in relatives for genetic analyses. *American Journal of Medical Genetics, 67*, 369–377.

Nigg, J.T., Hinshaw, S.P., Carte, E.T., & Treuting, J.J. (1998). Neuropsycholgical correlates of childhood Attention-Deficit/Hyperactivity Disorder: Explainable by comorbid disruptive behavior or reading problems? *Journal of Abnormal Psychology, 1107*, 468–480.

Olson, R.K., Wise, B., Conners, F., Rack, J., & Fulker, D.W. (1989). Specific deficits in component reading and language skills: Genetic and environmental influences. *Journal of Learning Disabilities, 22*, 339–348.

Pennington, B.F., Groisser, D., & Welsh, M.C. (1993). Contrasting cognitive deficits in attention-deficit hyperactivity disorder versus reading-disability. *Developmental Psychology, 29*, 511–523.

Pisecco, S., Baker, D.B., Silva, P.A.,, & Brooke, M. (1996). Behavioral distinctions in children with reading disability and/or ADHD. *Journal of the American Academy of Child and Adolescent Psychiatry, 35*, 1477–1484.

Purvis, K.L., & Tannock, R. (1997). Language abilities in children with Attention Deficit Hyperactivity Disorder, reading disabilities, and normal controls. *Journal of Abnormal Child Psychology, 25*, 133–144.

Rabin, M., Wen, X.L., Hepburn, M., Lubs, H.A., Feldman, E., & Duara, R. (1993). Suggestive linkage of developmental dyslexia to chromosome 1p34-p36. *Lancet, 342*, 178.

Reader, M.J., Harris, E.L., Schuerholz, L.J., & Denckla, M.B. (1995). Attention-deficit hyperactivity disorder and executive dysfunction. *Developmental Neuropsychology, 10*, 493–512.

Reynolds, C.A., Hewitt, J.K., Erickson, M.T., Silberg, J.L., Rutter, M., Simonoff, E., Meyer, J.M., & Eaves, L.J. (1996). The genetics of children's oral reading performance. *Journal of Child Psychology and Psychiatry, 37*, 425–434.

Rutter, M., & Yule, W. (1975). The concept of specific reading retardation. *Journal of Child Psychology and Psychiatry, 16*, 181–197.

Schulte-Korne, G., Grimm, T., Nothen, M.M., Muller-Myhsok, B., Propping, P., & Remschmidt, H. (1997). Evidence for linkage of spelling disability to chromosome 15. *American Journal of Medical Genetics, 63*, 279–282.

Semrud-Clikeman, M., Biederman, J., Sprich-Buckminster, S., Lehman, B.K., Faraone, S.V., & Norman, D. (1992). Comorbidity between ADDH and learning disability: A review and report in a clinically referred sample. *Journal of the American Academy of Child and Adolescent Psychiatry, 31*, 439–448.

Shaywitz, B.A., Fletcher, J.M., Holahan, J.M., Shneider, A.E., Marchione, K.E., Stuebing, K.K., Francis, D.J., Shankweiler, D.P., Katz, L., Liberman, I.Y., & Shaywitz, S.E. (1995). Interrelationships between reading-disability and attention-deficit hyperactivity disorder. *Child Neuropsychology, 1*, 170–186.

Smart, D., Sanson, A., & Prior, M. (1996). Connections between reading-disability and behavior problems—testing temporal and causal hypotheses. *Journal of Abnormal Child Psychology, 24*, 363–383.

Smith, S.D., Kimberling, W.J., & Pennington, B.F. (1991). Screening for multiple genes influencing dyslexia.. *Reading and Writing, 3*, 285–298.

Stanovich, K.E. (1994). Does dyslexia exist. *Journal of Child Psychology and Psychiatry, 35*, 579–595.

Smith, S.D., Kimberling, W.J., Pennington, B.F., & Lubs, H.A. (1983). Specific reading disability: Identification of an inherited form through linkage analysis. *Science, 219*, 1345–1347.

Stanovich, K.E., & Siegel, L.S. (1994). Phenotypic performance profile of children with reading disabilities: A regression-based test of the phonological-core variable-difference model. *Journal of Educational Psychology, 86*, 24–53.

Stevenson, J. (1988). Which aspects of reading-ability show a hump in their distribution. *Applied Cognitive Psychology, 2*, 77–85.

Stevenson, J. (1991). Which aspects of processing text mediate genetic effects? *Reading and Writing: An Interdisciplinary Journal, 3*, 249–269.

Stevenson, J. (1992). Evidence for a genetic etiology in hyperactivity in children. *Behavior Genetics, 22*, 337–344.

Stevenson, J. (1996). The hyperactive child at school. In S. Sandberg (Ed.), *Hyperactivity disorders of childhood* (pp. 382–432). Cambridge, UK: Cambridge University Press.

Stevenson, J., Graham, P., Fredman, G., & McLoughlin, V. (1987). A twin study of genetic influences on reading and spelling ability and disability. *Journal of Child Psychology and Psychiatry, 28*, 229–247.

Stevenson, J., Pennington, B.F., Gilger, J.W., DeFries, J.C., & Gillis, J.J. (1993). Hyperactivity and spelling disability—testing for shared genetic etiology. *Journal of Child Psychology and Psychiatry, 34*, 1137–1152.

Taylor, E., Sandberg, S., Thorley, G., & Giles, S. (1991). *The epidemiology of childhood hyperactivity*. Oxford, UK: Oxford University Press.

Warren, R.P., Odell, J.D., Warren, W.L., Burger, R.A., Maciulis, A., Daniels, W.W., & Torres, A.R. (1995). Reading-disability, attention-deficit hyperactivity disorder, and the immune-system. *Science, 268*, 786–787.

Warren, R.P., Singh, V.K., Averett, R.E., Odell, J.D., Maciulis, A., Burger, R.A., Daniels, W.W., & Warren, W.L. (1996). Immunogenetic studies in autism and related disorders. *Molecular and Chemical Neuropathology, 28*, 77–81.

Willcutt, E.G., & Pennington, B.F. (2000). Comorbidity of reading disability and attention-deficit/hyperactivity disorder: Differences by gender and subtype. *Journal of Learning Disabilities, 33*, 179–191.

Willcutt, E.G., Pennington, B.F., & DeFries, J.C. (2000). A twin study of the etiology of comorbidity between reading disability and attention-deficit/hyperactivity disorder. *American Journal of Medical Genetics, 96*(12), 293–301.

World Health Organisation. (1993). *International classification of disease—classification of mental and behavioural disorders: Diagnostic criteria for research* 10th rev. ed.). Geneva: Author.

# 7 Causes of the overlap among symptoms of Attention Deficit Hyperactivity Disorder, Oppositional Defiant Disorder, and Conduct Disorder

*Irwin D. Waldman, Soo Hyun Rhee, Florence Levy, and David A. Hay*

The taxonomy and aetiology of childhood psychiatric disorders have been of long-standing interest to researchers, clinicians, teachers, and parents. Of particular concern have been the externalising or disruptive behaviour disorders, namely attention-deficit hyperactivity disorder (ADHD), oppositional defiant disorder (ODD), and Conduct Disorder (CD). Compared with internalising problems (e.g., depression, anxiety disorders), externalising problems are more prevalent (Kazdin, 1987; Szatmari, Boyle, & Offord, 1989), often are more salient and disruptive, are more stable and more predictive of negative adult adjustment (Kohlberg, LaCrosse, & Ricks, 1972; Mannuzza, Klein, Bessler, Malloy, & LaPadula, 1993; Olweus, 1979; Parker & Asher, 1987; Robins, 1966), and may have greater societal costs (Kazdin, 1987). Accurate classification and a comprehensive understanding of aetiology are prerequisites to effective prevention of these behaviour problems and their sequelae.

One factor complicating such an understanding is the considerable overlap among these disorders. A number of studies have documented the overlap among the disruptive behaviour disorders of childhood in both clinical and non-clinical samples. For example, ADHD and CD were found to co-occur in 30–50% of children, and ADHD and ODD were found to co-occur in at least 35% of children, in both clinical and epidemiological samples in a review of relevant studies (Biederman, Newcorn, & Sprich, 1991). In a large epidemiological sample of 2697 children, 57% of children with CD also had ADHD, and 57% of children with ADHD also had CD (Szatmari et al., 1989). In a nonreferred sample of 222 children, 93% with CD or ODD also had ADHD, and 36% of children with ADHD also had CD or ODD (Bird, Gould, & Staghezza, 1993). Despite ample documentation of the substantial overlap among disruptive behaviour disorders, little is known regarding the causes of this overlap or of the disorders individually.

Among the many types of studies used to examine the aetiology of disorders, behaviour genetic designs (i.e., twin and adoption studies) are among the best, as they yield clearer causal inferences than almost any other design. Although both twin and adoption studies allow genetic and environmental influences on a trait or disorder to be disentangled, twin studies have certain advantages relative to adoption studies. These include greater accessibility and representativeness of samples to the general population, thus yielding greater generalisability of findings; contemporaneous measurement of relatives who are the same versus different ages (i.e., twin pairs versus adoptees and their biological and adoptive parents), which permits use of the same rather than different measures; and greater statistical power due both to larger sample sizes and greater genetic similarity between relatives. Twin studies examine the aetiology of a trait or disorder by estimating the magnitude of genetic influences (heritability or $h^2$), shared environmental influences (environmental influences that are experienced in common which make family members similar to one another; $c^2$), and nonshared environmental influences (environmental influences that are experienced uniquely, which make family members different from one another; $e^2$). These aetiological influences are estimated by comparing the similarity between monozygotic (MZ) twin pairs, who are genetically identical, and dizygotic (DZ) twin pairs, who are on average 50% genetically similar.

A number of previous twin studies have examined genetic and environmental influences on ADHD using a variety of measures and have estimated $h^2$ for ADHD to be moderate to high (i.e., 60–90%). Across most studies, shared environmental influences do not seem to contribute to the variance in ADHD symptoms (cf. Goodman & Stevenson, 1989), whereas nonshared environmental influences are small to moderate, contributing between 10% and 40% of the liability variance. In addition, a number of studies have found slight to moderate sibling contrast effects. Goodman and Stevenson (1989) conducted the first large twin study (102 MZ and 111 DZ twin pairs) of ADHD and reported heritability estimates for various measures of hyperactivity and inattention ranging from 32% to > 100%. In the Virginia Twin Study of Adolescent Behavioural Development (VTSABD), Eaves et al. (1997) found heritability estimates ranging from 60% to 80% and moderate nonshared environmental influences and slight contrast effects on ADHD symptoms assessed via maternal and paternal semi-structured interviews. Two twin studies also obtained high heritability estimates for hyperactivity on the Rutter A scale. In a sample of 376 twin pairs from the United Kingdom, Thapar, Hervas, and McGuffin (1995) estimated heritability at .88, with the remaining variation being due to nonshared environmental influences and a sibling contrast effect. Silberg et al. (1996) also obtained heritability estimates of 70% in the VTSABD study, with the remaining variance accounted for by nonshared environmental influences and a sibling contrast effect. These studies suggest that, however assessed, ADHD is highly heritable and is caused by nonshared, but not by shared, environmental influences.

There are few twin studies of CD, although many more studies of related constructs such as delinquency (e.g., Rowe, 1983) and aggression (e.g., van den Oord, Verhulst, & Boomsma, 1996) have been conducted. The majority of these studies find moderate genetic and shared and nonshared environmental influences on childhood or adolescent antisocial behaviour. Willcutt, Shyu, Green, and Pennington (1995) found that CD was influenced by additive genetic, shared environmental, and nonshared environmental influences ($h^2 = .34$ to $.38$, $c^2 = .29$ to $.38$, $e^2 = .24$ to $.37$). In the VTSABD, Eaves et al. (1997) found moderate heritability estimates for CD ranging from 23 to 69%, and moderate nonshared environmental influences ranging from 31 to 77%, depending on informant (i.e., mother, father, or child self-report). Shared environmental influences on CD symptoms were found only using father reports and were higher for boys than for girls ($c^2 = .37$ and $.09$, respectively). In a recent retrospective study of antisocial behaviour in 3226 adult twin pairs, Lyons et al. (1995) found minimal genetic influences and moderate shared and nonshared environmental influences on childhood (pre-15 years old) CD symptoms ($h^2 = .07$, $c^2 = .31$, $e^2 = .62$), but moderate genetic and nonshared environmental influences and minimal shared environmental influences on adult (post-15 years old) antisocial behaviour ($h^2 = .43$, $c^2 = .05$, $e^2 = .52$). In contrast to the above findings, Slutske et al. (1997) reported that according to their best fitting model, genetic influences on CD (assessed via retrospective report of childhood or adolescent antisocial behaviour) were substantial, but that there was no evidence for shared environmental influences ($h^2 = .71$, $c^2 = .00$, $e^2 = .29$).

There are very few twin studies of ODD, and most behaviour genetic studies of ODD symptoms have treated them as part of a composite with CD symptoms. Simonoff et al. (1995) examined American Psychiatric Association *Diagnostic and Statistical Manual of Mental Disorders*, third edition, revised (*DSM-III-R*; APA, 1987) ODD symptoms as part of a composite variable of ODD and CD symptoms which showed moderate genetic and nonshared environmental influences, but no shared environmental influence ($h^2 = .40$ to $.73$, $c^2 = .00$ to $.03$, $e^2 = .27$ to $.60$). Similarly, Silberg et al. (1996) examined oppositional problems, but these problems were part of the conduct problems factor of the Rutter A scale (Rutter, Tizard, & Whitmore, 1970, as cited in Silberg et al., 1996), which includes both oppositional and conduct problems. Silberg et al.'s (1996) analyses suggested moderate genetic and shared and nonshared environmental influences on the combination of oppositional and conduct problems ($h^2 = .25$ to $.66$, $c^2 = .04$ to $.42$, $e^2 = .29$ to $.33$). Unfortunately, the combination of ODD and CD symptoms in these studies obscures any differences in the aetiology of these disorders. Eaves et al. (1997) examined genetic and environmental influences on ODD symptoms in boys and girls across mother, father, and child self-reports. They found moderate genetic and nonshared environmental influences, but no shared environmental influences, across sex and informants ($h^2 = .21$ to $.65$, $e^2 = .36$ to $.79$). Willcutt et al. (1995) examined genetic and environmental influences on ODD symptoms in both reading disabled and control twin samples. They found moderate genetic, shared, and nonshared environmental influences in the reading disabled sample ($h^2 = .50$, $c^2 = .29$, $e^2 = .21$), and moderate genetic and nonshared environmental influences, but no shared environmental influences, in the control sample ($h^2 = .76$, $e^2 = .24$). These findings suggest the need for further behaviour genetic analyses to determine the magnitude of genetic influences on ODD, whether shared environmental influences are indeed present for ODD, and whether the aetiology of ODD is identical to that of CD.

There also are a few behaviour genetic studies of the overlap among the childhood disruptive disorders (Nadder, Silberg, Eaves, Maes, & Meyer 1998; Silberg et al., 1996; Willcutt et al., 1995). In these studies, emphasis is placed on determining the magnitude of common and specific aetiological influences on the two disorders. In addition, one also examines whether the common and specific aetiological influences are genetic, shared environmental, or nonshared environmental in nature. These studies have found that most of the covariation among symptoms of disruptive behaviour disorders is due to common additive genetic influences, with a moderate contribution of nonshared environmental influences. None the less, almost all of these studies (Nadder et al., 1998; Silberg et al., 1996) combined ODD and CD symptoms into a single scale and performed a bivariate genetic analysis of this combined scale and a separate scale corresponding to hyperactivity symptoms. The remaining study (Willcutt et al., 1995) performed analyses on *DSM* ADHD, ODD, and CD symptoms, treating the ODD and CD symptoms as separate, but conducted a series of three bivariate behaviour genetic analyses of the pairwise overlap among these disorders. This bivariate behaviour genetic analysis may not fully portray the commonality among aetiological influences underlying all three disruptive disorders.

Based on the findings reviewed here, there were three questions that we addressed in the current study. First, we sought to estimate the magnitude of genetic, shared environmental and nonshared environmental influences on ODD symptoms, as these are not well understood relative to the aetiology of ADHD and CD. The second question that we investigated was the aetiology of the overlap among all three childhood disruptive disorders. As in previous studies, we used multivariate behaviour genetic analyses to study the overlap among childhood disruptive disorders. The main difference between previous studies and the present study is the way in which ADHD, ODD, and CD symptoms were examined. Given the evidence that CD and ODD are developmentally related but clearly different, and that there are distinct covarying groups of CD and ODD symptoms (Loeber, Lahey, & Thomas, 1991), ODD and CD symptoms were examined separately in the present analyses. In addition, all three sets of symptoms were analysed simultaneously in the multivariate behaviour genetic analyses we conducted. A third question we investigated was whether all of the causes of ODD and CD symptoms are identical to those of ADHD symptoms, or whether ODD and CD also have genetic and environmental influences that are unique from those on ADHD. Given the substantial phenotypic overlap among ADHD, ODD, and CD found in previous studies, and the fact that ADHD shows an earlier age of onset than ODD and CD, it is conceivable that ODD and CD symptoms merely represent a later developmental manifestation of the same liability that underlies ADHD. We set up our multivariate behaviour genetic models (using a Cholesky decomposition; see Figure 7.1 on p. 122) specifically to test these alternative hypotheses regarding the presence or absence of causes on ODD and CD that were unique from those on ADHD.

## METHOD

### Participants

The participants were 3- to 15-year-old male and female same- and opposite-sex twin pairs and their non-twin siblings, aged 3 to 18 years. There were 1034 MZ pairs, 1009 DZ pairs, and 345 sibling pairs in families where there were at least two siblings in addition to the twin pair. Twins were recruited from the Australian National Health and Medical Research Council (NHMRC) funded Australian Twin Registry, a nationwide, population-based volunteer registry.

### Procedure

#### Zygosity determination.

Information on zygosity came from the mothers' responses to 11 questions regarding their twins' physical similarity. Responses to these questions yielded a physical similarity scale ranging from 0 to 17. The distribution of scores on this scale was bimodal, with the maximum discrimination between the two component distributions occurring between a score of 8 and 9. Hence, twin pairs who scored 0–8 on this scale were classified as DZs and twin pairs who scored 9–17 on this scale were classified as MZs. We used mothers' report of twins' physical similarity as the basis of zygosity determination in this study. Previous reports indicate the validity of such indices when compared with blood typing (e.g., Bonnelykke, Hauge, Holm, Kristoffersen, & Gurtler, 1989; Cohen, Dibble, Grawe, & Pollin, 1975) and DNA markers (Spitz et al., 1996).

#### Assessment of ADHD, ODD, and CD symptoms.

Mothers of twin and sibling pairs filled out a questionnaire (Levy & Hay, 1991) assessing the fourteen *DSM-III-R* ADHD symptoms, six CD symptoms, and four ODD symptoms. Each symptom was rated as "present" or "absent" for each twin and sibling. The six CD and four ODD symptoms were those that had the highest total predictive value for their respective disorders (Spitzer, Davies, & Barkley, 1990). Only half of the CD and ODD symptoms were used, as this questionnaire was designed as a brief rating scale in order to maximise the participation of twin families in the study. Although the inclusion of only half of the ODD and CD symptoms might raise concerns regarding the generalisability of results to the full set of symptoms, polychoric correlations estimated in a different sample between all of the symptoms and the reduced set analysed here were very high, approaching the reliabilities of the scales (for ODD, r = .96; for CD, r = .88). The within- and cross-twin (or sibling) correlations are shown in Table 7.1 for MZ and DZ twins and non-twin siblings.

## Data Analyses

There are a number of multivariate behaviour genetic models for analysing the causes underlying the correlations among multiple traits or disorders (for examples see Carey & DiLalla, 1994; Neale & Cardon, 1992; Waldman & Slutske, 2000). For this chapter we chose to investigate the genetic and environmental influences underlying the covariation among ADHD, ODD, and CD symptoms using a Cholesky decomposition, as this multivariate model has a number of desirable features. First, as described in more detail by Neale and Cardon (1992, pp. 249–253), the Cholesky decomposition possesses the desirable mathematical property that it ensures that the matrices of parameter estimates will be positive definite. This means that the resulting

*Table 7.1* Matrices of polychoric correlations for identical and fraternal twins and non-twin siblings

|  | ADHD | ODD | CD | ADHD | ODD |
|---|---|---|---|---|---|
| *MZ twins* | *Twin 1* | | | *Twin 2* | |
| ODD–T1 | 0.71 | | | | |
| CD–T1 | 0.64 | 0.66 | | | |
| ADHD–T2 | 0.90 | 0.66 | 0.58 | | |
| ODD–T2 | 0.67 | 0.86 | 0.59 | 0.74 | |
| CD–T2 | 0.60 | 0.59 | 0.86 | 0.62 | 0.68 |
| *DZ twins* | *Twin 1* | | | *Twin 2* | |
| ODD–T1 | 0.64 | | | | |
| CD–T1 | 0.56 | 0.60 | | | |
| ADHD–T2 | 0.41 | 0.32 | 0.30 | | |
| ODD–T2 | 0.33 | 0.41 | 0.33 | 0.66 | |
| CD–T2 | 0.26 | 0.26 | 0.60 | 0.54 | 0.60 |
| *Siblings* | *Sibling 1* | | | *Sibling 2* | |
| ODD–T1 | 0.70 | | | | |
| CD–T1 | 0.67 | 0.75 | | | |
| ADHD–T2 | 0.38 | 0.28 | 0.19 | | |
| ODD–T2 | 0.28 | 0.48 | 0.36 | 0.68 | |
| CD–T2 | 0.24 | 0.37 | 0.58 | 0.52 | 0.69 |

estimates of genetic and environmental variances and covariances cannot take on nonsensical values (e.g., a negative variance), as can often happen with other multivariate behaviour genetic models. Second, the Cholesky decomposition will exhaustively account for all of the genetic and environmental influences underlying the particular variables in the analysis, as well as underlying their covariation. Relative to other multivariate behaviour genetic models (e.g., the independent pathway model, Neale & Cardon, 1992), the Cholesky decomposition thus may be considered a largely exploratory technique, as minimal structure is imposed on the pattern of genetic and environmental influences. It attempts to explain as much of the variance in and covariance among the variables in the analysis (e.g., three variables: $V_1$, $V_2$, and $V_3$) in terms of a set of aetiological influences that explain the causes of $V_2$ and $V_3$ that are shared with $V_1$, a second set of uncorrelated residual aetiological influences on $V_3$ that are shared with $V_2$, and a final set of uncorrelated residual aetiological influences that are unique to $V_3$.

The ordering of $V_1$, $V_2$, and $V_3$ is very important. Although they could be exchanged with one another and the overall fit of the model would be unchanged, the parameter estimates from the model and their interpretation would change. *A priori* hypotheses and the conceptualisation of the analysis should determine the ordering of the variables in a Cholesky decomposition (Loehlin, 1996).

In contrast to the Cholesky decomposition, other multivariate behaviour genetic models proceed by imposing considerable structure on the pattern of genetic and environmental influences *a priori*, which reflects the specific substantive hypotheses of the investigator. In the independent pathway model, for example, the variables in the analysis load on only one common factor for each aetiological influence (e.g., additive genetic, shared, and nonshared environmental influences). We imposed some structure on the Cholesky decomposition by sequentially dropping sets of parameters in order to test substantive hypotheses regarding the genetic and environmental influences underlying the covariation among ADHD, ODD, and CD symptoms. We assessed the validity of these hypotheses by statistically contrasting the fit of these restricted models to the fit of the full Cholesky decomposition model.

The full Cholesky decomposition model is shown in Figure 7.1. As shown in the figure, there are as many factors for each source of variation as there are observed variables. Given that the model in Figure 7.1 is a multivariate ACE model (i.e., one that contains additive genetic and shared and nonshared environmental influences) and that there are three observed variables (i.e., ADHD, ODD, and CD symptoms), there are nine factors total in the full Cholesky decomposition model. For each source of variation, the first factor has loadings on all three observed variables, the second factor has loadings on only the second and third variables, and the third factor has a loading on only the third variable. As might be expected from such a structure, and as mentioned above, the ordering of the observed variables in the analysis is important, as different orderings can yield different patterns of

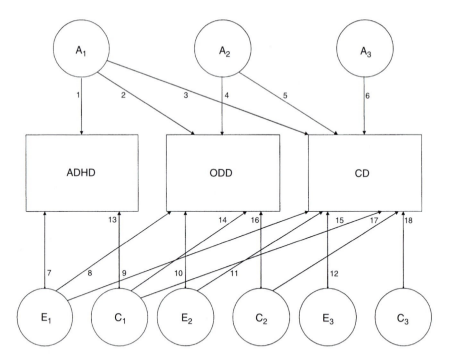

*Figure 7.1* Cholesky decomposition of disruptive behaviour disorder symptoms.

genetic and environmental influences and different interpretations as to the contribution of these influences to the covariation among the observed variables (Loehlin, 1996). We will describe the justification behind our ordering of the variables (i.e., ADHD, ODD, and CD) in the Results section later.

As shown in Figure 7.1, there are six path coefficients for each source of variation in the model, yielding a total of 18 estimated path coefficients in the full Cholesky decomposition model. Path coefficients 1–6 correspond to additive genetic influences, path coefficients 7–12 correspond to nonshared environmental influences, and path coefficients 13–18 correspond to shared environmental influences. The pathways connecting the diagnostic variables depicted in Figure 7.1 can be used to derive the expected correlations among ADHD, ODD, and CD symptoms in terms of their hypothesised causal influences. The expectations for the within-twin, cross-trait correlations (e.g., twin 1's ADHD symptoms with his or her ODD symptoms) are derived by multiplying the corresponding loadings on each aetiological factor on which the variables load and summing across all three sources of variation that influence the two disorders. Hence, the expected correlation between twin 1's ADHD and ODD is $1 * 2 + 7 * 8 + 13 * 14$. Similarly, the expected correlation between twin 1's ODD and CD is $2 * 3 + 4 * 5 + 8 * 9 + 10 * 11 + 14 * 15 + 16 * 17$. The additional products of loadings that are summed for the correlation between ODD and CD reflect the fact that they load on two factors for each source of variation in the analysis. In these equations, $1 * 2$, $2 * 3$, and $4 * 5$ represent the contribution of additive genetic influences, $7 * 8$, $8 * 9$, and $10 * 11$ represent the contribution of nonshared environmental influences, and $13 * 14$, $14 * 15$, and $16 * 17$ represent the contribution of shared environmental influences to the total expected phenotypic correlation between twin 1's ADHD and ODD symptoms, or twin 1's ODD and CD symptoms. The remaining expected correlations between ADHD and CD symptoms would be derived in a similar fashion.

As in other multivariate behaviour genetic models, the cross-twin, cross-trait correlations (e.g., twin 1's ADHD symptoms with twin 2's ODD symptoms) are crucial for resolving the causes of comorbidity. The expectations for the cross-twin, cross-trait correlations are similar to those for the within-twin, cross-trait correlations, except that they are multiplied by the coefficients of genetic relationship or of environmental similarity. Whereas the expectations for within-twin, cross-trait correlations are identical for MZ and DZ twins and non-twin siblings, the expectations for cross-twin, cross-trait correlations will differ for MZ and DZ twins and non-twin siblings due to the differences in their degrees of genetic relationship. For example, the expected cross-twin cross-trait correlation for twin 1's ADHD with twin 2's ODD for MZ twins is $(1 * 2) * 1$ (representing the contribution of additive genetic influences to comorbidity), $(13 * 14) * 1$ (representing the contribution of shared environmental influences), and $(7 * 8) * 0$ (representing the contribution of nonshared environmental influences). In contrast, the corresponding expected cross-twin, cross-trait correlation for DZ twins is $(1 * 2) * .5$ (representing the contribution of additive genetic influences), $(13 * 14) * 1$ (representing the contribution of shared environmental influences), and $(7 * 8) * 0$ (representing the contribution of nonshared environmental influences). Similarly, the expected cross-twin, cross-trait correlation for twin 1's ODD with twin 2's CD for MZ twins is $(2 * 3 + 4 * 5) * 1$ (representing the contribution of additive genetic influences to comorbidity), $(14 * 15 + 16 * 17) * 1$ (representing the contribution of shared environmental influences), and $(8 * 9 + 10 * 11) * 0$ (representing the contribution of nonshared environmental influences). In contrast, the corresponding expected cross-twin, cross-trait correlation for DZ twins is $(2 * 3 + 4 * 5) * .5$ (representing the contribution of additive genetic influences), $(14 * 15 + 16 * 17) * 1$ (representing the contribution of shared environmental influences), and $(8 * 9 + 10 * 11) * 0$ (representing the contribution of nonshared environmental influences). Although the contribution to the expected cross-correlation of additive genetic influences differs for DZ and MZ twins (i.e., by the multiplicative weights of .5 versus 1) due to their differing genetic relatedness, the contributions of shared and nonshared environmental influences are the same for both MZ and DZ twins (i.e., given similar multiplicative weights of 1 and 0), due respectively to the equal environments assumption and to the fact that environmental influences unique to each twin cannot contribute to cross-twin similarity.

Restricted versions of the Cholesky decomposition model can be tested by including different subsets of the compound pathways shown in Figure 7.1. For example, a multivariate AE model would include the pathways 1 * 2 and 7 * 8, as they contribute to the within-twin cross-trait correlation between twin 1's ADHD and twin 1's ODD, and (1 * 2) * 1 for MZs and (1 * 2) * .5 for DZs cross-twin, cross-trait correlation between twin 1's ADHD and twin 2's ODD. A multivariate ACE model would also include the pathway 13 * 14 for the contribution to the within-twin, cross-trait correlation, and (13 * 14) * 1 for both MZs and DZs for the contribution to the cross-twin, cross-trait correlation. In contrast, a multivariate additive genetic, dominant genetic, environmental (error) model (ADE) would substitute three dominance factors for the three shared environmental factors, and would thus include the pathway 13 * 14 for the contribution to the within-twin, cross-trait correlation, and the pathways (13 * 14) * 1 for MZs and (13 * 14) * .25 for DZs for the contribution to the cross-twin cross-trait correlation. These different expectations for the within- and cross-twin, cross-trait correlations form the basis of statistical tests of alternative models for the causes of comorbidity.

## RESULTS

As stated in the Introduction to this chapter, the major goal of these analyses was to examine whether all of the causes (i.e., genetic and environmental influences) on ODD and CD symptoms were identical to those on ADHD symptoms. In other words, we tested the very strong hypothesis that there were no additional causes of ODD and CD symptoms over and above those of ADHD symptoms. We performed this test separately for each source of variation in the analysis, so that we tested the hypotheses that there were no additional additive genetic or shared or nonshared environmental influences on ODD and CD symptoms above and beyond those on ADHD symptoms. We also tested a number of strong alternative hypotheses for each source of variation in our restricted Cholesky decomposition models. First, for each source of variation we tested the strongest alternative hypothesis, namely that all of its influences on each of the three sets of symptoms and their covariation could be dropped from the model. Second, for each source of variation we tested the alternative hypothesis that the causes contributed to each of the three disorders individually, but did not contribute to their covariation. Third, for each source of variation we tested the hypothesis mentioned first above, that all of the influences on ODD and CD symptoms were shared in common with ADHD symptoms, and that there were no influences on ODD and CD symptoms above and beyond those on ADHD symptoms. Fourth and finally, for each source of variation we tested the converse of the previous hypothesis, namely that the influences on ODD and CD symptoms were totally distinct from those on ADHD symptoms. We began this sequence of analyses by fitting the full Cholesky decomposition model and used it as a baseline to which the fit of the alternative restricted models described earlier could be compared.

We used a number of fit indices to assess the fit of particular models and the relative fit of alternative models. We chose these fit indices as they provide at least somewhat complementary information regarding the fit of structural equation models (Loehlin, 1992). These fit indices included the chi-square goodness of fit test and its associated $p$-value, the root mean square residual (RMR), and the Akaike Information Criterion (AIC). Models with a non-significant chi-square test are considered to fit the observed data well. Chi-square difference tests were also used to assess the relative fit of competing, hierarchically nested, alternative models. The RMR is a useful supplementary fit index as it indicates the average residual correlation among the variables in the model after their correlation due to the parameter estimates is accounted for. Values of RMR $\leq .05$ are considered suggestive of good model fit (Cole, 1987). The AIC is a useful supplementary fit index, especially for contrasting alternative models, as it does not require the alternative models being compared to be hierarchically nested, and it takes both the overall fit and model parsimony (i.e., the number of estimated parameters) into account (Loehlin, 1992; Neale & Cardon, 1992). The AIC is calculated as $\chi^2$ minus twice the degrees of freedom, and the alternative model with the lowest value of AIC is considered the best fitting model (Loehlin, 1992; Neale & Cardon, 1992).

In order to ensure identification of the full model, and thus obtain the fit statistics for it as well as standard errors and statistical tests for the parameter estimates, we had to drop the loading of CD symptoms on its own shared environmental influence factor (i.e., parameter 18). This seemed appropriate as well, given that this loading was equal to zero in the full model. This full model, minus parameter 18, fit the data fairly well ($\chi^2 = 42.63$, $df = 31$, $p = .080$, RMR $= .051$, AIC $= -19.37$). Parameter estimates for the full Cholesky decomposition model are shown in Figure 7.2. All of the parameter estimates for the additive genetic and nonshared environmental influences in the full model were significant (i.e., these parameter estimates were all greater than twice their standard errors), whereas none of the parameter estimates for the shared environmental influences were significant (i.e., all of these parameter estimates were 1.3 times their standard errors or less).

Based on the results of fitting the full Cholesky decomposition model, we began fitting restricted models by dropping sets of shared environmental influence parameters from the "C matrix", corresponding to the strong alternative hypotheses raised earlier. The fit of all models, and the results of the comparisons among the restricted models and between them and the baseline models, are shown in Table 7.2. Despite the fact that all of the parameter estimates in the full model corresponding to shared environmental influences

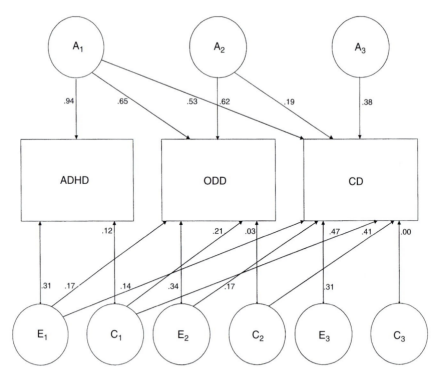

*Figure 7.2* Cholesky decomposition of disruptive behaviour disorder symptoms—
full model.

were nonsignificant, the strongest alternative model—in which shared environmental influences on all three variables and their overlap were dropped from the model—fit poorly relative to the full Cholesky model ($\Delta\chi^2 = 36.62$, $df = 5$, $p < .001$). The next alternative restricted model fitted specified that shared environmental influences acted on ADHD, ODD, and CD symptoms individually, but did not contribute to their overlap (i.e., dropping parameters 14, 15, and 17). Although this model fit well relative to the full Cholesky model ($\Delta\chi^2 = 3.64$, $df = 2$, $p > .10$), the loadings for ADHD and ODD were both estimated equal to zero. We next fit the alternative restricted model in which we retained only the first shared environmental influence factor on which ADHD, ODD, and CD symptoms all loaded (i.e., dropping parameters 16, 17, and 18). This model specifies that there are no shared environmental influences on ODD and CD symptoms unique from those that also influence ADHD symptoms. This model also fit the data well relative to the full Cholesky model ($\Delta\chi^2 = 0.87$, $df = 2$, $p > .50$), but only the loadings for ODD and CD symptoms were significant, whereas the loading for ADHD was merely equal to its standard error. We next fit the alternative restricted model in which we dropped the first shared environmental influence factor

Table 7.2 Fit statistics for alternative restricted Cholesky decomposition models

| Model | $\chi^2$ | df | p | RMR | AIC | Model comparisons[a] $\Delta\chi^2$ | $\Delta$df | p |
|---|---|---|---|---|---|---|---|---|
| Full Cholesky decomposition model | 42.63 | 31 | 0.080 | 0.051 | −19.37 | | | |
| *C matrix* | | | | | | | | |
| 1. Dropping all loadings in C matrix (drop parameters 13–18) | 79.26 | 36 | <0.001 | 0.059 | 7.26 | 36.62 | 5 | <0.001 |
| 2. Keep only diagonal elements of C (drop parameters 14, 15, and 17) | 46.28 | 33 | 0.062 | 0.050 | −20.28 | 3.64 | 2 | >0.10 |
| 3. Keep only first C factor (drop parameters 16, 17, and 18) | 42.72 | 33 | 0.120 | 0.050 | −24.28 | 0.87 | 2 | >0.50 |
| 4. Drop only first C factor (Drop parameters 13, 14, and 15) | 43.97 | 33 | 0.096 | 0.046 | −23.97 | 1.33 | 2 | >0.50 |
| 5. Drop only first C factor + specific CD loading (drop parameters 13, 14, 15, and 18) | 43.97 | 34 | 0.118 | 0.046 | −25.97 | 1.33 | 3 | >0.50 |
| *E matrix* | | | | | | | | |
| Baseline model (C matrix model 5) plus: | | | | | | | | |
| 1. Dropping all loadings in E matrix (drop parameters 7–12) | 116.82 | 40 | <0.001 | 0.065 | 36.82 | 70.54 | 6 | <0.001 |
| 2. Keep only diagonal elements of E (drop parameters 8, 9, and 11) | 83.20 | 37 | <0.001 | 0.052 | 9.20 | 39.23 | 3 | <0.001 |
| 3. Keep only first E factor (drop parameters 10, 11, and 12) | 64.67 | 37 | 0.003 | 0.054 | −10.67 | 20.70 | 3 | <0.001 |
| 4. Drop only first E factor, except for its loading for ADHD (drop parameters 8 and 9) | 71.58 | 36 | <0.001 | 0.052 | −1.58 | 27.62 | 2 | <0.001 |

Table 7.2 continued

| Model | $\chi^2$ | df | p | RMR | AIC | Model comparisons[a] | | |
|-------|----------|-----|-----|-----|-----|--------|-----|-----|
| | | | | | | $\Delta\chi^2$ | $\Delta$df | p |
| *A matrix* | | | | | | | | |
| Baseline model (C matrix model 5) plus: | | | | | | | | |
| 1. Dropping all loadings in A matrix (drop parameters 1–6) | 8051.13 | 40 | <0.001 | 0.162 | 7971.13 | 8007.16 | 6 | <0.001 |
| 2. Keep only diagonal elements of A (drop parameters 2, 3, and 5) | 1846.68 | 37 | <0.001 | 0.234 | 1772.68 | 1802.71 | 3 | <0.001 |
| 3. Keep only first A factor (drop parameters 4, 5, and 6) | 328.07 | 37 | <0.001 | 0.094 | 254.07 | 284.10 | 3 | <0.001 |
| 4. Drop only first A factor, except for its loading for ADHD (drop parameters 2 and 3) | 1838.87 | 36 | <0.001 | 0.236 | 1766.87 | 1794.91 | 2 | <0.001 |

*Note:*
a  All C Matrix models were compared to the Full Cholesky Decomposition model, whereas all E and A Matrix models were compared to the Baseline Model (C Matrix Model 5).

from the model, the converse of the model just presented (i.e., dropping parameters 13, 14, and 15). This model specifies that shared environmental influences only affect ODD and CD symptoms in common, and that there are no such influences on ADHD symptoms. This model also fit the data well relative to the full Cholesky model ($\Delta\chi^2 = 1.33$, $df = 2$, $p > .50$). None the less, only the loadings for ODD and CD symptoms on their common shared environmental influence factor were significant, whereas the loading for CD on its own factor (i.e., parameter 18) was estimated at zero. Like the results for the full Cholesky model, these results indicated that the loading for CD on its own factor (i.e., parameter 18) could be dropped from the model with no loss of fit. The best-fitting restricted model for shared environmental influences thus included only loadings of ODD and CD symptoms on their common shared environmental influence factor (i.e., parameters 16 and 17). This was in addition to all of the factor loadings corresponding to additive genetic and nonshared environmental influences (i.e., parameters 1–6 and 7–12, respectively). This model fit the data even better than the full Cholesky decomposition model ($\chi^2 = 43.97$, $df = 34$, $p = .118$, RMR = .046, AIC = 24.03), and was therefore used as the baseline model for the tests of restricted models for additive genetic and nonshared environmental influences shown later. It should be noted, however, that an even more parsimonious model, in which the loading of ODD symptoms on the common shared environmental influences factor (i.e., parameter 16) was dropped, fit almost as well as the previous model. Although no decrement in fit as a function of dropping this additional parameter could be detected using a chi-square difference test ($\Delta\chi^2 = 2.31$, $df = 1$, $p > .10$), the overall fit of this more parsimonious model was not as good as that of the baseline model ($\chi^2 = 46.28$, $df = 35$, $p = .096$, RMR = .050, AIC = −23.72).

We next fit the same series of restricted alternative models for the nonshared environmental influences in the "E matrix". The first restricted model we tested was the strongest alternative in which all nonshared environmental influences were dropped from the model (i.e., dropping parameters 7–12). This model did not fit as well as the baseline model ($\Delta\chi^2 = 70.54$, $df = 6$, $p < .001$). We next fit the alternative restricted model in which nonshared environmental influences affected only ADHD, ODD, and CD symptoms individually, but did not contribute to their overlap (i.e., dropping parameters 8, 9, and 11). This model also did not fit as well as the baseline model ($\Delta\chi^2 = 39.23$, $df = 3$, $p < .001$). The next alternative restricted model kept only the first nonshared environmental influences factor and specified that there were no nonshared environmental influences on ODD and CD symptoms unique from those on ADHD symptoms (i.e., dropping parameters 10, 11, and 12). This model also did not fit as well as the baseline model ($\Delta\chi^2 = 20.70$, $df = 3$, $p < .001$). The final restricted alternative model specified nonshared environmental influences contributing to the overlap of ODD and CD symptoms, with nonshared environmental influences on ADHD symptoms that did not contribute to its covariation with ODD and CD (i.e., dropping parameters 8 and 9). Once again, this model also did not fit as well as the baseline model, ($\Delta\chi^2 = 27.62$, $df = 2$, $p < .001$).

Finally, we fit the same series of restricted alternative models for the additive genetic influences in the "A matrix". The first restricted model we tested was the strongest alternative that dropped all additive genetic influences from the model (i.e., dropping parameters 1 to 6). This model fit very badly relative to the baseline model ($\Delta\chi^2 = 8007.16$, $df = 6$, $p < .001$). We next fit the alternative restricted model in which additive genetic influences affected only ADHD, ODD, and CD symptoms individually, but did not contribute to their overlap (i.e., dropping parameters 2, 3, and 5). This model also fit very badly relative to the baseline model ($\Delta\chi^2 = 1802.71$, $df = 3$, $p < .001$). The next alternative restricted model kept only the first additive genetic influences factor and specified that there were no additive genetic influences on ODD and CD symptoms unique from those on ADHD symptoms (i.e., dropping parameters 4, 5, and 6). This model also fit badly relative to the baseline model ($\Delta\chi^2 = 284.10$, $df = 3$, $p < .001$). The final restricted alternative model specified additive genetic influences contributing to the overlap of ODD and CD symptoms, with additive genetic influences on ADHD symptoms which did not contribute to its covariation with ODD and CD (i.e., dropping parameters 2 and 3). Once again, this model fit very badly relative to the baseline model ($\Delta\chi^2 = 1794.91$, $df = 2$, $p < .001$).

The results of these tests of restricted alternative models for both additive genetic and nonshared environmental influences indicated that none of the factor loadings for these sources of variation could be dropped from the baseline model, in contrast to the results for shared environmental influences. Thus, the best-fitting model was the baseline model resulting from the tests of restricted alternative models for shared environmental influences. This model contained all six parameters for additive genetic and nonshared environmental influences (i.e., parameters 1 to 6 and 7 to 12, respectively), as well as the two loadings of ODD and CD symptoms on their common shared environmental influences factor (i.e., parameters 16 and 17). The parameter estimates from this best-fitting model are presented in Figure 7.3 below.

The parameter estimates of the best-fitting model can be used to quantify the degree of genetic and environmental influences on ADHD, ODD, and CD symptoms, as well as underlying their covariation. Multiplication of each of the parameter matrices (i.e., the aforementioned "A", "C", and "E" matrices) by their transpose (i.e., AA', CC', and EE') yields additive genetic, shared environmental, and nonshared environmental covariance matrices (Neale & Cardon, 1992). The diagonal elements of these covariance matrices represent the additive genetic, shared environmental, and nonshared environmental variances for ADHD, ODD, and CD symptoms, which yield estimates of heritability ($h^2$), shared environmental influences ($c^2$), and nonshared environmental influences ($e^2$). For ADHD symptoms, genetic influences were of substantial magnitude ($h^2 = .90$), and the remaining variance was due to

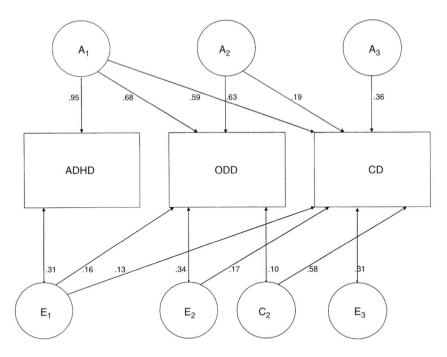

*Figure 7.3* Cholesky decomposition of disruptive behaviour disorder symptoms—best model.

nonshared environmental influences ($e^2 = .10$), as shared environmental influences did not contribute to ADHD. Similar estimates were found for ODD symptoms, as genetic influences also were of substantial magnitude ($h^2 = .85$), with almost all of the remaining variance being due to nonshared environmental influences ($e^2 = .14$); shared environmental influences contributed only minimally to ODD ($c^2 = .01$). A different picture emerged for CD symptoms, as both genetic and shared environmental influences were of moderate magnitude ($h^2 = .51$; $c^2 = .34$), with the remaining variance being due to nonshared environmental influences ($e^2 = .14$).

The contribution of genetic and environmental influences to the covariation among ADHD, ODD, and CD symptoms can be quantified in a number of different ways. Standardisation of the additive genetic, shared environmental, and nonshared environmental covariance matrices yields matrices of genetic, shared environmental, and nonshared environmental correlations among ADHD, ODD, and CD symptoms (Neale & Cardon, 1992). These genetic and environmental correlations represent the extent to which the same genes or (shared or nonshared) environments contribute to the phenotypic correlations among ADHD, ODD, and CD symptoms (Neale & Cardon, 1992). An example of the derivation of the genetic correlation between ODD and CD is shown in Box 7.1.

**Genetic correlation**

Calculation of the Genetic Correlation ($r_{Gij}$) between variables $i$ and $j$ follows the formula:

$$^rG_{ij} = \frac{g_{ij}}{\sqrt{g_{ii} \times g_{jj}}}$$

where $g_{ij}$ is the covariation between the variables due to genetic factors and $g_{ii}$ and $g_{jj}$ are the variances of variable $i$ and $j$ due to genetic factors.

For the genetic correlation between ODD and CD in Figure 7.3, $g_{ij}$ is estimated by tracing the paths between ODD and CD, which go through the Genetic factors, and $g_{ODD}$ and $g_{CD}$ are the paths from ODD or CD to themselves via genetic influences (see Box 2.1, chapter 2 for a description of tracing paths):

$$g_{ODD.CD} = (0.63 \times 0.19) + (0.59 \times 0.68) = 0.5209$$
$$g_{ODD} = 0.68^2 + 0.63^2 = 0.8593$$
$$g_{CD} = -.59^2 + 0.19^2 + 0.36^2 = 0.5138$$

Thus:

$$^rG_{ODD.CD} = \frac{g_{ODD.CD}}{\sqrt{g_{ODD} \times g_{CD}}}$$

$$= \frac{0.5209}{\sqrt{0.8593 \times 0.5138}}$$

$$= 0.7839$$

**Percentage of genetic covariation**

The total covariation can be partitioned into covariation between variables $i$ and $j$ due to genetic (G) and environmental (E) sources. The percentage of genetic covariation is the genetic covariance divided by the total covariance.

$$\% \, G_{ij} = \frac{G_{ij}}{G_{ij} + E_{ij}} \times 100$$

The percentage genetic covariation between ODD and CD in Figure 7.3, is:

$$\%G_{ODD.CD} =$$
$$\frac{(0.65 \times 0.53) + (0.62 \times 0.19)}{[(0.65 \times 0.53) + (0.62 \times 0.19)] + [(0.34 \times 0.17) + (0.17 \times 0.14)]} \times 100$$

$$= \frac{0.4623}{0.5439 \times 100} \times 100$$

$$= 85.00\%$$

*Box 7.1* Genetic correlation and genetic covariation

The genetic correlations among ADHD, ODD, and CD all were high ($r_{ADHD.ODD}$ = .73, $r_{ADHD.CD}$ = .82, $r_{ODD.CD}$ = .79), suggesting that a common set of genes influences the three disruptive behaviour disorders to a large extent. These common genetic influences affect ADHD, ODD, and CD to different degrees, however, as indicated by the differing heritabilities. The shared environmental correlation between ODD and CD was equal to unity, suggesting that the same shared environmental influences affect both of these disorders, albeit to very different degrees given their disparate $c^2$ estimates. The nonshared environmental correlations among ADHD, ODD, and CD all were moderate ($r_{ADHD.ODD}$ = .45, $r_{ADHD.CD}$ = .35, $r_{ODD.CD}$ = .55), suggesting that a common set of nonshared environments influences the three disruptive behaviour disorders to some extent. A different perspective on the contribution of genetic and environmental influences to the covariation among ADHD, ODD, and CD symptoms is provided by examining the percentage of the covariation between symptoms of each of the disorders that is due to genetic and environmental influences. For ADHD and ODD, as well as for ADHD and CD, 93% of their covariance is due to additive genetic influences and 7% to nonshared environmental influences. In contrast, for ODD and CD, 79% of their covariance is due to additive genetic influences, 9% to shared environmental influences, and 12% to nonshared environmental influences. An example of the derivation of the percentage of the covariation between ODD and CD that is due to common genetic influences is shown in Box 7.1.

## DISCUSSION

We addressed three questions in this chapter concerning the genetic and environmental influences underlying ADHD, ODD, and CD symptoms. The first question concerned the magnitude of genetic and environmental influences on ODD symptoms and the similarity of its aetiology to that of CD and ADHD. The variance components that emerged from our analyses suggested that genetic influences were of substantial magnitude for ODD as well as for ADHD ($h^2$ = .85 and .90, respectively), with almost all of the remaining variance being due to nonshared environmental influences ($e^2$ = .14 and .10, respectively). Shared environmental influences contributed minimally to ODD symptoms ($c^2$ = .01) and not at all to ADHD symptoms. The aetiology of ODD symptoms was quite different from that of CD symptoms, as genetic and shared environmental influences both were moderate for CD ($h^2$ = .51; $c^2$ = .34), with nonshared environmental influences that were similarly small in magnitude ($e^2$ = .14).

In this chapter we presented the results of a series of Cholesky decomposition analyses to test competing hypotheses regarding the contribution of genetic and environmental influences to the comorbidity among ADHD, ODD, and CD. With respect to additive genetic and nonshared environmental influences, none of the restricted alternative hypotheses provided an adequate fit to the data, thus indicating that a number of hypotheses regarding the comorbidity among the three disorders could be strongly rejected. Specifically, soundly rejected were the hypotheses that: (1) genetic or nonshared environmental influences do not cause the three disorders or their comorbidity; (2) all genetic or nonshared environmental influences act individually on the disorders without contributing to their comorbidity; (3) the only genetic or nonshared environmental influences on ODD and CD are those that also influence ADHD; (4) and the only genetic or nonshared environmental influences on ODD and CD are completely independent of ADHD. In contrast, the results suggested that the only shared environmental influences on ODD and CD are completely independent of ADHD, which is not caused by shared environmental influences.

The results of these multivariate behaviour genetic analyses also indicated that there was considerable overlap in the genetic and environmental influences on the three disorders. The shared environmental influences on ODD and CD overlapped completely, though the influence of these on CD was much greater than on ODD, which is caused only minimally by shared environmental influences. The genetic correlations suggested that most, but not all, of the genetic influences on the three disorders are shared in common, whereas the nonshared environmental correlations suggested that a moderate amount of the nonshared environmental influences on these disorders is shared in common but that many of these affect each disorder uniquely, albeit to a small extent. In addition, the majority of the overlap (93%) between ADHD on the one hand, and ODD and CD on the other hand, is due to common genetic influences, whereas the remainder (7%) is due to nonshared environmental influences. Slightly less of the overlap between ODD and CD is due to genetic influences (79%), with shared and nonshared environmental influences contributing much less to their overlap (9% and 12%, respectively).

It is interesting to speculate on the meaning of these results for molecular genetic analyses of childhood disruptive disorders. Given the high genetic correlations (ranging from .73 to .82), it seems likely that most of the specific candidate genes found to influence one of the disorders will influence the others as well. Indeed, the dopamine transporter gene (DAT1) which has been found to influence ADHD in a number of studies (Cook, Daly, Heron, Hawi & Fitzgerald 1995; Gill et al., 1997; Waldman, Rowe et al., 1998), recently has been found to influence ODD and CD symptoms as well (Waldman, Mohr et al., 1998). Interestingly, all of the effects of DAT1 on ODD and CD could be accounted for by its effects on the hyperactive-impulsive symptoms of ADHD. None the less, it is important to recognise that although the genetic correlations among these three disorders are high, all are less than unity. This suggests that there also will be some specific candidate genes that influence one of the disorders and not the others. Indeed, although the dopamine receptor D4 gene (DRD4) has been found in a number of studies to influence ADHD (LaHoste et al., 1996; Rowe et al., 1998; Smalley et al., 1998; Swanson et al., 1998), it appears to be unrelated to ODD and CD symptoms (Waldman, Mohr et al., 1998).

The present results also have implications for the search for specific "candidate" environmental influences on childhood disruptive disorders. First, all of the shared environmental influences found for CD should influence ODD, albeit to a very small extent given that shared environmental influences explained only 1% of its overall variance, at least in these analyses. Second, none of the shared environmental influences found for CD should influence ADHD, given that shared environmental influences explained none of its variance in these analyses. Third, some of the specific nonshared environmental influences—such as peer group influences, or parental treatment that is experienced uniquely by each twin or sibling in a family—can be expected to have a common influence on these disorders, although others can be expected to influence each disorder individually. Thus, being involved in a deviant peer group, or receiving insufficient supervision from one's parents, may have a common influence on one sibling's ODD and CD symptoms but not on the co-sibling, whereas, pre- or perinatal birth complications (such as those due to the twin transfusion syndrome in the extreme) may contribute to one of the twins' ADHD (but not ODD or CD) symptoms.

Our findings are similar to those of previous multivariate behaviour genetic studies (Nadder et al., 1998; Silberg et al., 1996; Willcutt et al., 1995) in finding that most of the covariation among symptoms of disruptive behaviour disorders is due to common additive genetic influences with a moderate contribution of nonshared environmental influences. There are a number of important differences between our study and the previous multivariate studies, however. First, whilst we used the Cholesky decomposition approach in our analyses, we tested a series of restricted alternative models that mapped explicitly on to a number of alternative substantive hypotheses of interest regarding the underlying causes of the comorbidity among the disruptive disorders. This allowed us to rule out a large number of alternative hypotheses concerning comorbidity among the three childhood disruptive disorders. Second, in contrast to a previous multivariate behaviour genetic analysis of *DSM* ADHD, ODD, and CD symptoms (Willcutt et al., 1995), we analysed symptoms of all three disorders together in a single multivariate behaviour genetic analysis, rather than in a set of three separate bivariate behaviour genetic analyses, thus yielding a more comprehensive and integrated set of results. Third, we treated symptoms of ODD and CD as separate symptom dimensions, in contrast to most previous behaviour genetic analyses (e.g., Nadder et al., 1998; Silberg et al., 1996; Simonoff et al., 1995). Our results suggested that the combination of ODD and CD symptoms into a single symptom dimension is unwarranted, given the dramatic differences in the magnitude of their underlying genetic and environmental influences, as well as the fact that the correlations of their additive genetic and nonshared environmental influences are high and moderate, respectively, but are both less than unity. This suggests that although there is substantial commonality in their underlying additive genetic and nonshared environmental influences, there are important unique influences on each disorder as well.

These results indicate the power of multivariate behaviour genetic analyses to illuminate the underlying causes of comorbidity among multiple related disorders showing some degree of phenotypic overlap. Such analyses can contrast the fit of alternative models representing alternative substantive conceptualisations of comorbidity. The results of multivariate behaviour genetic analyses of comorbidity also may be promising in guiding the search for specific candidate genes, and specific environmental variables, that influence multiple disorders and contribute to their overlap.

## REFERENCES

American Psychiatric Association. (1987). *Diagnostic and statistical manual of mental disorders* 3rd edn., rev. Washington, DC: Author.

Biederman, J., Newcorn, J., & Sprich, S. (1991). Comorbidity of Attention Deficit Hyperactivity Disorder with conduct, depressive, anxiety, and other disorders. *American Journal of Psychiatry, 148*, 564–577.

Bird, H.R., Gould, M.S., & Staghezza, B.M. (1993). Patterns of diagnostic comorbidity in a community sample of children aged 9 through 16 years. *Journal of the American Academy of Child and Adolescent Psychiatry, 31*, 361–368.

Bonnelykke, B., Hauge, M., Holm, N., Kristoffersen, K., & Gurtler, H. (1989). Evaluation of zygosity diagnosis in twin pairs below age seven by means of a mailed questionnaire. *Acta Geneticae Medicae et Gemellologiae, 38*, 305–313.

Carey, G., & DiLalla, D.L. (1994). Personality and psychopathology: Genetic perspectives. *Journal of Abnormal Psychology, 103*, 32–43.

Cohen, D.J., Dibble, E., Grawe, J.M., & Pollin, W. (1975). Reliably separating identical from fraternal twins. *Archives of General Psychiatry, 32*, 1371–1375.

Cole, D.A. (1987). Utility of confirmatory factor analysis in test validation research. *Journal of Consulting and Clinical Psychology, 55*, 584–594.

Cook, E.H., Stein, M.A., Krasowski, M.D., Cox, N.J., Olkon, D.M., Kieffer, J.E., & Leventhal, B.L. (1995). Association of attention-deficit disorder and the dopamine transporter gene. *American Journal of Human Genetics, 56*, 993–998.

Eaves, L.J., Silberg, J.L., Meyer, J.M., Maes, H.H., Simonoff, E., Pickles, A., Rutter, M., Neale, M.C., Reynolds, C.A., Erickson, M.T., Heath, A.C., Loeber, R., Truett, K.R., & Hewitt, J.K. (1997). Genetics and developmental psychopathology: 2. The main effects of genes and environment on behavioural problems in the Virginia Twin Study of Adolescent Behavioural Development. *Journal of Child Psychology and Psychiatry, 38*, 965–980.

Gill, M., Daly, G., Heron, S., Hawi, Z., & Fitzgerald, M. (1997). Confirmation of association between Attention Deficit Hyperactivity Disorder and a dopamine transporter polymorphism. *Molecular Psychiatry, 2*, 311–313.

Goodman, R., & Stevenson, J. (1989). A twin study of hyperactivity: II. The aetiological role of genes, family relationships and perinatal adversity. *Journal of Child Psychology and Psychiatry, 30* (5), 691–709.

Kazdin, A.E. (1987). Treatment of antisocial behaviour: Current status and future directions. *Psychological Bulletin, 102*, 187–203.

Kohlberg, L., LaCrosse, I., & Ricks, D. (1972). The predictability of adult mental health from childhood behavior. In B.B. Wolman (Ed.), *Manual of child psychopathology* (pp. 1217–1284). New York: McGraw-Hill.

LaHoste, G.J., Swanson, J.M., Wigal, S.B., Glabe, C., Wigal, T., King, N., & Kennedy J.L. (1996). Dopamine D4 receptor gene polymorphism is associated with Attention Deficit Hyperactivity Disorder. *Molecular Psychiatry, 1*, 121–124.

Levy, F., & Hay, D.A. (1991). *The Australian Twin Behaviour Rating Scale*. La Trobe University, Melbourne, Australia.

Loeber, R., Lahey, B.B., & Thomas, C. (1991). Diagnostic conundrum of oppositional defiant disorder and Conduct Disorder. *Journal of Abnormal Psychology, 100*, 379–390.

Loehlin, J.C. (1992). *Latent variable models* (2nd edn.). Hillsdale, NJ: Lawrence Erlbaum Associates Inc.

Loehlin, J.C. (1996). The Cholesky approach: A cautionary note. *Behavior Genetics, 26*, 65–69.

Lyons, M.J., True, W.R., Eisen, S.A., Goldberg, J, Meyer, J.M., Faraone, S.V., Eaves, L.J. & Tsuang, M.T. (1995). Differential heritability of adult and juvenile antisocial traits. *Archives of General Psychiatry, 52*(11), 906–915.

Mannuzza, S., Klein, R., Bessler, A., Malloy, P., & LaPadula, M. (1993). Adult outcome of hyperactive boys: Educational achievement, occupational rank, and psychiatric status. *Archives of General Psychiatry, 50*, 565–576.

Nadder, T.S., Silberg, J.L., Eaves, L.J., Maes, H.H., & Meyer, J.M. (1998). Genetic effects on ADHD symptomatology in 7- to 13-year-old twins: Results from a telephone survey. *Behavior Genetics, 28*, 83–99.

Neale, M.C., & Cardon, L.R. (1992). *Methodology for genetic studies of twins and families* . Dordrecht; The Netherlands: Kluwer Academic Publishers.

Olweus, D. (1979). Stability of aggressive reaction patterns in males: A review. *Psychological Bulletin, 86*, 852–875.

Parker, J.G., & Asher, S.R. (1987). Peer relations and later personal adjustment: Are low-accepted children at risk? *Psychological Bulletin, 102*, 357–389.

Robins, L.N. (1966). *Deviant children grown up* . Baltimore: Williams & Wilkins.

Rowe, D.C. (1983). Biometrical genetic models of self-reported delinquent behavior: A twin study. *Behavior Genetics, 13*, 473–489.

Rowe, D.C., Stever, C., Giedinghagen, L.N., Gard, J.M.C., Cleveland, H.H., Terris, S.T., Mohr, J.H., Sherman, S.L., Abramowitz, A., & Waldman, I.D. (1998). Dopamine DRD4 receptor polymorphism and Attention Deficit Hyperactivity Disorder. *Molecular Psychiatry, 3*, 419–426.

Silberg, J.L., Rutter, M., Meyer, J.M., Simonoff, E., Hewitt, J.K., Loeber, R., Pickles, A., Maes, H., & Eaves, L. (1996). Genetic and environmental influences on the covariation between hyperactivity and conduct disturbance in juvenile twins. *Journal of Child Psychology and Psychiatry and Allied Disciplines, 37* (7), 803–816.

Simonoff, E., Pickles, A., Hewitt, J.K., Silberg, J.L., Rutter, M., Loeber, L., Meyer, J.M., Neale, M.C., & Eaves, L. (1995). Multiple raters of disruptive child behavior: Using a genetic strategy to examine shared views and bias. *Behavior Genetics, 25*, 311–326.

Slutske, W.S., Heath, A.C., Dinwiddie, S.H., Madden, P.A.F., Bucholz, K.K., Dunne, M.P., Statham, D.J., & Martin, N.G. (1997). Modeling genetic and environmental influences in the etiology of Conduct Disorder: A study of 2,682 adult twin pairs. *Journal of Abnormal Psychology, 106* (2), 266–279.

Smalley, S.L., Bailey, J.N., Palmer, C.G., Cantwell, D.P., McGough, J.J., Del'Homme, M.A., Asarnow, J.R., Woodward, J.A., Ramsey, C., & Nelson, S.F. (1998). Evidence that the dopamine D4 receptor is a susceptibility gene in Attention Deficit Hyperactivity Disorder. *Molecular Psychiatry, 3,* 427–430.

Spitz, E., Moutier, R., Reed, T., Busnel, M.C., Marchaland, C., Roubertoux, P.L., & Carlier, M. (1996). Comparative diagnoses of twin zygosity by SSLP variant analysis, questionnaire, and dermatoglyphic analysis. *Behavior Genetics, 26,* 55–63.

Spitzer, R.L., Davies, M., & Barkley, R.A. (1990). The DSM III-R field trial of disruptive behavior disorders. *Journal of the American Academy of Child and Adolescent Psychiatry, 29,* 690–697.

Swanson, J.M., Sunohara, G.A., Kennedy J.L., Regino, R., Fineberg, E., Wigal, T., Lerner, M., Williams, L., LaHoste, G.J., & Wigal, S.B. (1998). Association of the dopamine receptor D4 (DRD4) gene with a refined phenotype of Attention Deficit Hyperactivity Disorder (ADHD): A family-based approach. *Molecular Psychiatry, 3,* 38–41.

Szatmari, P., Boyle, M., & Offord, D.R. (1989). ADDH and Conduct Disorder: Degree of diagnostic overlap and differences among correlates. *Journal of the American Academy of Child and Adolescent Psychiatry, 28,* 865–872.

Thapar, A., Hervas, A., & McGuffin, P. (1995). Childhood hyperactivity scores are highly heritable and show sibling competition effects: Twin study evidence. *Behavior Genetics, 25,* 537–544.

van den Oord, E.J.C.G., Verhulst, F.C., & Boomsma, D.I. (1996). A genetic study of maternal and paternal ratings of problem behaviors in 3-year-old twins. *Journal of Abnormal Psychology, 105*(3), 349–357.

Waldman, I.D., Mohr, J., Abramowitz, A., Sherman, S.L., Cleveland, H.H., Gard, J.M.C., Giedinghagen, L.N., Stever, C., & Rowe, D.C. (1998, October). *The relation between childhood antisocial behavior and the dopamine transporter and D4 receptor genes: Mediation via hyperactivity-impulsivity.* Paper presented at the World Congress of Psychiatric Genetics, Bonn, Germany.

Waldman, I.D., Rowe, D.C., Abramowitz, A., Kozel, S., Mohr, J., Sherman, S.L., Cleveland, H.H., Sanders, M.L., Gard, J.M.C., & Stever, C. (1998). Association and linkage of the dopamine transporter gene (DAT1) and Attention Deficit Hyperactivity Disorder in children: Heterogeneity due to diagnostic subtype and severity. *American Journal of Human Genetics, 63,* 1767–1776.

Waldman, I.D. & Slutske, W.S. (2000). Antisocial behavior and alcoholism: A behavioral genetic perspective on comorbidity. *Clinical Psychology Review, 20,* 255–287.

Willcutt, E.G., Shyu, V., Green, P., & Pennington, B.F. (1995; April). *Heritability of the disruptive behavior disorders of childhood.* Poster presented at the annual meeting of the Society for Research in Child Development, Indianapolis.

# 8 Aetiology of the sex difference
## *in the prevalence of DSM-III-R ADHD: A comparison of two models*[1]

*Soo Hyun Rhee, Irwin D. Waldman,*
*David A. Hay, and Florence Levy*

Attention-deficit hyperactivity disorder (ADHD) is a childhood disorder characterised by inattention, hyperactivity, and impulsivity. According to the American Psychiatric Association *Diagnostic and Statistical Manual of Mental Disorders*, fourth edition (APA,1994; *DSM-IV*), it affects approximately 3–5% of school-aged children, with more boys than girls affected. Reported sex ratios for ADHD range from 3:1 (e.g., Thorley, 1984) to 8:1 (e.g., Lambert, Sandoval, & Sassone, 1978). Little is known about the causes of ADHD, and even less is known about the aetiology of the sex difference in its prevalence. In this study we tested the predictions of two models that have been used to explain this difference in prevalence.

## DIFFERENCES BETWEEN ADHD BOYS AND GIRLS

The sex difference in the prevalence of ADHD has led many researchers to compare the cognitive functioning and behaviour problems of ADHD boys and ADHD girls. Researchers often cite evidence of poorer cognitive functioning in ADHD girls, and more severe behaviour problems in ADHD boys, but a review of gender comparisons reveals discrepant findings.

Ackerman, Dykman, and Oglesby (1983) used the Wechsler Intelligence Scale for Children—revised (WISC-R) and the Wide Range Achievement Test (WRAT) Arithmetic subtest to compare the cognitive functioning of hyperactive boys and hyperactive girls. They found that the boys' scores were significantly higher than the girls' scores. Berry, Shaywitz, and Shaywitz (1985) also found higher WISC-R scores in ADD-H boys than in ADD-H girls. James and Taylor (1990) found that girls meeting criteria for hyperkinetic syndrome on the World Health Organisation *International*

1  We would like to thank Scott O. Lillienfeld and Kim Wallen for their comments on this chapter. An earlier version of this chapter was presented at the meeting of the Behavior Genetics Association in 1995, and a more extensive version has been published in the *Journal of Abnormal Psychology, 108*, 24–41.

*Classification of Diseases*, ninth revision (WHO, 1979; *ICD-9*) scored significantly lower on IQ tests (WISC-R, Wechsler Preschool and Primary Scales Intelligence, or Merrill-Palmer) and had significantly higher rates of language disorders, and of neurological disorders than did their male counterparts. Supporting evidence comes from Brown, Madan-Swain, and Baldwin (1991), who found that ADHD girls had more cognitive (WISC-R Block Design; Kaufman Assessment Battery for Children Spatial Memory) and academic problems than did ADHD boys.

In contrast, deHass and Young (1984) did not find a statistically reliable difference between girls without ADD-H and girls with ADD-H on WISC-R Vocabulary, nor did deHass (1986) find statistically reliable differences between ADD-H boys and ADD-H girls on WISC-R Vocabulary, Block Design, and Digit Span. This is supported by Breen (1989), who found similar performance between ADHD boys and ADHD girls on the Kaufman Assessment Battery for Children, and by Horn, Wagner, and Ialongo (1989), who did not find statistically reliable differences between ADHD boys and ADHD girls in their performance on the Peabody Picture Vocabulary Test—revised, nor on the WRAT—revised.

Regarding behaviour problems, Ackerman et al. (1983) found that on the Conners Parent and Teacher Rating Scales, hyperactive boys were regarded by their parents, but not by their teachers, as more aggressive than were hyperactive girls. DeHass and Young (1984) found that hyperactive girls exhibited few conduct problems, and deHass (1986) found that hyperactive girls had fewer conduct problems than did hyperactive boys on the Conners Teacher Rating Scale. Berry et al. (1985) found more frequent disruptive and uncontrolled behaviours in ADD-H boys than in ADD-H girls.

On the other hand, Befera and Barkley (1985) found that ADD-H girls and ADD-H boys were similar in personality and emotional problems on the Personality Inventory for Children. Breen and Barkley (1988) found limited differences in ADD-H boys and ADD-H girls in delinquency and aggression on the Child Behavior Checklist, and Breen (1989) found similar levels of aggression in ADHD boys and ADHD girls on the Child Behavior Checklist. Horn et al. (1989), too, found no statistically reliable sex differences in behavioural problems.

Authors of more recent studies have attributed these discrepant findings to differences in sampling strategies, dependent measures, and requirements for diagnosis (e.g., Breen, 1989; Horn et al., 1989). The small sample sizes in these studies, especially of ADHD girls, could be a contributing factor. Whatever the source of these contradictory findings, there is a lack of consistent and conclusive evidence for sex differences in the cognitive and behavioural functioning of ADHD children.

## SEX DIFFERENCES IN THE PREVALENCE OF ADHD

The causes of the sex difference in the prevalence of ADHD are not clear. Researchers have examined possible aetiology of this sex difference by testing the assumptions of the polygenic multiple threshold model (e.g., Cloninger, Christiansen, Reich, & Gottesman, 1978), and the constitutional variability model (e.g., Taylor & Ounsted, 1972).

### Polygenic multiple threshold model

The polygenic multiple threshold model is based on the general multifactorial model of disease transmission (Carter, 1969, 1973). That is, if a disease or disorder has a multifactorial aetiology, instead of being caused by a single gene, multiple genetic and environmental factors are thought to be involved. The factors influencing the disorder may be several alleles at one locus, several gene loci, environmental factors, or any combination of these. All of these possible sources combine additively to make up the total liability for the disorder in question, and no assumptions are made about the relative importance of each. Individuals in the population differ in their degree of liability for the disorder, and this variation in liability represents the distribution of liability of the general population. The difference between being unaffected and being affected depends on whether the individual's liability exceeds a threshold, or a critical level of liability, needed for the manifestation of the disease.

The polygenic multiple threshold model provides an explanation for sex differences in the prevalence of a disorder. There may be multiple thresholds for different groups in the population, and the less frequently affected group (females, in the case of ADHD) presumably has a higher threshold for the disorder than does the more frequently affected group, (males, for ADHD). In ADHD, this higher threshold would indicate that females require a greater liability to manifest ADHD than do males.

The polygenic multiple threshold model of sex differences can be tested by comparing the prevalence of the disorder in the relatives of female probands versus male probands (see Figure 8.1).

In general, relatives of any proband have greater liability than do persons in the general population who do not have an affected relative. Consequently, the distribution of liability for the relatives of probands deviates from that of the general population. In the case of ADHD, a female proband would be more deviant in liability than would be a male proband, as females in general have a higher threshold for the disorder. Thus, female probands both require and transmit a greater liability than do male probands, and the distribution of liability for the relatives of female probands would be more deviant than that of the relatives of male probands. Thus, relatives of a female proband are more likely to have the disorder than are relatives of a male proband.

Kashani, Chapel, Ellis, and Shekim (1979) found a higher prevalence of

Distribution of Liability in Male and Female Population

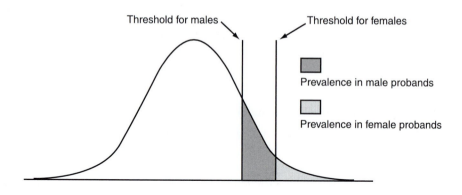

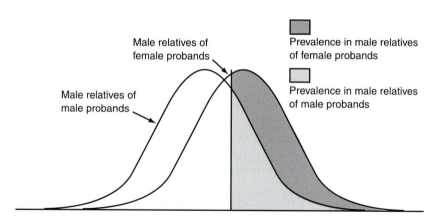

*Figure 8.1* Multifactorial multiple threshold model. Only male relatives of male and female probands are displayed. (From "Implications of sex differences in the prevalences of antisocial personality, alcoholism, and criminality for familial transmission", by C. R. Clonninger, K. O. Christiansen, T. Reich, and I. I. Gottesman, 1978, *Archives of General Psychology, 35,* p. 945. Copyright 1978 by the American Medical Association. Adapted with permission.)

psychopathology in the parents of hyperactive girls than in the parents of hyperactive boys, and suggested this finding as evidence for the polygenic multiple threshold model. These results were not replicated by Mannuzza and Gittelman (1984), who found a lower prevalence of psychopathology and retrospectively diagnosed hyperactivity among parents of hyperactive girls than among the parents of hyperactive boys. Biederman, Faraone, Keenan, Knee, and Tsuang (1990), who studied a sample of ADD boys, and Faraone,

Biederman, Keenan, and Tsuang (1991), who studied a sample of ADD girls, ascertained and evaluated their samples using the same method. The risk of ADD for the relatives (25%) of ADD boys was found to be slightly higher than the risk of ADD for the relatives (19.5%) of ADD girls. This result fails to support the polygenic multiple threshold model. Other confusing data come from James and Taylor (1990), who found that hyperactive girls were more likely than hyperactive boys to have relatives with a history of psychiatric disorders, but were less likely to have relatives with a history of hyperactivity. In addition, Silverthorn, Frick, Kuper, and Ott (1996) found evidence against the polygenic multiple threshold model in predicting the paternal history of ADHD and inconclusive evidence in predicting the maternal history of ADHD.

In the past, several researchers have found support for the polygenic multiple threshold model in antisocial personality disorder (e.g., Mednick, Gabrielli, & Hutchings, 1983; Sigvardsson, Cloninger, Bohman, & von Knorring, 1982). More recently, Faraone et al. (1995) assessed ADHD in the siblings of 140 ADHD probands and in 120 control subjects. A family was considered an "antisocial family" if the proband had Conduct Disorder or a parent had antisocial personality. They found that retrospectively diagnosed maternal ADHD was a stronger predictor for ADHD in the siblings of the probands than was retrospectively diagnosed paternal ADHD. This result was significant only in the "antisocial families".

One significant limitation of the studies just described is that ADHD was assessed in the adult relatives of ADHD children, which meant reliance on retrospective diagnoses of ADHD or on contemporaneous diagnoses of related adult disorders. It is also questionable whether evidence regarding general psychopathology in parents (e.g., Kashani et al., 1979) is useful in evaluating the polygenic multiple threshold model of ADHD. Although the polygenic multiple threshold model predicts a higher rate of *ADHD* in the relatives of female probands, it does not necessarily predict a higher rate of general psychopathology during adulthood in the relatives of female probands.

Rather than examining the risk for ADHD in the adult relatives of ADHD children, Goodman and Stevenson (1989) and Pauls, Shaywitz, Kramer, Shaywitz, and Cohen (1983) took a different approach. They examined the risk for ADHD in the siblings or co-twins of ADHD children. They found that the risk to the siblings of children with ADD was .35 (9 out of 26 siblings) if the proband was female, and .23 (22 out of 96 siblings) if the proband was male. This supports the polygenic multiple threshold model. Pauls and colleagues also found that the risk for ADD (assessed through family history) for the relatives of a hyperactive child was best explained by a model that included proband's sex in addition to the status of the parent (affected or not affected) and maternal positive family history as independent variables. Goodman and Stevenson compared the pairwise concordances (the proportion of twin pairs in which both members are affected) for hyperactivity in hyperactive boys and girls and in their dizygotic twin brother or sister. A boy had almost the same likelihood of being hyperactive if he had a hyperactive brother (27%) or a hyperactive sister (30%), a statistically unreliable difference. A girl, too, had almost the same likelihood of being hyperactive if she had a hyperactive brother (17%) or a hyperactive sister (13%), again a statistically unreliable difference.

It is questionable whether Goodman and Stevenson (1989) provide conclusive evidence against the polygenic multiple threshold model because of their use of pairwise concordance rates. First, because concordance rates are very sensitive to prevalence (A. Heath, personal communication), the same levels of concordance could indicate quite different degrees of shared liability, depending on males' and females' prevalence of ADHD. Second, the probandwise concordance rate (the probability that a twin will be affected given that his or her co-twin is affected) is preferable to the pairwise concordance rate (the probability that both members of a twin pair will be affected given that at least one member of the pair is affected) due to its clearer meaning and superior statistical properties (McGue, 1992). Third and most important, concordance rates are appropriate for diagnostic entities that are truly categorical. Many psychiatric disorders, including ADHD, lack this clear present–absent distinction at the phenotypic level. In ADHD a subject is given a diagnosis when the number of symptoms displayed exceeds an arbitrary criterion. If a quantitative variable—such as the number of symptoms—is treated as a categorical variable—such as presence or absence of a disorder—important information may be lost.

## Constitutional variability model

The polygenic multiple threshold model assumes that males and females differ in the prevalence of ADHD because females require a higher liability than do males—i.e., a greater amount of *the same causal factors* that affect males—to manifest a disorder. In contrast, the constitutional variability model assumes that males and females differ in the prevalence of ADHD because *different causal factors* are important for males and for females. Males are slower to develop and transcribe genomic information, and this is postulated to result in males potentially having more genomic information than do females, and thus greater genetic variability (Taylor & Ounsted, 1972). According to the constitutional variability model, males affected by a disorder are at the end of the continuum characterised by this greater variability. In ADHD, hyperactivity in boys and individual differences in the activity and attention of the general population are assumed to share the same aetiology. Hyperactivity in girls, on the other hand, is assumed to be caused by discrete pathological events such as brain damage (James & Taylor, 1990). Therefore, according to the constitutional variability model, the aetiology of female hyperactivity is different from that in the general population, and hyperactive girls should be affected more severely than are their male counterparts. Additionally, because the same factors that contribute to the male's disorder affect the general population, whereas females are affected via atypical causal events, more relatives of male probands should be affected than should be relatives of female probands. This prediction is the converse to that of the polygenic multiple threshold model (Eme, 1992).

As mentioned earlier, James and Taylor (1990) found that hyperkinetic girls had lower IQ scores and significantly higher rates of language disorders and of neurological disorders than did hyperkinetic boys. They asserted that this finding provided evidence for the constitutional variability model. Hyperkinetic girls had lower cognitive and neurological functioning, which suggested that an atypical pathological event, such as brain damage, may be the cause of their hyperkinesis. It is also possible, however, to interpret the lower IQs of ADHD girls as support for the polygenic multiple threshold model. Berry et al. (1985) suggested that girls with ADD-H may have lower IQs because they carry a higher biological loading of liability for ADD-H, which may affect not only ADD-H, but also cognitive and language functioning. In addition, it is difficult to support either the polygenic multiple threshold model or the constitutional variability model with evidence of sex differences in the cognitive functioning of ADHD children, given that research in this area has yielded conflicting findings.

## PRESENT STUDY

As stated previously, the polygenic multiple threshold model asserts that probands of the less frequently affected sex should have more affected relatives than should probands of the more frequently affected sex. In the present study, multiple regression analysis was used to test whether female probands or male probands have DZ co-twins and co-siblings with a higher number of ADHD symptoms. If having a sister with ADHD is a greater risk factor than having a brother with ADHD, this would be evidence for the polygenic multiple threshold model.

In doing this method of analysis, several other variables should be controlled for statistically. First, the number of ADHD symptoms in probands should be controlled for, because probands who have higher numbers of ADHD symptoms will tend to have co-twins/co-siblings with higher numbers of ADHD symptoms. Second, the sex of the co-twin/co-sibling also should be controlled for, because male co-twins/co-siblings are more likely to have greater numbers of ADHD symptoms than are female co-twins/co-siblings, given that males are more likely than females to have ADHD. Third, the interaction between the sex of the co-twin/co-sibling and the sex of proband should be examined, because the risk conveyed by having a sister or brother with ADHD symptoms could differ in males and in females.

Given the support for the polygenic multiple threshold model in antisocial personality disorder (Mednick et al. 1983; Sigvardsson et al. 1982), one may argue that if support for the polygenic multiple threshold model is found for ADHD, this may reflect the overlap between ADHD and Conduct Disorder. We examined this possibility by comparing the polygenic multiple threshold model and the constitutional variability model after restricting the sample to those DZ twin pairs and sibling pairs with no Conduct Disorder symptoms.

According to the constitutional variability model, the same factors that contribute to the males' disorder affect levels of ADHD symptoms in the general population of males, whereas females are affected by unusual pathological events, so that more relatives of male probands should be affected than should be relatives of female probands. Hence, if the multiple regression analysis comparing the risk of having a sister versus a brother with ADHD resulted in a finding opposing that predicted by the polygenic multiple threshold model (i.e., greater risk for ADHD in relatives of female probands), then the constitutional variability model would be supported.

The constitutional variablity model asserts that the genetic influences producing the *disorder of ADHD* in boys should be similar to the genetic influences producing *variation in ADHD symptoms* in the general male population. The genetic influences producing the disorder in girls, however, are thought to be different from the genetic influences producing the variation of ADHD symptoms in the general population of females, because the disorder in girls is supposedly caused by atypical events. Therefore, we contrasted, in males and females, the difference between the heritability for deviant ADHD scores ($h^2_g$) and the heritability for the variation of ADHD scores in the general population ($h^2$). According to the constitutional variability model, there should be no difference between $h^2_g$ and $h^2$ for boys. For girls, $h^2_g$ should be higher or lower than $h^2$. A higher $h^2_g$ would suggest that the atypical or anomalous event leading to ADHD in girls is a rare genetic influence, whereas a lower $h^2_g$ would indicate a rare environmental influence. In summary, if the difference between the two heritabilities is much smaller for males than for females, the constitutional variability model would be supported.

## Method

### Participants

The participants in the initial unselected sample were 3- to 15-year-old male and female same- and opposite-sex twin pairs and their non-twin siblings, aged 3–18 years (1034 MZ pairs, 1009 DZ pairs, and 348 sibling pairs in families where there were at least two siblings other than the twin pair). They were recruited from the National Health and Medical Research Council of Australia (NHMRC) Australian Twin Registry (ATR), a nation-wide, population-based volunteer registry. From this sample, we selected a group of ADHD children and their twins or siblings. The descriptive statistics for the sample are presented in greater detail in Table 8.1.

Table 8.1 Descriptive statistics of twin and sibling pairs

| Relationship | Number of pairs | Number of affected pairs | | | Age | | ADHD symptoms | | Correlation between pairs | |
|---|---|---|---|---|---|---|---|---|---|---|
| | | Neither affected | One affected | Both affected | Mean | SD | Mean | SD | Log-transformed data | Untransformed data |
| MZ pairs | 1,034 | 894 | 46 | 94 | 8.59 | 2.76 | 2.63 | 3.36 | 0.87 | 0.44 |
| Male pairs | 493 | 395 | 29 | 69 | 8.65 | 2.79 | 3.35 | 3.75 | 0.87 | 0.48 |
| Female pairs | 541 | 499 | 17 | 25 | 8.54 | 2.73 | 1.96 | 2.80 | 0.85 | 0.32 |
| DZ pairs | 1,009 | 839 | 138 | 32 | 8.53 | 2.79 | 2.74 | 3.21 | 0.35 | −0.13 |
| Male pairs | 291 | 232 | 48 | 11 | 8.37 | 2.78 | 3.23 | 3.36 | 0.32 | −0.07 |
| Female pairs | 261 | 232 | 22 | 7 | 8.80 | 2.80 | 2.22 | 2.82 | 0.44 | −0.28 |
| Opposite-sex pairs | 457 | 375 | 68 | 14 | 8.47 | 2.77 | 2.72 | 3.27 | 0.35 | −0.04 |
| Sibling sets | 348 | 305 | 38 | 5 | 10.41 | 3.42 | 1.67 | 2.84 | 0.23 | −0.26 |
| Male sib. sets | 96 | 82 | 14 | 0 | 10.27 | 3.50 | 1.84 | 3.03 | 0.04 | −0.23 |
| Female sib. sets | 90 | 79 | 11 | 0 | 10.30 | 3.28 | 1.57 | 2.72 | 0.17 | −0.40 |
| Opposite-sex sib. sets | 162 | 144 | 13 | 5 | 10.58 | 3.44 | 1.63 | 2.81 | 0.45 | 0.07 |

## Procedure

Information on zygosity came from the mothers' responses to 11 questions regarding their twins' physical similarity. The responses on these questions yielded a physical similarity scale ranging from 0 to 17. Given that the scale's distribution appeared to be bimodal with the maximal discrimination between the modes occurring between 8 and 9, twin pairs who scored 0–8 on this scale were assigned as DZ, and twin pairs who scored 9–17 on this scale were assigned as MZ. We used mothers' report of twins' physical similarity as an indicator of zygosity, given previous reports of the validity of such indices (e.g., Bonnelykke, Hauge, Holm, Kristofferson, & Gurtler, 1989; Cohen, Dibble, Grawe, & Pollin, 1975; Kasriel & Eaves, 1976).

The mothers of the twin pairs filled out a questionnaire based on ADHD diagnostic criteria of the American Psychiatric Association *Diagnostic and Statistical Manual of Mental Disorders*, third edition—revised (*DSM-III-R*; ADA, 1987) (see Table 8.2). As indicated by the *DSM-III-R*, if a participant had 8 or more of the 14 *DSM-III-R* symptoms for ADHD, the participant was considered a proband (i.e., diagnosed as having ADHD). Table 8.1 shows the number of MZ twin pairs, DZ twin pairs, and sibling twin pairs who were diagnosed using this method.

## Analyses

In order to test the polygenic multiple threshold model, in which females require greater liability than do males in order to manifest the same level of ADHD, Goodman and Stevenson (1989) tested the risk of ADHD for a DZ co-twin of male versus female probands using pairwise concordances. As mentioned earlier, concordance rates are sensitive to prevalence and can lead to loss of information if used with a quantitative variable, such as number of symptoms. Instead of concordance rates of presence and absence of ADHD, multiple regression analysis of ADHD symptom scores in the selected sample of DZ twins and siblings was used to assess the effect of proband's sex on the co-twin/co-sibling score. The following regression equation was used:

$$C = B_1 SP + B_2 P + B_3 SC + B_4 SPSC \tag{1}$$

Here, co-twin/co-sibling's score (C) was predicted from the sex of the proband (SP), the ADHD symptom score of the proband (P), the sex of the co-twin/co-sibling (SC), and the interaction between the sex of the proband and the sex of the co-twin/co-sibling (SPSC). $B_1$ is the effect of the proband's sex on the co-twin/sibling's score, controlling for the effects of the proband's score, co-twin/co-sibling's sex, and the interaction between the proband's sex and co-twin/co-sibling's sex. If having a sister with ADHD confers greater risk for ADHD to the co-twin/co-sibling than does having a brother with ADHD, then this provides evidence for the polygenic multiple threshold

*Table 8.2* DSM-III-R ADHD symptoms

| | *DSM-III-R ADHD symptoms* | *Items in the questionnaire* |
|---|---|---|
| 1 | Often fidgets with hands or feet or squirms in seat. | Often fidgets with hands or squirms in seat. |
| 2 | Has difficulty remaining seated when required to do so. | Often leaves seat in classroom or other situations in which remaining seated is expected. |
| 3 | Is easily distracted by extraneous stimuli. | Is easily distracted by external stimuli, e.g., noise or conversation. |
| 4 | Has difficulty awaiting turn in games or group situations. | Has difficulty awaiting turn in games or group situations. |
| 5 | Often blurts out answers to questions before they have been completed. | Often blurts out answers to questions before they have been completed. |
| 6 | Has difficulty following through on instructions from others, e.g., fails to finish chores. | Cannot follow through on instructions without close supervision, e.g., jobs around the house or school work. |
| 7 | Has difficulty sustaining attention in tasks or play activities. | Has difficulty keeping attention on tasks or play activities |
| 8 | Often shifts from one uncompleted activity to another. | Often shifts from one uncompleted activity to another. |
| 9 | Has difficulty playing quietly. | Has difficulty playing quietly. |
| 10 | Often talks excessively. | Often talks excessively. |
| 11 | Often interrupts or intrudes on others, e.g., butts into other children's games. | Often interrupts or intrudes on others. |
| 12 | Often does not seem to listen to what is said to him or her. | Often does not seem to listen to what is being said to him/her. |
| 13 | Often loses things necessary for tasks or activities at school or at home (e.g., toys, pencils, books, assignments). | Often loses things necessary for tasks or activities at home or school (e.g., pencils, toys, or tools) |
| 14 | Often engages in physically dangerous activities without considering possible consequences, e.g., runs into street without looking. | Often engages in physically dangerous activities without considering consequences e.g., running onto street without looking. |

model. If having a brother with ADHD confers greater risk for ADHD to the co-twin/co-sibling than does having a sister with ADHD, then this provides evidence for the constitutional variability model.

Another test of the constitutional variability model is whether $h^2_g$ is closer to $h^2$ for males than it is for females. DeFries and Fulker (1985, 1988) described two multiple regression models (the basic multiple regression model and the augmented multiple regression model) that can be used to estimate $h^2_g$, $h^2$ and $h^2_g - h^2$ if tested in a selected sample of probands and their co-twins. The basic multiple regression model is:

$$C = B_1 P + B_2 R + A \qquad (2)$$

where co-twin's score (C) is predicted from proband's score (P) and the coefficient of genetic relationship (R = 1 for monozygotic twins and .5 for dizygotic twins). $B_2$ is the regression coefficient representing the test of significance for genetic aetiology in ADHD, and the ratio of $B_2$ to $\bar{P}-\mu$ (the difference between the mean number of ADHD symptoms for the probands and the mean number of ADHD symptoms for the unselected population) yields $h^2_g$, the extent to which the ADHD in probands is heritable. DeFries and Fulker (1988) showed that when the scores of probands and co-twins are divided by $\bar{P}-\mu$ prior to fitting the basic model, $B_2$ directly estimates $h^2_g$.

In estimating $h^2_g$, the population mean of ADHD symptoms ($\mu$) is required. The sample mean of ADHD symptoms in the Australian Twin Registry was used as an estimate of the population mean (cf., Rende, Plomin, Reiss, & Hetherington, 1993).

The augmented multiple regression model, or the additive model, is:

$$C = B_3P + B_4R + B_5PR + A \qquad (3)$$

In which co-twin's score (C) is predicted from proband's score (P), the coefficient of genetic relationship (R), and the product of proband's score and the coefficient of genetic relationship (PR). $B_3$ is the direct estimate of $c^2$, the magnitude of shared environmental influences on ADHD symptoms. $B_5$ is the direct estimate of $h^2$, the magnitude of genetic influences on ADHD symptoms.

The difference between $h^2_g$ and $h^2$ tests whether the aetiology of extreme ADHD symptom scores differs from the aetiology of ADHD symptom variation within the normal range. DeFries and Fulker (1988) showed that, in the augmented model, $B_4$ will estimate $h^2_g-h^2$ directly if both proband and co-twin scores are expressed as a deviation from $\mu$ (the population mean), and divided by $\bar{P}-\mu$ (the mean of the probands minus the population mean), while $B_3$ and $B_5$ continue to estimate $c^2$ and $h^2$ respectively.

In order to test whether there was a sex difference in $h^2_g$, sex was tested as a moderator in the regression equation estimating $h^2_g$. This analysis was limited to the same-sex twin and sibling pairs. This regression equation is:

$$C = B_6P + B_7R + B_8S + B_9PS + B_{10}RS + A \qquad (4)$$

where C, P, and R are as before, and S is a dummy variable for sex (e.g., S = 0 for males and 1 for females). $B_{10}$ tests whether $h^2_g$ differs in males and females.

Next, sex was tested as a moderator in the augmented regression equation to test for sex differences in $h^2$ and $h^2_g-h^2$. This analysis was limited to the same-sex twin and sibling pairs. This regression equation is:

$$C = B_6P + B_7R + B_8S + B_9PR + B_{10}PS + B_{11}RS + B_{12}PRS + A \qquad (5)$$

where C, P, R, PR, and S are as before. $B_{11}$ tests whether $h^2_g-h^2$ differs for males and females, and $B_{12}$ tests whether $h^2$ differs for males and females. The rest of the regression coefficients are not examined here as they are irrelevant for examining the predictions of the constitutional variability model.

A twin was considered a proband if his or her number of ADHD symptoms exceeded the *DSM-III-R* threshold of eight or more symptoms. Given that twin pairs in this study were not selected with respect to the level of twins' ADHD symptoms, defining either the first or second member of the twin pair as a proband would be arbitrary. Hence, twin pairs were "double-entered" into the data file, such that each twin gets a chance to be "proband" and "co-twin". Due to the artificial increase in the degrees of freedom, regression analyses of "double-entered" data require a correction of the regression coefficients' standard errors (e.g., Stevenson, Batten, & Cherner, 1992), using the following equation:

corrected standard error = obtained standard error

$$\times \sqrt{N_d - K - 1 \, / \, N_s - K - 1}_{[NF\&SR1]} \qquad (6)$$

where $N_d$ = number of twin pairs including those double entered, $N_s$ = actual number of twin pairs, and K = number of coefficients in the regression equation.

The standard errors of the regression coefficients were corrected for double-entry in all of the analyses, given that all of the analyses were conducted for "double-entered" data.

## RESULTS

### Comparison of the polygenic multiple threshold model and the constitutional variability model

The polygenic multiple threshold model and the constitutional variability model were compared using equation 1 in DZ twin pairs and sibling pairs in the selected sample. The regression coefficient for the effect of proband sex was positive and significant when proband score, co-twin sex, and the interaction between proband sex and co-twin sex were controlled, $t(245) = 2.211$, $p = .03$. Co-twins or co-siblings of female probands had a higher number of ADHD symptoms on average (mean = 5.54, SD = 4.35) than did co-twins or co-siblings of male probands (mean = 4.24, SD = 4.00). The effect size for the difference between these means, $d$, was .27. Analysis of covariance was used to derive adjusted means for co-twins' or co-siblings' ADHD symptoms after controlling for the proband score, co-twin sex, and the interaction between proband sex and co-twin sex. These adjusted means were 5.55 for the co-twins and co-siblings of female probands, and 4.22 for the co-twins and co-siblings of male probands.

In order to address the hypothesis that support for the polygenic multiple threshold model in ADHD may be simply be a reflection of ADHD's overlap with Conduct Disorder, the polygenic multiple threshold model and the constitutional variability model were compared for DZ twin pairs and for sibling pairs in that subset of the selected sample with no Conduct Disorder symptoms. In this subsample, the regression coefficient for the effect of proband sex was positive but not statistically significant when proband score, co-twin sex, and the interaction between proband sex and co-twin sex were controlled, $t(80) = .882$, $p = .38$. The lack of statistical significance of this result may be due to the reduced size of the sample of ADHD children with no Conduct Disorder symptoms. Again, co-twins or co-siblings of female probands had a higher number of ADHD symptoms on average (mean = 5.47, SD = 4.29) than did co-twins or co-siblings of male probands (mean = 3.51, SD = 3.81). The effect size for the difference between these means, $d$, was .45. The adjusted means for co-twins' or co-siblings' ADHD symptoms after controlling for the proband score, co-twin sex, and the interaction between proband sex and co-twin sex were 5.96 for the co-twins and co-siblings of female probands and 3.02 for the co-twins and co-siblings of male probands.

### Test of a sex difference in $h^2_g$–$h^2$

Sex moderation of the basic and augmented model was tested for same-sex twin and sibling pairs. In the basic model we found that there was no statistically significant sex difference in the $h^2_g$ estimate, $t(359) = .428$, $p = .67$, and in the augmented model we found that there was no statistically significant sex difference in the $h^2$ estimate, $t(357) = .316$, $p = .75$, nor in the $h^2_g$–$h^2$ estimate, $t(357) = -.253$, $p = .80$. These findings were very similar when sibling pairs were excluded.

### DISCUSSION

As suggested in the Introduction of this chapter, sex differences in the transmissability of ADHD provide a strong test of the validity of two competing models for the aetiology of sex differences in ADHD, viz., the polygenic multiple threshold model and the constitutional variability model. Analyses of DZ twin and sibling data, in which co-twin's or co-sibling's ADHD scores are regressed on proband's sex, afford such a test. When co-twin's and co-sibling's score were regressed on proband's sex, co-twin's sex, proband's score, and the interaction between proband's sex and co-twin's sex in DZ twin pairs and sibling pairs, the regression coefficient for proband sex was positive and significant. This means that a DZ co-twin or co-sibling of a proband had a higher number of ADHD symptoms if the proband was female than if the proband was male, regardless of the proband's number of ADHD symptoms or of the co-twin's or co-sibling's own sex. Hence, having a sister with ADHD was a greater risk factor than was having a brother with

ADHD. This result supports the polygenic multiple threshold model, which asserts that probands of the less frequently affected sex (females in the case of ADHD) should have more affected relatives than should probands of the more frequently affected sex.

The constitutional variability model predicts a sex difference in the distinction between genetic influences on deviant scores and genetic influences on normal variability (i.e., $h^2_g$–$h^2$ should be greater in females than males). The sex moderation of $h^2_g$, $h^2$, or $h^2_g$–$h^2$ was not significant. This result is evidence against the constitutional variability model.

These results in general support the polygenic multiple threshold model's explanation for sex differences in the prevalence of ADHD. According to this model, an individual is affected with ADHD if he or she exceeds a certain threshold of liability. Females are less likely to be affected with ADHD because they require a greater threshold of liability to manifest ADHD than do males.

One possible explanation for the support of the polygenic multiple threshold model is that adults might be more sensitive to ADHD symptoms in boys and might be more likely to label a boy as having ADHD than to label a girl as having ADHD. In other words, factors that might influence the parents' and teachers' report of boys' symptoms in the general population might be similar to those influencing their report of girls' symptoms in the general population. None the less, their report of boys' symptoms in the extreme levels might be affected by a special labelling phenomenon absent in their report of girls' symptoms in the extreme levels. One can test this hypothesis by comparing the difference between the heritability for extreme scores and the heritability for ADHD symptoms in the general population in boys versus girls. The results suggest that the heritability for extreme scores and the heritability for ADHD symptoms are both high, and that the difference between the two estimates is not significantly different in boys compared to girls. This does not support the hypothesis of a special labelling phenomenon, which provides a simple explanation for the finding of support for the polygenic multiple threshold model.

It was possible that support for the polygenic multiple threshold model may have reflected ADHD's overlap with Conduct Disorder. This possibility was examined by comparing the polygenic multiple threshold model and the constitutional variability model after restricting the sample to those DZ twin and sibling pairs with no Conduct Disorder symptoms. Support for the polygenic multiple threshold was found also in the "pure" ADHD cases. Although it was not statistically significant, the difference between the means for ADHD symptoms in co-twins or co-siblings of male and female probands was actually higher in this sample than in the entire selected sample (effect size, $d = .45$ in the selected sample with no Conduct Disorder symptoms versus .27 in the entire selected sample). The statistical insignificance of this result is most likely due to the small sample size ($N = 70$) of the "pure" ADHD sample. This conclusion is inconsistent with that reached in Faraone et al.'s (1995) family study, in that Faraone et al. assert finding evidence for the polygenic multiple threshold model only in ADHD families that also were characterised by relatively high levels of antisocial behaviour.

One possible reason for this inconsistency in findings may be that Faraone et al. (1995) did not attribute their nonsignificant finding to their small sample size. They reported that in antisocial families ($N = 33$), the odds of sibling ADHD was 9.7 times greater in families with maternal ADHD compared with those without maternal ADHD ($p = .002$), whereas the similar odds ratio assessing the paternal ADHD effect was not significant (odds ratio = 1.5, $p = .58$). In non-antisocial families ($N = 73$), a statistical trend was found for the odds ratio for the maternal ADHD effect (odds ratio = 2.9, $p = .08$), whereas the odds ratio for the paternal ADHD effect was similar to that for antisocial families (odds ratio = 1.5, $p = .87$). Another possible reason for the inconsistency in the findings is the difference in the assessment of ADHD symptoms. First, Faraone et al. relied on contemporaneous report of the children's ADHD symptoms but retrospective report of the parents' ADHD symptoms, whereas we relied solely on contemporaneous report of ADHD symptoms. Second, Faraone et al. used face-to-face structured interviews in their assessment, whereas we used the questionnaire method. Although the use of different assessment methods may lead to differences in our findings, our questionnaire has been validated against a structured interview. This comparison yielded moderate agreement between the questionnaire and interview, suggesting that it is unlikely to be the major source of differences in results.

In conclusion, the tests of the assumptions of the polygenic multiple threshold model and the constitutional variability model found evidence in support of the polygenic multiple threshold model and against the constitutional variability model. This suggests that males are more likely to be affected by ADHD than are females because they have a lower threshold for the liability required to express the disorder of ADHD. The present study also found evidence for the polygenic multiple threshold model in a sample of twin and sibling pairs with no Conduct Disorder symptoms, suggesting that the evidence for the polygenic multiple threshold model for ADHD is not due to the overlap of ADHD and Conduct Disorder, and that it is not restricted to only those ADHD children who also have Conduct Disorder.

## REFERENCES

Ackerman, P.T., Dykman, R.A., & Oglesby, D.M. (1983). Sex and group differences in reading and attention disordered children with and without hyperkinesis. *Journal of Learning Disabilities, 16*, 407–415.

American Psychiatric Association. (1987). *Diagnostic and statistical manual of mental disorders* (3rd ed., rev.). Washington, DC: Author.

American Psychiatric Association. (1994). *Diagnostic and statistical manual of mental disorders* (4th ed.). Washington, DC: Author.

Befera, M.S. & Barkley, R.A. (1985). Hyperactive and normal girls and boys: Mother–child interaction, parent psychiatric status and child psychopathology. *Journal of Child Psychology and Psychiatry, 26,* 439–452.

Berry, C.A., Shaywitz, S.E., & Shaywitz, B.A. (1985). Girls with attention deficit disorder: A silent minority? A report on behavioral and cognitive characteristics. *Pediatrics, 76,* 801–809.

Biederman, J., Faraone, S.V., Keenan, K., Knee, D., & Tsuang, M.T.(1990). Family genetic and psychosocial risk factors in DSM-III attention deficit disorder. *Journal of the American Academy of Child and Adolescent Psychiatry, 29,* 526–533.

Bonnelykke, B., Hauge, M., Holm, N., Kristoffersen, K., & Gurtler, H.(1989). Evaluation of zygosity diagnosis in twin pairs below age seven by means of a mailed questionnaire. *Acta Geneticae Medicae et Gemellologiae, 38*(3–4), 305–313.

Breen, M.J. (1989). Cognitive and behavioral differences in ADHD boys and girls. *Journal of Child Psychology and Psychiatry, 30,* 711–716.

Breen, M.J. & Barkley, R.A. (1988). Child psychopathology and parenting stress in girls and boys having attention deficit disorder with hyperactivity. *Journal of Pediatric Psychology, 13,* 265–280.

Brown, R.T., Madan-Swain, A., & Baldwin, K. (1991). Gender differences in a clinic-referred sample of attention-deficit-disordered children. *Child Psychiatry and Human Development, 22,* 111–128.

Carter, C.O. (1969). Genetics of common disorders. *British Medical Bulletin, 25,* 52–57.

Carter, C.O. (1973). Multifactorial genetic disease. In V.A. McKusick & R. Clairborne (Eds.), *Medical genetics* (pp. 199–208). New York: H.P. Publishing.

Cloninger, C.R., Christiansen, K.O., Reich, T., & Gottesman, I.I. (1978). Implications of sex differences in the prevalences of antisocial personality, alcoholism, and criminality for familial transmission. *Archives of General Psychiatry, 35,* 941–951.

Cohen, D.J., Dibble, E., Grawe, J.M., & Pollin, W. (1975). Reliably separating identical from fraternal twins. *Archives of General Psychiatry, 32,* 1371–1375.

DeFries, J.C., & Fulker, D.W. (1985). Multiple regression analysis of twin data. *Behavior Genetics, 15,* 467–473.

DeFries, J.C., & Fulker, D.W. (1988). Multiple regression analysis of twin data: Etiology of deviant scores versus individual differences. *Acta Geneticae Medicae et Gemellologiae, 37,* 205–216.

deHass, P.T. (1986). Attention styles and peer relationships of hyperactive and normal boys and girls. *Journal of Abnormal Child Psychology, 14,* 457–467.

deHass, P.T., & Young, R.D. (1984). Attention styles of hyperactive and normal girls. *Journal of Abnormal and Child Psychology, 12,* 531–546.

Eme, R.F. (1992). Selective female affliction in the developmental disorders of childhood: A literature review. *Journal of Clinical Child Psychology, 21,* 354–364.

Faraone, S.V., Biederman, J., Chen, W.J., Milberger, S., Warburton, R., & Tsuang, M.T. (1995). Genetic heterogeneity in attention-deficit hyperactivity disorder (ADHD): Gender, psychiatric comorbidity, and maternal ADHD. *Journal of Abnormal Psychology, 104,* 334–345.

Faraone, S.V., Biederman, J., Keenan, K., & Tsuang, M.T. (1991). A family-genetic study of girls with DSM-III attention deficit disorder. *American Journal of Psychiatry, 148,* 112–117.

Goodman, R., & Stevenson, J. (1989). A twin study of hyperactivity—II. The aetiological role of genes, family relationships and perinatal adversity. *Journal of Child Psychology and Psychiatry, 30,* 691–709.

Horn, W.F., Wagner, A.E., & Ialongo, N. (1989). Sex differences in school-aged children with pervasive Attention Deficit Hyperactivity Disorder. *Journal of Abnormal Child Psychology, 17,* 109–125.

James, A., & Taylor, E. (1990). Sex differences in the hyperkinetic syndrome of childhood. *Journal of Child Psychology and Psychiatry, 31,* 437–446.

Kashani, J., Chapel, J.L., Ellis, J., & Shekim, W.O. (1979). Hyperactive girls. *Journal of Operational Psychiatry, 10,* 145–148.

Kasriel, J., & Eaves, L. (1976). The zygosity of twins: Further evidence on the agreement between diagnosis by blood groups and written questionnaires. *Journal of Biosocial Science, 8,* 263–266.

Lambert, N.M., Sandoval, J., & Sassone, D. (1978). Prevalence of hyperactivity in elementary school children as a function of social system definers. *American Journal of Orthopsychiatry, 48,* 446–463.

Mannuzza, S., & Gittelman, R. (1984). The adolescent outcome of hyperactive girls. *Psychiatry Research, 13,* 19–29.

McGue, M. (1992). When assessing twin concordance, use the probandwise not the pairwise rate. *Schizophrenia Bulletin, 18,* 171–176.

Mednick, S.A., Gabrielli, W.F., & Hutchings, B. (1983). Genetic influences in criminal behavior: Evidence from an adoption cohort. In K.T. Van Dusen & S.A. Mednick (Eds.), *Prospective studies of crime and delinquency* (pp. 39–56). Boston: Kluwer-Nijhof.

Pauls, D.L., Shaywitz, S.E., Kramer, P.L., Shaywitz, B.A., & Cohen, D.J. (1983). Demonstration of vertical transmission of attention deficit disorder. *Annals of Neurology, 14,* 363.

Rende, R.D., Plomin, R., Reiss, D., & Hetherington, E.M. (1993). Genetic and environmental influences on depressive symptomatology in adolescence: Individual differences and extreme scores. *Journal of Child Psychology and Psychiatry, 34,* 1387–1398.

Sigvardsson, S., Cloninger, C.R., Bohman, M., & von Knorring, A.L. (1982). Predisposition to petty criminality in Swedish adoptees: III. Sex differences and validation of the male typology. *Archives of General Psychiatry, 39,* 1248–1253.

Silverthorn, P., Frick, P.J., Kuper, K., & Ott, J. (1996). Attention Deficit Hyperactivity Disorder and sex: A test of two etiological models to explain the male predominance. *Journal of Clinical Child Psychology, 25*(1), 52–59.

Stevenson, J., Batten, N., & Cherner, M. (1992). Fears and fearfulness in children and adolescents: A genetic analysis of twin data. *Journal of Child Psychology and Psychiatry, 33,* 977–985.

Taylor, D., & Ounsted, C. (1972). The nature of gender differences explored through ontogenetic analyses of sex ratios in disease. In C. Ounsted & D. Taylor (Eds.), *Gender differences: Their ontogeny and significance* (pp. 215–240). London: Churchill Livingstone.

Thorley, G. (1984). Hyperkinetic syndrome of childhood: Clinical characteristics. *British Journal of Psychiatry, 144,* 16–24.

Wechsler, D. (1989). *Wechsler Preschool and Primary Scale of Intelligence—Revised.* San Antonio, TX: Psychological Corporation.

World Health Organisation. (1979). *International classification of diseases.* 9th rev. ed.; *(ICD-9). Classification of mental and behavioural disorders, diagnostic criteria.* Geneva: Author.

# 9   Single gene studies of ADHD

*Alan Zametkin, Monique Ernst, and
Robert Cohen*

## INTRODUCTION

Over the past 25 years, it has become apparent that neuropsychiatric syndromes as diverse as Huntington's disease, Fragile-X syndrome, and Lesch Nyhan disorder, are caused by single genes. On the other hand, to date no single gene has been identified for complex behavioural conditions such as schizophrenia, bipolar illness, Tourette syndrome or Attention Deficit Hyperactivity Disorder (ADHD), despite concerted efforts by international research programmes.

This chapter presents an overview of the strategies for single gene studies of ADHD. We then review proposed modes of inheritance for the disorder, and describe current knowledge of the association between several diseases that present with attentional difficulties, and are caused by single gene abnormalities. These disorders are Generalised Resistance to Thyroid Hormone (GRTH), and Fragile-X syndrome. Finally, we will discuss the potential implications, for research and therapy, of single gene studies.

## GENETICS

Perhaps the strongest support for a neurobiological basis for ADHD are the many studies supporting the concept that the disorder runs in families. Dating back to the early 1970s, studies of adoption, twins, families, and, most recently, molecular investigations point toward genetic influences as one mechanism underlying symptoms of ADHD. This has been discussed in some of the earlier chapters of this book.

Many models for the inheritance of ADHD have been proposed, including single gene, polygenic, and multifactorial models. Amongst the earliest models was that of Deutsch, Matthysse, Swanson & Farkas (1990), in which a genetic latent structure analysis of dysmorphology was performed. They reported that the autosomal dominant model best fit the data.

Family studies with 140 ADHD probands and 368 first-degree relatives, were consistent with a model of highly penetrant autosomal dominant gene transmission (Faraone et al., 1992). An important point from this study was that female members of the family seemed to be linked to an increased familial risk of the disorder. Additionally, if a parent had ADHD, the risk was 6.6 times greater for sisters, and 1.5 times greater for brothers. The authors rejected the hypothesis of a more severe genetic disorder in girls. Their model speculated that in the males, a proportion of the cases was caused by environmental rather than genetic factors.

More recent data from the Colorado Reading Project (Stevenson, Pennington, Gilger, DeFries, & Gillis, 1993), suggested that ADHD in these reading disabled families, and in the controls, followed the pattern of either a single dominant gene, or a single major gene. Finally, more recent family studies report a higher risk for ADHD in siblings of ADHD probands (20.8%), than in siblings of normal probands (5.6%) (Biederman et al., 1992).

## MOLECULAR STUDIES

As will be discussed later, a series of studies has attempted to identify single gene causes of ADHD. It will become apparent that no clear-cut candidate gene has been definitively identified, thus the cause of ADHD is unlikely to be a single gene. How then, can studies of disorders that are caused by single genes, and that have attentional difficulties as symptoms, elucidate the aetiology of ADHD?

Perhaps one of the most interesting observations in the pursuit of a molecular basis of attentional difficulties was the original description of Resistance to Thyroid Hormone (RTH), first described by Refetoff, DeWind and DeGroot in 1967. The disorder is characterised by decreased pituitary and tissue responsiveness to thyroid hormone. Patients typically have elevated free and total triiodothyronine (T3) and thyroxine (T4) levels, and inappropriately normal or elevated thyroid stimulating hormone (TSH) levels. Refetoff, Weiss, and Usala (1993) described the phenotype as heterogenous, including ADHD, growth delay, and tachycardia. Although sporadic cases do occur, the syndrome is usually transmitted in an autosomal dominant manner. In 1988, linkage between RTH and the thyroid hormone receptor (hTR β) gene was shown (Usala et al., 1988).

Alhough unknown, the prevalence of RTH in the general population is thought to be quite low. The phenotype is highly heterogenous and ranges from highly symptomatic to subclinical. The earliest descriptions of the syndrome alluded to hyperactivity, behavioural problems, and cognitive deficit (see Elia, Gulotta, Rose, Marin, & Rapoport, 1994, and Refetoff, 1990, for a review).

In the first large and rigorous study of the behavioural manifestations of the syndrome in a genetically well characterised sample of 18 kindreds, Hauser and colleagues (1993) reported some interesting associations between the genotype and phenotypic expression. In this study, 42% of adults and

70% of minors, positive for RTH, were diagnosed with ADHD. Of note was the finding in the study that both the affected and unaffected males had a three times increased risk of ADHD, consistent with the accepted fact that this disorder is more prevalent among males. Although RTH is an exceedingly rare condition, and unlikely to be associated with routine cases of ADHD, RTH serves as an interesting model for a genetic pathway to symptoms of ADHD.

By what mechanism could abnormalities in the hTR β gene lead to symptoms of ADHD? As Hauser and colleagues (1993, p. 1000) pointed out, thyroid hormone is essential for normal brain development, and its absence in the most extreme case causes mental retardation.

> In the human fetus the concentration of $T_3$ receptors is low at 10 weeks of gestation, but increases 10-fold by the 16th week, coincidentally with neuroblast proliferation. . . . The regulation of the expression of myelin basic protein mRNA (in rat) and the expression of the NGFI-A gene, an immediate early-response gene implicated in the control of brain cell proliferation and aspects of brain development, is directly regulated by $T_3$ in the brains of neonatal, but not adult, rats. Taken together, these studies suggest the importance of the thyroid receptor-β protein in brain development. Theoretically, mutations of the hTR β gene could result in behavioural abnormalities through several different mechanisms, including potentially irreversible effects on axonal routing, neuronal proliferation and migration, and the regulation of gene expression during critical periods of brain development.
>
> In addition to its putative role in brain development, the thyroid receptor–thyroid hormone complex may influence catecholamine neurotransmitter systems thought to be involved in the pathphysiology of attention deficit hyperactivity disorder.

In an interesting experiment, Rovet and Alvarez (1996) examined a cohort of 85 7-year-old children born with congenital hypothyroidism (CH), who had been treated since birth. Unfortunately, there was no unaffected control group. In reviewing the literature on what is known about this disorder, Rovet and Alvarez reported several studies that found that these children performed more poorly in cognitive, neuromotor, and behavioural areas, including tasks of attention. They were also more active than normal. The investigators concluded that: "Such problems are typically associated with onset severity and duration of disease as well as early treatment adequacy. Some also appear to reflect later levels of thyroid hormone" (p. 580).

Kooistra, van der Meere, Vulsma, and Kalverboer (1996) showed that the ability to maintain attention over time—in children with CH treated early—reflected severity of initial hypothyroidism. They were interested in the correlation between circulating hormone levels and behaviour as measured by the Child Behavior Checklist (CBCL), the Conners Rating Scale, and subtests of the WISC (the mean of performance on Arithmetic, Digit Span, and Coding). Therefore, they subdivided all of their patients into four groups, by the level of $T_4$ and TSH. The results of the study showed that poorer attention (as assessed on the WISC subtests) was associated with higher levels of $T_4$, and to a lesser degree TSH, consistent with the finding in RTH. They noted, however, that the higher $T_4$ TSH profile contributed to less deviance on the "hyperactive" scales (which feature items of both hyperactivity and attention—Conners and Child Behavior Check List), when rated by parents. Of particular interest to us is their report that, in older treated CH adolescents, when compared to normals on the Continuous Performance Task (CPT), it was Errors of Commission—not of Omission—that distinguished CH from normals. One word of caution is in order. The Rovet and Alvarez (1996) study had no way to control for compliance with thyroid supplementation, and the values that they obtained may not reflect the more chronic status of their patients.

The Hauser et al. (1993) report generated considerable interest, as well as additional research reports, mostly on the incidence of thyroid abnormalities in ADHD children at large. This is an interesting question in itself, but not much relevant to the core question of how abnormalities in the thyroid bTR β gene might lead to symptoms of ADHD.

In a series of studies that followed Hauser's original report, certain findings became apparent. In an attempt to ascertain whether ADHD individuals have an increase in thyroid hormone abnormalities, Weiss, Stein, Trømmer, and Refetoff (1993) reported that no cases of GRTH were found in 277 children with ADHD. However, a prevalence rate of 5.4% of ADHD subjects with some thyroid abnormality was noted, higher than that expected by chance alone (less than 1% in the general population). Weiss et al. reported that: "The 5–10 fold increased prevalence of ADHD in patients with GRTH compared with that in the general population suggests an association between these two conditions. In 11 of 98 families, the diagnosis of GRTH was suspected in the proposition because of learning disabilities or hyperactivity or both" (p. 541). Their results offered support for a link between thyroid function abnormalities and the cognitive behavioural manifestation of ADHD.

It should be noted that if appropriately diagnosed ADHD children from the general population are screened one is unlikely to find individuals with GRTH. This is confirmed in studies by Elia et al. (1994) and Spencer et al. (1995). The Elia et al. study retrospectively reviewed thyroid indices of 53 well-characterised ADHD boys and compared them to normal controls. Spencer and colleagues found no evidence of GRTH in 123 ADHD subjects. However, these findings would be expected given the extreme rarity of GRTH in the general population.

Cook et al. (1995) described an association of ADD and the Dopamine Transporter Gene (DAT). The authors cite two lines of evidence that they claimed did not support the Hauser et al. (1993) finding. First, they cited that

GRTH is extremely rare in ADHD individuals. (Weiss et al., 1993). Although this observation is accurate, Hauser did not claim that GRTH was *common* in the ADHD population, but that in the GRTH population ADHD is common. Cook cited another Weiss paper (Weiss et al. 1994) as evidence that low intelligence, but not ADHD, is associated with GRTH by a mutation in the R316H in the Thyroid Hormone Receptor or the β gene. However, Cook and collegues failed to report that the Weiss et al. study involved only one kindred with 16 members, which is insufficient support for the contention that subsequent studies have failed to show genetic linkage of ADHD and GRTH.

## RECENT STUDIES INVESTIGATING SINGLE GENES

The major drawback of association studies, such as that of Cook et al. (1995) cited above, is that affected individuals are compared with controls who may be selected from different populations with different allele frequencies (i.e., population stratification). To avoid this problem, Cook et al. used the haplotype-based haplotype relative risk (HHRR) method. They tested for association between a variable number of tandem repeats (VNTR) polymorphism at DAT1 in *DSM-III-R* diagnosed ADHD ($N = 49$) and undifferentiated ADHD ($N = 8$) subjects. In this study, they utilised trios of family members, including 24 mother–child diads, 4 father–child diads, and 27 mother–father–child triads. The finding that certain stimulants, which so dramatically ameliorate the symptoms of ADHD, bind to and inhibit the dopamine transporter (Volkow et al., 1995), led the investigators to study the DAT1 locus as a primary candidate gene. They reported that there was a significant association between the 480 base pair DAT1 allele and ADHD. In a subsequent report, LaHoste, Swanson, and Wigal (1996) did not confirm this finding.

Another problem with the Cook et al. (1995) study was the fact that many of the comparisons included only one parent, thus information about the other parent's allele was not available. Added to this, the allele status of unaffected siblings would have made a far more convincing case. Finally, this study did not examine the gene directly, and as the authors suggested, the association could have been with an ADHD susceptibility gene close to *but not* the Dopamine transporter gene.

Waldman et al. (1998) reported a study of 101 children referred to a psychiatric clinic for behavioural and learning problems, including—but not limited to—ADHD. These children also had extreme scores on the Inattentive and/or Hyperactive-impulsive *Diagnostic and Statistical Manual of Mental Disorders*, fourth edition (*DSM-IV*; American Psychiatric Association, 1994) dimensions. Using the transmission disequilibrium test (TDT) analysis, the authors suggested that ADHD was associated with the DAT1 gene more strongly at severe levels of ADHD symptoms. Additionally, the

DAT1 gene was more strongly associated with the Combined type, and with the Hyperactive-Impulsive type, than with the Inattentive ADHD subtype.

## GENE TO BRAIN

What is known about brain morphology and physiology of individuals with RTH? Are these findings consistent with what is known about the anatomical localisation of attention and previous brain imaging studies of ADHD?

The only anatomical study of the brain in RTH compared 20 affected males to 23 affected females, and to 32 unaffected first-degree relatives (18 male, 14 female) (Leonard, Martinez, Weintraub, & Hauser 1995). Of the affected males, 72% had ADHD, and 50% of the affected females had ADHD. The data analysis was limited to blinded qualitative assessment of presence or absence of extra or missing gyri in the parietal bank of the Sylvian fissure (multimodal association cortex), and the presence or absence of single or multiple Heschl's transverse gyri (primary auditory cortex). The results demonstrated a significant increase in the frequency of anomalous Sylvian fissures in the left hemisphere in males with RTH, at twice the rate of the other groups (70% of affected males v approximately 30% of affected females). Additionally, they reported an increased frequency of anomalous multiple Heschl's gyri in either hemisphere in males with RTH (50% of affected males v 9% of affected females and 0% in unaffected females). However, RTH with anomalies did not have an increased frequency of ADHD, as compared with RTH subjects with no anomalies. The findings were interpreted to show that in males, foetal abnormalities of thyroid hormone action may produce grossly observable cerebral anomalies of the left hemisphere.

Matochik, Zametkin, Cohen, Hauser, & Weintraub (1996) used Flourodeoxyglucose Positron Emission Tomography (FDG PET) to measure both attentional abilities and brain metabolism in 13 adult RTH patients versus 13 normal controls. The attention measure consisted of an auditory three-tone discrimination task. The anatomical localisation of brain metabolism during execution of this task had previously been well documented to the right lateral prefrontal cortex (increased metabolism), and the middle cingulate (decreased activation). They showed very poor performance on the auditory attention task in the RTH group, with significantly fewer correct identifications (attributed to inattentiveness), and significantly more false alarms (attributed to impulsivity). This aside, the most interesting differences in cerebral glucose metabolism were those showing that in the RHT group, compared to the control group, significantly higher metabolic rates were evident in the anterior cingulate and in the right parietal cortex during execution of the task. A number of other investigators who used blood-flow methods (see Matochik et al., 1996) have shown anterior cingulate to be activated during a variety of attentional tasks, so the anterior cingulate system has clearly been postulated as being important in attentional regulation. In the group with RTH, Matochik speculated that: "the higher functional activity of the anterior cingulate during sustained attention may reflect a decreased signal to noise ratio of the neural processing of the target stimuli. Thus our data is consistent with the hypothesis that decreased activity of the anterior cingulate during a sustained attention task is required for efficient performance" (p. 27).

We have recently reviewed both anatomical Magnetic Resonance Imaging (MRI) and FDG PET studies in ADHD adults and adolescents who do not carry the gene for RTH (Zametkin & Liotta, 1997). In synthesising this growing literature, it is safe to say that no study of quantitative morphology of ADHD brain has *failed* to detect difference between ADHD and normals. However, the findings have been inconsistent in the directions of the differences, and in the brain structures that differ. The corpus callosum tends to be the structure most likely to differ in this population, although total brain volume seems to be smaller in ADHD children.

In a study of adult ADHD, Zametkin et al. (1990) showed widespread reductions in metabolism not confined to cingulate or parietal cortex, but few significant regional differences (Ernst et al., 1994) in brain metabolism, in teenagers with and without ADHD, were noted in later studies.

## FRAGILE-X SYNDROME

A common genetic disorder, Fragile-X syndrome, is one of more than seven neurological diseases discovered in the 1990s to be caused by expansion in the genetic code (DNA) of a trinucleotide or triplet repeat (e.g., CAGCAG-CAGCAG). That is, an increase in the length of a repeating sequence in a specific chromosomal location. These diseases include Huntington's disease, spinocerebellar ataxia, and myotonic dystrophy. Many excellent reviews of this area have appeared in the last few years, and the reader is referred to these for further detail (La Spada, 1997; Paulson & Fischbeck, 1996; Reddy & Housman, 1997; Tsuji, 1997; Warren & Ashley, 1995). In brief, human mutations leading to increases beyond a certain size in these repeat sequences—that is, beyond the size variation found in the DNA of normal individuals—are usually unstable. This leads to further changes in successive generations (this phenomenon is sometimes referred to as "augmentation"). The mutations are often dominant, i.e., inheritance of a single allele, or copy of the mutated gene, is sufficient to cause the disease, or are located on the X chromosome. The most common form of this type of human mutation is the expansion of a triplet repeat of CAG in the coding region, in other words, in the part of the gene that determines the amino acid sequence of the protein. This leads to an abnormally long run within the protein of polyglutamine, coded for and resulting in a progressive neurodegeneration. It is believed that it is the alteration of the properties of the protein coded by the gene that leads to the abnormal phenotype.

The mutation in Fragile-X disease, however, is an expansion of the trinucleotide repeat in the promotor. This is the area of the gene involved in the regulation of transcription, and not coding for the sequence of amino acids, of the FMR1 gene, located on the X chromosome (Kremer et al., 1991; Verkerk et al., 1991). The mutation appears to lead to an alteration of expression of the protein. That is, the amount of protein that is formed in the cell, and the abnormal phenotype is likely to be the result of an alteration in development rather than a result of neurodegeneration. Fragile-X is subclassified as a premutation if the expansion consists of 150–600 base pairs, or as a full mutation if an amplification to 600–3000 (200 or more triplet repeats) base pairs occurs. Although alleles become expanded primarily through female gametocyte formation, expansion can also occur post-zygotically. In this latter process, the sex of the embryo also appears to affect expansion, being greater in male than in female embryos. The full mutation causes the range of physical and behavioural symptoms that has, in general, been associated with the Fragile-X syndrome. The specific neuropsychological profile of individuals with the Fragile-X syndrome is one of relatively poorer visual-spatial, visual-motor coordination, and attentional-organisational deficits, compared to verbal abilities (Crowe & Hay, 1990; Freund, Abrams, & Reiss, 1991; Freund & Reiss, 1991; Mazzocco, Pennington, & Hagerman, 1993; Prouty et al., 1988; Reiss & Freund, 1990). Children with the Fragile-X syndrome also have impairments in social functioning, including problems establishing and maintaining peer relationships, and difficulties with nonverbal communication. Stereotypic behaviour is common. In females these symptoms can occur in the presence of normal IQ scores (Crowe & Hay, 1990; Freund et al., 1991; Freund & Reiss, 1991; Mazzocco et al., 1993; Prouty et al., 1988; Reiss & Freund, 1990). Most males with the disorder suffer from mental retardation. On the contrary females are generally less affected, and show a much greater range of IQ effects from little to severe (mental retardation) (Freund et al., 1991; Freund & Reiss, 1991; Hagerman, 1996b; Prouty et al., 1988; Reiss & Freund, 1990).

Hyperactivity is reportedly present by 2 years of age. In some studies, more than 70% of boys with Fragile-X syndrome have met criteria for ADHD (Baumgardner, Reiss, Freund, & Abrams, 1995; Borghgraef, Fryns, Dielkens, Pyck, & Van den Berghe, 1987; Bregman, Leckman, & Ort, 1988). Hyperactivity appears to diminish before puberty or during puberty, although the attentional difficulties are likely to persist. In contrast, longitudinal studies of IQ in males suggest a decline in IQ that occurs between the ages of 6 and 15 years (Bennetto & Pennington, 1996). Although hyperactivity can be the presenting symptom of a child with Fragile-X syndrome, Hagerman (1996b) has suggested that DNA testing is only appropriate in children who have additional features typical of either pan-developmental disorder or Fragile-X syndrome. These include large or prominent ears, hand-flapping, and so on. ADHD symptoms are also found in girls with Fragile-X syndrome; however, the frequency of symptoms may not be increased over age and

IQ-matched female controls (Freund, Reiss, & Abrams, 1993; Hagerman et al., 1992).

The treatment of ADHD in Fragile-X children does not, in principle, differ from that of ADHD in the general population. A combined treatment approach that includes behavioural interventions that foster a positively reinforcing structured environment, cognitive therapy, and medication, is generally successful in reducing ADHD symptoms. The medications of first choice are the central nervous system (CNS) stimulants (e.g., methylphenidate, amphetamine, and pemoline). Other medications that have had reported success include the tricyclic antidepressants, the selective serotonin re-uptake inhibitors, clonidine, and folic acid (Hagerman, 1996a).

It is the overlap in both the symptomatology and treatment of ADHD, with and without the Fragile-X syndrome, that makes this single gene disorder a potentially valuable model for increasing our understanding of the pathophysiology of ADHD. Perhaps first and foremost, knowledge of the single gene that causes Fragile-X syndrome allows for the possibility of creating a mouse model that shares at least part of the neuropsychological profile of the human disorder. However, to understand the mouse model, as well as the phenotypic variation that is observed in the clinical disorder, an expanded discussion of the defect that results from the expansion of the triplet repeat in the promoter region of the FMR1 gene is required (de Vries et al., 1996). The expansion associated with the full-mutation allele leads to a hypermethylation of the CpG island of the FMR1 gene that is not present in the premutation and normal alleles (Bell et al., 1991; Vincent et al., 1991). Methylation of the CpG island is correlated with transcriptional inactivity of the FMR1 gene (Pieretti et al., 1991; Sutcliffe et al., 1992) and a reduction in the FMRP. The FMR1 protein is known to play an important role in RNA processing and perhaps intraneuronal localisation of the RNA. As such it is likely that the protein is involved in the maturation of brain neurons. It is the absence of the FMR1 protein, the product of the FMR1 gene, which is normally expressed in a variety of tissues and at high levels in the brain (Abitbol et al., 1993; Hinds et al., 1993; Verkerk et al., 1991), that leads to the spectrum of physical disabilities, mental retardation, and the rest of the neuropsychological profile associated with the Fragile-X mutation. Transgenic mutant mice that are no longer able to make stable FMR1 mRNA and protein as a direct result of a knockout of the Fragile-X gene (FMR1) experience a similar loss of function (Kooy et al., 1996) as that which is observed as a result of the trinucleotide expansion of the FMR1 gene in the human. Similar to males with the Fragile-X Syndrome, male knockout mice suffer from macro-orchidism, hyperactivity, and visual spatial disabilities as measured with the Morris Water Maze.

Just as the mouse model is likely to reveal new information about the pathophysiology of attention, phenotypic variation in the clinical disorder presents an opportunity to associate changes in normal brain physiology with attention deficits. Because Fragile-X mutation in the female is characterised by relative preservation of IQ in the presence of greater phenotypic variation, association studies of females may be particularly rewarding. Briefly, the variation in females could result from the size of the repeat region (Rousseau et al., 1994) and/or a variation in X chromosome inactivation (Carpenter, Leichtman, & Say, 1982; Knoll, Chudley, & Gerrard, 1984; Malmgren et al., 1992; Paul, Froster-Iskenius, Moje, & Schwinger, 1984; Rocchi et al., 1990; Rousseau, Heitz, Oberle, & Mandel, 1991a; Uchida, Freeman, Jamro, Partington, & Soltan, 1983; Uchida & Joyce, 1982). For example, females who are heterozygous for the full mutation have one normal X chromosome capable of producing a normal amount of FMRP in those cells in which the abnormal X chromosome is inactivated. Thus, by chance, individuals with identical expansions might have very different percentages of cells in the brain producing FMRP. Alternatively, female variation might be caused by differences in the length of repeats, resulting in methylation pattern changes in the promoter region (CpG island) and as a result differences in FMR1 protein production.

Reiss, Freund, Baumgardner, Abrams, and Denckla (1995) demonstrated that lymphocyte activation status of the FMR1 gene, and not repeat size, was correlated with IQ measures in girls 6–17 years of age with the full mutation. The effect of activation status was greatest for those intellectual functions most affected by the full mutation. The rationale for this work was based on the assumption that lymphocyte activation patterns (i.e., methylation patterns) reflect similar patterns in the brain. Correlations between different activation patterns of the FMR1 mutation across different tissues from human fetuses (Wohrle, Hennig, Vogel, & Steinbach, 1993) lends some support to this approach as well as findings from other studies that lymphocyte Fragile-X chromosome activation patterns are associated with cognitive outcome in other studies (McConkie-Rosell et al., 1993; Sobesky et al., 1996; Webb & Jacobs, 1990). The power of this approach may be weakened as subjects get older, because the selection process that occurs in blood favours the production of blood cells with inactivation of the Fragile-X chromosome (Rousseau, Heitz, Oberle, & Mandel, 1991b).

It is less clear how an absence of FMR1 protein in the brain leads to the neurobehavioral syndrome of Fragile-X. Increased cerebral and ventricular volumes point to a general effect of the absence of the FMR1 protein on brain development. Specific effects in the caudate nucleus, cerebellar vermis, hippocampus, and superior temporal gyrus may be superimposed on these general ones. An MRI study of the temporal lobe (Reiss, Lee, & Freund, 1994) showed that the right and left hippocampal volumes were significantly enlarged in Fragile-X syndrome males and females, and increased with age. However, although the volume of the superior temporal gyrus was abnormally large, it decreased with age. Reiss et al. suggested that the abnormally larger hippocampal regions could be the result of either prenatal interference with the normal aspects of neuronal migration, leading to an overproliferation or misalignment of neurons, or from interference with the normal pruning of selected neurons or synapses that normally occurs much later in time. Increased volume of the thalamus in females with Fragile-X has also been reported (Abrams & Reiss, 1995). In a PET study of regional glucose metabolic rate (FDG-PET) of Fragile-X subjects, increased activity was found in the caudate, thalamus, cerebellar vermis, and in the premotor cortex (Schapiro et al., 1995). The neuroimaging findings are consistent with the morphological and biochemical data obtained in rodents and in foetuses. Abnormalities in the morphology of dendritic spines of Fragile-X subjects have been reported by some investigators (Hinton, Brown, Wisniewski, & Rudelli, 1991; Jenkins et al., 1984; Rudelli et al., 1985). The highest levels of FMR1 gene expression in the mouse have been found in the granular layers of the hippocampus and cerebellum. In the human foetus particularly high expression has been observed in the neurons of the nucleus basalis magnocellularis, the pyramidal neurons of the hippocampus, thalamus, e.g., in the GABAergic neurons of the reticular nuclei, and subthalamus (Abitbol et al., 1993).

The MRI evidence of selectivity of brain effects, along with the data suggesting selectivity in FMR1 gene expression in many of the areas known to be related to attention, makes it likely that functional brain imaging studies of Fragile-X subjects during the performance of tasks requiring attention could reveal abnormalities in those structures that contribute to the deficits in attention found in Fragile-X syndrome. To gather more specific data in this regard we have initiated a PET study of women with the FMR1 premutation and full mutation, which will measure brain regional functional activities in the resting state, and whilst they were doing a CPT. The neuroanatomical determinants of CPT that can be assessed by the FDG-PET procedure have been reported and include the frontal cortex, cingulate, and basal ganglia (Cohen, Semple, Gross, King, & Nordahl, 1992). The increased variance of the neuropsychological syndrome in females should allow us to more readily evaluate whether any regional metabolic differences found between the patients and controls are related to general intellectual function and/or CPT performance.

Although the approaches discussed here relate to single-gene studies of conditions with some phenotypic feature of ADHD, they also provide some insight into the pathophysiological processes involved in attention, and models that might further research and understanding of ADHD.

## REFERENCES

Abitbol, M., Menini, C., Delezoide, A.L., Rhyner, T., Vekemans, M., & Mallet, J. (1993). Nucleus basalis magnocellularis and hippocampus are the major sites of FMR-1 expression in the human fetal brain. *Nature Genetics, 4*, 147–153.

Abrams, M., & Reiss, A.L. (1995). Quantitative brain imaging studies of fragile X syndrome. *Developmental Brain Dysfunction, 8*, 187–198.

American Psychiatric Association. (1987). *Diagnostic and statistical manual of mental disorders* (3rd ed.-revised). Washington, DC: American Psychiatric Association.

American Psychiatric Association. (1994) *Diagnostic and statistical manual of mental disorders* (4th ed.). Washington, DC: American Psychiatric Association

Baumgardner, T.L., Reiss, A.L., Freund, L.S., & Abrams, M.T. (1995). Specification of the neurobehavioral phenotype in males with fragile X syndrome. *Pediatrics, 95,* 744–752.

Bell, M.V., Hirst, M.C., Nakahori, Y., MacKinnon, R.N., Roche, A., Flint, T.J., Jacobs, P.A., Tommerup, N., Tranebjaerg, L., Froster-Iskenius, U., Kerr, B., Turner, G., Undenbaum, R.H., Winter, R., Pembrey, M.E., Thibodeaus, S., & Davies, K.E. (1991). Physical mapping across the fragile X: Hypermethylation and clinical expression of the fragile X syndrome. *Cell, 64,* 861–866.

Bennetto, L., & Pennington, B.F. (1996). The neuropsychology of fragile X syndrome. In R.J. Hagerman & A.C. Cronister (Eds.), *Fragile X syndrome: Diagnosis, treatment and research* (pp. 211–248). Baltimore: Johns Hopkins University Press.

Biederman, J., Faraone, S.V., Keenan, K., Benjamin, J., Krifcher, B., Moore, C., Sprich-Buckminster, S., Ugaglia, K., Jellinek, M.S., Steingard, R., Spencer, T.J., Norman, D., Kolodny, R., Kraus, I., Perrin, J., Keller, M., & Tsuang, M.T. (1992). Further evidence for family-genetic risk factors in attention deficit hyperactivity disorder: Patterns of comorbidity in probands and relatives in psychiatrically and pediatrically referred samples. *Archives of General Psychiatry, 9,* 728–738.

Borghgraef, M., Fryns, J.P., Dielkens, A., Pyck, K., & Van den Berghe, H. (1987). Fragile (X) syndrome: a study of the psychological profile in 23 prepubertal patients. *Clinical Genetics, 32,* 179–186.

Bregman, J.D., Leckman, J.F., & Ort, S.I. (1988). Fragile X syndrome: Genetic predisposition to psychopathology. *Journal of Autism and Developmental Disorders, 18,* 343–354.

Carpenter, N.J., Leichtman, L.G., & Say, B. (1982). Fragile X-linked mental retardation. *American Journal of Diseases of Childhood, 136,* 392–398.

Cohen, R.M., Semple, W.E., Gross, M., King, A.C., & Nordahl, T.E. (1992). The metabolic brain pattern of sustained auditory discrimination. *Experimental Brain Research, 92,* 165–172.

Cook, E.H., Stein, M.A., Krasowski, M.D., Cox, N.J., Olkon, D.M., Kieffer, J.E., & Leventhal, B.L. (1995). Association of attention-deficit disorder and the dopamine transporter gene. *American Journal of Human Genetics, 56,* 993–998.

Crowe, S.F., & Hay, D.A. (1990). Neuropsychological dimensions of the fragile X syndrome: Support for a non-dominant hemisphere dysfunction hypothesis. *Neuropsychologia, 28,* 9–16.

Deutsch, C.K., Matthysse, S., Swanson, J.M., & Farkas, L.G. (1990). Genetic latent structure analysis of dysmorphology in attention deficit disorder. *Journal of the American Academy of Child and Adolescent Psychiatry, 29,* 189–194.

de Vries, B.B., Jansen, C.C., Duits, A.A., Verheij, C., Willemsen, R., van Hemel, J.O., van den Ouweland, A.M., Niermeijer, M.F., Oostra, B.A., & Halley, D.J. (1996). Variable FMR1 gene methylation of large expansions leads to variable phenotype in three males from one fragile X family. *Journal of Medical Genetics, 33,* 1007–1010.

Elia J., Gulotta C., Rose S., Marin, G., & Rapoport, J.L. (1994). Thyroid function and Attention-Deficit Hyperactivity Disorder. *Journal of the American Academy of Child and Adolescent Psychiatry, 33,* 169–172.

Ernst, M., Liebenauer L.L., King, A.C., Fitzgerald, G.A., Cohen, R.M., & Zametkin, A.J. (1994). Reduced brain metabolism in hyperactive girls. *Journal of the American Academy of Child and Adolescent Psychiatry*, *33*, 858–868.

Faraone, S.V., Biederman, J., Chen, W.J., Krifcher, B. Lehman, B., Keenan, K., Moore, C., Sprich, S., & Tsuang, M.T. (1992). Segregation analysis of attention deficit-hyperactivity disorder: evidence for single gene transmission. *Psychiatric Genetics*, *2*, 257–275.

Freund, L., Abrams, M., & Reiss, A.L. (1991). Brain and behavior correlates of the fragile X syndrome. *Current Opinions in Psychiatry*, *4*, 667–673.

Freund, L.S., & Reiss, A.L. (1991). Cognitive profiles associated with the fra(X) syndrome in males and females. *American Journal of Medical Genetics*, *38*, 542–547.

Freund, L.S., Reiss, A.L., & Abrams, M.T. (1993). Psychiatric disorders associated with fragile X in the young female. *Pediatrics*, *91*, 321–329.

Hagerman, R.J. (1996a). Medical follow-up and pharmacotherapy. In R.J. Hagerman & A.C. Cronister (Eds.), *Fragile X syndrome: Diagnosis, treatment and research* (2nd ed., pp. 283–331). Baltimore: Johns Hopkins University Press.

Hagerman, R.J. (1996b). Physical and behavioral phenotype. In R.J. Hagerman & A.C. Cronister (Eds.), *Fragile X syndrome: Diagnosis, treatment and research* (2nd ed., pp. 3–87). Baltimore: Johns Hopkins University Press.

Hagerman, R.J., Jackson, C., Amiri, K., Silverman, A.C., O'Connor, R., & Sobesky, W.E. (1992). Fragile X girls: Physical and neurocognitive status and outcome. *Pediatrics*, *89*, 395–400.

Hauser, P., Zametkin, A.J, Martinez, P., Vitiello, B., Matochik, J.A., Mixon, A.J., & Weintraub, B.D. (1993). Attention deficit-hyperactivity disorder in people with generalized resistance to thyroid hormone. *New England Journal of Medicine*, *328*, 997–1001.

Hinds, H.L., Ashley, C.T., Sutcliffe, J.S., Nelson, D.L., Warren, S.T., Housman, D.E., & Schalling, M. (1993). Tissue specific expression of FMR1 provides evidence for a functional role in fragile X syndrome. *Nature Genetics*, *3*, 36–43.

Hinton, V.J., Brown, W.T., Wisniewski, K., & Rudelli, R.D. (1991). Analysis of neocortex in three males with the fragile X syndrome. *American Journal of Medical Genetics*, *41*, 289–294.

Jenkins, E.C., Brown, W.T., Brooks, J., Duncan, C.J., Rudelli, R.D., & Wisniewski, H.M. (1984). Experience with prenatal fragile X. *American Journal of Medical Genetics*, *17*, 215–239.

Knoll, J.H., Chudley, A.E., & Gerrard, J.W. (1984). Fragile (X) X-linked mental retardation: II. Frequency and replication patttern of fragile (X)(q28) in heterozygotes. *American Journal of Human Genetics*, *36*, 640–645.

Kooistra L., van der Meere J.J., Vulsma T., & Kalverboer, A.F. (1996). Sustained attention problems in children with early-treated congenital hypothyroidism. *Acta Paediatrica*, *85*, 425–429.

Kooy, R.F., D'Hooge, R., Reyniers, E., Bakker, C.E., Nagels, G., De Boulle, K., Storm, K., Clincke, G., De Deyn, P.P., Oostra, B.A., & Willems, P.J. (1996). Transgenic mouse model for the fragile X syndrome. *American Journal of Medical Genetics*, *64*, 241–245.

Kremer, E.J., Pritchard, M., Lynch, M., Yu , S., Holman, K., Baker, E., Warren, S.T., Schlessinger, D., Sutherland, G.R., & Richards, R.I. (1991). Mapping of DNA instability at the fragile X to a trinucleotide repeat sequence p(CCG)n. *Science*, *252*, 1711–1714.

La Spada, A.R. (1997). Trinucleotide repeat instability: Genetic features and molecular mechanisms. *Brain Pathololgy*, *7*, 943–963.

LaHoste, G.F., Swanson, J.M., & Wigal, S.B. (1996). Dopamine D4 receptor gene polymorphism is associated with attention deficit hyperactivity disorder. *Molecular Psychiatry*, *1*, 121–124

Leonard, C.M., Martinez, P., Weintraub, B.D., & Hauser, P. (1995). Magnetic resonance imaging of cerebral anomalies in subjects with resistance to thyroid hormone. *American Journal of Medical Genetics*, *60*, 238–243

Malmgren, H., Steen-Bondeson, M.L., Gustavson, K.H., Seemanova, E., Holmgren, G., Oberle, I., Mandel, J.L., Pettersson, U., & Dahl, N. (1992). Methylation and mutation patterns in the fragile X syndrome. *American Journal of Medical Genetics*, *43*, 268–278.

Matochik, J.A., Zametkin, A.J., Cohen, R.M., Hauser, P., & Weintraub, B.D. (1996). Abnormalities in sustained attention and anterior cingulate metabolism in subjects with resistance to thyroid hormone. *Brain Research*, *723*, 23–28.

Mazzocco, M.M., Pennington, B.F., & Hagerman, R.J. (1993). The neurocognitive phenotype of female carriers of fragile X: Additional evidence for specificity. *Journal of Developmental and Behavioural Pediatrics*, *14*, 328–335.

McConkie-Rosell, A., Lachiewicz, A.M., Spiridigliozzi, G.A., Tarleton, J., Schoenwald, S., Phelan, M.C., Goonewardena, P., Ding, X., & Brown, W.T. (1993). Evidence that methylation of the FMR-1 locus is responsible for variable phenotypic expression of the fragile X syndrome. *American Journal of Human Genetics*, *53*, 800–809.

Paul, J., Froster-Iskenius, U., Moje, W., & Schwinger, E. (1984). Heterozygous female cariers of the marker X chromosome: IQ estimation and replication status of fra(X)(q). *Human Genetics*, *66*, 344–346.

Paulson, H.L., & Fischbeck, K.H. (1996). Trinucleotide repeats in neurogenetic disorders. *Annual Review of Neuroscience*, *19*, 79–107.

Pieretti, M., Zhang, F.P., Fu, Y.H., Warren, S.T., Oostra, B.A., Caskey, C.T., & Nelson, D.L. (1991). Absence of expression of the FMR-1 gene in fragile X syndrome. *Cell*, *66*, 817–822.

Prouty, L.A., Rogers, R.C., Stevenson, R.E., Dean, J.H., Palmer, K.K., Simensen, R.J., Coston, G.N., & Schwartz, C.E. (1988). Fragile X syndrome: Growth, development, and intellectual function. *American Journal of Medical Genetics*, *30*, 123–142.

Reddy, P.S., & Housman, D.E. (1997). The complex pathology of trinucleotide repeats. *Current Opinion in Cell Biology*, *9*, 364–372.

Refetoff, S., Weiss, R.E., & Usala, S.J. (1993). The syndromes of resistance to thyroid hormone. *Endocrine Reviews*, *14*(3), 348–399.

Refetoff, S. (1990). Resistance to thyroid hormone. *Thyroid Today*, *13*, 1–11

Refetoff, S., DeWind, L.T., & DeGroot, L.J. (1967).Familial syndrome combining deaf-mutism, stuppled epiphyses, goiter and abnormally high PBI: possible target organ refractoriness to thyroid hormone. *Journal of Clinical Endocrinology and Metabolism*, *27*,279–294.

Reiss, A.L., & Freund, L. (1990). Fragile X syndrome. *Biological Psychiatry*, *27*, 223–240.

Reiss, A.L., Freund, L.S., Baumgardner, T.L., Abrams, M.T., & Denckla, M.B. (1995). Contribution of the FMR1 gene mutation to human intellectual dysfunction. *Nature Genetics*, *11*(3), 331–334.

Reiss, A.L., Lee, J., & Freund, L. (1994). Neuroanatomy of fragile X syndrome: The temporal lobe. *Neurology, 44,* 1317–1324.

Rocchi, M., Archidiacono, N., Rinaldi, A., Filippi, G., Bartolucci, G., Fancello, G.S., & Siniscalco, M. (1990). Mental retardation in heterozygotes for the fragile-X mutation: Evidence in favor of an X inactivation-dependent effect. *American Journal of Human Genetics, 46,* 738–743.

Rousseau, F., Heitz, D., Oberle, I., & Mandel, J.-L. (1991a). Selection in blood cells from female carriers of the fragile X syndrome: Inverse correlation between age and proportion of active of active X chromosomes carrying the full mutation. *Journal of Medical Genetics, 28,* 830–836.

Rousseau, F., Heitz, D., Oberle, I., & Mandel, J.-L. (1991b). Selection in blood cells from female carriers of the fragile X syndrome: Inverse correlation between age and proportion of active X chromosomes carrying the full mutation. *Journal of Medical Genetics, 28,* 830–836.

Rousseau, F., Heitz, D., Tarleton,, J., MacPherson, J., Malmgren, H., Dahl, N., Barnicost, A., Mathew, C., Mornet, E., Teuada, I., Maddalena, A., Spiegel, R., Schinzel, A., Marcos, J.A.G., Schorderet, D.F., Schaap, T., Maccioni, L., Russo, S., Jacobs, P.A., Schwartz, C.E., & Mandel, J.L. (1994). A multicenter study on genotype–phenotype correlations in the fragile X syndrome, using direct diagnosis with probe StB12.3: the first 2,253 cases. *Journal of Medical Genetics, 55,* 225–237.

Rovet, J., & Alvarez, M. (1996). Thyroid hormone and attention in school-age children with congential hypothyroidism. *Association for Child Psychology and Psychiatry, 37,* 579–585.

Rudelli, R.D., Brown, W.T., Wisniewski, K., Jenkins, E.C., Laure-Kamionowska, M., Connell, F., & Wisniewski, H.M. (1985). Adult fragile X syndrome: Clinico-neuropathologic findings. *Acta Neuropathologica, 67,* 289–95.

Schapiro, M.B., Murphy, D.G., Hagerman, R.J., Azari, N.P., Alexander, G.E., Miezejeski, C.M., Hinton, V.J., Horwitz, B., Haxby, J.V., Kumar, A., White, B., & Grady, C.L. (1995). Adult fragile X syndrome: Neuropsychology, brain anatomy, and metabolism. *American Journal of Medical Genetics, 60,* 480–493.

Sobesky, W.E., Taylor, A.K., Pennington, B.F., Bennetto, L., Porter, D., Riddle, J., & Hagerman, R.J. (1996). Molecular/clinical correlations in females with fragile X. *American Journal of Medical Genetics, 64,* 340–345.

Spencer, T.J., Biederman, J., Wilens, T.E., Guite, J., & Harding, M. (1995). ADHD and thyroid abnormalities: A research note. *Journal of Child Psychology and Psychiatry, 36,* 879–885.

Stevenson, J., Pennington, B.F., Gilger, J.W., DeFries, J.C., & Gillis, J.J. (1993). Hyperactivity and spelling disability: Testing for shared genetic aetiology. *Journal of Child Psychology and Psychiatry, 34,* 1137–1152.

Sutcliffe, J.S., Nelson, D.L., Zhang, F.P., Pieretti, M., Caskey, C.T., Saxe, D., & Warren, S.T. (1992). DNA methylation represses FMR1 transcription in fragile X syndrome. *Human Molecular Genetics, 1,* 397–400.

Tsuji, S. (1997). Molecular genetics of triplet repeats: Unstable expansion of triplet repeats as a new mechanism for neurodegenerative diseases. *Internal Medicine, 36,* 3–8.

Uchida, I.A., Freeman, V., Jamro, H., Partington, M., & Soltan, H. (1983). Additional evidence for fragile X activity in heterozygous carriers. *American Journal of Human Genetics, 35,* 861–868.

Uchida, I.A., & Joyce, E.M. (1982). Activity of the fragile X in heterozygous carriers. *American Journal of Human Genetics, 34*, 286–293.

Usala, S., Bale, A.E., Gesundheit, N., Weinberger, C., Lash, R.W., Wondisford, F.E., McBride, O.W., & Weintraub, B.D. (1988) Tight linkage between the syndrome of generalized thyroid hormone resistance and the human -cerAB gene. *Molecular Endocrinology, 2*, 1217–1220

Verkerk, A.J., Pieretti, M., Sutcliffe, J.S., Fu, Y.H., Kuhl, D.P., Pizzuti, A., Reiner, O., Richards, S., Victoria, M.F., Zhang, F.P., Eussen, B.E., VanOmmen, G., Blonden, L., Riggins, G.J., Chastain, J.L., Kunst, C.B., Galjaard, H., Caskey, C.T., Oostra, B.A., & Warren, S.T. (1991). Identification of a gene (FMR-1) containing a CGG repeat coincident with a breakpoint cluster region exhibiting length variation in fragile X syndrome. *Cell, 65*, 905–914.

Vincent, A., Heitz, D., Petit, C., Kretz, C., Oberle, I., & Mandel, J.L. (1991). Abnormal pattern detected in fragile-X patients by pulsed-field gel electrophoresis. *Nature, 349*, 624–626.

Volkow, N.D., Ding, Y., Fowler, J.S., Wang, G.J., Logan, T., Gatley, S.J., Schlyer, D.J., & Pappas, N. (1995). A new PET ligand for the dopamine transporter: Studies in the human brain. *Journal of Nuclear Medicine, 36*, 2162–2168.

Waldman, I.D., Rowe, D.C., Abramowitz, A., Kozel, S., Mohr, J.H., Sherman, S.L., Cleveland, H.H., Sanders, M.L., Gard, J.M., & Stever, C. (1998). Association and linkage of the dopmaine transporter and attention deficit hyperactivity disorder in children: Heterogeneity owing to diagnostic sybtype and severity. *American Journal of Human Genetics, 63*, 1767–1776.

Warren, S.T., & Ashley, C.T., Jr. (1995). Triplet repeat expansion mutations: The example of fragile X syndrome. *Annual Review of Neuroscience, 18*, 77–99.

Webb, T., & Jacobs, P.A. (1990). Fragile Xq27.3 in female heterozygotes for the Martin-Bell syndrome. *Journal of Medical Genetics, 27*, 627–631.

Weiss, R.E., Stein, M., Duck, S., Chyna, B., Phillips, W., O'Brien, T., Gutermuth, L., & Refetoff, S. (1994). Low intelligence but not attention deficit hyperactivity disorder is associated with resistance to thyroid hormone caused by mutation R316H in the thyroid hormone receptor gene. *Journal of Clinical Endocrinology and Metabolism, 78*, 525–1528.

Weiss, R.E., Stein, M., Trommer, B., & Refetoff, S. (1993). Attention-deficit hyperactivity disorder and thyroid function. *Journal of Pediatrics, 123*, 539–545.

Wohrle, D., Hennig, I., Vogel, W., & Steinbach, P. (1993). Mitotic stability of fragile X mutations in differentiated cells indicates early post-conceptional trinucleotide repeat expansion. *Nature Genetics, 4*, 140–142.

Zametkin, A.J., & Liotta, W. (1997). The future of brain imaging in child psychiatry. *Child Adolescent Psychiatric Clinics of North America, 6*, 447–460.

Zametkin, A.J., Nordahl, T.E., Gross, M., King, A.C., Semple, W.E., Rumsey, J., Hamburger, S., & Cohen, R.M. (1990). Cerebral glucose metabolism in adults with hyperactivity of childhood onset. *New England Journal of Medicine, 323*, 1361–1366.

# 10  Molecular genetics of ADHD

*Cathy Barr, James Swanson and*
*James Kennedy*

## INTRODUCTION

Attention Deficit Hyperactivity Disorder (ADHD) is considered the most prevalent mental health disorder of childhood. Its prevalence depends on the diagnostic criteria and procedures used for assessment, and variations in classification methods have resulted in a 20-fold (1% to 20%) difference in reports in the literature (Swanson, Sergeant, et al., 1998).

A large cross-national difference in administrative prevalence (recognition rate) exists, but when the same criteria and methods are used, similar values for epidemiological prevalence have been reported. For strict criteria of severe developmentally inappropriate levels of inattention, impulsivity, and overactivity, confirmed by two sources to produce impairment at home and at school, the prevalence is about 3% of the school-aged population.

Prospective follow-up studies have documented poor outcome in education (years of school completed), social adjustment (arrest rate), and other important areas of functioning in adolescence and adulthood (Mannuzza, Klein, Bessler, Malloy, & LaPadula, 1998; Satterfield, Swanson, Schell, & Lee, 1994). ADHD is also associated with a variety of co-occurring disorders. These include Conduct Disorder, learning disability, depression, anxiety disorder, and oppositional defiant disorder, and in clinical samples more that half of the cases have one or more comorbid disorders (Multimodal Treatment Study of Children with ADHD; (MTA Cooperative Group, 1999). Multiple negative impacts on family, academic, social and occupational functioning demand treatment. The primary treatments are with stimulant medication and behaviour modification (Arnold et al., 1997), but these treatments are considered to be symptomatic treatments intended to provide temporary control of symptoms and typically not to normalise behaviour. The long-term benefits or risks of treatment are unknown but are now under investigation (MTA Cooperative Group, 1999).

The use of stimulant drugs (methylphenidate or amphetamine) is more widespread in North America than in other geographical locations (WHO, 1993). Despite 50 years of clinical experiences and research (see Wigal et al.,

1999) this pharmacological intervention is still controversial (Greenhill, Halperin, & Abikoff, 1999; Greenhill & Osmon, 2000). One reason for the controversy is the lack of a confirmed biological basis of the disorder that might provide a rationale for pharmacological intervention (Swanson & Castellanos, 1998).

Biological bases for ADHD have been proposed. One of the earliest and most prominent of these being the dopamine (DA) hypothesis of ADHD (Levy, 1991; Wender, Epstein, Kopin, & Gordon 1971). This theory holds that the mesolimbic and nigrostriatal dopamine pathways in the brain are underactive, resulting in abnormal functioning of cortical-striatal-thalamic loops involved in the control of sensory-motor and cognitive brain functions (Castellanos, 1997).

This theory is based on a site of action of stimulant drugs, which bind to the dopamine transporter protein and inhibit re-uptake of synaptic dopamine (Volkow et al., 1998), as well as stimulate release of dopamine from presynaptic dopamine terminals in the basal ganglia and frontal cortex (Patrick, Mueller, Gualtieri, & Breese, 1987). These dopamine agonist effects have suggested that ADHD may be the consequence of a dopamine deficit, which is corrected by stimulant medication. Acquired brain lesions (e.g., brain damage during foetal development, Lou, 1996; and structure of dopamine receptors, e.g., allelic variation in dopamine genes, Swanson, Sergeant, et al., 1998; Swanson, Sunohara, et al., 1998) have been suggested as biological aetiologies for these abnormal brain functions that produce hyperactivity, inattention, and impulsivity (the clinical symptoms of ADHD). In this chapter, we will discuss methods for the investigation of molecular genetic bases of ADHD. Family (e.g., Biederman et al., 1992; Faraone, Biederman, & Milberger, 1994), adoption (e.g., Deutsch et al., 1982), and twin (for review see Thapar, Holmes, Poulton, & Harrington, 1999) studies agree that genetic factors play an important role in the aetiology of ADHD (Levy, Barr, & Sunohara, 1998; Thapar et al., 1999).

All twin studies to date have supported a substantial genetic influence contributing to ADHD, or the components of ADHD (Thapar et al., 1999). Early studies examined the concordance in monozygotic (MZ) twins compared to dizygotic (DZ) twins and observed a higher concordance in the former. Large MZ to DZ twin concordance differences have been reported for a number of twin studies and this is most striking in the two early studies (Lopez, 1965; Willerman, 1973). In particular, the Willerman study found no concordant DZ twins. These extreme MZ–DZ differences may have been the result of small sample sizes in these two studies. However low DZ concordance has also been observed in larger twins studies. Preconceived ideas of greater MZ than DZ twin similarity (particularly in maternal raters) may also explain the inflated the MZ to DZ ratios.

The heritability estimates from twin studies range from 0.54 to 0.91 (Thapar et al., 1999). This wide range in heritability estimates is influenced by diagnostic differences, the person rating the behaviours—which is related to the situation in which the behaviour is observed—and sibling competition effects (Thapar et al., 1999).

The twin study of Goodman and Stevenson (1989a, b) estimated a heritability of 64% for broadly defined hyperactivity based on a concordance rate for ADHD of 51% for same-sex monozygotic twins and 33% for dizygotic twins. MZ twins were found to be more alike than same-sex DZ pairs on parent and teacher ratings of hyperactivity and on objective measures of attentiveness. The common environmental effects appeared to be less substantial, accounting for between 0% and 30% of the variance suggesting that family resemblances on these measures appear to owe more to shared genes than shared environment (Goodman, 1989a, b).

Gillis, Gilger, Pennington, and DeFries (1992), used a basic regression model for the analysis of selected twin data from reading disabled twins with at least one of the twins having ADHD (37 MZ twins and 37 DZ twins). Seventy-nine per cent of MZ twins and thirty-two per cent of DZ twins were concordant for ADHD, suggesting that ADHD is highly heritable in this comorbid group. Adjusting the scores for either IQ or reading performance difference did not substantially change parameter estimates (Gillis et al., 1992).

Using a sample of 91 pairs of MZ and 105 pairs of same-sex DZ twins, Stevenson (1992) showed significant evidence for genetic contributions to the components of ADHD; i.e. high activity levels and poor attention abilities.

A significant genetic influence on competence in school, and on all areas of problem behaviour, was reported by Edelbrock, Rende, Plomin, and Thompson (1995). They used the Child Behavior Checklist (CBCL) in a sample of 99 MZ and 82 same-sex DZ twins. A correlation of .68 for MZ and .29 for DZ was found for attention problems.

Thapar, Hervas, and McGuffin (1995), systematically ascertained a population-based sample of twin pairs between 8 and 16 years of age. Hyperactivity scores were found to be substantially heritable based on maternal-rated hyperactivity scores. In addition, this study supported the importance of sibling interaction effects in hyperactivity (Thapar et al., 1995).

Gjone, Stevenson, and Sundet (1996) examined parental ratings of the CBCL in five Norwegian cohorts of same-sex twins (526 MZ and 389 DZ pairs). The results suggest substantial genetic influence on attention problems across sex, age, and severity. Heritability estimates ranged from 0.73 in boys aged 5 to 9 years, to 0.76 in girls of the same age range.

The largest population-based twin cohort studied to date consisted of 1938 families with twin and siblings aged 4 to 12 years (Levy, Hay, McStephen, Wood, & Waldman, 1997). Heritability estimates from regression techniques ranged from 0.75 to 0.91, which was robust across familial relationships. The heritability of ADHD in twins where at least one met criteria for ADHD showed no significant difference regardless of whether ADHD was treated as a trait or a category. These findings suggest that ADHD is an extreme behaviour that varies genetically throughout the entire population, rather than a disorder with discrete determinants.

In order to determine whether the symptoms of ADHD were continuously distributed or categorically discrete, Hudziak et al. (1998) performed latent class and factor analysis on data on ADHD symptoms. They used a large general population sample of 1549 female twin pairs. Latent class and factor analyses were consistent with the presence of separate continuous domains of inattention, hyperactivity-impulsivity, and combined problems with attention and hyperactivity-impulsivity. The results from this study suggest that *DSM-IV* ADHD subtypes can be thought of as existing on separate continua of inattention, hyperactivity-impulsivity, and combined type problems.

Individuals with ADHD are frequently diagnosed with comorbid reading disabilities and/or language impairment (Humphries, Koltun, Malone, & Roberts, 1994; Tannock & Brown, in press; Tannock & Schachar, 1996). However, the estimate of the frequency varies between 10% (August & Holmes, 1984) and 92% (Silver, 1981).

The genetic relationship between these two disorders is unclear and surprisingly has not been extensively investigated. The possibility of a common genetic aetiology for the reported association of ADHD and reading disabilities was examined in a study of reading-disabled twin pairs (Gilger, Pennington, & DeFries, 1992). Substantial heritability was evident in their sample for ADHD (81% for MZ and 29% for DZ twins) and reading disabilities (84% for MZ and 64% for DZ twins). However the cross-concordance for the combination of reading disabilities and ADHD was low (44% and 30% for MZ and DZ twins, respectively), and was interpreted as evidence for a genetically mediated subtype of reading disabilities—ADHD.

Despite the intensive investigation from twin and family studies on ADHD, and the genetic relationship between the ADHD and comorbid disorders, these studies do not identify specific genes responsible for the susceptibility to these disorders. Recently, molecular genetic studies have been conducted to investigate the molecular genetic basis of ADHD. In this chapter, we will explain some of the basic terms and methods used in this effort to find specific genes that contribute to ADHD.

## CHARACTERISATION OF THE ADHD PHENOTYPE FOR GENETIC STUDIES

The phenotype (the observable appearance of the genotype) of ADHD is very complex and the genetics will probably prove to be likewise. One of the primary concerns for a genetic study is to correctly classify an individual into a group whose members share characteristics. This is in order to enhance the possibility of detecting a gene that is involved in determining that characteristic or trait. This trait, or phenotype, may be as simple as wrinkled versus smooth peas (as studied by Mendel), or as complex as the syndrome of ADHD.

Significant problems exist in the definition of the ADHD phenotype. First, the *DSM* rationale purposely ignores aetiology, and is based only on phenomenology, so there is no overt attempt to define phenotypes of disorders with genetic bases. Second, the *DSM* revision process generates changing phenotypes of disorders. The ADHD phenotype has changed three times over the past 20 years, as the *DSM* manuals and criteria were revised in 1980 (*DSM-III*; American Psychiatric Association), 1987 (*DSM-III-R*; APA), and 1994 (*DSM-IV*; APA). Third, the *DSM* phenotype is not identical to the hyperkinetic phenotype defined by the *International Classification of Diseases* (*ICD*; World Health Organisation) process. *DSM* revisions have been paralleled by changes in the *ICD* diagnostic manuals in 1979 (*ICD-9*; WHO) and 1992 (*ICD-10*; WHO), which use the label Hyperkinetic Disorder (HKD). Despite some convergence in specific symptoms, the decision rules about subtypes of the disorder and comorbid conditions still differ (Swanson & Castellanos, 1998; Swanson, Sergeant, et al., 1998). The two current diagnostic manuals (*DSM-IV*; APA, 1994 and *ICD-10*; WHO, 1992) now specify the same 18 symptoms for ADHD and Hyperkinetic Disorder. However, the "decision rules" differ across settings and cultures. For example, *DSM-IV* allows multiple subtypes based on partial syndrome, but *ICD-10* does not, and *DSM-IV* encourages diagnosis of many comorbid disorders. The *ICD-10* lists one specific comorbid condition (Hyperkinetic Conduct Disorder) and discourages the rest. The complex rules for *DSM-IV* and *ICD-10* are provided in Table 10.1. The various combinations of inclusion criteria based on symptom domains (i.e., combined, inattentive, and hyperactive/impulsive subtypes) and comorbid conditions (i.e., the externalising disorders of conduct and oppositional defiant disorder, and the internalising disorders such as anxiety and depression) produce 12 possible phenotypes of ADHD (see Table 10.1). Fourth, some genetic studies use rating of behaviours rather than diagnosis of disorder to define the phenotype (see for example Gjone et al., 1996; Waldman et al., 1998).

There is no consensus on which of these variants of the ADHD phenotype should be accepted for biological studies of ADHD. For most studies of brain imaging, a refined phenotype (ADHD—Combined type without serious comorbidities other than Oppositional Defiant Disorder (ODD) has been used, which is close to the definition of HKD in *ICD-10*. A similar acceptance of a refined phenotype of ADHD has not been characteristic of genetic studies of ADHD.

Once a phenotype is defined that can reliably be identified across individuals, a DNA laboratory can test genes of interest to investigate their role in determining the presence of the phenotype. For psychiatric disorders, the approach has generally been categorical in that an individual is considered as either affected, unaffected or of unknown status. As discussed earlier for ADHD/HKD, there are many complexities in defining "affected" versus "unaffected" status—including deciding upon the criteria by which an individual will be categorised, and determining whether a particular person meets these criteria. For psychiatric disorders, the criteria for classifying an

Table 10.1 ADHD subgroups based on DSM-IV and ICD-10 criteria[1]

| Symptom subtype | Comorbidity | | DSM-IV[4] | | ICD-10 | |
| | Externalising[2,6] | Internalising[3,5] | Label | Codes[8,9] | Label[7] | Codes[10] |
|---|---|---|---|---|---|---|
| Consensus subgroups | | | | | | |
| Combined | -CD/ODD | -A/M | ADHDc | 314.1/F90.0 | HKDaa | F90.0 |
| Combined | +CD/ODD | -A/M | ADHDc | 314.1/F90.0 | HKDcd | F90.1 |
| Nonconsensus subgroups | | | | | | |
| Combined | -CD/ODD | +A/M | ADHDc | 314.1/F90.0 | A or M | F3 or F4 |
| Combined | +CD/ODD | +A/M | ADHDc | 314.1/F90.0 | Mixed | F92 |
| Hyper/Imp | -CD/ODD | -A/M | ADHDh | 314.1/F90.0 | Other | F98.8 |
| Hyper/Imp | +CD/ODD | -A/M | ADHDh | 314.1/F90.0 | CD/ODD | F91 |
| Hyper/Imp | -CD/ODD | +A/M | ADHDh | 314.1/F90.0 | A or M | F3 or F4 |
| Hyper/Imp | +CD/ODD | +A/M | ADHDh | 314.1/F90.0 | Mix C/E | F92 |
| Inattentive | -CD/ODD | -A/M | ADHDi | 314.0/F98.8 | Other | F98.8 |
| Inattentive | +CD/ODD | -A/M | ADHDi | 314.0/F98.8 | CD/ODD | F91 |
| Inattentive | -CD/ODD | +A/M | ADHDi | 314.0/F98.8 | A/M | F3 or F4 |
| Inattentive | +CD/ODD | +A/M | ADHDi | 314.0/F98.8 | Mix C/E | F92 |

Notes:
1 Minor differences in criteria for total and diversity of symptoms from hyperactive and impulsive subdomains.
2 Conduct Disorder or Oppositional Defiant Disorder (CD/ODD).
3 Anxiety, Mood, or Pervasive Developmental disorders (A/M).
4 DSM-IV guidelines recommend exclusion if ADHD symptoms are present "only at home" or have "late onset".
5 Unanticipated in the Clinical Criteria (1992) and excluded in the Research Criteria (1993) of ICD-10.
6 If criteria for both CD/ODD and HKD are met in ICD-10, the HKD diagnosis takes precedence.
7 "aa" refers to disorder of attention and activity; "cd" refers to Conduct Disorder or Oppositional Defiant Disorder.
8 In DSM-IV ICD-9 codes are used in the body.
9 ICD-10 codes are listed in an appendix of DSM-IV, but not all listed codes are consistent with the ICD-10.
10 By international treaty, by the year 2000 ICD-10 codes should be implemented in the USA.

individual as affected are often the *DSM* or *ICD* criteria, but it is important to consider that this "gold standard" is not based on the underlying genetic mechanism. Despite acknowledged limitations, the current *DSM* or *ICD* ADHD phenotypes provide reliability of diagnosis, and thus can be used successfully to discriminate individuals with a genetic susceptibility. However, other approaches may also be used. For example, Morton and Frith (1995) have used a causal modelling approach to define possibilities of differences at neural, cognitive, and behavioural levels of analysis (see Figure 10.1). They lay out the possibilities in this causal model framework, and describe three types of disorder. These are the "A" type, with one neural cause but multiple behavioural manifestations, the "V" type, with multiple neural causes but one behavioural manifestation, and the "X" type, with multiple neural causes of a single cognitive deficit that produces multiple behavioural manifestations. They argue that the cognitive level of analysis may be the key for defining the phenotype of a disorder such as ADHD, and they propose that the "X" type may best describe a disorder as complicated as ADHD.

A person who expresses the behavioural phenotype and who does not have the risk alleles is considered to be a phenocopy (an individual whose affected

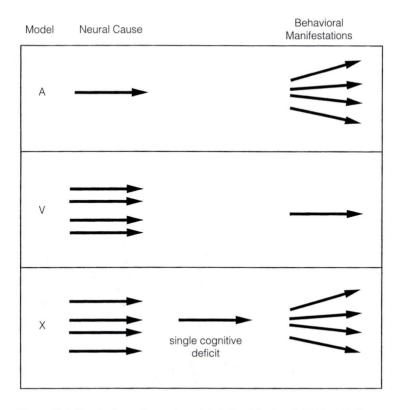

*Figure 10.1* Illustration of causal models (after Morton & Frith, 1995).

status is due to nongenetic factors). Thus, some individuals have the same disorder but have different aetiologies, so an "X" model would apply. To give a more concrete example for ADHD, a child meeting criteria for the behaviour phenotype of ADHD combined type, with comorbid ODD, may have acquired the symptoms due to prenatal exposure to risk factors, and foetal maldevelopment of brain regions involved in executive function. Another child who manifests the complex phenotype and executive function difficulties may have acquired the phenotype due to variation in dopamine genes.

Additionally, individuals that carry ADHD risk alleles may not express the behaviour symptoms of hyperactivity or inattention. From the less than 100% concordance in MZ twins (for a review see Thapar et al., 1999), it is evident that an individual may carry the genes and not show the behaviour. The genetic expression is presumed to be influenced by one or more risk or protective factors in the environment. The percentage of people who carry the risk alleles of a susceptibly gene, and who show the phenotype, is termed the penetrance. Those who carry the risk allele and who don't manifest the phenotype are called nonpenetrant carriers.

At this point, as with other psychiatric and behavioural disorders, there are no biological markers for ADHD. The diagnosis is based on a description of a person's behaviour. In the case of childhood ADHD, typically parents and teachers are the informants by interview or questionnaire, and the subjective nature of this information allows for informant bias. For example, parents with high tolerance levels may not rate the child as hyperactive, whereas those parents with low tolerance may rate a nonhyperactive child as hyperactive. To confirm the presence of the child's symptoms in at least two settings, a teacher interview may be necessary, to resolve parent–teacher discrepancies in ratings of ADHD symptoms (Teacher Telephone Interview—IV, TTI; Schachar & Tannock, 1990; Swanson, Lerner, March & Gresham, 1999). If telephone discussions are not sufficient to resolve differences, it may be necessary for a trained clinician to make observations of the child in the natural school environment (or an approximation to it).

Another issue impacting on the study of the genetics of ADHD is the presence of comorbid conditions in ADHD probands and their family members. The possibility exists that ADHD combined with a comorbid condition is a homogenous subtype with one gene having multiple impacts (an "A" type model). Alternatively, it is possible that a child with a comorbid condition such as depression, reading disability, or anxiety may meet the criteria for ADHD but the symptoms are the expression of the comorbid disorder with different underlying aetiology. This would be a phenocopy, and fit a "V" type model.

According to *DSM-IV* (APA, 1994), if the behaviour can best be explained by the comorbid condition, then this meets exclusionary criteria for ADHD. The difficulty of course is determining the "true" nature of the observable behaviour. The genetic relationship of ADHD with comorbid disorders has been investigated using family studies (Biederman et al., 1992; Biederman, Faraone, Keenan, Steingard, & Tsuang, 1991; Biederman, Faraone, Keenan, & Tsuang 1991; Faraone, Biederman, Jetton, & Tsuang., 1997, Faraone et al., 1993; Faraone, Biederman, Mennin, & Russell, 1998.; Faraone, Biederman, Mennin, Wozniak, & Spencer, 1997.; Wozniak, Biederman, Mundy, Mennin, & Faraone, 1995). These studies suggest that ADHD with some comorbid conditions may represent genetic subtypes of ADHD but the exact genetic relationship has yet to be established. Likewise, the subtypes of ADHD (inattentive only, hyperactive/impulsive, or combined) may reflect different genetic aetiologies, but again, the situation is not clear. Another complicating factor is that these subtypes do not appear to breed true in families (Smalley, personal communication; Szatmari, Boyle, & Offord, 1993).

In the future we may be able to distinguish genetic versus environmental cases and subtypes of ADHD families by refining the phenotypes with more sensitive behavioural and nonbehavioural measures such as neurocognitive, neuroimaging, neurophysiological, and biochemical markers. For example, the investigator could characterise the subjects on performance on a sustained attention task, or a behavioural inhibition task, or by some measurable characteristics of response to stimulant medication. Instead of using a categorical diagnosis by *DSM-IV* or *ICD-10* criteria, the subjects' placement on a dimension may be used to define the phenotype.

## DESIGN OF STUDIES FOR MOLECULAR GENETICS

The hope of molecular genetic studies is that they may untangle the issues of genetic subtypes in the future, but the degree to which we will have success identifying these genetic susceptibility factors will in part be determined by the complexity of the genetics and the degree to which we can correctly address these issues in the planning and design of the study. In this section, we will address some key issues that should be considered in the design of molecular genetic studies of ADHD.

When designing an investigation of a phenotype with extensive genetic heterogeneity, provision for a large sample size is imperative. That is, if there are a number of different genes that can influence the phenotype, then a large number of families will be required in order to have the statistical power to detect each gene. Risch and Merikangas (1996) have estimated the number of families that is required to detect a gene of various genotypic risk ratios. At this point for ADHD, we do not know the number of genes that contribute to the phenotype or the impact that each gene has on the expression of the phenotype. It is therefore difficult to specify *a priori* an appropriate sample size.

Another factor to consider in the design of a genetic study is the penetrance. Given the previous discussion of reduced penetrance and the possibility that an individual could carry ADHD susceptibility genes without expressing the phenotype, then a strategy should be chosen to prevent complications from incomplete penetrance. In other words, some family members may carry the susceptibility genes without expressing the behaviours. For example, a collection of large multi-generational families may be unwise in that the diagnosis of some members of the pedigree may be difficult to specify with certainty; possibly because they are older and no longer symptomatic. Likewise, some individuals may be symptomatic but may not achieve a research criteria (i.e., family members who manifest only five symptoms of inattention, and thus do not exceed the established criteria of six or more of the nine symptoms on this domain). Therefore, it may not be possible to correctly classify all individuals into either an affected or unaffected category. Also critical to the use of large multi-generational pedigrees is the diagnosis of adult members of the pedigree which is known to be problematic (see Chapter 4, by Hay, McStephen, & Levy). Misdiagnosis of a critical member of a pedigree can substantially change the results of the linkage analysis, as was demonstrated by the change in linkage results by orders of magnitude for affective disorder (Egeland et al., 1987; Kelsoe et al., 1989).

One strategy would be to include only subjects that can unequivocally be designated as affected, such as an affected sibling pair design. This type of design avoids the difficulties of the requirement to be clear as to which family members definitely do not have the phenotype.

## MOLECULAR GENETICS

There are variations in the DNA sequence that differ among individuals in a population. The variants at a specific polymorphic site are called alleles and the position of the site on the genetic map is termed the locus (plural is loci). These sequence variants are termed polymorphisms if the less common allele has a population frequency of more than 5% (but a less stringent criteria of 1% is often used) (Ott, 1991). If the sequence variant has a population frequency for the less common allele of less than 5% (1%) then the sequence change is termed a mutation.

A mutation or polymorphism is termed functional if the allele results in changes in gene expression or protein structure. The DNA sequence variation may result in changes in the level of cell type specific expression of the transcription of a gene, splicing or processing of the messenger RNA (mRNA). On the other hand, if the variation is in the coding region of the gene that determines the amino acid sequence, then a change in the protein structure may result. Any of these changes in the expression or in the amino acid sequence may result in a change of protein function and observable phenotypic changes. Generally, DNA sequence variations do not result in any type of phenotypic variation. This is because they are not in coding or regulatory region of a gene, or the change is conservative (e.g., does not change the amino acid or changes to a similar amino acid).

The majority of sequence variants (polymorphisms or mutations) used for genetic study do not result in a change of function for a gene. Because of evolutionary pressure to preserve the function of a gene, coding and regulatory regions are less likely to have variation than other nonfunctional regions of the DNA. For linkage studies, the more polymorphic a site is, the more likely the inheritance pattern of the chromosomal region can be determined among members of a family, and therefore the site is a more useful one for a genetic study. Polymorphisms in areas outside the functional region of the gene can be used to track the inheritance of the specific location on the chromosome and provide evidence for linkage without having to be the DNA variant responsible for the phenotype.

The polymorphisms with known chromosomal location (markers) can be used to define the region of a chromosome that contains an as yet unknown gene that confers risk for a disorder (see Figure 10.2). These genetic markers follow a Mendelian mode of inheritance, i.e., the inheritance obeys Mendel's laws. In contrast, the observed inheritance of a complex phenotype may not follow these laws. However the inheritance of the phenotype can be inferred, based on the observation of the inheritance pattern of the phenotype in families. Because of the usefulness of these markers for genetic studies, a considerable effort in the human genome mapping programme has been dedicated to the discovery and localisation of large numbers of these markers, see for example (Dib et al., 1996; Utah Marker Development Group, 1995).

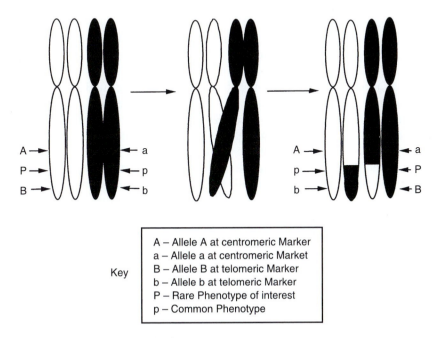

*Figure 10.2* Meiotic recombination.

If a specific biochemical pathway or gene is suspected then the search for genetic susceptibility factors can target these genes. For ADHD, a direction is suggested by a pharmacological model, and a site of action hypothesis, related to stimulant medication. This implicates the dopamine system, and suggests known dopamine genes as "candidates". As described in more detail later, several genes in the dopamine system have now been studied and polymorphisms in these genes have been reported to be associated with ADHD.

One can also carry out a comprehensive search of all the chromosomes by typing markers at regular intervals. This approach is called a genome scan. Generally the markers are chosen such that the largest interval between markers is 10 centimorgans (cM) requiring roughly 400 markers to cover the approximately 4000 cM length of the total complement of human chromosomes. However, the distance between markers chosen for the genome scan is dependent on the power and structure of the pedigrees available.

## GENETIC DATA ANALYSES

The basis of both linkage and association is that the marker is located physically close on the chromosome to the gene responsible for the phenotype. The smaller the distance between the marker and the aetiological gene, the less likely that recombination will separate the marker and the gene during meiosis (see Figure 10.2) and these marker alleles and the phenotype will co-segregate. For linkage studies, the co-segregation is measured in families. The distance from the marker that linkage can detect depends on the power of the pedigree (size, structure, number, and phenotypes of pedigree members) and the informativeness of the marker.

Association studies on the other hand depend on the marker not being separated by recombination during meiosis over many generations such that the marker allele and the allele responsible for the phenotype remain together in a population. Therefore, the marker must necessarily be located much closer to the etiological gene than in a linkage study. The finding of an association depends on the marker allele either being the disease causing DNA variant or being in linkage disequilibrium (LD) with the sequence variant. Several factors are involved in determining linkage disequilibrium. These include the distance between the disease and the marker locus, the age of the disease mutation in the population, marker and disease locus mutation rates, population growth rates, effective population sizes, and a host of evolutionary processes. Because LD requires that the marker be physically close to the disease-causing mutation, the causative gene must either be selected by an *a priori* hypothesis (specific candidate), or a very dense map of markers must be used.

The most useful approach when investigating a candidate gene or region is to use functional polymorphisms, as these may be the aetiological site. These functional DNA variants can be used in combination with closely linked highly polymorphic markers that allow the unambiguous determination of the inheritance of the chromosome from the parents. The combination of alleles across a group of polymorphisms in a small region on one chromosome constitutes a haplotype.

The simplest approach in an association strategy is to compare a group of cases with a group of controls. The alleles of subjects with the disorder are compared to the alleles of matched controls screened for the absence of the disorder. If such a study is attempted, the controls must be matched carefully for ethnic ancestry, because false positives and false negative results can occur easily due to population stratification, reviewed in Khoury and Yang (1998).

Frequencies of alleles for most genes are different across ethnic groups; see, for example, Barr & Kidd (1993), and Lichter et al. (1993). Thus, if the clinical setting used to collect the affected subjects has a different ethnic distribution than the control sample, this can result in a significant difference between the two groups that is not related to the presence or absence of the disorder.

Alternative strategies to control for ethnic differences have been developed with the use of family-based controls; see, for example Falk and Rubinstein (1987), Spielman and Ewens (1998), and Thomson (1995). In this type of approach the case is assessed as before to determine the phenotype (typically a research diagnosis). After this DNA samples are obtained from the case and from his or her biological relatives; typically a parent but for some types of statistics other relatives, in particular siblings, can be used (Spielman & Ewens, 1998). These types of statistics have become increasingly utilised in genetic studies in the past few years and this is reflected in the study of ADHD (see, for example, Cook et al., 1995; Gill, Daly, Heron, Hawi, & Fitzgerald, 1997; Smalley et al., 1998; Swanson, Sunohara, et al., 1998).

One particular type of family-based control association study, the haplotype relative risk (HRR) statistic, has been used in several molecular studies of ADHD (Cook et al., 1995; Gill et al., 1997; Swanson, Sunohara, et al., 1998). The HRR counts parental marker alleles (or haplotypes) transmitted to an affected child and compares them with those parental alleles not transmitted (Falk & Rubinstein, 1987; Terwilliger & Ott, 1992).

Another statistic frequently used in the study of ADHD is the transmission disequilibrium test (TDT; Spielman, McGinnis, & Ewens, 1993), that tests for linkage in the presence of linkage analysis. The TDT test considers parents who are heterozygous for an allele and evaluates the frequency with which an allele is transmitted to an affected offspring compared to an alternative allele. Under the null hypothesis each allele should have an equal change of being transmitted and deviations from this equal transmission is indicative of linkage. The appeal of the TDT is the simplicity as well as being quite powerful (Speer, 1998; Spielman et al., 1993).

A major strength of association studies is that if there is linkage disequilibrium then this strategy has much more power than a linkage strategy to find genes of small or moderate effect. That is, more families are required for linkage studies to find a gene of the same effect (Risch & Merikangas, 1996). To illustrate this point we can take an example from their paper. To detect a gene with a genotypic risk ratio of 4.0 and a disease allele frequency of 0.80, the authors estimate that it would require 2013 families (consisting of an affected child and both parents), using a linkage approach compared to 222 families for an association study.

## MOLECULAR GENETIC STUDIES OF ADHD

In the last decade of the 20th century, there has been increased interest in molecular genetic studies of ADHD. The first molecular studies centered on the role of the thyroid hormone receptor (see Chapter 9 by Zametkin, Ernst, & Cohen). More recently, the role of the dopamine system genes have been the focus of interest. The first dopamine gene to be studied, the dopamine transporter, is a good candidate based on the site of action of stimulant medications. The dopamine transporter, located on chromosome 5p15.3, has several polymorphisms. One of these, a 40 bp repeat in the 3' untranslated region, has been reported to be associated with ADHD (Cook et al., 1995; Gill et al., 1997; Rowe, Stever, Gard, et al., 1998).

There are two common alleles of this 40 bp repeat, one with 10 copies of the repeat and one with 9 copies of the repeat (Vandenbergh et al., 1992). In the Cook et al. (1995) study of the dopamine-transporter gene the investigators reported an association using the haplotype relative risk method of the 10-repeat allele (the more frequent allele) in the ADHD cases, compared to the frequency of the 9-repeat allele using a sample of 49 ADHD subjects and parents (chi-squared = 7.29, 1 $df$, $p = .007$). This association was replicated (chi-squared = 6.07, 1 $df$., $p = .014$) in a sample taken in Ireland of 40 nuclear families comprised of 26 probands with both parents and 14 probands with a single parent (Gill et al., 1997).

Waldman et al. (1998) also examined the relationship between DAT and ADHD. Within-family analysis of linkage disequilibrium using the transmission disequilibrium test suggested association and linkage of ADHD with DAT, and this relationship was especially strong for the hyperactive-impulsive subtype but not the inattentive subtype. Siblings discordant ($n = 12$) for the 10-repeat allele differed markedly in the level of both hyperactive-impulsive and inattentive symptoms, such that siblings with the higher number of 10-repeat alleles had much higher symptom levels. The authors also examined the probands ($n = 112$) symptoms and regressed these symptoms on the number of 10-repeat alleles for each proband. The number of 10-repeat alleles was significantly related to the number of hyperactive-impulsive symptoms, but not inattentive symptoms.

Molecular genetic studies have also focused on two dopamine receptors, D2 and D4. In 1991, using a case control association study design, Comings et al. reported an association between a polymorphism in the D2 receptor in Caucasian subjects with ADHD, compared to controls. This study found an increase in the frequency of the A1 allele of a TaqI restriction fragment length polymorphism (RFLP) at the dopamine D2 receptor locus (DRD2) in patients with ADHD, as well as individuals with Tourette Syndrome, alcoholism, autistic disorder, and post-traumatic stress disorder compared to controls.

Since this polymorphism is known to have a wide range of frequencies in different populations (Barr & Kidd, 1993), association studies using this polymorphism may be complicated by the variability in different populations. Care must therefore be taken in matching samples versus controls by ethnic background. A better design to avoid this population variability in allele frequencies would be to use family-based controls as discussed previously. Thus far there have been no additional published studies on the dopamine D2 receptor and ADHD.

The D4 receptor has received considerable attention in the past few years. This gene, located on chromosome 11p15.5, has several polymorphisms, but the one receiving the most attention is located in the coding region and consists of 48 bp repeats in the third exon (Van Tol et al., 1992). This repeat is highly polymorphic and results in considerable amino acid changes in the protein (Lichter et al., 1993).

Functional differences in the intracellular signaling system have been reported for these protein variants (Asghari et al., 1995), and the 7-repeat allele may be subsensitive to endogenous dopamine (Asghari et al., 1994). This blunted response of the 7-repeat allele to dopamine is consistent with the ameliorative effects of methylphenidate treatment, in that synaptic dopamine levels are raised by methylphenidate, possibly compensating for the blunted response.

A case control study conducted by LaHoste et al. (1996) revealed an increased frequency of the 7-repeat allele in the ADHD sample. Subsequently, proband/parent trios were collected and the same allele was found to occur at a higher frequency in probands than in the nontransmitted alleles of the parents (Swanson, Sunohara, et al., 1998). Further support for this gene in ADHD has come from three recently published studies (Faraone et al., 1999; Rowe, Stever, Giedinghagen et al., 1998; Smalley et al., 1998).

In addition to the published studies, we have further support for biased transmission of the 7-repeat allele using the TDT test, using a sample of 107 families collected in Toronto (Sunohara et al., in press). A fourth study did not find any evidence of an association using a case control approach using 41 children with ADHD and 56 controls matched for ethnicity and sex (Castellanos et al., 1998).

The study of Rowe, Stever, Giedinghagen, et al. (1998) used a number of different statistical approaches to investigate the relationship between ADHD and DRD4 including the TDT, quantitative TDT, and a comparison of discordant sibling pairs. Using a case control approach, the 7-repeat allele occurred more frequently in children with the ADHD—inattentive subtype than in controls. However, interpretation of these findings should show caution, as the controls were not ethnically matched to the subjects. Using family data, the authors also examined the transmission of alleles using both a categorical and quantitative TDT test. No significant evidence was found for biased transmission of the 7-repeat allele using either a categorical or a quantitative approach; however, a positive correlation of inattentive symptoms and the 7-repeat allele was reported using a quantitative TDT. In genetically discordant sibling pairs, the sibling with a greater number of 7-repeat alleles displayed more inattentive symptoms than did his or her co-sibling with fewer 7-repeat alleles.

A study by Faraone et al. (1999) reported the results from 27 triads (ADHD children and both their parents), that were collected through a clinically referred parent with ADHD. The chi-square test of cells containing the 7-repeat allele found only one pair significantly contributed to the significance. The 7-repeat allele *was* transmitted and the 4 allele *was not* transmitted a greater number of times than the number of times the 4 repeat allele *was* transmitted and the 7-repeat allele *was not* (chi-squared = 7.4, $df = 1$, $N = 1$, $p = .007$).

Smalley et al. (1998) genotyped 133 families, consisting of 49 with a single ADHD proband, and 84, with at least one additional affected sibling. No significant evidence for identity-by-descent sharing of alleles was found. However, when the 89 informative meioses were stratified into those with ($n = 44$) and without ($n = 45$) the 7-repeat allele, a trend emerged with increased allele sharing among the sibling pairs from parental meioses in which the 7-repeat was present, $p = .07$.

## SUMMARY AND FUTURE DIRECTIONS

If additional linkage and association studies continue to support these genes as susceptibility factors in ADHD then the next step is to determine the molecular mechanism by which these genes contribute to the phenotype. For, it is possible that the polymorphism in the dopamine transporter gene associated with ADHD is in a transcriptional regulatory element and the repeat number influences the rate of transcription of the gene. This hypothesis can be checked by standard molecular studies of transcription regulation. However, it is more likely that the association can be explained by the polymorphic repeat being in linkage disequilibrium with another DNA sequence variant that directly changes the protein structure. The aetiological DNA sequence variant can be determined by screening the gene by various molecular methods inlcuding direct sequencing. Likewise, the number of 48 bp repeats in exon 3 of the dopamine receptor D4 may be responsible for the phenotype. Another possibility is that the sequence composition of the repeats is important or alternatively that the 7-repeat allele may be in linkage disequilibrium with another sequence variant in another part of the gene responsible for the phenotype. Further studies are required to determine which of these alternative hypotheses are true.

In summary, the molecular genetic findings presented thus far should be considered preliminary at this time, due to small sample sizes (for a genetic study of a complex phenotype), heterogeneity in populations, subject ascertainment, and diagnostic assessment. It is critical that all researchers in this field use caution in the interpretation of any molecular finding. This is particularly the case when speaking with lay audiences, as the subtleties of the complex issues discussed in this chapter will not be recognised and misunderstandings will undoubtedly result. Further studies are needed, and the molecular mechanism determined before we can make definitive conclusions about the role of any gene in ADHD. Despite the critical limitations, a good start has been achieved and many groups are active and collaborating in this research.

## REFERENCES

American Psychiatric Association. (1980). *Diagnostic and statistical manual of mental disorders*, (3rd ed.). Washington, DC: Author.

American Psychiatric Association. (1987). *Diagnostic and statistical manual of mental disorders*, (3rd ed. rev.). Washington, DC: Author.

American Psychiatric Association. (1994). *Diagnostic and statistical manual of mental disorders*, (4th ed.). Washington, DC: Author.

Arnold, L.E., Abikoff, H.B., Cantwell, D.P., Conners, C.K., Elliott, G., Greenhill, L.L., Hechtman, L., Hinshaw, S.P., Hoza, B., Jensen, P.S., Kraemer, H.C., March, J.S., Newcorn, J.H., Pelham, W.E., Richters, J.E., Schiller, E., Severe, J.B., Swanson, J.M., Vereen, D., & Wells, K.C. (1997). National Institute of Mental Health Collaborative Multimodal Treatment Study of Children with ADHD (the MTA). Design challenges and choices. *Archives of General Psychiatry*, *54*, 865–870.

Asghari, V., Sanyal, S., Buchwaldt, S., Paterson, A., Jovanovic, V., & Van Tol, H.H. (1995). Modulation of intracellular cyclic AMP levels by different human dopamine D4 receptor variants. *Journal of Neurochemistry*, *65*, 1157–1165.

Asghari, V., Schoots, O., van Kats, S., Ohara, K., Jovanovic, V., Guan, H.C., Bunzow, J.R., Petronis, A., & Van Tol, H.H. (1994). Dopamine D4 receptor repeat: Analysis of different native and mutant forms of the human and rat genes. *Molelecular Pharmacology*, *46*, 364–373.

August, G.J., & Holmes, C.S. (1984). Behavior and academic achievement in hyperactive subgroups and learning-disabled boys: A six-year follow-up. *American Journal of the Disabled Child*, *138*, 1025–1029.

Barr, C.L., & Kidd, K.K. (1993). Population frequencies of the A1 allele at the dopamine D2 receptor locus. *Biological Psychiatry*, *34*, 204–209.

Biederman, J., Faraone, S.V., Keenan, K., Benjamin, J., Krifcher, B., Moore, C., Sprich-Buckminster, S., Ugaglia, K., Jellinek, M.S., Steingard, R., Spencer, T.J., Norman, D., Kolodny, R., Kraus, I., Perrin, J., Keller, M.B., & Tsuang, M.T. (1992). Further evidence for family-genetic risk factors in Attention Deficit

Hyperactivity Disorder: Patterns of comorbidity in probands and relatives psychiatrically and pediatrically referred samples. *Archives of General Psychiatry, 49,* 728–738.

Biederman J., Faraone, S.V., Keenan, K., Steingard, R., & Tsuang, M.T. (1991). Familial association between attention deficit disorder and anxiety disorders. *American Journal of Psychiatry, 148,* 251–256.

Biederman, J., Faraone, S.V., Keenan, K., & Tsuang, M.T. (1991). Evidence of familial association between attention deficit disorder and major affective disorders. *Archives of General Psychiatry, 48,* 633–642

Castellanos, F.X. (1997). Toward a pathophysiology of attention-deficit/hyperactivity disorder. *Clinical Pediatrics (Phila), 36,* 381–393

Castellanos, F.X., Lau, E., Tayebi, N., Lee, P., Long, R.E., Giedd, J.N., Sharp, W., Marsh, W.L., Walter, J.M., Hamburger, S.D., Ginns, E.I., Rapoport, J.L., & Sidransky, E. (1998). Lack of an association between a dopamine-4 receptor polymorphism and attention-deficit/hyperactivity disorder: Genetic and brain morphometric analyses. *Molecular Psychiatry, 3,* 431–434.

Comings, D.E., Comings, B.G., Muhleman, D., Dietz, G., Shahbahrami, B., Tast, D., Knell, E., Kocsis, P., Baumgarten, R., Kovacs, B.W., Levy, D.L., Smith, M., Borison, R.L., Evans, D., Klein, D.N., MacMurray, J.P., Tosk, J.M., Sverd, J., Gysin, R., & Flanagan, S.D. (1991). The dopamine D2 receptor locus as a modifying gene in neuropsychiatric disorders. *Journal of the American Medical Association, 266,* 1793–1800.

Cook, E.H., Jr., Stein, M.A., Krasowski, M.D., Cox, N.J., Olkon, D.M., Kieffer, J.E., & Leventhal, B.L. (1995). Association of attention-deficit disorder and the dopamine transporter gene. *American Journal of Human Genetics, 56,* 993–998.

Deutsch, C.K., Swanson, J.M., Bruell, J.H., Cantwell, D.P., Weinberg, F., & Baren, M. (1982). Overrepresentation of adoptees in children with the attention deficit disorder. *Behavior Genetics, 12,* 231–238.

Dib, C., Faure, S., Fizames, C., Samson, D., Drouot, N., Vignal, A., Millasseau, P., Marc, S., Hazan, J., Seboun, E., Lathrop, M., Gyapay, G., Morissette, J., & Weissenbach, J. (1996). A comprehensive genetic map of the human genome based on 5,264 microsatellites. *Nature, 380,* 152–154.

Edelbrock, C., Rende, R.D., Plomin, R., & Thompson, L.A. (1995). A twin study of competence and problem behavior in childhood and early adolescence. *Journal of Child Psychology and Psychiatry, 36,* 775–785.

Egeland, J.A., Gerhard, D.S., Pauls, D.L., Sussex, J.N., Kidd, K.K., Allen, C.R., Hostetter, A.M., & Housman, D.E. (1987). Bipolar affective disorders linked to DNA markers on chromosome 11. *Nature, 325,* 783–787

Falk, C.T., & Rubinstein, P. (1987). Haplotype relative risks: An easy reliable way to construct a proper control sample for risk calculations. *Annals Human Genetics, 51,* 227–233.

Faraone, S.V., Biederman, J., Jetton, J.G., & Tsuang, M.T. (1997). Attention deficit disorder and Conduct Disorder: Longitudinal evidence for a familial subtype. *Psychological Medicine, 27,* 291–300.

Faraone, S.V., Biederman, J., Keenan, K., & Tsuang, M.T. (1991). Separation of DSM-III attention deficit disorder and Conduct Disorder: Evidence from a family-genetic study of American child psychiatric patients. *Psychological Medicine, 21,* 109–121.

Faraone, S.V., Biederman, J., Lehman, B.K., Keenan, K., Norman, D., Seidman, L.J.,

Kolodny, R., Kraus, I., Perrin, J., & When, W.J. (1993). Evidence for the independent familial transmission of Attention Deficit Hyperactivity Disorder and learning disabilities: Results from a family genetic study. *American Journal of Psychiatry, 150*, 891–895.

Faraone, S.V., Biederman, J., Mennin, D., & Russell, R. (1998). Bipolar and antisocial disorders among relatives of ADHD children: Parsing familial subtypes of illness. *American Journal of Medical Genetics, 81*, 108–116.

Faraone, S.V., Biederman, J., Mennin, D., Wozniak, J., & Spencer, T.J. (1997). Attention-deficit hyperactivity disorder with bipolar disorder: A familial subtype? *Journal of the American Academy of Child and Adolescent Psychiatry, 36*, 1378–1387, 1387–1390.

Faraone, S.V., Biederman, J., & Milberger, S. (1994). An exploratory study of ADHD among second-degree relatives of ADHD children. *Biological Psychiatry, 35*, 398–402.

Faraone, S.V., Biederman, J., Weiffenbach, B., Keith, T., Chu, M.P., Weaver, A., Spencer, T.J., Wilens, T.E., Frazier, J., Cleves, M., & Sakai, J. (1999). Dopamine D4 gene 7-repeat allele and Attention Deficit Hyperactivity Disorder. *American Journal of Psychiatry, 156*, 768–770.

Gilger, J.W., Pennington, B.F., & DeFries, J.C. (1992). A twin study of the etiology of comorbidity: Attention-deficit hyperactivity disorder and dyslexia? *Journal of the American Academy of Child and Adolescent Psychiatry, 31*, 343–348.

Gill, M., Daly, G., Heron, S., Hawi, Z., & Fitzgerald, M. (1997). Confirmation of association between Attention Deficit Hyperactivity Disorder and a dopamine transporter polymorphism. *Molecular Psychiatry, 2*, 311–313.

Gillis, J.J., Gilger, J.W., Pennington, B.F., & DeFries, J.C. (1992). Attention deficit disorder in reading-disabled twins: Evidence for a genetic etiology. *Journal of Abnormal Child Psychology, 20*, 303–315.

Gjone, H., Stevenson, J., & Sundet, J.M. (1996). Genetic influence on parent-reported attention-related problems in a Norwegian general population twin sample? *Journal of the American Academy of Child and Adolescent Psychiatry, 35*, 88–96, 596–598.

Goodman, R., & Stevenson, J. (1989a). A twin study of hyperactivity—I. An examination of hyperactivity scores and categories derived from Rutter teacher and parent questionnaires. *Journal of Child Psychology and Psychiatry, 30*, 671–689.

Goodman, R., & Stevenson, J. (1989b). A twin study of hyperactivity—II. The aetiological role of genes, family relationships and perinatal adversity. *Journal of Child Psychology and Psychiatry, 30*, 691–709.

Greenhill, L., & Osmon, B. (2000). *Ritalin: Theory and practice* . Larchmont, NY: M.A. Liebert Publishers.

Greenhill, L.L., Halperin, J.M., & Abikoff, H. (1999). Stimulant medications. *Journal of the American Academy of Child and Adolescent Psychiatry, 38*, 503–512.

Hudziak, J.J., Heath, A.C., Madden, P.A.F., Reich, W., Bucholz, K.K., Slutske, W., Bierut, L.J., Neuman, R.J., & Todd, R.D. (1998). Latent class and factor analysis of DSM-IV ADHD: A twin study of female adolescents. *Journal of the American Academy of Child and Adolescent Psychiatry, 37*, 848–857.

Humphries, T., Koltun, H., Malone, M., & Roberts, W. (1994). Teacher-identified oral language difficulties among boys with attention problems. *Journal of Developmental Behavhavior Pediatrics, 15*, 92–98.

Kelsoe, J.R., Ginns, E.I., Egeland, J.A., Gerhard, D.S., Goldstein, A.M., Bale, S.J.,

Pauls, D.L., Long, R.T., Kidd, K.K., Conte, G., Houseman, D.E., & Paul, S.M. (1989). Re-evaluation of the linkage relationship between chromosome 11p loci and the gene for bipolar affective disorder in the Old Order Amish. *Nature, 342,* 238–243

Khoury, M.J., & Yang, Q. (1998). The future of genetic studies of complex human diseases: an epidemiologic perspective. *Epidemiology, 9,* 350–354.

LaHoste, G.J., Swanson, J.M., Wigal, S.B., Glabe, C., Wigal, T., King, N., & Kennedy, J.L. (1996). Dopamine D4 receptor gene polymorphism is associated with Attention Deficit Hyperactivity Disorder. *Molecular Psychiatry, 1,* 121–124.

Levy, F. (1991). The Dopamine theory of Attention Deficit Hyperactivity Disorder (ADHD). *Australian and New Zealand Journal of Psychiatry, 25,* 277–283.

Levy, F., Barr, C., & Sunohara, G.A. (1998). Directions of aetiologic research on Attention Deficit Hyperactivity Disorder. *Australian and New Zealand Journal of Psychiatry, 32,* 97–103

Levy, F., Hay, D.A., McStephen, M., Wood, C., & Waldman, I.D. (1997). Attention-deficit hyperactivity disorder: A category or a continuum? Genetic analysis of a large-scale twin study. *Journal of the American Academy of Child and Adolescent Psychiatry, 36,* 737–744

Lichter, J.B., Barr, C.L., Kennedy, J.L., Van Tol, H.H., Kidd, K.K., & Livak, K.J. (1993). A hypervariable segment in the human dopamine receptor D4 (DRD4) gene. *Human Molecular Genetics, 2,* 767–773.

Lopez, R.E. (1965). Hyperactivity in twins. *Canadian Psychiatric Association Journal, 10,* 421–426.

Lou, H.C. (1996). Etiology and pathogenesis of attention-deficit Hyperactivity Disorder (ADHD): Significance of prematurity and perinatal hypoxi-haemodynamic encephalopathy. *Acta Paediatrica, 85,* 1266–1271

Mannuzza, S., Klein, R.G., Bessler, A., Malloy, P., & LaPadula, M. (1998). Adult psychiatric status of hyperactive boys grown up. *American Journal of Psychiatry, 155,* 493–498

Morton, J., & Frith, U. (1995). Causal modeling: A structural approach to developmental psychology. In D. Cicchetti & D.J. Cophen (Eds.), *Manual of developmental psychopathology,* (Vol. 2, pp. 357–390). New York: John Wiley.

MTA Cooperative Group. (1999). A 14-month randomized clinical trial of treatment strategies for Attention-Deficit/Hyperactivity Disorder. *Archives of General Psychiatry, 56,* 1073–1086.

Ott, J. (1991). *Analysis of human genetic linkage.* Baltimore/London: Johns Hopkins University Press.

Patrick, K.S., Mueller, R.A., Gualtieri T.C., & Breese, G.R. (1987). Pharmacokinetics and actions of methylphenidate. In H.Y. Meltzer (Ed.), *Psychopharmacology: 3rd generation of progress.* New York: Raven Press.

Risch, N., & Merikangas, K. (1996). The future of genetic studies of complex human diseases. *Science, 273,* 1516–1517.

Rowe, D.C., Stever, C., Gard, J.M., Cleveland, H.H., Sanders, M.L., Abramowitz, A., Kozol, S.T., Mohr, J.H., Sherman, S.L. & Waldman, I.D. (1998). The relation of the dopamine transporter gene (DAT1) to symptoms of internalizing disorders in children. *Behavior Genetics, 28,* 215–225.

Rowe, D.C., Stever, C., Giedinghagen, L.N., Gard, J.M., Cleveland, H.H., Terris, S.T., Mohr, J.H., Sherman, S.L., Abramowitz, A., & Waldman, I.D. (1998). Dopamine

DRD4 receptor polymorphism and Attention Deficit Hyperactivity Disorder. *Molecular Psychiatry*, *3*, 419–426.

Satterfield, J., Swanson, J.M., Schell, A., & Lee, F. (1994). Prediction of antisocial behaviour in Attention-Deficit Hyperactivity Disorder boys from aggression/defiance scores. *Journal of the American Academy of Child and Adolescent Psychiatry*, *33*, 185–190.

Schachar, R., & Tannock, R. (1990). *Teacher telephone interview*. Toronto: Department of Psychiatry, The Hospital for Sick Children.

Silver, L.B. (1981). The relationship between learning disabilities, hyperactivity, distractibility, and behavioral problems: A clinical analysis *Journal of the American Academy of Child and Adolescent Psychiatry*, *20*, 385–397.

Smalley, S.L., Bailey, J.N., Palmer, C.G., Cantwell, D.P., McGough, J.J., Del'Homme M.A., Asarnow, J.R., Woodward, J.A., Ramsey, C., & Nelson, S.F. (1998). Evidence that the dopamine D4 receptor is a susceptibility gene in Attention Deficit Hyperactivity Disorder. *Molecular Psychiatry*, *3*, 427–430.

Speer, M.C. (1998). Sample size and power. In J.L. Haines & M.A. Pericak-Vance (Eds.), *Approaches to gene mapping in complex human diseases* (pp. 161–200). New York: Wiley-Liss.

Spielman, R.S., & Ewens, W.J. (1998). A sibship test for linkage in the presence of association: The sib transmission/disequilibrium test. *American Journal of Human Genetics*, *62*, 450–458

Spielman, R.S., McGinnis, R.E., & Ewens, W.J. (1993). Transmission test for linkage disequilibrium: The insulin gene region and insulin-dependent diabetes mellitus (IDDM). *American Journal of Human Genetics*, *52*, 506–516.

Stevenson, J. (1992). Evidence for a genetic etiology in hyperactivity in children. *Behavior Genetics*, *22*, 337–344.

Sunohara, G.A, Roberts, W., Malone, M., Schachar, R., Tannock, R., Basile, V., Wigal, T., Wigal, S.B., Schuck, S., Moriarty, B.A., Swanson, J.M., Kennedy, J.L., & Barr, C.L. (in press). Linkage of the Dopamine D4 receptor gene and Attention-Deficit Hyperactivity Disorder. *Journal of the American Academy Child and Adolescent Psychiatry* .

Swanson, J.M., Lerner, M., March, J., & Gresham, F.M. (1999). Assessment and intervention for attention-deficit/hyperactivity disorder in the schools: Lessons from the MTA study. *Pediatric Clinics North America*. *46*, 993–1009.

Swanson, J.M., & Castellanos, F.X. (1998). *Biological bases of ADHD: Neuroanatomy, genetics, and pathophysiology*. Abstract of paper presented at Diagnosis and treatment of Attention Deficit Hyperactivity Disorder, NIH Consensus Conference, Bethesda, Md.

Swanson, J.M., Sergeant, J.A., Taylor, E., Sonuga-Barke, E.J., Jensen P.S., & Cantwell, D.P. (1998). Attention-deficit hyperactivity disorder and hyperkinetic disorder. *Lancet*, *35*, 429–433.

Swanson, J.M., Sunohara, G.A., Kennedy, J.L., Regino, R., Fineberg, E., Wigal, T., Lerner, M., Williams, L., LaHoste, G.J., & Wigal, S.B. (1998). Association of the dopamine receptor D4 (DRD4) gene with a refined phenotype of Attention Deficit Hyperactivity Disorder (ADHD): A family- based approach. *Molecular Psychiatry*, *3*, 38–41.

Szatmari, P., Boyle, M.H., & Offord, D.R. (1993). Familial aggregation of emotional and behavioral problems of childhood in the general population. *American Journal of Psychiatry*, *150*, 1398–1403.

Tannock, R., & Brown, T.E. (in press). Attention Deficit Disorders with Learning Disorders. In T.E. Brown (Ed.), *Attention Deficit Disorder and comorbidities in children, adolescents and adults*. Washington, D.C.: American Psychiatric Press.

Tannock, R., & Schachar, R. (1996). Executive dysfunction as an underlying mechanism of behavior and language problems in Attention Deficit Hyperactivity Disorder. In J.H. Beitchman, N. Cohen, M.M. Konstantareas, R. Tannock (Eds.). *Language, learning, and behavior disorders: Developmental, biological, and clinical perspectives* (pp. 128–155). New York: Cambridge University Press.

Terwilliger, J.D., & Ott, J. (1992). A haplotype-based "haplotype relative risk" approach to detecting allelic associations. *Human Heredity, 42*, 337–346.

Thapar, A., Hervas, A., & McGuffin, P. (1995). Childhood hyperactivity scores are highly heritable and show sibling competition effects: Twin study evidence. *Behavior Genetics, 25*, 537–544.

Thapar, A., Holmes, J., Poulton, K., & Harrington, R. (1999). Genetic basis of attention deficit and hyperactivity. *British Journal of Psychiatry, 174*, 105–111.

Thomson, G. (1995). Mapping disease genes: Family-based association studies. *American Journal of Human Genetics, 57*, 487–498.

Utah Marker Development Group. (1995). A collection of ordered tetranucleotide-repeat markers from the human genome. *American Journal of Human Genetics, 57*, 619–628.

Vandenbergh, D.J., Persico, A.M., Hawkins, A.L., Griffin, C.A., Li, X., Jabs, E.W., & Uhl, G.R. (1992). Human dopamine transporter gene (DAT1) maps to chromosome 5p15.3 and displays a VNTR. *Genomics, 14*, 1104–1106.

Van Tol, H.H., Wu, C.M., Guan, H.C., Ohara, K., Bunzow, J.R., Civelli, O., Kennedy, J., Seeman, P., Niznik, H.B., & Jovanovic, V. (1992). Multiple dopamine D4 receptor variants in the human population. *Nature, 358*, 149–152.

Volkow, N.D., Wang, G.J., Fowler, J.S., Gatley, S.J., Logan, J., Ding, Y.S., Hitzemann, R., & Pappas, N. (1998). Dopamine transporter occupancies in the human brain induced by therapeutic doses of oral methylphenidate. *American Journal of Psychiatry, 155*, 1325–1331.

Waldman, I.D., Rowe, D.C., Abramowitz, A., Kozel, S.T., Mohr, J.H., Sherman, S.L., Cleveland, H.H., Sanders, M.L., Gard, J.M., & Stever, C. (1998). Association and linkage of the Dopamine transporter gene and Attention-Deficit Hyperactivity Disorder in children: Heterogeneity owing to diagnostic subtype and severity. *American Journal of Human Genetics, 63*, 1767–1776.

Wender, P.H., Epstein, R.S., Kopin, I.J., & Gordon, E.K. (1971). Urinary monoamine metabolites in children with minimal brain dysfunction. *American Journal of Psychiatry, 127*, 1411–1415.

Wigal, T., Swanson, J.M., Regino, R., Lerner, M.A., Soliman, I., Steinhoff, K., Gurbani, S., & Wigal, S.B. (1999). Stimulant medications for the treatment of AHDH: Efficacy and limitations. *Mental Retardation and Developmental Disabilities Research Reviews, 5*, 215–224.

Willerman, L. (1973). Activity level and hyperactivity in twins. *Child Development, 44*, 288–293.

World Health Organization. (1979). *International Classification of Diseases, ninth revision, clinical modification*. Geneva: WHO.

World Health Organization. (1992). *ICD-10 Classification of behavioural disorders: Clinical descriptions and diagnostic guidelines*. Geneva: WHO.

World Health Organization. (1993). *International classification of diseases. 10th revision (ICD-10). Classification of mental and behavioural disorders, diagnostic criteria for research* (10th rev. ed.) [*ICD-10*]. Geneva: WHO.

Wozniak, J., Biederman, J., Mundy, E., Mennin, D., & Faraone, S.V. (1995). A pilot family study of childhood-onset mania. *Journal of the American Academy of Child and Adolescent Psychiatry, 34*, 1577–1583.

# 11 The genetic relationship between ADHD and Gilles de la Tourette syndrome[1]

*David Pauls, Nancy Fredine, Kimberly Lynch, Charles R. Hurst, John P. Alsobrook II*

The Gilles de la Tourette syndrome (GTS) is a chronic and complex neuropsychiatric disorder defined by the cardinal features of fluctuating motor and phonic tics. A range of behavioural and cognitive disorders often accompanies these tics. These include some forms of Attention Deficit Hyperactivity Disorder (ADHD), and obsessive compulsive disorder (OCD). Originally described over 100 years ago, GTS was for many years considered to be rare, some researchers questioning the biological basis of the syndrome. However, GTS has since emerged as a model neuropsychiatric disorder, and in the late 1960s it was demonstrated that haloperidol was effective in the treatment of this syndrome. This observation renewed interest in the biological basis of GTS, and subsequent research has contributed to a large body of knowledge regarding the natural history of the syndrome and the importance of biological/genetic factors in its aetiology (Leckman & Cohen, 1999).

Although the precise pathogenic mechanisms remain unclear, a picture is emerging from accumulated evidence that, in most cases, GTS occurs in those individuals with a genetically determined vulnerability.

Tics usually begin in middle childhood (average age 7 years) with motor tics often preceding the onset of phonic tics (Leckman, King, & Cohen, 1999). The prevalence for GTS has been estimated to be between 0.5 and 36 per 10,000 (Zohar et al., 1999). Milder variants, such as chronic tics (CT), occur more frequently (Zohar et al., 1999). The expression of GTS is gender-dependent, with boys being more commonly affected with tics than girls.

The range of symptoms is quite broad, and enormously varied. The most common tics involve the muscles of the eyes, face, neck, and shoulders, and include eye blinking and head jerking (Jagger et al., 1982; Leckman et al., 1999). Vocal tics most often consist of repetitive throat clearing, sniffling, or grunting, although more complex phonic tics—such as word repetition, nonsense syllables, or abrupt changes in rhythm or tone of voice—can be observed. More extreme symptoms, such as bouts of cursing (copralalia),

1  This work was supported in part by grants MH00508 (an RSA to Dr Pauls from NIMH), NS16648, MH 49351, HD 03008, and MH 03029.

occur in a minority of patients with GTS (Leckman et al., 1999). Although "involuntary", motor and phonic tics are suppressible for brief periods of time.

Tics often occur in bouts and can be exacerbated by stress and anxiety. Symptoms are frequently at their most severe before puberty. A majority of patients experience a significant reduction, or at least a stabilisation, of their tic repertoire during adolescence and young adulthood, although a minority of patients show severe and/or progressive symptoms into adulthood (Leckman et al., 1998). A few individuals become chronically disabled by constant paroxysms of tics, including coprolalia and self-injurious tics (Shapiro, Shapiro, Young, & Feinberg, 1988).

In contrast to the increased clarity that has emerged for the natural history of GTS, a less clear picture has developed regarding the associated disorders that may occur in conjunction with this disorder. It is evident from many studies that GTS is often found in children and adults who have additional psychiatric symptoms and diagnoses (Leckman & Cohen, 1999). What is not yet resolved is the relationship between these comorbid conditions and GTS.

In 1982, Jagger and colleagues reported that symptoms of inattention and hyperactivity were among the first observed in a large percentage of clinic patients. Given that at least 50% of clinic cases of GTS were reported to have ADHD, Comings and Comings (1987) proposed that ADHD represented a variant expression of the aetiologic factors responsible for the manifestation of GTS and CT. Findings from our work (Pauls et al., 1986; Pauls, Leckman, & Cohen, 1993) do not fully support this hypothesis. In this chapter, we review the data examining the relationship between GTS and ADHD.

Although the data regarding the genetic relationship between GTS and ADHD remain somewhat controversial, it is becoming clear that children with both GTS and ADHD (GTS + ADHD) have more difficulties than do children with GTS alone. Children with GTS and ADHD may have a different profile of cognitive abilities and worse social adjustment than do children with GTS alone (Carter et al., 2000; Dykens et al., 1990; Stokes, Bawden, Camfield, Backman, & Dooley, 1991). The co-occurrence of ADHD among clinical patients may be conceptualised as reflecting a more general disturbance in the maturation of systems that underlie self-regulation, including the coordination of attention, motor activity, and emotional responsivity (Cohen, 1990).

## PHENOMENOLOGY AND NATURAL HISTORY OF ADHD

Attention Deficit Hyperactivity Disorder (ADHD) is a prevalent neuropsychiatric syndrome of childhood onset. Children with ADHD are typically described as having chronic difficulties in the areas of inattention, impulsivity, and overactivity. They usually display these characteristics early in life to a degree that is inappropriate for their age or developmental level. The symptoms are manifested across a variety of situations, and tax the children's capacity to pay attention, inhibit their impulses, and restrain their movement (Towbin & Riddle, 1993). Definitions have varied considerably throughout the history of this disorder, as have the recommended criteria for obtaining a diagnosis. The current recommended criteria listed in the *Diagnostic and Statistical Manual of Mental Disorders*, fourth edition (*DSM-IV*; American Psychiatric Association, 1994) emphasise two parallel symptom lists, one focusing on inattention, poor concentration, and disorganisation, and the other focusing on symptoms related to hyperactivity and behavioural impulsivity. The diagnosis of ADHD therefore can reflect predominantly inattentive type, a hyperactive-impulsive type, or a combined type. Symptoms must be developmentally extreme, and must lead to clear impairment in at least two key domains (school, home, work).

Epidemiological studies suggest that ADHD may be among the most common childhood psychiatric disorders. Prevalence estimates from studies using modern methodology range from approximately 2% to 9% (Anderson, Williams, McGee, & Silva, 1987; Costello et al., 1988). As with GTS, males are more commonly affected with ADHD than are females. Estimates of the ratios of males to females range from 3 : 1 to 8 : 1 (McGee, Williams, & Silva, 1987; Reeves, Werry, Elkind, & Zametkin, 1987; Szatmari, Offord, & Boyle, 1989; Werry, Reeves, & Elkind, 1987). The causes of ADHD are unknown. Data from a number of studies suggest multiple aetiologies, and genetic factors have been demonstrated as being important (Biederman et al., 1986, 1992; Faorone et al., 1992).

In the past it was believed that all children with ADHD "outgrew their problem" at puberty. Recent data suggests that this is probably not true for some individuals (Biederman et al., 1995). In fact, as early as 1985 Cantwell suggested three potential types of outcomes of ADHD in childhood:

1   a "developmental delay" outcome, in which the individuals no longer manifest any functionally impairing ADHD symptoms after adolescence
2   a "continual display" outcome, in which individuals remained functionally impaired into adult life, and who experience a variety of different types of social and emotional difficulties
3   a "developmental decay" outcome, in which individuals experience the core ADHD symptoms and continue to develop more serious psychopathology in adulthood (e.g., alcoholism, substance abuse, and antisocial personality disorder).

## NEUROPSYCHOLOGICAL ASSESSMENT OF GTS AND ADHD

A number of studies have examined the neuropsychological functioning of individuals with GTA and/or ADHD. The following section summarises findings for individuals with GTS and compares them to those observed for individuals with ADHD.

## Neuropsychology of GTS

Although the majority of children with GTS are of normal intelligence, many studies have reported neuropsychological abnormalities in individuals with GTS (Bornstein, 1990; Schultz et al., 1998; Schultz, Carter, Scahill, & Leckman, 1999). The most consistently observed deficits have involved tasks that measure visuomotor integration or visual-graphic ability. These abilities have been examined in at least 12 different studies from 1967 to the present. Lucas, Kauffman, and Morris (1967) reported that 8 out of 15 adolescents with GTS drew abnormal drawings when given the Bender Gestalt Test. Shapiro, Shapiro, and Clarkin (1974) gave the Bender Gestalt to 30 individuals with GTS. They found that 24 out of the 30 drawings showed some deficits. A later replication study from the same group (Shapiro, Shapiro, Bruun, & Sweet, 1978), examined 50 GTS subjects and 50 non-GTS psychiatric outpatients. Forty per cent of the GTS subjects scored in the organically impaired range on the Bender Gestalt compared to only fourteen per cent of the non-GTS individuals. Similar findings for the Bender Gestalt were reported by Ferrari, Matthews, and Barabas (1984), Hagin, Beecher, Pagano, and Kreeger (1982), and Incagnoli and Kane (1981). Comparable results were reported by Brookshire, Butler, Ewing-Cobbs, and Fletcher (1994), who examined GTS individuals with the Beery Test of Visual-Motor Integration (VMI). Children with GTS scored 0.75 standard deviations below the normative mean, even though their IQs were average. When compared to a motor free visual-perceptual task (Benton Judgement of Line Orientation), their VMI scores were significantly lower, suggesting a deficit in integration of visual and motor abilities, rather than just a deficit in visual-perceptual abilities. Carter, Gladstone, and Schultz (1992) found similar differences on the VMI. However, they reported that weaknesses on the VMI were related to depressive symptomatology. Finally, Schultz et al. (1998) also reported significant differences between GTS children and controls on the VMI. Furthermore, these findings held even when controlling for the presence of ADHD and depressive symptomatology. Finally, the Rey-Osterrieth Complex Figure Test (Rey Figure) was used in five studies to examine the visual-perceptual and motor skills of GTS individuals. The Rey Figure, in addition to measuring visuomotor skills, also examines skills important in executive functioning and organisational abilities. Findings are equivocal. Sutherland, Kolb, Schoel, Whishaw, and Davies (1982) reported that individuals with GTS were significantly impaired when compared to controls. Harris et al. (1995) found that children with GTS and ADHD scored significantly worse than did children with GTS alone (GTS–ADHD). Children with GTS alone scored slightly higher than the normative mean, whereas children with GTS + ADHD scored SD 0.75 below the mean. Schuerholz,

Baumgardner, Singer, Reiss, and Denckla (1996) also reported that children with GTS–ADHD were superior on the Rey Figure, when compared to children with GTS + ADHD, and to a group of unaffected control children. These findings were not replicated by Schultz et al. (1998).

In addition to examining visuomotor abilities, there have been a number of other studies of GTS individuals that have focused on executive functioning. The domain of executive functioning (EF) includes planning, goal-directed behavior, maintenance of cognitive set, cognitive flexibility, impulse control, sustained attention, and self-regulation. Thus, EF does not refer to a single ability, but rather to a range of related abilities. Nevertheless, given that GTS individuals are characterised by an inability to inhibit urges to move and vocalise, inhibitory processes and related executive functions are logical topics of investigation.

Compared to visuomotor integration, the findings with regard to EF in GTS individuals are much less clear. At least 13 studies of GTS individuals have incorporated measures of EF (Baron-Cohen, Cross, Crowson, & Robertson, 1994; Bornstein, 1990, 1991; Bornstein, Baker, Bazylewich, & Douglas, 1991; Channon, Flynn, & Robertson, 1992; Georgiou, Bradshaw, Phillips, & Chiu, 1996; Harris et al., 1995; Ozonoff, Strayer, McMahon, & Filloux, 1994; Randolph, Hyde, Gold, Goldberg, & Weinberger, 1993; Schultz et al., 1998; Shucard, Benedict, Tekpkkilic, & Lichter, 1997; Silverstein, Como, Palumbo, West, & Osborn, 1995; Sutherland et al., 1982; Yeates & Bornstein, 1994). Although some studies find EF differences on selected measures, there are inconsistencies across studies. For example, in tests of mental flexibility no consistent finding has emerged. On the other hand, a consistent result has been observed in response time during continuous performance tests (CPT; Como & Kurlan, 1991; Harris et al., 1995; Shucard et al., 1997). Children with GTS consistently respond more slowly during CPT. This was observed even when the presence of attentional difficulties was controlled for (Harris et al., 1995). Of interest is that whereas response time measures appear to be related to GTS, omission and commission errors do not (Como & Kurlan, 1991; Harris et al., 1995; Randolph et al., 1993; Schultz et al., 1998; Shucard et al., 1997).

In summary, studies that have looked at neuropsychological functioning in children with Tourette's Syndrome have found very similar patterns of results. Intellectual functioning is largely average to above average. In spite of this, psychomotor and visual-perceptual deficits are routinely observed in children with GTS. Fine-motor, executive functioning, and attention deficits are also present. Many of these deficits lend support to the notion that basal ganglia abnormalities are involved in the manifestation of Tourette's Syndrome. However, a caveat for all published reports on GTS and associated features needs to be mentioned. All current studies have been done with clinic-referred children. Comprehensive prospective assessment of attention, impulsivity and neuropsychological functioning in a sample of unaffected children at risk is needed to understand the developmental course of the GTS and related conditions.

**Neuropsychology of ADHD**

As noted previously, executive functioning encompasses abilities related to planning, goal-directed behaviour, maintenance of cognitive set, cognitive flexibility, impulse control, sustained attention, and self-regulation. Thus, it is not surprising that it has been hypothesised that individuals with ADHD may show some executive function deficits.

Seidman et al. (1995) administered the Rey Figure to 65 boys with ADHD and 45 age-, grade-, and socioeconomic-status-matched controls. ADHD children, when copying the Rey figure, were less accurate in their drawings, leaving out significantly more details of the figure than did the control children. Furthermore, ADHD children were significantly impaired on the organisation of the copy, which assesses the extent to which the elements of the figure were organised in relation to one another. When asked to reproduce the figure from memory, children with ADHD and control subjects did not differ significantly in the number of elements they were able to remember, nor in the extent to which elements were organised in relation to one another. However, a significantly larger percentage of the control children used a configurational style when recalling the figure.

Loge, Staton, and Beatty (1990) examined 20 children meeting *Diagnostic and Statistical Manual of Mental Disorders*, third edition, revised (*DSM-III-R*; American Psychiatric Association, 1987) criteria for ADHD, and 20 sex- and age-matched controls free of learning disabilities, neurological, or psychiatric illnesses. The tests administered included the Wechsler Intelligence Scale for Children—Revised (WISC-R), the Reading Comprehension Test (a subtest of the Woodcock-Johnson reading group), the Benton Line Orientation Test, the Parietal Lobe Drawings, the Gordon Diagnostic System (GDS), the Symbol Digit Modalities Test (SDMT), Verbal Fluency, Design Fluency, the Wisconsin Card Sorting Test (WCST), the Peterson-Brown Short-Term Memory Test, and the California Verbal Learning Test (CVLT).

Although all children in both groups scored in the normal range on the WISC-R full-scale IQ measure, the children in the ADHD group scored significantly lower than did the children in the control group. In addition, the children in the ADHD group performed poorly on a test of reading comprehension, and on measures of verbal learning (CVLT) and memory (Peterson-Brown Test). ADHD subjects also made more errors of commission, on both the Vigilance Task and the Distractibility Task, than did control children.

The ADHD children in this study generally performed normally on the various tests of frontal lobe dysfunction (Verbal Fluency, Category Fluency, Design Fluency, WCST). Thus, these researchers concluded that the cognitive performance of children with ADHD did not appear to be characterised by predominant, generalised, or severe frontal lobe dysfunction. They proposed that the frontal lobe physiological abnormalities that occur in ADHD were probably due to widely distributed circuits involved in the executive control of attention.

Grodinsky and Diamond (1992) too looked specifically at executive functioning in boys with ADHD. Their subjects were 130 boys (66 ADHD and 64 controls) between the ages of 6 and 11 years. They administered tests of inhibition/impulsivity (the Gordon Diagnostic System-Vigilance Task, the Stroop Colour–Word Interference Test), tests of cognitive flexibility (the Trail Making Test and the WCST), and tests of planning and organisation (Controlled Oral Word Association Test [COWAT]—a verbal fluency task), Porteus Mazes, and the Rey Figure.

The results revealed that ADHD boys were inferior to controls on both tasks of inhibition/impulsivity and planning and organisation. In contrast, the two tests considered to be sensitive to cognitive flexibility failed to yield positive results. Improvements with age were seen on almost all tasks in the battery. The age effects were consistent for both ADHD boys and control boys.

Fischer, Barkley, Edelbrock, and Smallish (1990) followed 100 hyperactive children and 60 community controls prospectively over an 8-year period into adolescence. The children ranged in age from 4 to 12 years at the initial evaluation, and were 14–20 years old at follow-up. The neuropsychological instruments used were the Selective Reminding Test—to test verbal learning and memory; the WCST—to assess abstract conceptualization and problem solving; and the COWAT—to measure verbal fluency.

No differences were found between the hyperactive and control groups at follow-up on any of the three neuropsychological measures. This was an unexpected finding, and the authors suggested that the deficits found in younger children dissipated as the child matured. Future studies following children with ADHD over time, and testing them more frequently, are needed.

Weyandt and Willis (1994) studied 115 children aged 6–12 years, with either ADHD ($n = 36$), developmental language disorder ($n = 34$), or no disability ($n = 45$). Using six measures of executive functioning, they found that children with ADHD performed more poorly than did control children on two of those measures. Significant differences were found on the Matching Familiar Figures Test and the Tower of Hanoi, but not on measures of verbal fluency, visual search, WCST, or mazes. These findings are consistent with those of Loge et al. (1990), but differ from those of Grodinsky and Diamond (1992).

Consistent with the report of Fischer et al. (1990), Weyandt and Willis (1994) observed age-related changes in executive function performance across three different age groups. Improved performance was associated with increasing age. Children aged 10–12 years performed better than did children aged 8–9 years, who performed better than children aged 6–7 years.

To address age related changes, Seidman, Biederman, Faraone, Weber, and Ouellette (1997) examined the neuropsychological functioning of both younger ( < 15 years) and older ( ≥ 15 years) children with ADHD. Their subjects included 118 male participants aged 9–22 years, and 99 male controls. Full-scale IQ was estimated from the Vocabulary and Block Design subtests of the WISC-R, and academic achievement was assessed with the Reading and Arithmetic tests of the Wide Range Achievement Test—Revised (WRAT-R). Specific neuropsychological tests included the Rey Figure, Finger Tapping Test, auditory Continuous Performance Test, Wide-Range Achievement Test of Memory and Learning (WRAM-L) for children under 17 years, the CVLT for children 17 years of age and older, the computerised WCST, the Stroop test, and the scattered-letters version of the visual cancellations test.

Results indicated that the boys with a *DSM-III-R* diagnosis of ADHD were significantly more impaired in neuropsychological functioning compared to age-matched controls without ADHD. Specifically, the children with ADHD performed worse on measures of various tasks of attention and executive functioning. These findings were found across the two age groups, suggesting that neuropsychological deficits were not restricted to younger children with ADHD. However, Seidman and colleagues (1997) found that the cognitive impairments in younger and older boys with ADHD occurred in the context of overall better neuropsychological performance for older participants, regardless of group membership. The impairment was most pronounced on the Stroop Test, the WCST, and the Rey Figure, all tests of executive function.

Pennington and Ozonoff (1996), in their review of neuropsychological deficits in children with developmental disorders, found that in 15 out of 18 studies significant differences between ADHD subjects and controls were found on measures of executive function. A total of 60 executive function measures was used across the reviewed studies, and for 40 (67%) of these there was significantly worse performance by the ADHD subjects. Among the measures most sensitive to ADHD were the Tower of Hanoi, Stroop test, Matching Familiar Figures Test number of errors, and Trail Making Test Part B. Also sensitive were measures of motor inhibition, such as the Go No-Go, the Stopping Task, the Anti-Saccade task, the Conflict Motor task, and the Neuropsychological Assessment of Children Inhibition measure.

Thus, in contrast to the findings with GTS individuals, where the predominant findings were of visuomotor integration deficits, the studies of ADHD individuals suggested more deficits in EF. There is some overlap however, and more work is needed in which individuals with GTS alone, ADHD alone and GTS + ADHD are compared. Only when these individuals are directly assessed, and comparisons are made using the same experimental paradigms, will it be possible to determine the overlap of deficits between these two disorders.

## Neuropsychology of comorbid GTS and ADHD

Four studies (Harris et al., 1995; Schuerholz et al., 1996; Schultz et al., 1998; Yeates & Bornstein, 1994) have compared GTS individuals with ADHD (GTS + ADHD) to GTS individuals without ADHD (GTS–ADHD), whereas one compared GTS + ADHD individuals to those with ADHD alone (Como & Kurlan, 1991).

Schuerholz and colleagues (1996) studied 65 children between the ages of 6 and 14 years. *DSM-IV* criteria were used to assign a diagnosis of GTS and/or ADHD, along with subsequent parent report measures (Conner's Abbreviated Parent Symptom Questionnaire, and the Achenbach Child Behavior Checklist [CBCL]. Twenty-one children were diagnosed with GTS only, and nineteen children with GTS + ADHD. The remaining 25 children were those for whom a diagnosis of ADHD was not clearly established, but who had clear ADHD characteristics by at least one criterion. These children were considered highly suspect in terms of ADHD, and were given the diagnosis of GTS ± ADHD. In addition, a comparison group was formed from 27 unaffected siblings of children involved in other research at the same institution. ADHD, along with other major cognitive or neurological disorders, was ruled out in all 27 of these children.

A comprehensive battery of tests was given—it measured IQ, language and reading skills, visual-spatial processing, executive functioning, and self-regulatory processes. The GTS–ADHD group had the highest mean full-scale IQ (117), with the GTS ± ADHD group second, and the comparison and the GTS + ADHD group with the lowest full-scale IQ scores. There was a significant difference between the GTS–ADHD group and the GTS + ADHD group in full-scale IQ. There were no learning disabilities found in the GTS–ADHD group, although 15 children from the other two experimental groups had at least one learning disability.

The only significant differences observed between the GTS–ADHD and GTS + ADHD groups were for measures of self-regulation, visual-spatial processing, executive functioning, and phoneme segmentation.

Yeates and Bornstein (1994) found that 16 individuals with GTS + ADHD were significantly more impaired on some measures of cognitive flexibility (Trail Making A and B), but not on others (the WCST), than were 34 children with GTS–ADHD. On the other hand, Schultz et al. (1999) reported no differences on Trail Making or WCST. In contrast, Harris et al. (1995) and Silverstein et al. (1995) found greater impairment on the WCST among GTS + ADHD individuals when compared to GTS–ADHD individuals.

Impulsivity was also examined in these groups. Harris et al. (1995) found that GTS + ADHD subjects were significantly more impulsive than were GTS–ADHD subjects, as did Schultz et al. (1998). Moreover, the latter investigators found that visuomotor integration skill and inhibitory control together were able to classify 80% of the GTS–ADHD and 82% of the controls. Como and Kurlan (1991) examined whether EF measures differed between GTS + ADHD and ADHD individuals without tics, and found that children with ADHD alone performed significantly worse on a number of dimensions, including speed of response and number of CPT commission errors.

In sum, there appears to be some overlap of deficits in GTS and ADHD individuals, but the similarities are not completely understood. The similarities that have been noted may have occurred in those GTS individuals with comorbid ADHD, although in a few more recent studies this does not appear to explain all similarities. It is also quite clear that there are very specific differences between GTS and ADHD individuals. The most obvious result of the work that has been done to date is that more work is needed. Although a few studies have been reported that examined individuals with each disorder separately, more are needed. Future studies need to examine representative samples, and not samples that have come from clinic populations. These studies also need to examine children prospectively.

## Familial relationship between GTS and ADHD

The familial/genetic relationship between GTS and ADHD is controversial. As noted earlier, Comings and Comings (1987) proposed that ADHD represented a variant expression of the underlying genetic factors important for the manifestation of GTS. In 1993, Pauls et al. reported the results of a family study that found no evidence of a genetic relationship between GTS and ADHD. Their analysis addressed the question of whether or not the occurrence of ADHD among first degree relatives was dependent upon the attention-deficit status of the proband, and hence whether or not these diagnoses represent true genetic pleiotropy rather than separate inheritance mechanisms. Pauls et al. used a family genetic design to measure the rate of ADHD in two categories of first-degree relatives: those of GTS probands with comorbid ADHD, and those of GTS probands without comorbid ADHD. The rate of ADHD among relatives of GTS probands with ADHD (GTS + ADHD probands) was 15.9% (24 out of 151 relatives), whereas the rate among relatives of GTS probands without ADHD (GTS–ADHD probands) was only 3.2% (6 out of 187 relatives). These results were significantly different at the $p = .0001$ level ($\chi^2$ 1 = 15.1); the attentional status of the relatives was significantly associated with the attentional status of the GTS proband. Thus, since the rate of ADHD alone was not elevated among non-GTS affected relatives, these data suggested that ADHD did not represent a pleiotropic expression of a susceptibility gene for GTS.

The design of the Comings and Comings (1987) study, in which the authors proposed ADHD as a variant expression of the spectrum of GTS, was quite different from the study reported by Pauls and colleagues (1993). Whereas the data reported by Pauls et al. (1993) were from direct personal interviews, and best estimate diagnoses, the data reported by Comings and Comings (1987) came primarily from a single informant in the proband's family. The data as presented in the initial Comings and Comings report could not be re-analysed to allow for a direct comparison between the two studies. However, in a subsequent paper, Knell and Comings (1993) provided some family data that could be analysed in a comparable way. The most informative analysis for this type of data is not to make separate comparisons of each group of relatives with a control group (as these authors did). Rather, it is preferable directly to compare the rate of ADHD in the relatives of GTS + ADHD probands with the rate of ADHD in relatives of GTS–ADHD probands. If an attentional deficit is inherited as part of the Tourette's diathesis, then the attentional status of the GTS–ADHD proband should have no effect on the rates of ADHD in the first-degree relatives.

Analysing the data reported by Knell and Comings (1993) in this way reveals that their data show very similar patterns to those reported by Pauls et al. (1993). In the Knell and Comings data, 34 out of 194 relatives (17.5%) of GTS + ADHD probands had ADHD, compared to only 14 out of 144 relatives (9.7%) of GTS–ADHD probands. This difference is significant (Fishers Exact Test $p = .02$). Thus, similar to the result reported by Pauls et al. the relatives of GTS + ADHD probands were at significantly greater risk for ADHD than were the relatives of GTS–ADHD probands. Taken at face value, these findings do not support the hypothesis that there is a genetic relationship between GTS and ADHD. However, the rate of ADHD among the relatives of GTS–ADHD probands in the Knell and Comings sample was elevated over some estimates of the population prevalence for ADHD and thus the results are inconclusive regarding a genetic relationship between GTS and ADHD.

It is possible that individuals with GTS + ADHD may represent a subtype of disorder that is in part distinct from GTS and/or ADHD alone. Our data (Pauls et al., 1993) suggested that there may be two different types of individuals with GTS and ADHD. Although the morbid risks among family members did not suggest a genetic relationship between GTS and ADHD, further analyses were performed to determine if individuals with GTS + ADHD might represent a distinct subtype of the syndrome. To examine this hypothesis, logistic regression analyses were undertaken. Logistic regression analyses allow the examination of relationships between categorical data much in the same way as traditional regression analyses are used to examine quantitative data. The initial full model predicted the occurrence of ADHD, and included age as a covariate; gender of the individual; ADHD diagnosis of the proband; GTS or CT diagnosis of the relative; whether the individual was a relative of a GTS proband or control; and all possible interactions. Stepwise selection by simple deletion of effects produced the most parsimonious model that included ADHD diagnosis of the GTS proband ($p < .0001$), gender ($p < .0019$), and diagnosis of GTS ($p < .014$). No interactions reached statistical significance. These results again demonstrated the fact that ADHD occurred most often among the relatives of GTS probands who themselves had a diagnosis of ADHD (15.9% vs 3.2%). As well as this, more males than females had ADHD (odds ratio of 1.9), and there was a higher than expected occurrence of ADHD among those relatives who had a diagnosis of GTS (25.0% vs 8.9% overall). There was no suggestion that ADHD alone was a variant manifestation of the GTS spectrum.

On the other hand, these results suggested that individuals who have GTS were at greater risk for exhibiting symptoms of inattention and impulsivity. It is possible that GTS and some forms of ADHD share some common pathways of expression. Alternatively, it is possible that having GTS interferes with an individual's ability to attend appropriately to stimuli in the surrounding environment. Arguing against this explanation is the fact that many GTS patients appear to have symptoms of inattention prior to onset of tics. It follows that not all of the attentional problems experienced by individuals with GTS are secondary to the expression of GTS.

In an attempt to determine if there were differences among relatives who had both GTS and ADHD, several comparisons were made. First, relatives with both ADHD and GTS were compared to relatives who had ADHD without tics. The age at onset of ADHD for relatives with both disorders was compared to the age at onset of ADHD among relatives who had only ADHD. It should be noted that the sample of relatives was too small to allow meaningful statistical comparisons, but the preliminary results provided some interesting trends. First, there was a difference in the reported age at onset for ADHD among relatives who also had GTS, when compared to relatives who had only ADHD. The average age at onset of ADHD was 6.3 for relatives with both GTS and ADHD, compared to 5.5 for relatives with ADHD alone. Furthermore, examining the actual ages at onset for all relatives with both diagnoses revealed that, for all but one individual, the onset for ADHD occurred, either simultaneously with the onset of tics, or after the onset of tics. This suggested that the ADHD experienced by relatives with GTS might be secondary to the onset of GTS.

It could be hypothesised that earlier onset ADHD is more likely to be aetiologically independent of GTS. If that be so, then to the extent that ADHD is familial, the risk of ADHD alone among relatives of GTS probands with early onset ADHD should be higher than the risk of ADHD alone among relatives of GTS probands who have later onset ADHD. Examining the relatives in these two types of families revealed that the rate of ADHD alone, among relatives of GTS probands with earlier onset ADHD, was 25.0% compared to only 12.2% among the relatives of GTS probands with later onset ADHD ($\chi^2 = 3.85$, $p < .05$). These findings suggested that there might be at least two types of GTS probands with ADHD:

(1) those who have a form of ADHD independent of GTS (probands with onset of ADHD prior to onset of GTS)
(2) those who have a form that is secondary to the expression of GTS (probands with concurrent or later onset of ADHD).

A caveat regarding these data is that all ages at onset were obtained retro-spectively. Retrospective data about age at onset is not optimal. Thus, these findings regarding the sequence of onset of GTS and ADHD should be considered as hypothesis generating. In future work designed to more fully understand the relationship between GTS and ADHD, it will be important to study younger individuals who are closer to their onset age as well as their families. Another alternative is to prospectively follow very young children at risk for GTS to collect data about the early developmental and clinical course of these individuals. This will allow for a more rigorous examination of this hypothesis.

Prospective longitudinal studies of very young children at risk are needed in order to understand more fully the connection between GTS and ADHD. By following children at risk, and evaluating them in several different domains, it should be possible to obtain data to elucidate the relationship between these two syndromes. A prospective longitudinal study of children at risk, that documents shared and unique environments, is needed. Prospective data would help to document whether ADHD represents the first symptoms of GTS, or whether it reflects a broader response of children to the combination of pathophysiologic vulnerability and environmental stressors.

## MOLECULAR GENETIC STUDIES OF GTS AND ADHD

Comings and others (see, for example, Comings et al., 1996) have reported associations with other dopamine receptors. These findings have not been replicated by other investigators. Results from association studies, using a case-control paradigm, are difficult to interpret, and have been shown to be particularly susceptible to false positive results due to population stratification (Gelernter, Goldman, & Risch, 1993).

As described elsewhere in this volume (Barr, Swanson, & Kennedy, Chapter 10), there have been several studies of ADHD in which associations have been reported with several different genes. One such association has been reported for the "7" allele of DRD4 receptor gene. This allele has also been reported to be associated with GTS (Grice et al., 1996). The association was observed in only three small nuclear families that were part of several large multigenerational families, and has not been replicated in other more repre-sentative samples (Hebebrand et al., 1997; van de Wetering, personal communication).

## SUMMARY

In sum, although the neuropsychological data suggest some similarities between GTS and ADHD, there is no compelling data to support the hypothesis that there is a genetic relationship between GTS and ADHD.

Neither the family data nor the molecular genetic data provide convincing evidence for a simple genetic relationship. As noted, more data collected in a prospective longitudinal way are needed to examine more completely the aetiological relationship between these two interesting and complex disorders of childhood.


## REFERENCES

American Psychiatric Association. (1987). *Diagnostic and statistical manual of mental disorders* (3rd ed.). Washington, DC: Author.

American Psychiatric Association. (1994). *Diagnostic and statistical manual of mental disorders* (4th ed.). Washington, DC: Author.

Anderson, J.C., Williams, S., McGee, R., & Silva, P.A. (1987). DSM-III disorders in pre-adolescent children: Prevalence in a large sample from the general population. *Archives of General Psychiatry, 44*, 69–76.

Baron-Cohen, S., Cross, P., Crowson, M., & Robertson, M.M. (1994). Can children with Gilles de la Tourette syndrome edit their intentions? *Psychological Medicine, 24*, 29–40.

Biederman, J., Faraone, S.V., Keenan, K., Benjamin, J., Krifcher, B., Moore, C., Sprich-Buckminster, S., Ugaglia, K., Jellinek, M.S., Steingard, R., Spencer, T.J., Norman, D., Kolodny, R., Kraus, I., Perrin, J., Keller, M.B., & Tsuang, M.T. (1992). Further evidence for family genetic risk factors in Attention Deficit Hyperactivity Disorder: Patterns of comorbidity in probands and relatives in psychiatrically and pediatrically referred samples. *Archives of General Psychiatry, 49*, 728–738.

Biederman, J., Faraone, S.V., Mick, E., Spencer, T.J., Wilens, T.E., Kiely, K., Guite, J., Ablon, J.S., Reed, E., & Warburton, R. (1995). High risk for Attention Deficit Hyperactivity Disorder among children of parents with childhood onset of the disorder: A pilot study. *American Journal of Psychiatry, 152*, 431–435.

Biederman, J., Munir, K., Knee, D., Habelow, W., Armentano, M., Autor, S., Hoge, S.K., & Waternaux, C. (1986). A family study of patients with Attention Deficit Disorder and normal controls. *Journal of Psychiatry Research, 20*, 263–274.

Bornstein, R.A. (1990). Neuropsychological performance in children with Tourette's Syndrome. *Psychiatry Research, 33*, 78–81.

Bornstein, R.A. (1991). Neuropsychological performance in adults with Tourette's syndrome. *Psychiatric Research, 37*, 229–236.

Bornstein, R.A., Baker, G.B., Bazylewich, T., & Douglas, A.B. (1991). Tourette syndrome and neuropsychological performance. *Acta Psychiatrica Scandinavica, 84*, 212–216.

Bornstein, R.A., King, G., & Carroll, A. (1983). Neurological abnormalities in Gilles de la Tourette's Syndrome. *Journal of Nervous and Mental Disease, 171*, 497–502.

Brookshire, B.L., Butler, I.J., Ewing-Cobbs, L., & Fletcher, J.M. (1994). Neuropsychological characteristics of children with Tourette syndrome: Evidence for a nonverbal learning disability? *Journal of Clinical and Experimental Neuropsychology, 16*, 289–302.

Cantwell, D.P. (1985). Hyperactive children have grown up: What have we learned about what happens to them? *Archives of General Psychiatry, 42*, 1026–1028.

Carter, A.S., Gladstone, M., & Schultz, R. T. (1992). *Neurological functioning of children affected with Tourette's Syndrome*. Paper presented at the National Academy of Neuropsychologists, Pittsburgh, PA.

Carter, A.S., O'Donnell, D.A., Schultz, R.T., Scahill, L., Leckman, J.F., & Pauls, D.L. (2000). *Social and emotional adjustment in children affected with Gilles de la Tourette's syndrome: Associations with ADHD and family functioning. Journal of Child Psychology and Psychiatry*, *41*, 215–223.

Channon, S., Flynn, D., & Robertson, M.M. (1992). Attentional deficits in Gilles de la Tourette syndrome. *Neuropsychiatry, Neuropsychology and Behavioral Neurology*, *5*, 170–177.

Cohen, D.J., (1990). *Tourette's syndrome: Developmental psychopathology of a model psychiatric disorder of childhood*. The 27th annual Institute of Pennsylvania Hospital Award Lecture in Memory of Edward A. Strecker.

Comings, D.E. & Comings, B.G. (1987). A controlled study of Tourette syndrome: I. Attention-deficit learning disorders, and school problems. *American Journal of Human Genetics*, *41*, 701–741.

Comings, D.E., Wu, S., Chiu, C., Ring, R.H., Gade, R., Ahn, C., MacMurray, J.P., Dietz, G., & Muhleman, D. (1996). Polygenic inheritance of Tourette syndrome, stuttering, attention deficit hyperactivity, conduct, and oppositional defiant disorder: The additive and subtractive effect of the three dopaminergic genes—DRD2, D beta H, and DAT1. *American Journal of Medical Genetics (Neuropsychiatric Genetics)*, *67*, 264–288.

Como, P.G., & Kurlan, R. (1991). An open-label trial of fluoxetine for obsessive-compulsive disorder in Gilles de la Tourette's syndrome. *Neurology*, *41*, 872–874.

Costello, E.J., Costello, A.J., Edelbrock, C., Burns, B.J., Dulcan, M.K., Brent, D., & Janiszewski, S. (1988). Psychiatric diagnoses in pediatric primary care: Prevalence and risk factors. *Archives of General Psychiatry*, *45*, 1107–1116.

Dykens, E., Leckman, J., Riddle, M.A., Hardin, M., Schwartz, S., & Cohen, D. (1990). Intellectual, academic, and adaptive functioning of Tourette Syndrome children with and without Attention Deficit Disorder. *Journal of Abnormal Child Psychology*, *18*, 607–615.

Faraone, S.V., Biederman, J., Chen, W.J., Krifcher, B., Keenan, K., Moore, C., Sprich, S., & Tsuang, M.T. (1992). Segregation analysis of Attention Deficit Hyperactivity Disorder: Evidence for single gene transmission. *Psychiatric Genetics*, *2*, 257–275.

Ferrari, M., Matthews, W.S., & Barabas, G. (1984). Children with Tourette's Syndrome: Results of psychological tests given prior to drug treatment. *Developmental and Behavioral Pediatrics*, *5*, 116–119.

Fischer, M., Barkley, R.A., Edelbrock, C.S., & Smallish, L. (1990). The adolescent outcome of hyperactive children diagnosed by research criteria: II. Academic, attentional, and neuropsychological status. *Journal of Consulting and Clinical Psychology*, *58*, 580–588.

Gelernter, J., Goldman, D., & Risch, N. (1993). The A1 allele at the D2 dopamine receptor gene and alcoholism: A reappraisal. *Journal of the American Medical Association*, *269*, 1673–1677.

Georgiou, N., Bradshaw, J.L., Phillips, J.G., & Chiu, E. (1996). The effect of Huntington's disease and Gilles de la Tourette's syndrome on the ability to hold and shift attention. *Neuropsycholgia*, *34*, 843–851.

Grice, D.E., Leckman, J.F., Pauls, D.L., Kurlan, R., Kidd, K.K., Pakstis, A.J., Chang, F.M., Cohen, D.J., & Gelernter, J. (1996). Linkage disequilibrium between an allele at the dopamine D4 receptor locus with Tourette's syndrome by the transmission disequilibrium test. *American Journal of Human Genetics, 59,* 644–652.

Grodinsky, G.M., & Diamond, R. (1992). Frontal lobe functioning in boys with attention-deficit hyperactivity disorder. *Developmental Neuropsychology, 8,* 427–445.

Hagin, R.A., Beecher, R., Pagano, G., & Kreeger, H. (1982). Effects of Tourette syndrome on learning. *Advances in Neurology, 35,* 323–328.

Harris, E.L., Schuerholz, L.J., Singer, H.S., Reader, M.J., Brown, J.E., Cox, C., Mohr, J., Chase, G.A., & Denckla, M.B. (1995). Executive function in children with Tourette syndrome and/or Attention Deficit Hyperactivity Disorder. *Journal of the International Neuropsychological Society, 1,* 511–516.

Hebebrand, J., Nothen, M.M., Ziegler, A., Klug, B., Neidt, H., Eggermann, K., Lehm-kuhl, G., Poustka, F., Schmidt, M.H., Propping, P., & Remschmidt, H. (1997). Nonreplication of linkage disequilibrium between the dopamine D4 receptor locus and Tourette syndrome. *American Journal of Human Genetics, 61,* 238–239.

Incagnoli, T., & Kane, R.L. (1981). Neuropsychological functioning in Gilles de la Tourette's syndrome. *Journal of Clinical Neuropsychology, 3,* 167–171.

Jagger, J., Prusoff, B.A., Cohen, D.J., Kidd, K.K., Carbonari, C.M., & John, K. (1982). The epidemiology of Tourette's syndrome: A pilot study. *Schizophrenia Bulletin, 8,* 267–277.

Knell, E.R., & Comings, D.E. (1993). Tourette's syndrome and attention-deficit hyperactivity disorder: Evidence for a genetic relationship. *Journal of Clinical Psychiatry, 54,* 331–337.

Leckman, J.F., & Cohen, D.J. (1999). *Tourette Syndrome: Tics, obsessions, compulsions.* New York: Wiley & Sons.

Leckman, J.F., King, R.A., & Cohen, D.J. (1999). Tics and tic disorders. In: J.F. Leckman & D.J. Cohen (eds.), *Tourette Syndrome: Tics, obsessions, compulsions* (pp. 23–42). New York: Wiley & Sons.

Leckman, J.F., Zhang, H., Vitale, A., Lahnin, F., Lynch, K., Bondi, C., Kim, Y.-S., & Peterson, B.S. (1998). Trajectories of tic severity in Tourette's syndrome: The first two decades. *Pediatrics, 102,* 14–19.

Loge, D.V., Staton, R.D., & Beatty, W.W. (1990). Performance of children with ADHD on tests sensitive to frontal lobe dysfunction. *Journal of the American Academy of Child and Adolescent Psychiatry, 29,* 540–545.

Lucas, A.R., Kauffman, P.E., & Morris, E.M. (1967). Gilles de la Tourette disease: A clinical study of fifteen cases. *Journal of the American Academy of Child and Adolescent Psychiatry, 6,* 700–722.

McGee, R., Williams, S., & Silva, P.A. (1987). A comparison of girls and boys with teacher-identified problems of attention. *Journal of the American Academy of Child and Adolescent Psychiatry, 26,* 711–717.

Ozonoff, S., Strayer, D.L., McMahon, W.M., & Filloux, F. (1994). Executive function abilities in autism and Tourette syndrome: An information processing approach. *Journal of Child Psychology and Psychiatry, 35,* 1015–1032.

Pauls, D.L., Hurst, C.R., Kidd, K.K., Kruger, S.D., Leckman, J.F., & Cohen, D.J. (1986). Tourette syndrome and Attention Deficit Disorder: Evidence against a genetic relationship. *Archives of General Psychiatry, 43,* 1177–1179.

Pauls, D.L., Leckman, J.F., & Cohen, D.J. (1993). Familial relationship between Gilles de la Tourette's Syndrome, Attention Deficit Disorder, Learning Disabilities, Speech Disorders, and Stuttering. *Journal of the American Academy of Child and Adolescent Psychiatry, 32,* 1044–1050.

Pennington, B.F., & Ozonoff, S. (1996). Executive functions and developmental psychopathology. *Journal of Child Psychology, Psychiatry, and Allied Disciplines, 37,* 51–87.

Randolph, C., Hyde, T.M., Gold, J.M., Goldberg, T.E., & Weinberger, D.R. (1993). Tourette's syndrome in monozygotic twins: Relationship of tic severity to neuropsychological function. *Archives of Neurology, 50,* 725–728.

Reeves, J.C., Werry, J.S., Elkind, G.S., & Zametkin, A.J. (1987). Attention deficit, conduct, oppositional, and anxiety disorders in children: II. Clinical characteristics. *Journal of the American Academy of Child and Adolescent Psychiatry, 26,* 144–155.

Schuerholz, L.J., Baumgardner, T.L., Singer, H.S., Reiss, A.L., & Denckla, M.B. (1996). Neurological status of children with Tourette's syndrome with and without Attention Deficit Hyperactivity Disorder. *Neurology, 46,* 958–965.

Schultz, R.T., Carter, A.S., Gladstone, M., Scahill, L., Leckman, J.F., Peterson, B.S., Zhang, H., Cohen, D.J., & Pauls, D.L. (1998). Visual-motor integration, visuoperceptual and fine motor functioning in children with Tourette syndrome. *Neuropsychology, 12,* 134–145.

Schultz, R.T., Carter, A.S., Scahill, L., & Leckman, J.F. (1999). Neuropsychological findings. In J.F. Leckman & D.J. Cohen (Eds.), *Tourette Syndrome: Tics, obsessions, compulsions (pp. 80–103).* New York: Wiley & Sons.

Seidman, L.J., Benedict, K.B., Biederman, J., Bernstein, J.H., Seiverd, K., Milberger, S., Norman, D., Mick, E., & Faraone, S.V. (1995). Performance of children with ADHD on the Rey-Osterreith Complex Figure: A pilot neuropsychological study. *Journal of Child Psychology, Psychiatry, and Allied Disciplines, 36,* 1459–1473.

Seidman, L.J., Biederman, J., Faraone, S.V., Weber, W., & Ouellette, C. (1997). Toward defining a neuropsychology of attention deficit-hyperactivity disorder: Performance of children and adolescents from a large clinically referred sample. *Journal of Consulting and Clinical Psychology, 65,* 150–160.

Shapiro, A.K., Shapiro, E.S. Bruun, R.D., & Sweet, R.D. (1978). *Gilles de la Tourette Syndrome.* New York: Raven Press.

Shapiro, A.K., Shapiro, E.S. Young, J.G., & Feinberg, T. (1988). *Gilles de la Tourette Syndrome* (2nd ed.). New York: Raven Press.

Shapiro, E.S., Shapiro A.K., & Clarkin, J. (1974). Clinical psychological testing in Tourette's syndrome. *Journal of Personality Assessment, 38,* 464–478.

Shucard, D.W., Benedict, R.H.B., Tekpkkilic, A., & Lichter, D.G. (1997). Slowed reaction time during a continuous performance test in children with Tourette's syndrome. *Neuropsychology, 11,* 147–155.

Silverstein, M.S., Como, P.G., Palumbo, D.R., West, L.L., & Osborn, L.M. (1995). Multiple sources of attentional dysfunction in adults with Tourette's syndrome: Comparison with attention deficit-hyperactivity disorder. *Neuropsychology, 2,* 157–164.

Stokes, A., Bawden, H.N, Camfield, P.R., Backman, J.E., & Dooley, M.B. (1991). Peer problems in Tourette's disorder. *Pediatrics, 87,* 936–942.

Sutherland, R.J., Kolb, B., Schoel, W.M., Whishaw, I.Q., & Davies, D. (1982). Neuropsychological assessment of children and adults with Tourette syndrome: A comparison with learning disabilities and schizophrenia. *Advances in Neurology, 35,* 311–321.

Szatmari, P., Offord, D.R., & Boyle, M.H. (1989). Ontario child health study: Prevalence of Attention Deficit Disorder with hyperactivity. *Journal of Child Psychology and Psychiatry, 30,* 219–230.

Towbin, K.E., & Riddle, M.A. (1993). Attention deficit hyperactivity disorder. In R. Kurlan (Ed.), *Handbook of Tourette's Syndrome and related tic and behavioral disorders*. New York: Marcel Dekker.

Werry, J.S., Reeves, J.C., & Elkind G.S. (1987). Attention deficit, conduct, oppositional, and anxiety disorders in children: I. A review of research on differentiating characteristics. *Journal of the American Academy of Child and Adolescent Psychiatry, 26*, 133–143.

Weyandt, L.L., & Willis, W.G. (1994). Executive functions in school-aged children: Potential efficacy of tasks in discriminating clinical groups. *Developmental Neuropsychology, 10*, 27–38.

Yeates, K.O., & Bornstein, R.A. (1994). Attention Deficit Disorder and neuropsychological functioning in children with Tourette's syndrome. *Neuropsychology, 8*, 65–74.

Zohar, A.H., Apter, A., King, R., Pauls, D.L., Leckman, J.F., & Cohen, D.J. (1999). Epidemiological studies. In J.F. Leckman & D.J. Cohen (Eds.), *Tourette Syndrome: Tics, obsessions, compulsions* (pp. 177–193). New York: Wiley & Sons.

# 12  Implications of genetic studies of attentional problems for education and intervention

*David A. Hay and Florence Levy*

The impact of developments in genetic research is achieving ever more public attention and scrutiny. The Human Genome Project is well on target with its plans to sequence the entire human genetic complement—the announcement was made in June 2000 that the initial sequencing goal had been attained. This is pointed out by Rutter in Chapter 13 of this volume. Although in actuality this means only that the entire genetic code has been described, it is being interpreted in the wider community as implying that the genes for *all* traits have been mapped and sequenced. The media have already gone beyond this, vigorously promoting such possibilities as choosing (or changing) the genes that will give your baby the desired attributes in such areas as intelligence, personality, and sporting ability. Will ADHD be added to this list? Although this may seem fanciful, the fact is that families are already associating work on the genetics of ADHD with the potential for genetic manipulation and clinicians should be prepared to answer such questions in an informed manner.

Until now this volume has focused on what is known about the genetics of attentional problems and issues that stand in our way of the advancement of genetic knowledge. It is clear that significant problems remain in defining the phenotype of ADHD, especially at different ages, and it is even more difficult to identify exactly how many genetically distinct subtypes of ADHD exist. Constantly emerging themes of chapters in this text are that ADHD has a very high genetic component, and it is associated with many comorbid conditions. Potential implications of these findings cannot be ignored. We may be a far distance from genetic engineering by which ADHD and other genes are identified very early and manipulated, but there is none the less an accumulating body of knowledge about the genetics of ADHD and its consequences. Implications are already apparent for both clinical practice and education, as well as in the focus of future research.

Chapters in this volume raise many such issues that have a bearing on clinical and educational intervention. In this chapter, we focus on a few key questions that should be seen in the context of recent, broader texts on the aetiology and management of children with ADHD and their families (Accardo, Blondis, Whitman, & Stein, 1999; Sandberg, in press).

# DIAGNOSIS

The continuum versus category issue has implications for the level of symptoms required for diagnosis and for future treatment strategies. As discussed in Chapter 2 of this volume, the fourth edition of the *Diagnostic and Statistical Manual* (*DSM-IV*, American Psychiatric Association, 1994) diagnosis of ADHD—Combined type requires 12 symptoms. However, a child with five symptoms in one or both of the Inattentive and Hyperactive-Impulsive subtypes fails meet criteria for a formal diagnostic label. This fine differentiation makes for difficulty at both the research and clinical levels where categorical diagnoses may be required.

The concept of ADHD as a continuum has been proven for the unitary diagnosis of the American Psychiatric Association. *Diagnostic and Statistical Manual of Mental Disorders*, third edition, revised (*DSM-III-R*; American Psychiatric Association, 1987) (Levy, Hay, McStephen, Woods & Waldman, 1997 and Chapters 2 and 3, this volume). None the less, much remains unclear about the three *DSM-IV* categories and their genetic relationship. At least three competing models exist, implicitly if not explicitly:

(1) the concept of two continua, one of Inattention and one of Hyperactivity-Impulsivity, with the Combined type being the fusion of the two
(2) Barkley's (1997) view that the Hyperactive-Impulsive type is the developmental precursor of the Combined type, with the Inattentive type being a different disorder
(3) Neuman et al.'s (1999) conclusion from their latent class analysis that the Combined type may represent a third continuum, possibly genetically distinct (Chapter 3, this volume) from both Inattention and Hyperactivity-Impulsivity.

At present, conclusions from both quantitative and molecular genetic research are equivocal.

Neale and Kendler (1995) propose elegant genetic models that can test these alternative hypotheses. Our preliminary analyses favour their random multiformity model, where the combined type can result either from an increased risk for one subtype due to presence of the other, or from those individuals who, by chance, are high scorers on both the Inattentive and Hyperactivity–Impulsivity continua. Are there clinical implications for the possibility that there might thus be two forms of the combined type?

Clearly, ADHD is not a single genetic entity. However, how many types actually exist, and on what basis are they defined? This might be of less concern for the clinician, dealing with the immediate needs of children and their families, were it not for the issue of comorbidity. Often the problems comorbid with ADHD are the most difficult to treat. Several chapters in this text have dealt with the most common comorbidities of ADHD. These include learning problems (Chapter 5—speech and language, Chapter 6—reading and spelling), and Oppositional Defiant Disorder (ODD) and Conduct Disorder (CD) (Chapter 7). None the less, the question remains as to whether ADHD subtypes, with or without such additional problems, are genetically distinct. As summarised in Hagemann, Hay, and Levy (in press) genetic analyses need more integration with the growing body of neuropsychological and associated information about heterogeneity within ADHD. This should be done whether this be at the level of reading disability (Tannock, 1998), school behaviour (Gaub & Carlson, 1997), or motor deficits (Piek, Pitcher, & Hay, 1999).

## COMORBIDITY

Taylor (1998) has argued that comorbidity is an important source of heterogeneity in ADHD. For example, the presence or absence of CD is a key clinical distinction, but whether this distinction is associated primarily with family factors or with neurodevelopmental impairment has been a source of contention. Behaviour genetic studies can help to untangle such questions related to symptom overlap.

Waldman, Rhee, Levy, and Hay (Chapter 7, this volume) have shown that most genetic influences on ADHD, ODD, and CD are shared ($r_{ADHD.ODD}$ = .73, $r_{ADHD.CD}$ = .82, $r_{ODD.CD}$ = .79). The findings in relation to the genetic overlap between ADHD and ODD could suggest that both conditions would benefit from similar treatments, including medication and behavior management. This is an important clinical question, in relation to use of medication for subthreshold ADHD comorbid with ODD.

As indicated by the authors, shared environmental influences contributed minimally to ODD symptoms and moderately to CD. However, because the prevalence of CD symptoms in 4- to 12-year-olds is low, it is difficult to draw conclusions about CD. Issues about treatment are ultimately clinical questions, but genetic studies can help to explain clinical findings and guide further research into genetic phenotypes.

## INTERVENTION

A key issue is whether treatment should differ for *DSM-IV* subtypes. To date most treatment studies have been based on *DSM-III-R* symptomatology, as have quantitative and molecular analyses. The authors of several chapters in this text suggest that ADHD subtypes may be genetically distinct, e.g., the finding that the *DSM-IV* subtypes appear to breed true (Chapter 3, this volume) raises issues in relation to clinical treatment. Another issue relating to treatment strategies is the finding that the Inattentive (I) and Hyperactive/Impulsive (HI) subtypes differ in the degree of common family environmental influence (Chapters 3 and 4, this volume). As discussed in Chapter 3, behaviour management may be more important for those symptoms where common enviroment is relatively more significant, and where the behaviour of one twin or sibling may be influencing the other.

Taylor (1998) has discussed findings by Ho et al. (1996) suggesting that the associations of hyperactivity differ according to the situation in which they are recorded. Home-specific behaviour was associated with Oppositional Defiant Disorder (ODD). In contrast, problems specific to school showed a relationship with written language difficulties, and pervasive problems were associated with language delays. In the present text, Levy, McStephen, and Hay (Chapter 3) found differences in genetic and environmental influences, at symptom and subtype levels, between HI and I, which may help explain clinical findings of situational specificity. Varying influences on subtypes may result in different situational responses, with different treatment implications.

## FAMILY DYNAMICS

There is a growing body of evidence concerning the impact on the family of a child with ADHD. Although this is usually seen as environmental, the high heritability of ADHD, and the growing body of knowledge on the manifestations of ADHD in adulthood, may lead to a re-evaluation. To date, the largest body of information comes from the family studies of Biederman and his colleagues (Biederman et al., 1993). Unfortunately family data cannot differentiate cause nor consequences in the relationship between parental and child behaviour.

At the same time, genetic issues must be considered in family-based intervention. Hay and colleagues (Chapter 4, this volume) discuss psychopathology and personality features in adult relatives of ADHD probands, as well as the putative association of the DRD4 gene with novelty seeking (Benjamin et al., 1996). How does parental personality impact upon the child? This may well be one of the first demonstrations of gene–environment correlation (see Rutter, Chapter 13 of this volume), with the parents providing both genes and a parenting style that facilitates the expression of these genes.

## LANGUAGE AND ADHD

The findings by Stevenson (Chapter 6, this volume) in relation to comorbidity of ADHD with reading and spelling disability, as well as Lewis's work on language and ADHD (Chapter 5, this volume) raise issues of both prevention and education. Preventative language approaches may be appropriate at an early stage of development. It is also likely that educational approaches, general and remedial, would differ for different groups. For example, the work of Grigorenko et al. (1997) indicates linkage of different genes to different aspects of reading, which may be differentially involved in ADHD. In addition, Stevenson's emphasis on the importance of phonological processing and spelling disability in comorbidity studies provides a direction for future remedial work. He points out that some studies have shown that children with comorbid ADHD and reading disability are similar to children with reading disability alone in having a deficit in phonological processing.

The question of independent versus co-transmission of ADHD and Learning Disability raised by Biederman et al. (1993) is also addressed by Stevenson in Chapter 6 of this volume, where he proposes co-transmission of ADHD and spelling. Stevenson, Pennington, Gilger, DeFries, & Gillis (1993) estimated that 75% of the covariation between reading and hyperactivity arose from shared genetic factors.

Recently there have been reports of differences in language between ADHD children with and without reading disability (Tannock, 1998), and comorbidity differences between subtypes for social impairment and school-related problems (Hudziak et al., 1998). This supports the notion that comorbidity may be important in targeting specific interventions, or at least in guiding "best practice" in evaluation.

In Chapter 4, Hay, McStephen, and Levy point out that considerably more work needs to be done in the area of the developmental genetics of ADHD. They suggest that different genes may be operative at different stages of development, and that factors such as learning problems and Conduct Disorder may modify outcome. This too raises the question of whether diagnostic and treatment approaches should differ significantly at different stages of development, with implications for adult ADHD as a personality dimension. We need to establish whether early interventions influence later personality outcome, so that the most effective treatment strategies can be implemented. As well as this, there are implications for management of ADHD children by parents who might themselves display ADHD-related psychopathology.

## COMORBIDITY AND SCHOOLING

Bailey (1997) has pointed out that comorbidity issues have considerable educational implications. First, the implications of being *both* learning disability *and* ADHD may be overlooked when a student is treated for one condition and not the other. Learning disability may include reading, arithmetic, and/or language disorder, each of which may require an individual intervention programme. Language-disabled children may have impaired pragmatics, resulting in poor communication and social skills. The management of individual differences in an educational setting requires both administrative support and curriculum planning. For example, the issue of the extent to which learning-disabled students require separate tuition versus support teaching in the general classroom has both cost and planning implications.

Bailey (1997) also points out that the *DSM-IV* subtypes may require differential educational planning. Although children with the Hyperactive/ Impulsive subtype are difficult to ignore, the needs of Inattentive children may be overlooked, particularly when they require remedial support for learning difficulty. As well as this, the work of Hudziak et al. (1998) and Neuman et al. (1999) suggests a separate continuum for the Combined subtype, where children may have special needs related to degree of disability.

Gender differences are also discussed in Bailey (1997). Here, Chapter 8 by Rhee and colleagues, provides some insights. The authors show that gender differences in *DSM-III-R* ADHD symptomatology relate to threshold differences for manifestation of symptoms, rather than to constitutional differences. This notwithstanding, we still know little about the reasons for comorbidity differences, in which respect further *DSM-IV* related studies should provide greater insights. Sensitivity to gender issues is required at the level of classroom balance and teacher attitudes.

Adolescents require special consideration. As Hay and colleagues indicate (Chapter 4, this volume) the transition from the structure of primary school to the demands of high school is particularly difficult for ADHD children. Lack of planning to avoid failure to cope may result in school-dropout and/ or delinquency. It is also important to bear in mind that adolescents are particularly sensitive to peer-pressure and differences. They may resent taking medication at school, and wish to avoid other suggestions of difference, such as special schooling. The poor communication and social skills mentioned earlier may be particularly disabling at the secondary-school level. Even students preparing for university have special needs, for instance entrance exams will require assessments for special examination supports, such as readers and writers. Educators and clinicians should be sensitive to all of these factors, and it is necessary that they be appropriately trained to manage them.

Finally, relationships between support personnel, teachers and parents are potential minefields in that there are numerous situations that might give rise to misunderstanding and tensions. In this respect, the sensitive and educated clinician has an important role in providing support for parents and educators, as well as defusing tensions that may arise. Genetics may well enter this situation. It may lead to families seeing ADHD as a "biological" problem about which they can do little or it may lead to a genetic "witch hunt" trying to trace the history of ADHD to one or other family.

## IMPLICATIONS OF MOLECULAR GENETICS

Molecular genetic studies can have considerable impact in two areas:

(1) Relatively cheap genomic screening procedures, such as single nucleotide

polymorphism chips (SNPs—minute genetic variations that occur throughout human DNA), raises the possibility of determining early behaviour genetic markers, or molecular markers for vulnerability to ADHD. For instance, the SNP Consortium Ltd is a non-profit making entity and collaborative effort to create a genome-wide map of SNP genetic markers. These data are available free of charge, and for unrestricted use, to biomedical researchers throughout the world. Such a map of genetic signposts will enable researchers to navigate the genome faster and with greater efficiency as they search of genes associated with disorders such as ADHD. (The Consortium's SNP data set can be accessed via the Internet through The SNP Consortium's website— http://snp.cshl.org). Access can also be attained via dbSNP, the public database maintained by the National Institutes of Health's National Center for Biotechnology Information—http://www.ncbi.nlm.nih.gov/ SNP)

(2) SNP-based and other gene-based research has the potential to assist in the development of "pharmacogenomic" approaches (Schmidt, 1998). For example, gene testing may help to indicate why a particular individual responds or fails to respond to particular medications, may answer some diagnostic questions. This approach may also help in the development of "tailored" medications for particular behavioural traits. Already the findings related to dopamine receptor (La Hoste et al., 1996) and dopamine transporter (Cook et al., 1995) genes are drawing attention to the importance of dopaminergic systems. Barr, Swanson and Kennedy, (Chapter 10, this volume) have outlined a pharmacological model, based on stimulant therapy and the dopamine hypothesis, allowing a convergence of brain imaging and genetic approaches. Our understanding of the physiology and pathophysiology of ADHD, and thus targeted treatments, should improve as a result of this.

An important study by Winsberg and Comings (1999) has reported an association of the dopamine transporter gene (DAT1) with poor methylphenidate response. They investigated an African-American sample diagnosed with ADHD. The sample included 16 responders and 14 nonresponders to methylphenidate, based on *DSM-III-R*. They found a significant increase in the frequency of individuals homozygous for the 10-repeat allele of the dopamine transporter gene in the nonresponder group (86%), compared with the responder group (31%). According to Cook (1999), this study is the first that directly examines the relationship of genetic variation and response to pharmacological intervention in children with a psychiatric disorder. As such is likely to be a prelude to further advances in the field of child pharmacogenomics.

## ETHICAL ISSUES

The molecular genetic approach raises ethical questions, perhaps even greater than those often discussed for the pharmacological treatment of ADHD in the past (Levy, 1989). Already, the patenting of DNA findings is a controversial issue (Schmidt, 1998). The era of "DNA politics" is yet to emerge in relation to testing for vulnerability and treatment, as well as issues of ownership.

At this point, speculation should be positive. There is little doubt from the present text that multivariate behaviour genetic analysis can make an important contribution to best practice in child behaviour management, by analysing latent aetiogical factors that determine complex behaviours. None the less, such analyses are complex and often not user-friendly for clinicians, nor acceptable to those who make the final decisions about funding and support.

It should be asked whether there is a possibility of early behaviour genetic markers, and ultimately of molecular markers, for the development of ADHD. Furthermore, when and if such markers are discovered, they will only be of real use if acceptable interventions are available. The problems of wrongly labelling a child are significant. On the other hand, markers for early detection of speech and reading problems may well lead to significant early interventions. Rutter (Chapter 13, this volume) discusses some of the issues surrounding the implications of molecular markers. The obvious next step is appropriate genetic counselling. In one of the very first texts that deals with genetic counselling in psychiatry, Faraone, Tsuang, and Tsuang (1999) indicate some of the problems that can and do exist. One issue they deal with is precisely our concern here, namely the extent of heterogeneity both in aetiology and symptomatology. It is difficult enough to discuss this among the disparate professions involved in behaviour genetics. It is much more difficult to convey to families.

## AGENDA FOR PSYCHIATRIC GENETICS

Ongoing advances in psychiatric genetics and DNA technology are now making it possible to find specific genes and gene variants that play critical roles in complex disorders. Because of this, the National Institute of Mental Health convened a work group "to facilitate the search for genes that influence mental disorders". The conclusions are discussed by Barondes (1999) and associated commentaries. The recommendations about data-sharing are laudable. However, the reported "general agreement" that schizophrenia and bipolar disorder be the preferred candidates for large-scale studies aimed at finding the relevant susceptibility genes may reflect a lack of representation in the group of behaviour-geneticists studying childhood psychopathology. In particular in the area of ADHD, where enormous advances are currently being made. Certainly, there is considerable potential for international collaborative studies, given the degree of current interest in this topic. For example, we have not examined the issue of cross-cultural differences in ratings of ADHD, nor cross-Atlantic differences in diagnostic practice, areas where genetic approaches, both behavioural and molecular, are likely to be of interest. The optimal would be to combine these with the appropriate collaboration also on intervention, since differences in diagnoses are combined and confounded with differences in treatment.

## CONCLUSION

At present, the management of the comorbid behaviour problems associated with ADHD is probably a greater problem for clinicians than are the core symptoms. The untangling of influences on these complex behaviours should help develop more rational treatment strategies.

How is this best achieved? There are three complementary strategies.

### Clearer identification of ADHD subtypes

Much has happened since the 1994 *DSM-IV* subtyping, but more needs to be done with the reliable separation of the subtypes. This text has demonstrated just how crucial this is for diagnosis and intervention.

### Comorbidity

As explained in most chapters of this text, the development of "best practice" that routinely includes in the assessment of ADHD the adequate assessment of possible comorbid conditions. At the same time, this assessment needs to consider the source of such information, given potential problems with data from parents who might have experienced the same problems as their children.

### The family

Complementing the discussion by Rutter (Chapter 13, this volume), any role of genetics in counselling, as well as intervention, must consider both the psychosocial and the direct role of parents (it is very interesting that so few studies have formally sought family information). The message that family information implies both genetics and environmental influences requires clarification. There is no doubt that future clinical and research models will embrace the complexity of these influences on the child with ADHD and the family.

# REFERENCES

Accardo, P.J., Blondis, T.A., Whitman, B.Y., & Stein, M.A. (1999). *Attention deficits and hyperactivity in adults* (2nd ed.). New York: Marcel Decker.

American Psychiatric Association. (1987). *Diagnostic and statistical manual of mental disorders* (3rd ed., rev.). Washington, DC: Author.

American Psychiatric Association. (1994). *Diagnostic and statistical manual of mental disorders* (4th ed.). Washington, DC: Author.

Bailey, J. (1997). Mapping the research and development agenda for AD/HD. In J. Bailey & D. Rice (Eds.), *Attention Deficit/Hyperactivity Disorder: Medical, psychological and educational perspectives*. Sydney: Australian Association of Special Education Inc.

Barkley, R.A. (1997). *ADHD and the nature of self-control.* New York: Guilford Press.

Barondes, S.H. (1999) An agenda for psychiatric genetics. *Archives of General Psychiatry, 56,* 549–552.

Benjamin, J., Li, L., Patterson C., Greenberg B.D., Murphy D.L., & Hamer, D.H. (1996). Population and familial association between the D4 dopamine receptor gene and measures of novelty seeking. *Nature Genetics, 12,* 81–84.

Biederman, J., Faraone, S.V., Spencer, T.J., Wilens, T.E., Norman, D., Lapey, K.A., Mick, E., Lehman, B.K., & Doyle, A. (1993). Patterns of psychiatric comorbidity, cognition and psychosocial functioning in adults with Attention-Deficit Hyperactivity Disorder. *American Journal of Psychiatry, 150,* 1792–1798.

Cook, E.H. (1999). The early development of child psychopharmacogenetics: Commentary. *Journal of the American Academy of Child and Adoleccent Psychiatry, 38,* 1478–1481.

Cook, E.H., Jr., Stein, M.A., Krasowski, M.D., Cox, N.J., Olkon, D.M., Kieffer, J.E., & Leventhal, B.L. (1995). Association of attention-deficit disorder and the dopamine transporter gene. *American Journal of Human Genetics, 56,* 993–998.

Faraone, S.V., Tsuang, M.T., & Tsuang, D.W. (1999). *Genetics of mental disorders: A guide for students, clinicians and researchers.* New York: Guilford Press.

Gaub, M., & Carlson, C.L. (1997). Behavioral characteristics of DSM-IV ADHD in a school-based population. *Journal of Abnormal Child Psychology, 25,* 1036–1045.

Grigorenko, E.L., Wood, F.B., Meyer, M.S., Hart, L.A., Speed, W.C., Shuster, A., & Pauls, D.L. (1997). Susceptibility loci for distinct components of developmental dyslexia on chromosomes 6 and 15. *American Journal of Human Genetics, 60,* 27–39.

Hagemann, E., Hay, D.A., & Levy, F. (in press). Cognitive aspects and learning. In S. Sandberg (Ed.), *Hyperactivity and attention disorders of childhood* (2nd ed.). Cambridge, UK: Cambridge University Press.

Ho, T.P., Luk, E.S.L., Leung, P.W.L., Taylor, E., Mak, F.L. & Bacon-Shone, J. (1996). Situational versus pervasive hyperactivity in a community sample. *Psychological Medicine, 26,* 309–321.

Hudziak, J.J., Heath, A.C., Madden, P.A.F., Reich, W., Bucholz, K.K., Slutske, W., Bierut, L.J., Neuman, R.J. & Todd R.D. (1998). Latent class and factor analysis of DSM-IV ADHD: A twin study of female adolescents. *Journal of the American Academy of Child and Adolescent Psychiatry, 37,* 848–857.

LaHoste, G.J., Swanson, J.M., Wigal, S.B., Glabe, C., Wigal, T., King, N., & Kennedy, J.L. (1996). Dopamine D4 receptor gene polymorphism is associated with Attention Deficit Hyperactivity Disorder. *Molecular Psychiatry, 1,* 121–124.

Levy, F. (1989). CNS stimulant controversies. *Australian and New Zealand Journal of Psychiatry*, *23*, 497–502.

Levy, F., Hay, D., McStephen, M., Wood, C., & Waldman, I.D. (1997). Attention Deficit Hyperactivity Disorder (ADHD): A category or a continuum? Genetic analysis of a large scale twin study. *Journal of the American Academy of Child and Adolescent Psychiatry*, *36*, 737–744.

Neale, M.C., & Kendler, K.S. (1995). Models of comorbidity for multifactorial disorders. *American Journal of Human Genetics*, *57*, 935–953.

Neuman, R.J., Todd, R.D., Heath, A.C., Reich, W.C., Hudziak, J.J., Bucholz, K.K., Madden, P.A.F., Begletter, H., Porjesz, B., Kuperman, S., Hesselbrock, V., & Reich, T. (1999). Evaluation of ADHD typology in three contrasting samples: A latent class approach. *Journal of the American Academy of Child and Adolescent Psychiatry*, *38*, 25–33.

Piek, J.P., Pitcher, T.M. & Hay, D.A. (1999). Motor coordination and kinaesthesis in boys with Attention Deficit Hyperactivity Disorder. *Developmental Medicine and Child Neurology*, *41*, 159–165.

Sandberg, S. (in press). Psychosocial contributions. In S. Sandberg (Ed.), *Hyperactivity and attention disorders in childhood* (2nd ed.). Cambridge, UK: Cambridge University Press.

Schmidt, K. (1998). Just for you. *New Scientist*, November, 32–36.

Stevenson, J., Pennington, B.F., Gilger, J.W., DeFries, J.C., & Gillis, J.J. (1993). Hyperactivity and spelling disability—testing for shared genetic etiology. *Journal of Child Psychology and Psychiatry*, *34*, 1137–1152.

Tannock, R. (1998). Attention Deficit Disorder: Advances in cognitive, neurobiological, and genetic research. *Journal of Child Psychology and Psychiatry*, *19*, 65–99.

Taylor, E. (1998). Clinical foundations of hyperactivity research. *Behavioural Brain Research*, *94*, 11–24.

Winsberg, B.G., & Comings, D.E. (1999). Association of the dopamine transporter gene (DAT1) with poor methylphenidate response. *Journal of the American Academy of Child and Adolescent Psychiatry*, *38*, 1474–1477.

# 13 Child psychiatry in the era following sequencing the genome

*Michael Rutter*

## INTRODUCTION

Earlier chapters in this volume have clearly outlined the strengths and potential of quantitative and molecular genetic research strategies. The findings with respect to ADHD have been consistent in showing relatively high heritabilities, with estimates in the range 50%–90% (Rutter, Silberg, O'Connor, & Simonoff, 1999b; Thapar, Holmes, Poulton, & Harrington, 1999). The evidence is compelling that there are strong genetic influences on the dimension of hyperactivity/inattention and on individual variation in liability to ADHD. Moreover, there are replicated findings of genes involved in the dopamine system that are implicated in susceptibility to ADHD. There is every reason to be optimistic that, in the years ahead, other susceptibility genes will be discovered, and that molecular genetics findings will do much to increase our understanding of the role of genetic influences on ADHD.

In the immediately preceding chapter (Chapter 12, this volume), Hay and Levy look ahead to some of the clinical opportunities that are likely to be provided by these expected advances in knowledge. There is every reason to suppose that the molecular genetic revolution will indeed change clinical practice in psychiatry (Plomin & Rutter, 1998; Rutter & Plomin, 1997).

On the day that I wrote these words, the announcement was made that the rough draft of the complete sequencing of the human genome has been attained. There is no doubt that this constitutes a remarkable accomplishment (although the dating of it is rather arbitrary), as well as one that, in sharp contrast to the usual state of affairs, has been achieved far sooner than originally anticipated. Newspapers abound with speculation as to how this will make possible all sorts of medical discoveries that will transform current notions of what can be done in the realm of prevention and treatment of disease and disorder. Psychiatry, together with the rest of medicine, will share in those benefits and, because of its high heritability, ADHD is likely to be among the conditions for which the gains will be greatest. In this concluding chapter, I consider in more detail the nature of these benefits, the risks involved, and research challenges that must be met if the benefits are to be obtained.

## CLINICAL CONCEPTS

### ADHD as a diagnostic category

Levy, McStephen, and Hay (Chapter 3, this volume) outline some of the uncertainties regarding the diagnostic concept of ADHD. There is no doubt, of course, that many individuals show the clinical picture that constitutes the diagnostic concept. It is also clear that it involves substantial social impairment that persists over time, is associated with a considerably increased risk for antisocial behaviour, and that sequelae often extend into adult life (Barkley, 1997; Rutter, Maughan, et al., 1997b; Schachar & Tannock, in press; Tannock, 1998). Queries concern the boundaries of the disorder, its nature, and the extent of its heterogeneity. One of the difficulties is that overactivity and inattention are very common nonspecific indicators of psychological disturbance (for instance, mania and anxiety are accompanied by restlessness and marked difficulties in concentration), as well as being diagnostically specific symptoms of a particular mental disorder (ADHD) (Rutter, Roy, & Kreppner, in press-b). In a real sense, the phenomena constitute the psychiatric equivalents of fever, malaise; and fatigue as indicators of somatic dysfunction. This makes it difficult to know what conclusions to draw from reports that children with the Fragile—X anomaly, or the resistance to thyroid syndrome, show high rates of ADHD (see Zametkin, Ernst, & Cohen, Chapter 9, this volume), or that inattention/overactivity is particularly common in institution-reared children (Rutter et al., in press-b). It is noteworthy that only a tiny proportion of children with ADHD show any of these risk factors. Do the associations reflect a form of psychopathology that is qualitatively different from "ordinary" ADHD, or even if accounting for only a small proportion of cases, do they provide valuable clues to the same risk processes? Will advances in genetics help to provide an answer? I shall revisit the latter question after considering some of the genetic evidence.

There are also uncertainties concerning the breadth and pattern of the diagnostic concept. The *International Classification of Diseases*, 10th revision (*ICD-10*; World Health Organization, 1992) favours a narrow concept, giving rise to a population incidence of 1%–2%. The *Diagnostic and Statistical Manual of Mental Disorders*, fourth edition (*DSM-IV*; American Psychiatric Association, 1994), on the other hand, favours a broader concept, giving rise to incidence rates that are much higher. Some clinical and epidemiological evidence suggests that the validity of the former may be somewhat greater, but genetic findings tend to point to a wider diagnostic concept (Rutter, Maughan, et al., 1997b). Indeed, both genetic (Levy, Hay, McStephen, Wood, & Waldman 1997) and epidemiological (Rutter, Giller, & Hagell, 1998) findings are consistent with a view that ADHD may be more appropriately viewed as a continuously distributed quantitative dimension, than as a qualitatively distinct categorical disorder.

As Levy et al. (Chapter 3, this volume) bring out, other uncertainties concern the possible heterogeneity of ADHD. In particular, is the purely inattentive variety part of the same construct as is the hyperactive/impulsive subtype, or is it a rather different disorder? Genetic findings indicate that, overall, inattention and overactivity reflect the same genetic liability (Nadder, Silberg, Rutter, Maes, & Eaves, in press), but they do not rule out the possibility that a purely inattentive disorder may be relatively genetically distinct.

It may seem odd to be raising queries about a diagnostic concept that has proved so useful in clinical practice, that has given rise to a reasonably consistent set of research findings, and for which there is a well-validated treatment method—namely stimulant medication, as indicated by the Multimodal Treatment Study of Children with ADHD Cooperative Group (MTA Cooperative Group, 1999a, b). Nevertheless, it remains the case that we do not know the pathophysiology of ADHD. It is also unclear whether genetic risk factors will prove to have a degree of unity, or whether they will apply to many different facets or dimensions. As Levy, McStephen, and Hay (chapter 3, this volume) emphasise, ADHD might be relatively homogeneous in terms of phenotypic criteria, yet genetically heterogeneous (see also Nadder et al., in press).

### ADHD as a multifactorial disorder

Misleading "hype" by scientists and journalists often involves reference to "genes for ADHD", or for schizophrenia, or for bipolar disorder. The implication is one of a deterministic action by which genes directly *cause* the psychological condition. This notion is also inappropriately applied to multifactorial disorders such as ADHD. There is no one direct cause—either genetic or nongenetic. Rather, the reality is a complex interacting admixture of multiple genes and multiple environmental risk factors. That is what is meant by multifactorial causation. It is implied by a heritability that is well short of unity. It is possible that within the broad group of ADHD disorders there are a few due to direct gene effects operating in Mendelian fashion but, if so, it is highly probable that these account for a tiny proportion of cases. Rather, the likely scenario is of individual susceptibility genes that increase the risk of ADHD, but whether or not ADHD actually develops depend on the presence or absence of other genes, and of nongenetic risk factors. At the moment, we do not know whether this mixture of genetic and nongenetic risk factors operates additively (i.e., no particular factor has to be present; rather it is a question of how many out of a large pool are operating) or synergistically (i.e., the emergence of disorder is dependent on the catalytic interplay among particular groups of risk factors).

### ADHD as a comorbid disorder

Along with most other child psychiatric disorders (Angold, Costello, & Erkanli, 1999), it is very common for ADHD to be accompanied by (be comorbid with) supposedly separate and different forms of psychopathology. Thus, it co-occurs with language deficits (see Lewis, Chapter 5, this volume), reading difficulties (see Stevenson, Chapter 6, this volume), and with oppositional/defiant and Conduct Disorders (see Waldman, Rhee, Levy, & Hay, Chapter 7, this volume). There is also less consistent association with other disorders such as Tourette's syndrome (Pauls, Fredine, Lynch, Hurst, & Alsobrook, Chapter 11, this volume). There are many possible explanations for these comorbid patterns (Caron & Rutter, 1991; Rutter, 1997), each of which has rather different clinical implications. It could be, for example, that they share some key risk factors—such as a genetically influenced sensation-seeking trait, or family adversity, or scapegoating—with the syndromic outcomes being different because of other risk factors that are not shared. On the other hand, it could be that the various associated disorders constitute alternative, interchangeable, manifestations of the same genetic liability. In that connection, it is important to recognise that the phenomena might change developmentally, even though the genetic risk factors do not, or *vice versa* (see Eaves, Maes, Rutter, & Silberg, in press; Hay, McStephen, & Levy, Chapter 4, this volume; Nadder, Silberg, Maes, Rutter & Eaves, 2000). Yet again, it could be that an earlier behaviour, such as inattention or overactivity, provides a risk for a later one, such as antisocial behaviour. This could be either because it serves to put children into risk circumstances, or to render them more susceptible to environmental hazards. The last possibilities involve various forms of gene–environment correlation (rGE) or interaction (G × E). These are discussed in greater detail below, but the point that needs to be made here is that although they crucially implicate the environment in the causal process, standard genetic analyses will identify the effect as purely genetic (see Rutter, Silberg, & Simonoff, 1993; Silberg, Rutter, Neale, & Eaves, in press). In order to differentiate these G × E interplay causal processes from effects solely attributable to a shared genetic liability, it is necessary to have longitudinal data over the relevant age span. It is also necessary to have discriminating measures of the environment, and to use appropriate methods of data analysis. In many ways, the key question is whether a MZ co-twin of a child with ADHD. who does not him- or herself show ADHD, has an increased risk of ODD/CD (or whatever comorbid disorder is being considered). It will be appreciated, however, that such an analysis immediately requires the need to consider measurement error and the arbitrariness of categorical diagnostic thresholds. For obvious reasons, the identification of specific susceptibility genes will help, but only to the extent that, in combination, these genes account for a substantial proportion of the genetic variance.

## ADHD as a predominantly male disorder

As Rhee, Waldman, Levy, and Hay (Chapter 8, this volume) emphasise, ADHD is several times more common in males than in females. Their data suggest that a polygenic threshold model may be operating, in which females require a higher genetic "dose" to manifest the disorder. Nevertheless, despite their elegant and well-targeted analyses, they note that there is conflicting evidence, and the issue remains to be fully resolved. Two further points need to be added. First, gender differences in psychopathology are very common (see Moffitt, Caspi, Rutter, & Silva, in press). Thus, autism, ADHD, dyslexia, and developmental language disorders are all far more common in males. They tend to be conceptualised as varieties of neurodevelopmental disorder. Is the explanation of their male preponderance the same for all of these conditions? Conversely, depression and anorexia/bulimia nervosa are more common in females. Does this have a different explanation? Second, even if the threshold liability model is correct, what is its explanation at the molecular level? This remains a hugely important and under explored area.

## GENETIC RISK MECHANISMS

### Mode of operation of genetic risk factors

At least five different mechanisms could be involved in the operation of genetic risk factors. First, they could create a relatively direct risk for the disorder as such. Of course, genes do not have any direct effects on behaviour. Rather, their effects are on proteins, but if the protein products are directly implicated in the causal process for disorder, the net effect could be a mechanism that led more or less directly to an increased risk for the disorder. This would constitute an approximation to the ways in which Mendelian disorders function, but with the difference that the effects are probabilistic rather than determinative (even with Mendelian inheritance the effects may not be completely determinative). It is not known if there are genes that function in this way in relation to psychopathology, but they may exist.

Second, genes may have relatively direct effects on part functions that, when combined with other functions, serve to make up the disorder (Flint, 1999). It is thought that this may be the case with elements of dyslexia (see Stevenson, Chapter 6, this volume), and it could be so with different components of ADHD, such as hyperactivity, inattention, and impulsivity.

Third, genes may influence temperamental (or other) dimensions that, in themselves, do not constitute the disorder, but which serve indirectly to increase the risk of disorder when combined with other risk factors. That is thought to be the case with respect to the role of neuroticism in the increased risk for affective and anxiety disorders (Kendler, 1996). It is also quite likely to be the case with respect to sensation seeking or novelty seeking in the risk for ADHD. The implication is that the gene or genes influence some personality feature that involves no direct risk for disorder but which, in some circumstances, may predispose to disorder. Thus, novelty or sensation seeking could foster creative science, or risky sports such as rock climbing, or gambling, or drug-taking, or entrepreneurial business ventures, or antisocial behaviour. Which of these was the outcome would depend on other factors or circumstances.

Fourth, genes may act through their role in increasing (or decreasing) environmental risk exposure. This may come about through passive, active or evocative gene–environment correlations (Rutter, Dunn, et al., 1997a). Passive correlations reflect the fact that parents both pass on genes to their children, and create environments for their upbringing. Thus, it has been well demonstrated that parents with personality disorder have a much increased likelihood of providing their children with a discordant, conflict-ridden family environment (Rutter & Quinton, 1984), and that parents with depression have an increased likelihood of being impaired in their parenting (Silberg & Rutter, in press). Of course, the genes do not cause the environmental risks directly but, through their effects on the parental phenotype, they will serve to make environmental risk exposure for the children more or less likely.

Active gene–environment correlations (rGE) refer to the mechanisms by which our genetically influenced behaviour leads us to select (or avoid) certain sorts of environments. The examples of possibilities given earlier with respect to novelty or sensation seeking illustrate this effect. Evocative rGE cover the mechanisms by which our own genetically influenced behaviour elicits particular responses from the people with whom we interact (Bates, Pettit, Dodge, & Ridge, 1998; Ge et al., 1996; O'Connor, Deater-Deckard, Fulker, Rutter, & Plomin, 1998). This is shown, for example, in the ways in which adopted children's disruptive behaviour (shown to be related to their biological parentage) provokes negative responses from their adoptive parents with whom they do not share genes (other than to the extent found in any two biologically unrelated individuals). The point about rGE effects is that the genetic risks may come about only (or largely) because they predispose the person to experience risk environments. The genes, in those circumstances, do not increase the risk of psychopathology directly but only do so through their influence on environmental risk exposure.

Fifth, genes may exert their effects through influences on susceptibility to environmental risks—gene–environment interactions ($G \times E$). Twin and adoptee studies have shown the existence of such $G \times E$ interactions with respect to both life stresses and depression (Kendler et al., 1995; Silberg et al., in press), and family discord/disruption/negativity and antisocial behaviour (Bohman, 1996; Cadoret, 1985; Cadoret, Yates, Troughton, Woodworth, & Stewart, 1995). However, it is likely that $G \times E$ is more pervasively present than has been demonstrated so far. The point is that it has been shown over and over again that there are huge individual differences in response to all manner of environmental risks—both physical and psychosocial (Rutter, 2000a). It must also be expected that there are genetic influences on those variations in vulnerability. Molecular genetic studies in the field of internal medicine are beginning to document specific genetic risks in relation to infections (Hill, 1998), allergies (Anderson & Cookson, 1998), immune responses

(Todd, in press), outcome after head injury (Teasdale, Nicoll, Murray, & Fiddes, 1997), and cigarette smoking (Talmud, Bujac, Hall, Miller, & Humphries, 2000). Indeed, it has been argued that the main potential for molecular genetic research in the field of multifactorial disorders lies in the provision of greater understanding of environmental risk mediation (Weatherall, 1992).

It is very apparent that evidence of high heritability, or even of specific susceptibility genes, in and of itself provides no information on the nature of risk processes. Genetic findings provide a hugely helpful lead but they constitute the beginning, and not the end, of research into causal mechanisms.

## Universality of genetic risks

It might be supposed that, though genes operate in diverse ways, there is at least a high predictability for genetic effects. Just as male sex is always determined by a gene on the Y chromosome, so should there be genes that always lead to inattention, or risk-taking, or overactivity. That could be the case, but it is very unlikely to often be so. To begin with, it is known that population groups vary greatly with respect to the incidence of particular genetic allelic variations (Malhotra & Goldman, 1999; Motulsky, 1999; Todd, 1999). For example, those associated with thalassaemia vary markedly by geography (Gay, Phillips, & Kazazian, 1996), and those linked with breast cancer vary by ethnicity (Hartge, Struewing, Wacholder, Brody, & Tucker, 1999; Szabo & King, 1997). In addition, populations vary in the extent to which particular allelic variations are associated with disease susceptibility. For example, this has been shown with respect to Apo-E-4 and the risk of Alzheimer's disease, which varies across ethnic groups (Farrer et al., 1997). Furthermore, for most diseases (even Mendelian conditions) there is not one gene responsible, but many. Thus, cystic fibrosis is associated with hundreds of allelic variations (Cutting, 1996), and retinitis pigmentosa (Inglehearn, 1998) with several quite different and distinct genes that involve contrasting patterns of Mendelian inheritance. A practical consequence of this state of affairs is that it is much easier to be sure that an individual has a susceptibility gene, than to be sure that the individual does not have such a gene. A negative finding could mean that the detection techniques have not been adequate to pick up all relevant genes, or that there are susceptibility genes not yet discovered.

## Strength of genetic effects

Sometimes it is supposed that, if heritability is high, susceptibility genes are likely to have large effects. It would certainly make life easier if that were the case, but probably this will prove to be the exception. Most single genes account for a tiny proportion of the variance in disease liability (Plomin, DeFries, McClearn, & Rutter, 1997). This is evident for example in relation to genetic effects on novelty seeking, and it is likely to be so in most other instances. No single susceptibility gene will account for disease occurrence, although the combined effect of many genes may do so.

## "Good" genes and "bad" genes

Sometimes, people expect that the genetic revolution will lead to the identification of the "bad" susceptibility genes that predispose to disease and, therefore, that genetic advances should lead to interventions to counter the effects of those "bad" genes or, more heroically, to use gene therapy to replace them. Particularly with respect to multifactorial disorders, this categorisation of genes into "good" and "bad" is quite misleading. Many genes have rather varied (pleiotropic) effects on several functions, and these may include both adaptive and maladaptive consequences. Sometimes, too, heterozygotic status may involve protective effects on some different outcome. The best known example is the protective effect of thalassaemia heterozygote status against malaria, but there are others (Rotter & Diamond, 1987). In addition, a single genetically influenced trait may be risky for some outcomes, but protective for others. For example, an anxious, emotionally hyper-responsive temperament constitutes a risk for anxiety disorders, but a protection against antisocial behaviour (Hirschfeld et al., 1992; Lahey, McBurnett, Loeber, & Hart, 1995). Sometimes, too, the concept of "good" and "bad" genes is extrapolated to the potential to identify genetically high risk and low risk individuals, with the assumption that genetic profiling of foetuses should enable parents to choose which pregnancies to terminate. That possibility raises important ethical issues (Rutter, 1999) but, more crucially, it would be impractical. The point is that diseases derive from the action of multiple genes. The very strong likelihood is that *everyone* carries important susceptibility genes for some undesirable outcome. It would be necessary to balance an increased risk, let us say, for diabetes but a reduced risk for something like schizophrenia, for instance. That aside, whether or not a particular genetic susceptibility will actually lead to disease will depend in part on environmental risks. Not only are the risks probabilistic, they are also contingent upon circumstances.

## SEARCHING FOR SUSCEPTIBILITY GENES

### Linkage strategies

Barr, Kennedy, and Swanson (Chapter 10, this volume) have described the two main molecular genetic research approaches, linkage analyses and association studies, which constitute inter-related but different strategies. The rationale of each is different, and they have a contrasting mixture of strengths and weaknesses (Rutter, Silberg, O'Connor, & Simonoff, 1999a). In essence, linkage studies test for co-inheritance, that is whether the inheritance of a particular trait "goes with" the inheritance of a particular gene location.

Extended family pedigree studies were powerful in the case of well-defined phenotypes for which the mode of inheritance was known, but of less use for the study of multifactorial disorders (although there have been successes). In contrast, affected relative pair strategies are readily applicable and avoid most of the problems, although they have less statistical power. Their main strength, however, is also their key weakness. That is, they have the great merit of being able to detect genetic effects over a substantial span of each chromosome (so making total genome scans practical). The down side to this is that they can detect only rather large genetic effects, and that when a gene locus has been identified it covers a huge distance, and therefore incorporates a vast number of possible susceptibility genes. The consequence is that going from a positive lod score (implying an area likely to include one or more suscepibility genes) to identification of the specific gene(s) responsible is quite an arduous process. It will usually involve moving on to association methods.

## Association methods

Association strategies work on a different principle. That is, they test whether the particular mix of alleles that is most commonly associated with a particular trait or disorder differs significantly from the mix found in the general population (or some other control group). The great advantage of association methods is that they can detect much weaker genetic effects than is possible with linkage methods (Edwards, 1965; Risch & Merikangas, 1996). The down side is that they can do so only if the relevant gene is placed very closely to the genetic markers used in the search. Up to now, this has usually meant a focus on specific candidate genes (meaning genes known to have an effect on physiological functions that play a part in the causal process involved in the disease under study). The problem has been that in most psychiatric conditions the pathophysiology is unknown so that, strictly speaking, there are no candidate genes. As well as this, insofar as anything is known about the pathophysiology, the gene search has had to focus on the tiny bits of existing knowledge rather than on the huge areas of ignorance. This does not provide a very powerful way of forward progression.

A concern in association studies has been the possible distortion created by stratification biases (Gelernter, Goldman, & Risch, 1993; Gelernter, Kranzier, & Cubells, 1997). That is, if cases and controls differ in their genealogical origins, this may result in differences in allelic frequencies that have nothing to do with the disease or disorder being investigated. It has proven quite difficult to determine the extent of this possible bias, added to which it is likely to vary according to the make-up of the population being studied (Risch, 2000). Three main considerations predominate. First, there is the question of whether the main concern relates to false positive or false negative findings. If the former predominates, the answer lies in the use of family controls of one sort or another. The disadvantages of this are a loss of statistical power, and that either parents or siblings must be available for genotyping. In addition, the costs of studies of trios—i.e., both parents and probands—are inevitably substantially greater than are studies of singletons and controls (Morton & Collins, 1998; Page & Amos 1999). The second consideration concerns the expectation that the susceptibility genes will involve common polymorphic allelic variations (in which case stratification biases are likely to be minor), or rare mutant allelic variations (for which stratification biases may be considerable). The distinction between the two is to a considerable extent arbitrary. In an evolutionary sense, all allelic variations are mutations. Nevertheless, the implications are rather different (Risch, 2000). Third, rather than focus on how to deal with stratification biases, there may be advantages to concentrating on genetically isolated populations when seeking to map susceptibility genes for complex multifactorial disorders (Wright, Carothers, & Pirastu, 1999).

An even greater problem with association studies has been created by the extremely narrow focus, and the consequent need to focus on candidate genes. Two methodological advances carry the promise of overcoming this problem. First, the availability of single nucleotide polymorphisms (SNPs) has meant that there has been a massive increase in the markers that could be used to cover the genome. There is an unresolved controversy over the map density of markers required for this purpose (Kruglyak, 1999; Owen, Cardno, & O'Donovan, 2000; Risch, 2000), but it seems likely that the true position is somewhere midway between the most optimistic and most pessimistic extremes.

The second advance has been provided by DNA pooling (Barcellos et al., 1997; Daniels et al., 1998). The principle is straightforward. All cases are combined, as are all controls, so greatly simplifying the comparison and greatly increasing the statistical power. There are various methodological issues that need to be dealt with (Kirov, Williams, Sham, Craddock, & Owen, 2000), but the main constraint is provided by the requirement of a yes–no decision on affected status. If, for example, genetic effects varied by age of onset, severity, pattern of comorbidity, or stage in the disease process, DNA pooling would result in a considerable loss of power, and not a gain. It constitutes a promising technique, but one that is not problem free.

## Quantitative trait loci (QTL) approaches

There has been an increasing awareness that many of the risk factors in both internal medicine and psychopathology operate as continuously distributed dimensions. Thus, variations in cholesterol level are associated with differences in the risk of coronary artery disease across the whole range, and not just at supposedly abnormal high levels. Similarly, this probably applies to temperamental features, such as neuroticism or sensation seeking, in relation to mental disorder. It is possible to apply molecular genetic methods to the study of these quantitative trait loci (QTL) (Abecasis, Cardon, & Cookson, 2000; Allison, 1997; Rabinowitz, 1997). Potentially, the method should have increased statistical power, either from obtaining leverage from variations across the whole range, or from a focus on extremes both low and high (Eaves & Meyer, 1994; Risch & Zhang, 1995). However, considerable challenges remain in obtaining reliable and valid measures of the relevant attributes within the range of normal variation. We may well already have reasonable measures of this kind (such as for neuroticism or possible sensation seeking), but it may prove more difficult with respect to autism (see Bailey, Palferman, Heavey, & Le Couteur, 1998), or schizophrenia (Lenzenweger & Korfine, 1996). Nevertheless, the notion that genes do operate in relation to QTL seems valid, and undoubtedly this constitutes one more way forward in the search for susceptibility genes.

The underlying message is that molecular genetics includes a range of powerful research strategies. None are without problems but, in combination, they are likely to prove quite powerful. The future search for susceptibility genes will not be easy nor straightforward, nevertheless, it is likely to deliver the goods—albeit probably over a longer time frame than suggested by the genetic enthusiasts.

## FINDING OUT WHAT GENES DO

### How will sequencing the genome help?

Completion of the awesome task of sequencing the genome has been greeted in some quarters as if it provided the answers to the questions of understanding how genes operate. On its own, it will not do that. It has been described, reasonably, as the book of life. However, it is a book in which we have identified all the words, and how they fit together, but we have little notion as to the meaning of the words. Nevertheless, sequencing the genome will help in a very important way because, for the first time, we know what genes are present. It may be somewhat like looking for needles in a haystack, but at least we know precisely the number of hidden needles, and their form. That is bound to be of significant assistance. In fact, the gains go far beyond that because we have information on the genomes of other species, and on the effects of numerous protein alterations. That is where bioinformatics comes in (Eisenberg, Marcotte, Xenarios, & Yeates, 2000). In essence, bioinformatics is a way of making multiple links among huge data banks of diverse genetic information. This cannot possibly be done through the operation of a human mind alone making relevant conceptual connections (although that is an indispensable part of the process). Rather it requires massive "data crunching" to bring out connections that had not been anticipated. It is a new technology, and one for which the rules are still being devised. Nevertheless, it is a fast evolving technology, which is crucial in gaining momentum. Much the same applies to the use of DNA arrays and microbeads, in which levels of gene expression can be measured for thousands of genes simultaneously (Brenner et al., 2000; Lockhart & Winzeler, 2000).

## How do genes function?

Let us assume that future research has succeeded in identifying a substantial number of validated susceptibility genes. Where does that leave us, and of what use will this be in improving clinical practice? For all the reasons already discussed, the answer has to be "not much". That is because identification of a genetic effect is, on its own, uninformative on the crucial question of what genes do. Two somewhat separate issues are involved. First, there is the question of the effects of genes on proteins and, through those effects, on the phenotype (see Rutter, 2000b). Animal studies are crucial in that connection. It is only through experimental gene "knock-out" and "insertion" studies in species such as the mouse (that are genetically quite similar to humans) that we can progress (Flint, 1999; Sibilia & Wagner, 1996; Wicker, Todd, & Peterson, 1995). The object of the exercise is to manipulate the genes in one way or another in order to understand the biological effects, with the aim of determining how they influence behaviour. It needs to be appreciated that, for this to succeed, it is not necessarily essential to create an animal model that closely mimics the human psychopathological disorder. That would be difficult for ADHD, and even more difficult for conditions such as autism or schizophrenia. Rather the need, albeit still quite a difficult one, is to have a model that reflects the genetic alterations, and which gives rise to a behavioural picture that recreates essential components of the human condition. It has not proven easy to do this in the field of internal medicine and it will be even more difficult to do so with disorders such as ADHD. Nevertheless, that *is* what is needed. The immediate way forward is for molecular genetic studies in humans to lead on to transgenic investigations in other species—and this is just the beginning.

Molecular genetics and transgenics in the near future will be supplemented by proteomics—the study of the interplay among proteins (Pandey & Mann, 2000). This requires the very different discipline of protein chemistry, and other elements of so-called functional genomics.

Let us suppose that all of this is successful (and it has not yet been so in a field of medicine), where does that leave us? The main (and huge) unresolved issue will then be gene–environment interplay (meaning both rGE and G × E). In other words, to the extent that genetic effects are dependent upon some combination with environmental risk factors, epidemiological research that brings the two together will be imperative. This means that a full understanding of genetic risk processes will necessitate accurate identification of environmental risk factors. For that to be possible, research designs must be capable of differentiating environmentally mediated risk from genetically mediated risk, and be able to separate environmental effects on the individual from person effects on the environment. Research designs with these attributes are available (see Rutter, Pickles, Murray, & Eaves, in press-a), and they have succeeded in identifying true environmentally mediated risks (see Rutter, 2000a). Nevertheless, our knowledge on these is much more limited than is sometimes appreciated.

A good deal of evidence is available on risk indicators, but far less on risk *mechanisms*. That is, data are available on which environmental factors are statistically associated with ADHD (Sandberg, in press), but not on how they operate. For example, to what extent do associations between parental negativity and ADHD reflect genetic mediation (stemming from, say, personality qualities in the parents representing the adult sequelae of their own ADHD), or the effect of disruptive child behaviour on the parents? In addition, insofar as environmental effects are long lasting, what mechanism is involved in maintaining them? What are the effects of environmental risks on the organism? Are there neural effects? Do environmental effects operate through the same brain processes as do genetic effects, or do they function differently? For example, what are the effects of either or both on cognitive processing or mind sets? Do they operate on the risks for the origin of ADHD, or rather on its course?

It will be appreciated that answering these questions will require enormous general population samples (many tens of thousands, and possibly hundreds of thousands) that include environmental high-risk groups, and the use of high-quality discriminating measures of environmental risk. A considerable challenge remains in devising or adopting existing environmental risk measures so that they can be used in samples as large as those envisaged, as well as having the capacity to index environmental risk in a reliable and valid manner.

## CLINICAL BENEFITS OF GENETIC RESEARCH

### Understanding of neural processes

At least with respect to highly heritable neurodevelopmental disorders such as autism, schizophrenia, and ADHD, the most important product of molecular genetic research is likely to be the lead provided for biological studies that could delineate the causal neural processes that constitute the biological underpinning of the disorders. Up to now, the findings from biological research in psychiatry have been singularly inconclusive on specifics (see Bailey, Phillips, & Rutter, 1996 for a discussion of this point with regard to autism; Harrison, 1997, regarding schizophrenia; and Tannock, 1998, regarding ADHD). Findings have been consistent in indicating abnormalities of brain structure or function. However, they have either been inconsistent on the details, or too general to be of much help in delineation of diagnosis-specific pathophysiology, or even nonspecific brain processes that truly mediate psychopathological risk, albeit risk that spans several diagnoses. The detection of susceptibility genes, alone, will not provide an answer. This notwithstanding, the determination of their function (through transgenics and proteomics) could do much to provide the leads that are needed to redirect biological studies. It will be appreciated that achieving the objective of determining causal neural processes will require a long and difficult research journey in which finding the genes (difficult though that has been) may prove to be the easiest step (Rutter, 2000b).

## Pharmacogenetics

Related to the understanding of neural processes is the possibility of developing more effective pharmacological interventions. Of course, with respect to ADHD we already have drugs that make a real and worthwhile difference (MTA Cooperative Group, 1999a, b). Stimulants do much to alleviate key problems. There are, however, three limitations. First, the benefits are not diagnosis-specific and this must raise uncertainties over whether or not the medication addresses the basic underlying pathophysiology. Second, stimulants are not uniformly successful with respect to all the problems associated with ADHD. Third, not all children with ADHD respond dramatically to stimulant medication. Marked individual variability in response to drugs is a phenomenon that pervades medicine in its entirety. We know a good deal about which groups of drugs tend to benefit which groups of patients, but we know far less about what differentiates those within those groups who do and do not respond. Molecular genetic findings could help greatly in elucidating this, as well as providing leads on which new types of drugs might be useful—the growing field of pharmacogenetics (Evans & Relling, 1999).

## Nature–nurture interplay

The point has been made that, in child psychiatry, we are largely dealing with multifactorial disorders, and the involvement of both genetic and environmental risk factors. Another point made is that the causal processes often rely on interplay between the two, deriving from gene–environment correlations and interactions. Several points emerge from these considerations. First, insofar as genetic risks operate indirectly through effects on environmental risk exposure or susceptibility, the detection of genetic risks will be greatly facilitated by a focus on environmental high risk groups. That requires, of course, good quality measurement of environmental risks in genetic studies. Second, the identification of environmentally mediated risks will be much easier if there is a focus on subgroups of the population who are most vulnerable to such risks, and if an identification of specific genetic risks (through knowledge regarding susceptibility genes) can allow a more valid identification of risk mediation that is not genetic (Plomin & Rutter, 1998). The major practical problem in this endeavour will be the fact that, in almost all instances, there will be *many* susceptibility genes. Partialling out the specific effects of identified genes will depend on identification of all (or at least most of) the relevant genes and not just a few of them. That will constitute a substantial challenge, and will not be achieved easily. Nevertheless, in the long run, there is no doubt that much of the potential of molecular genetics will lie in its value for investigation of nature–nurture interplay.

It should be added that identification of the underlying causal neural processes should help in sorting out environmental mechanisms and, in particular, the effects of environmental adversities on the organism. Thus, for example, insofar as institutional rearing predisposes to inattention/overactivity, does it do so by affecting the same neural processes as "ordinary ADHD" or is the pathophysiology quite different?

One further consideration with respect to environmental influences is the reminder that it is necessary to extend possibilities to physical influences. These include maternal alcohol consumption (Maier, Miller, & West, 1999; Streissguth & Kanter, 1997), obstetric/perinatal complications (Geddes & Lawrie, 1995; Murray & Woodruff, 1995), and minor developmental aberrations as indexed by minor congenital anomalies (Meyers, Elias, & Arrabel, 1995; Waldrop & Halverson, 1971) or dermatoglyphic asymmetry (Davis & Bracha, 1996).

## DIAGNOSIS

Given all the problems of psychiatric diagnosis, and the lack of any kind of external criterion to validate it, there has been a hope that molecular genetic findings could help define boundaries, diagnostic criteria, and demarcations. It is indeed likely that they will be of some value in that connection (Rutter & Plomin, 1997). Thus, identification of the bulk of the set of susceptibility genes for autism should assist determination of which social and communicative abnormalities are part of the same genetic liability as autism (and hence truly part of a broader phenotype) and which due to something quite different. The same should apply to schizotypy and schizophrenia. In comparable fashion, it should be of assistance in sorting out whether syndromes of inattention without hyperactivity are truly part of ADHD, and whether hyperactivity with high anxiety, or associated with mental retardation, or accompanied by Tourette's syndrome, reflect the same genetic liability. These constitute major advantages.

Nevertheless, three caveats require expression. First, the method works best when there is a major gene that *directly* causes the disease (as is the case with Mendelian conditions) but this applies to very few psychiatric disorders. Second, with multifactorial disorders they rely on the identification of *most* of the relevant susceptibility genes and not just one of them. Third, it is important to appreciate that most medical diagnoses are *not* based on a primary cause; rather they are based on the unifying pathophysiology. Thus, insulin-dependent diabetes is diagnosed on the basis of the underlying abnormality in glucose metabolism and not on whether or not the individual has one or other of the several susceptibility genes. Even more strikingly, tuberous sclerosis is diagnosed on the basis of the key clinical functions and not on which of the two known genes is responsible. Cystic fibrosis is diagnosed on the physiological abnormality and not on which of the numerous allelic mutations is responsible. In short, the real progress in psychiatric diagnosis will come from understanding the causal neural processes that will be facilitated by molecular genetic research, rather than from identification of the susceptibility genes as such (Owen et al., 2000).

## Genetic screening

In some quarters, there are high expectations of what could be achieved in the future through genetic screening. The Star Wars scenario is that when all genetic information is gathered (which is likely to be a lengthy process), each person could be given a genetic profile. This purportedly will specify whether or not that individual will develop ADHD, or bipolar disorder, or asthma, or diabetes. However, in reality it will not work quite like that for two rather different reasons.

First, the specification of disease liability will depend not on one main gene alone, but rather on several susceptibility genes (often needing to work in combination), and of a particular polygenic background. Of course, eventually genetic research could meet some of these expectations, but that will not be possible in the near future. Second, even when the full picture of genetic liability is available, the prediction of disease outcome will still depend on whether or not the person encounters particular environmental hazards. The ways in which multifactorial disorders function will not lend them easily to a deterministic approach. What the genetic data will do, however, is to provide invaluable leads on which environmental manipulations could *lower* the risk of a disease outcome. That constitutes the really valuable potential.

## Counselling

Many of the same considerations apply to genetic counselling. Such counselling first developed on the basis of knowledge regarding the relative risks associated with the various forms of Mendelian single gene transmission. The aim was to provide information about the likelihood that a particular individual with a family history of a Mendelian disorder might themselves develop the condition, the likelihood that they might be a carrier, and hence the risks for other family members, and the risks for further pregnancies or for a child *in utero*. Molecular genetics advanced the field in a major way because the identification of disease genes meant that predictions could be made with respect to each person (on the basis of individual molecular genetic findings) and not just on the basis of population averages. Unfortunately, the situation is very much more complex with multifactorial disorders because, even with precise genetic data, the risks are probabilistic (not deterministic) and are contingent upon future life circumstances. At present, problems of diagnosis abound (because of uncertainties over the boundaries of broader phenotypes), but even when these are resolved, the uncertainties deriving from the unknowns about future environments will remain. Genetic counselling will constitute an even more important speciality than it does now, but the range of skills required will be much wider than they have been in the past.

## Ethical issues

Finally, it is necessary to consider some of the most crucial ethical issues that will arise as a result of genetic advances in the future. They are many and varied, but should be manageable if properly handled. Certainly, they should not constitute a barrier to further genetic research (Farmer & McGuffin, 1998; Rutter, 1999). One concern is that excessive focus on the priorities of molecular genetic research could result in a dangerous neglect of research into environmental risk mechanisms. This is a realistic risk that deserves serious attention. What is essential is research into *both* genetic and environmental risk factors, with a specific emphasis on their interplay.

A second and related concern is that genetic research will lead to a misleading genetic determinism that will hinder political steps, policy initiatives, and practical innovations in their attempts to deal with the serious environmental hazards that need remediation—poverty, social inequity, racial discrimination, family breakdown, poor parenting, child neglect, and child abuse. Although a real risk, this is one that arises from a *mis*understanding of the messages of genetic research, and not from the research outcomes as such. The evidence from research is clear-cut in indicating the veracity and importance of environmental risks (Rutter, 2000a), and in highlighting the fact that genetic findings apply to individual differences within existing populations living in prevailing environmental circumstances, and not necessarily to effects on the level of disorder as it varies over time or across populations (Rutter & Smith, 1995). We need to pay careful attention to the realities of genetic findings, and not jump to conclusions on what we think genetics *might* mean.

A third somewhat similar concern is that the "medicalisation" of social problems could lead to an excessive use of drug treatments to the neglect of treatments (or preventative interventions) focused on psychosocial risk factors. Although the stimulus for this tendency has had nothing whatsoever to do with genetics, it has to be said that the risk is real if only because drug treatments (at least as provided by those in the community lacking the prerequisite expertise) are cheap, undemanding and save time (see Zito et al., 2000). However, one of the key messages of genetic research is that genetic factors are *not* concerned only with disease. To the contrary, they affect all human behaviour and carry no implications with respect to medicalisation.

A somewhat different worry is that genetic findings could increase psychiatric stigma. Of course, that could happen, but it is a curious expectation because the existing stigma probably arises in considerable part from an attitude that mental disorders are manifest because people are acting irresponsibly and not taking adequate control of their lives, not coping when they should, and not trying hard enough. Evidence that, as in other things, they are influenced by their biological predisposition could well *reduce* stigma, rather than increase it (see Farmer & McGuffin, 1998).

A parallel anxiety is that genetic determinism undermines the notion of free will and therefore implies that people need no longer take responsibility for their actions. As noted earlier, the genetic findings indicate a probabilistic effect and not a deterministic one. As discussed elsewhere (Rutter, 1999) the genetic evidence is neutral on free will. There is no reason to suppose that there is any undermining effect.

Yet another concern is that genetic information will disadvantage individuals with respect to health or life assurance (Royal Society, 1997). That is a reasonable concern, but two main points need to be made. First, the probabilistic, contingent nature of genetic risks in relation to multifactorial disorders means that it is not obvious that genetic data could be truly disadvantaging if properly used. The real danger lies in their misuse and misunderstanding. Second, society needs to consider whether it wishes the costs of genetic risk to be borne by society or by the individual. That is a real choice. In many countries, the nation absorbs the costs that are inherent in the fact that some individuals have much greater educational or health needs than others. That is the essence of a universal system of general and special education and of national health care. Should not the same apply to insurance (Rutter, 1999)?

## CONCLUSION

This volume summarises what is known on the genetics of ADHD, and on how it relates to the complex clinical phenomena of this important and puzzling condition. In this final chapter I have sought to look ahead to where this might lead us in the future. The potential for substantial clinical benefits is real, but there are some important hazards that we must learn to avoid if we are to capitalise optimally on the huge research potential provided by genetics.

## REFERENCES

Abecasis, G.R., Cardon, L.R., & Cookson, W.O.C. (2000). A general test of association for quantitative traits in nuclear families. *American Journal of Human Genetics, 66,* 279–292.

Allison, D.B. (1997). Transmission-disequilibrium tests for quantitative traits. *American Journal of Human Genetics, 60,* 676–690.

American Psychiatric Association. (1994). *Diagnostic and statistical manual of mental disorders,* (4th ed.). Washington, DC: Author.

Anderson, G., & Cookson, W. (1998). The genetics of asthma and atopy. In I.A. Hughes & R.M. Gardiner (Eds.), *Doctors to the genome: From conception to maturity* (pp. 137–153). London: Royal College of Physicians.

Angold, A., Costello, E.J., & Erkanli, A. (1999). Comorbidity. *Journal of Child Psychology and Psychiatry, 40*, 55–87.

Bailey, A., Palferman, S., Heavey, L., & Le Couteur, A. (1998). Autism: The phenotype in relatives. *Journal of Autism and Developmental Disorders, 28*, 381–404.

Bailey, A., Phillips, W., & Rutter, M. (1996). Autism: Towards an integration of clinical, genetic, neuropsychological, and neurobiological perspectives. *Journal of Child Psychology and Psychiatry Annual Research Review, 37*, 89–126.

Barcellos, L.F., Klitz, W., Field, L.L., Tobias, R., Bowcock, A.M., Wilson, R., Nelson, M.P., Nagatomi, J., & Thomson, G. (1997). Association mapping of disease loci by use of a pooled DNA genomic screen. *American Journal of Human Genetics, 61*, 734–747.

Barkley, R.A. (1997). *ADHD and the nature of self-control.* New York/London: Guilford Press.

Bates, J.E., Pettit, G.S., Dodge, K.A., & Ridge, B. (1998). Interaction of temperamental resistance to control and restrictive parenting in the development of externalizing behavior. *Developmental Psychology, 34*, 982–995.

Bohman, M. (1996). Predisposition to criminality: Swedish adoption studies in retrospect. In G.R. Bock & J.A. Goode (Eds.), Ciba Foundation Symposium 194; *Genetics of criminal and antisocial behaviour.* (pp. 99–114). Chichester, UK: Wiley.

Brenner, S., Williams, S.R., Vermaas, E.H., Storck, T., Moon, K., McCollum, C., Mao, J.I., Luo, S., Kirchner, J.J., Eletr, S., DuBridge, R.B., Burcham, T., & Albrecht, G. (2000). *In vitro* cloning of complex mixtures of DNA on microbeads: Physical separation of differentially expressed cDNAs. *PNAS, 97*, 1665–1670.

Cadoret, R.J. (1985). Genes, environment and their interaction in the development of psychopathology. In T. Sakai & T. Tsuboi (Eds.), *Genetic aspects of human behavior* (pp. 165–175). Tokyo: Igaku-Shoin.

Cadoret, R.J., Yates, W.R., Troughton, E., Woodworth, G., & Stewart, M.A.W. (1995). Genetic-environmental interaction in the genesis of aggressivity and Conduct Disorders. *Archives of General Psychiatry, 52*, 916–924.

Caron, C., & Rutter, M. (1991). Comorbidity in child psychopathology: Concepts, issues and research strategies. *Journal of Child Psychology and Psychiatry, 32*, 1063–1080.

Cutting, G.R. (1996). Cystic fibrosis. In D.L. Rimoin, J.M. Connor, & R.E. Pyeritz (Eds.), *Emery and Rimoin's principles and practice of medical genetics* (Vol. 2, 3rd ed., pp. 2685–2717). New York: Churchill Livingstone.

Daniels, J., Holmans, J., Williams, N., Turic, D., McGuffin, P., Plomin, R., & Owen, M.J. (1998). A simple method for analyzing microsatellite allele image patterns generated from DNA pools and its application to allelic association studies. *American Journal of Human Genetics, 62*, 1189–1197.

Davis, J.O., & Bracha, H.S. (1996). Prenatal growth markers in schizophrenia: A monozygotic co-twin control study. *American Journal of Psychiatry, 153*, 1166–1172.

Eaves, L.J., Maes, H., Rutter, M., & Silberg, J.L. (in press). Genetic and environmental causes of covariation in interview assessments of disruptive behavior in child and adolescent twins. *Behavior Genetics.*

Eaves, L.J., & Meyer, J. (1994). Locating human quantitative trait loci: Guidelines for the selection of sibling pairs for genotyping. *Behavior Genetics, 24,* 443–455.

Edwards, J.H. (1965). The meaning of the associations between blood groups and disease. *Annals of Human Genetics, 29,* 77–83.

Eisenberg, D., Marcotte, E.M., Xenarios, I., & Yeates, T.O. (2000). Protein function in the post-genomic era. *Nature, 405,* 823–826.

Evans, W.E., & Relling, M.V. (1999). Pharmacogenomics: Translating functional genomics into rational therapeutics. *Science, 286,* 487–491.

Farmer, A., & McGuffin, P. (1998). Ethics and psychiatric genetics. In S. Block (Ed.), *Ethics and psychiatry* (3rd ed., pp. 479–493). Oxford, UK: Oxford University Press.

Farrer, L.A., Cupples, L.A., Haines, J.L., Hyman, B., Kukull, W.A., Mayeux, R., Myers, R., Pericak-Vance, M.A., Risch, N., van Duijn, C.M., for the APOE and Alzheimer Disease Meta Analysis Consortium. (1997). Effects of age, sex, and ethnicity on the association between apolipoprotein E genotype and alzheimer disease. *Journal of the American Medical Association, 278,* 1349–1356.

Flint, J. (1999). The genetic basis of cognition. *Brain, 122,* 2015–2031.

Gay, J.C., Phillips, J.A., III, & Kazazian, H.H., Jr. (1996). Hematoglobinopathies and thalassemias. In D.L. Rimoin, J.M. Connor, & R.E. Pyeritz (Eds.), *Emery and Rimoin's principles and practice of medical genetics* (Vol. II, 3rd ed., pp. 1599–1626). New York: Churchill Livingstone.

Ge, X., Conger, R.D., Cadoret, R.J., Neiderhiser, J.M., Yates, W.R., Troughton, E., & Stewart, M.A.W. (1996). The developmental interface between nature and nurture: A mutual influence model of child antisocial behavior and parenting. *Developmental Psychology, 32,* 574–589.

Geddes, J.R., & Lawrie, S.M. (1995). Obstetric complications and schizophrenia: A meta-analysis. *British Journal of Psychiatry, 167,* 786–793.

Gelernter, J., Goldman, D., & Risch, N. (1993). The A1 allele at the $D_2$ dopamine receptor gene and alcoholism: A reappraisal. *Journal of the American Medical Association, 269,* 1673–1677.

Gelernter, J., Kranzler, H., & Cubells, J.F. (1997). Serotonin transporter protein (SLC6A4) allele and haplotype frequencies and linkage disequilibria in African- and European-American and Japanese populations and in alcohol-dependent subjects. *Human Genetics, 101,* 243–246.

Harrison, P.J. (1997). Schizophrenia: A disorder of neurodevelopment? *Current Opinion in Neurobiology, 7,* 285–289.

Hartge, P., Struewing, J.P., Wacholder, S., Brody, L.C., & Tucker, M.A. (1999). The prevalence of common BRCA1 and BRCA2 mutations among Ashkenazi Jews. *American Journal of Human Genetics, 64,* 963–970.

Hill, A.V.S. (1998). Genetics and genomics of infectious disease susceptibility. *British Medical Bulletin, 55,* 401–413.

Hirschfeld, D.R., Rosenbaum, J.F., Biederman, J., Bolduc, E.A., Faraone, S.V., Snidman, N., Reznick, J.S., & Kagan, J. (1992). Stable behavioral inhibition and its association with anxiety disorder. *Journal of the American Academy of Child and Adolescent Psychiatry, 31,* 103–111.

Inglehearn, C.F. (1998). Molecular genetics of human retinal dystrophies. *Eye, 12,* 571–579.

Kendler, K.S. (1996). Major depression and generalised anxiety disorder. Same genes, (partly) different environments—revisited. *British Journal of Psychiatry, 168* (Suppl. 30), 68–75.

Kendler, K.S., Kessler, R.C., Walters, E.E., MacLean, C., Neale, M.C., Heath, A.C., & Eaves, L.J. (1995). Stressful life events, genetic liability, and onset of an episode of major depression in women. *American Journal of Psychiatry, 152*, 833–842.

Kirov, G., Williams, N., Sham, P., Craddock, N., & Owen, M.J. (2000). Pooled genotyping of microsatellite markers in parent-offspring trios. *Genome Research, 10*, 105–115.

Kruglyak, L. (1999). Prospects for whole-genome linkage disequilibrium mapping of common disease genes. *Nature Genetics, 22*, 139–144.

Lahey, B.B., McBurnett, K., Loeber, R., & Hart, E.L. (1995). Psychobiology of Conduct Disorders. In G.P. Scholevar (Ed.), *Conduct Disorders in children and adolescents: Assessments and intervention* (pp. 27–44). Washington, DC: American Psychiatric Press.

Lenzenweger, M.F., & Korfine, L. (1996). Tracking the taxon: On the latent structure and base rate of schizotypy. In A. Raine, T. Lencz, & S.A. Mednick (Eds.), *Schizotypal personality* (pp. 135–167). New York: Cambridge University Press.

Levy, F., Hay, D.A., McStephen, M., Wood, C., & Waldman, I.D. (1997). Attention-deficit hyperactivity disorder (ADHD): A category or a continuum? Genetic analysis of a large-scale twin study. *Journal of the American Academy of Child and Adolescent Psychiatry, 36*, 737–744.

Lockhart, D.J., & Winzeler, E.A. (2000). Genomics, gene expression and DNA arrays. *Nature, 405*, 827–836.

Maier, S.E., Miller, J.A., & West, J.R. (1999). Prenatal binge-like alcohol exposure in the rat results in region-specific deficits in brain growth. *Neurotoxicology and Teratology, 21*, 285–291.

Malhotra, A.K., & Goldman, D. (1999). Benefits and pitfalls encountered in psychiatric genetic association studies. *Biological Psychiatry, 45*, 544–550.

Meyers, C., Elias, S., & Arrabal, P. (1995). Congenital anomalies and pregnancy loss. In L.G. Keith, E. Papiernik, D.M. Keith, & B. Luke (Eds.), *Multiple pregnancy: Epidemiology, gestation and perinatal outcome* (pp. 73–92). New York: Parthenon Publishing.

Moffitt, T.E., Caspi, A., Rutter, M., & Silva, P. (in press). *Sorting out sex differences in antisocial behaviour: Findings from the first two decades of the Dunedin Longitudinal Study*. Cambridge, UK: Cambridge University Press.

Morton, N.E., & Collins, A. (1998). Tests and estimates of allelic association in complex inheritance. *Proceedings of the National Academy of Science USA, 95*, 11389–11393.

Motulsky, A.G. (1999). If I had a gene test, what would I have and who would I tell? *Lancet, 354*(Suppl. I), 35–37.

MTA Cooperative Group. (1999a). A 14-month randomized clinical trial of treatment strategies for attention-deficit/hyperactivity disorder. *Archives of General Psychiatry, 56*, 1073–1086.

MTA Cooperative Group. (1999b). Moderators and mediators of treatment response for children with attention-deficit/hyperactivity disorder: The multimodal treatment study of children with attention-deficit/hyperactivity disorder. *Archives of General Psychiatry, 56*, 1088–1096.

Murray, R.M., & Woodruff, P.W.R. (1995). Developmental insanity or demantia praecox: A new perspective on an old debate. *Neurology, Psychiatry and Brain Research, 3*, 167–175.

Nadder, T.S., Silberg, J.L., Maes, H.H., Rutter, M., & Eaves, L.J. (2000). Genetic effects on the variation and covariation of ADHD and ODD/CD symptomat-ologies across informant and occasion of measurement. *Manuscript submitted.*

Nadder, T.S., Silberg, J.L., Rutter, M., Maes, H.H., & Eaves, L.J. (in press). Comparison of multiple measures of ADHD symptomatology: A multivariate genetic analysis. *Journal of Child Psychology and Psychiatry.*

O'Connor, T.G., Deater-Deckard, K., Fulker, D., Rutter, M., & Plomin, R. (1998). Early adolescence: Antisocial behavioral problems and coercive parenting. *Developmental Psychology, 34*, 970–981.

Owen, M.J., Cardno, A.G., & O'Donovan, M.C. (2000). Psychiatric genetics: Back to the future. *Molecular Psychiatry, 5*, 22–31.

Page, G.P., & Amos, C.I. (1999). Comparison of linkage-disequilibrium methods for localization of genes influencing quantitative traits in humans. *American Journal of Human Genetics, 64*, 1194–1205.

Pandey, A., & Mann, M. (2000). Proteomics to study genes and genomes. *Nature, 405*, 837–846.

Plomin, R., DeFries, J.C., McClearn, G.E., & Rutter, M. (1997). *Behavioral Genetics.* New York: W.H. Freeman & Co.

Plomin, R., & Rutter, M. (1998). Child development, molecular genetics, and what to do with genes once they are found. *Child Development, 69*, 1223–1242.

Rabinowitz, D. (1997). A transmission disequilibrium test for quantitative trait loci. *Human Heredity, 47*, 342–350.

Risch, N. (2000). Searching for genetic determinants in the new millennium. *Nature, 405*, 847–856.

Risch, N., & Merikangas, K. (1996). The future of genetic studies of complex human diseases. *Science, 273*, 1516–1517.

Risch, N., & Zhang, H. (1995). Extreme discordant sib pairs for mapping quantitative trait loci in humans. *Science, 268*, 1584–1589.

Rotter, J.I., & Diamond, J.M. (1987). What maintains the frequencies of human genetic diseases? *Nature, 329*, 289–290.

Royal Society. (1997). Human genetics: Uncertainties and the financial implications ahead: A discussion organized and edited by R.N. Anderson. *Philosophical Transactions of the Royal Society of London: Biological Sciences, 352*, 1035–114.

Rutter, M. (1997). Comorbidity: Concepts, claims and choices. *Criminal Behaviour and Mental Health, 7*, 265–285.

Rutter, M. (1999). Genes and behaviour: Health potential and ethical concerns. In A. Carroll & C. Skidmore (Eds.), *Inventing heaven?: Quakers confront the challenges of genetic engineering* (pp. 66–88). Reading, UK: Sowle Press.

Rutter, M. (2000a). Psychosocial influences: Critiques, findings and research needs. *Development and Psychopathology, 12*, 375–405.

Rutter, M. (2000b). Genetic studies of autism: From the 1970s into the Millennium. *Journal of Abnormal Child Psychology, 28*, 3–14.

Rutter, M., Dunn, J., Plomin, R., Simonoff, E., Pickles, A., Maughan, B., Ormel, J., Meyer, J.M., & Eaves, L. (1997a). Integrating nature and nurture: Implications of person–environment correlations and interactions for developmental psychology. *Development and Psychopathology, 9*, 335–364.

Rutter, M., Giller, H., & Hagell, A. (1998). *Antisocial behavior by young people.* New York: Cambridge University Press.

Rutter, M., Maughan, B., Meyer, J.M., Pickles, A., Silberg, J.L., Simonoff, E., & Taylor, E. (1997b). Heterogeneity of antisocial behavior: Causes, continuities, and consequences. In R. Dienstbier (Series Ed.) & D.W. Osgood (Vol. Ed.), *Nebraska symposium on motivation: Vol. 44. Motivation and delinquency* (pp. 45–118). Lincoln, NE: University of Nebraska Press.

Rutter, M., Pickles, A., Murray, R., & Eaves, L. (in press-a). Testing hypotheses on specific environmental causal effects on behavior. *Psychological Bulletin.*

Rutter, M., & Plomin, R. (1997). Opportunities for psychiatry from genetic findings. *British Journal of Psychiatry, 171*, 209–219.

Rutter, M., & Quinton, D. (1984). Parental psychiatric disorder: Effects on children. *Psychological Medicine, 14*, 853–880.

Rutter, M., Roy, P., & Kreppner, J. (in press-b). Institutional care as a risk factor for inattention/overactivity. In S. Sandberg (Ed.), *Hyperactivity and attention disorders in childhood* (2nd ed.). Cambridge, UK: Cambridge University Press.

Rutter, M., Silberg, J.L., O'Connor, T., & Simonoff, E. (1999a). Genetics and child psychiatry: I. Advances in quantitative and molecular genetics. *Journal of Child Psychology and Psychiatry, 40*, 3–18.

Rutter, M., Silberg, J.L., O'Connor, T., & Simonoff, E. (1999b). Genetics and child psychiatry: II. Empirical research findings. *Journal of Child Psychology and Psychiatry, 40*, 19–55.

Rutter, M., Silberg, J., & Simonoff, E. (1993). Whither behavioral genetics? A developmental psychopathology perspective. In R. Plomin & G.E. McClearn (Eds.), *Nature, nurture, and psychology* (pp. 433–456). Washington, DC: APA Books.

Rutter, M., & Smith, D.J. (1995). *Psychosocial disorders in young people: Time trends and their causes.* Chichester, UK: Wiley.

Sandberg, S. (in press). Psychosocial contributions. In S. Sandberg (Ed.), *Hyperactivity and attention disorders in childhood* (2nd ed.). Cambridge, UK: Cambridge University Press.

Schachar, R., & Tannock, R. (in press). Syndromes of hyperactivity and attention deficit. In M. Rutter & E. Taylor (Eds.), *Child and adolescent psychiatry: Modern approaches* (4th ed.). Oxford, UK: Blackwell Scientific.

Sibilia, M., & Wagner, E.F. (1996). Transgenic animals. *European Review, 4*, 371–392.

Silberg, J.L., & Rutter, M. (in press). Nature–nurture interplay in the risks associated with parental depression. In S.H. Goodman & I.H. Gotlib (Eds.), *Children of depressed parents: Alternative pathways to risk for psychopathology.* New York: APA.

Silberg, J.L., Rutter, M., Neale, M.C., & Eaves, L. (in press). Genetic moderation of environmental risk for depression and anxiety in adolescent girls. *British Journal of Psychiatry.*

Streissguth, A.P., & Kanter, J. (1997). *The challenge of fetal alcohol syndrome: Overcoming secondary disabilities.* Seattle: University of Washington Press.

Szabo, C.I., & King, M.-C. (1997). Population genetics of BRCA1 and BRCA2. *American Journal of Human Genetics, 60*, 1013–1020.

Talmud, J.P., Bujac, S.R., Hall, S., Miller, G.J., & Humphries, S.E. (2000). Substitution of asparagine for aspartic acid at residue 9 (D9N) of lipoprotein lipase markedly augments risk of ischaemic heart disease in male smokers. *Atherosclerosis, 149*, 75–81.

Tannock, R. (1998). Attention Deficit Hyperactivity Disorder: Advances in cognitive, neurobiological, and genetic research. *Journal of Child Psychology and Psychiatry and Allied Disciplines, 39*, 65–99.

Teasdale, G.M., Nicoll, J.A.R., Murray, G., & Fiddes, M. (1997). Association of apolipoprotein E polymorphism with outcome after head injury. *Lancet, 350,* 1069–1071.

Thapar, A., Holmes, J., Poulton, K., & Harrington, R. (1999). Genetic basis of attention deficit and hyperactivity. *British Journal of Psychiatry, 174,* 105–111.

Todd, J.A. (1999). From genome to aetiology in a multifactorial disease, type 1 diabetes. *BioEssays, 21,* 164–174.

Todd, J.A. (in press). Multifactorial diseases: Ancient gene polymorphism at quantitative trait loci and a legacy of survival during our evolution. In C.R. Scriver, A. Beaudet, W.S. Sly, D. Valle, B. Vogelstein, & B. Childs (Eds.), *The metabolic and molecular basis of inherited disease.* New York: McGraw-Hill.

Waldrop, M., & Halverson, C. (1971). Minor physical anomalies and hyperactive behaviour in young children. In J. Hellmutt (Ed.), *Exceptional infant.* New York: Bruner/Mazel.

Weatherall, D. (1992). *The Harveian oration: The role of nature and nurture in common diseases: Garrod's legacy.* London: Royal College of Physicians.

Wicker, L.S., Todd, J.A., & Peterson, L.B. (1995). Genetic control of autoimmune diabetes in the NOD mouse. *Annual Review of Immunology, 13,* 179.

World Health Organization. (1992). *ICD-10 categories F00–F99 mental and behavioural disorders (including disorders of psychological development): Clinical descriptions and diagnostic guidelines.* Geneva: WHO.

Wright, A.F., Carothers, A.D., & Pirastu, M. (1999). Population choice in mapping genes for complex diseases. *Nature Genetics, 23,* 397–404.

Zito, J.M., Safer, D.J., dos Reis, S., Gardner, J.F., Bates, M., & Lynch, F. (2000). Trends in the prescribing of psychotropic medications to preschoolers. *Journal of the American Medical Association, 283,* 1025–1030.

# Author index

# Subject index

NOTE: For certain general areas such as brain structures, questionnaires and tests, all items are listed under one heading rather than being referenced separately.